T0076090

Get the eBook FREE!

(PDF, ePub, Kindle, and liveBook all included)

We believe that once you buy a book from us, you should be able to read it in any format we have available. To get electronic versions of this book at no additional cost to you, purchase and then register this book at the Manning website.

Go to https://www.manning.com/freebook and follow the instructions to complete your pBook registration.

That's it!
Thanks from Manning!

Praise for the first edition

BDD in Action

SECOND EDITION

JOHN FERGUSON SMART
JAN MOLAK
Foreword by DANIEL TERHORST-NORTH

MANNING

SHELTER ISLAND

For online information and ordering of this and other Manning books, please visit
www.manning.com. The publisher offers discounts on this book when ordered in quantity.
For more information, please contact

> Special Sales Department
> Manning Publications Co.
> 20 Baldwin Road
> PO Box 761
> Shelter Island, NY 11964
> Email: orders@manning.com

Manning Publications Co.
20 Baldwin Road
PO Box 761
Shelter Island, NY 11964

Development editors:	Helen Stergius and Marina Michaels
Technical development editor:	Nick Watts
Review editor:	Mihaela Batinić
Production editor:	Keri Hales
Copy editor:	Michele Mitchell
Proofreader:	Jason Everett
Technical proofreader:	Srihari Sridharan
Typesetter:	Dennis Dalinnik
Cover designer:	Marija Tudor

ISBN: 9781617297533
Printed in the United States of America

Deliberate Discovery—A "Sonnet"

Uncertainty's the muse of all that's new,
And ignorance the space in which she plays;
A year's enough to prove a vision true,
But we could prove it false in only days.
We dream, and chase our dream, and never fear
To fail, and fail. Up, up! And on again,
But ask us to pursue another's goals
And failure makes us mice where we were men.
Ah, best laid plans! Where were you at the end
Who chained us and constrained us from the start?
We knew you made a fickle, fragile friend;
You tricked us when you claimed you had a heart!
We thought less travelled roads would see us winning
In places other fools had feared to stray—
If only we had known from the beginning
The ignorance we found along the way.
And yet, a list of dangers and disasters
Filled out, and scanned, and added to some more
Would still have left out some of what we mastered—
We didn't know we didn't know before.

We planned our way with maps we'd made already
Assuming the terrain would be the same,
Expecting well-paved roads to keep us steady
And any local creatures to be tame.
We loaded up our caravans and wagons
With good advice, best practices and tools
But didn't spot the legend—"Here be dragons!"
So we got burnt, again. They say that fools
Rush in, and yet we count ourselves as wise,
We praise each other's skill and raise a glass
To intellect—ignoring the demise
Of expeditions just as skilled as ours.
When they return, worn out, their pride in shreds,
We laugh and say, "A death march! You expect
Such things to fail." And in our clever heads
It's obvious—at least in retrospect.
The dragons of our ignorance will slay us
If we don't slay them first. We could be brave
And work for kings who don't refuse to pay us
When we're delayed because we found their cave.

They say that matter cannot be created,
A fundamental principle and law,
While dragons keep emerging, unabated;
As many as you slay, there's still one more.
Our ignorance is limitless—be grateful,
Or else we'd find we've nothing left to learn;
To be surprised by dragons may be fateful,
But truth be told, it's best laid plans that burn.
We could seek out the dragons in their dungeons
And tread there softly, ready to retreat;
We could seek other roads, postponing large ones,
And only fight the ones we might defeat.
The world could be a world of dragon slayers
And stand as men and women, not as mice;
The joy that comes from learning more should sway us;
The fiercest dragons won't surprise us twice.
Discover tiny dragons, be they few,
And all the mightiest, with equal praise—
Uncertainty's our muse of all that's new,
And ignorance the space in which she plays.

—Liz Keogh

contents

vii

foreword

Welcome to the second edition of John Ferguson Smart's comprehensive *BDD in Action*. When I wrote the foreword to the first edition in 2014, it was with a mixture of relief and delight that someone had taken on the mammoth task of capturing the landscape of BDD methods, tools, and techniques. John's approach was to carefully, thoughtfully, and thoroughly document what he saw and experienced, as a practitioner, coach, consultant, and trainer, and I was excited to write the foreword that introduced this book to the world.

Fast-forward to 2023, and we are living in a world in which everything has changed. A global pandemic has seen an unprecedented increase in the use of the word "unprecedented." Teams and organizations are adopting distributed and hybrid working patterns, making collaboration on knowledge work simultaneously more important and more challenging than ever before.

Behavior-Driven Development seems to be a perfect fit for this new world. Its focus on communication across the entire product development cycle means we have living documentation as shared artifacts between team members and other stakeholders separated by geography and time zones. The team can agree on a feature, discuss its scope in the form of scenario titles ("The one where . . ."), and get into the detail of acceptance criteria, while having automated assurance that what they agreed is indeed how the application behaves. Tie this into your version control and path to live and you are well on the way to full continuous compliance!

In this updated edition of the book, John and Jan have revisited all the existing content, improving its clarity and flow for both the first-time reader and the returning practitioner. But the world does not stand still; since 2014 there have been several exciting new developments in the world of BDD.

Example Mapping is a simple yet powerful way of exploring a feature, surfacing uncertainty, and capturing assumptions, business rules, questions, and, of course, examples. I will admit that when it was first described to me, I reacted with a polite but confused "So what?" It seemed too simple to be useful. But then many of the best ideas are, and it has since become a staple of my BDD tool kit.

The Screenplay Pattern is another obvious-when-you-say-it-out-loud technique. Most UI automation frameworks use the language of the UI—buttons, fields, forms, and so forth—known as a page model. Screenplay flips this on its head and says, "Why not describe UI interactions in the language of the business domain, like we do everywhere else?" You won't go back.

John and Jan describe these and other valuable techniques with their customary clarity and detail, providing worked examples that guide the reader through not only theory but tangible practice. I found myself nodding along with much of this new material, as well as having a couple of *Aha!* moments myself.

I am delighted that BDD still has this much traction and interest nearly 20 years on (!), and I am grateful to John and Jan for producing this second edition of such a comprehensive resource.

—Daniel Terhorst-North, practitioner consultant

preface

Like many projects, when I started working on a new edition to *BDD in Action* in 2019, I thought it would be easy: a few library updates here and there, and maybe a couple of new sections on the more recent requirement discovery practices.

But as I reread the material I'd written about BDD in 2013–2014, I realized that a *lot* of things had evolved. To paraphrase Roy Scheider's character in *Jaws*, I was going to need a bigger book. The core tenets remained the same, as the fundamental ideas behind BDD are still as solid, and as useful, as ever.

But the way we do BDD has evolved quite a bit. We've learned how to facilitate requirements discovery sessions more effectively, with techniques such as Example Mapping, Feature Mapping, and Journey Mapping. We have also seen so many teams misinterpret and misunderstand BDD and suffer as a consequence, so some clarification of the core principles seemed useful. In 2015, I was introduced to the Screenplay Pattern for the first time, and for me this was a game-changer in writing cleaner, more maintainable test automation code.

JavaScript has grown massively since the first edition; I've teamed up with Jan Molak, author of *Serenity/JS* (the TypeScript implementation of the Screenplay pattern), to take a deeper look at how to practice the technical side of BDD in JavaScript and TypeScript projects.

In this edition, no chapter remained untouched, many chapters were completely rewritten, and there are several entirely new ones. Enjoy!

acknowledgments

A little like a film, a book has a cast of hundreds, from minor roles to people whose contributions made this book possible. Our thanks go to the dedication, professionalism, and attention to detail of all the folks at Manning: Michael Stephens, Melissa Ice, Rebecca Rinehart, Paul Spratley, Eleonor Gardner, and many others. Helen Stergius and Marina Michaels, our development editors, were unflagging, courteous, and helpful—all the way to the final chapter—in the drive to push this book into production. Thanks to Nick Watts and Srihari Sridharan, who did an exemplary job as technical proofreaders and came up with some great suggestions along the way.

The reviewers also deserve special mention—this book would not be what it is without their help: Alain Couniot, Alessandro Campeis, Alex Lucas, Andy Wiesendanger, Burk Hufnagel, Christian Kreutzer-Beck, Conor Redmond, Craig Smith, David Paccoud, Goetz Heller, Hilde Van Gysel, Jared Duncan, Jean-François Morin, Jeff Smith, John Booth, John Guthrie, John Kasiewicz, Julien Pohie, Kelum Prabath Senanayake, Kelvin Johnson, Kevin Liao, Lorenzo De Leon, Phillip Sorensen, Richard Vaughan, Ronald Borman, Santosh Shanbhag, and Viorel Moisei.

We owe much of what we know about BDD to the BDD community: Gojko Adzic, Nigel Charman, Andrew Glover, Liz Keogh, Chris Matts, Dan North, Richard Vowles, and many others—not to mention the broader Agile and open source communities: Dan Allen, John Hurst, Paul King, Aslak Knutsen, Bartosz Majsak, Gáspár Nagy, Seb Rose, Alex Soto, Renee Troughton, Matt Wynne, and more. Thanks for so many fruitful conversations, email exchanges, pair coding sessions, and Skype chats! Special thanks to Daniel Terhorst-North for contributing the foreword to the book.

A special thanks also goes to Antony Marcano and Andy Palmer, who introduced us to the idea of the Screenplay Pattern and helped to take our automation coding to another level.

Much of the content of the book is inspired by work done and conversations held over the years with clients, friends, and colleagues in many different organizations: Anthony O'Brien, Parikshit Basrur, Tom Howard, Ray King, Ian Mansell, Peter Merel, Michael Rembach, Simeon Ross, Tim Ryan, Tong Su, Peter Suggitt, Marco Tedone, Peter Thomas, Trevor Vella, Gordon Weir, John Singh, and many others.

FROM JOHN: A very special thanks to my dedicated spouse, Chantal, and my boys, James and William, without whose patience, endurance, support, and encouragement this book would simply not have been possible.

FROM JAN: I want to thank my amazing wife, Anna, for her love, support, and patience. She was as important to this book getting done as I was. I also want to thank my two wonderful daughters, Alexandra and Victoria, for their encouragement and for believing in their dad.

about this book

The goal of this book is to help get teams up and running with effective BDD practices. It aims to give you a complete picture of how BDD practices apply at all levels of the software development process, including discovering and defining high-level requirements, implementing the application features, and writing executable specifications in the form of automated acceptance and unit tests.

Who should read this book

This book has a broad audience. It's aimed both at teams who are completely new to BDD and at teams who are already trying to roll out BDD or related practices, like acceptance test–driven development or specification by example. It's for teams who struggle with misaligned and changing requirements, time wasted due to defects and rework, and product quality. It's for practitioners whose job is to help these teams, and it's for everyone who shares a passion for discovering better ways to build and deliver software.

Different people will get different things out of this book:

- *Business analysts and testers* will learn more effective ways of discovering requirements in collaboration with users, and of communicating these requirements to development teams.
- *Developers* will learn how to write higher-quality, more maintainable code with fewer bugs, how to focus on writing code that delivers real value, and how to build automated test suites that provide documentation and feedback for the whole team.

- *Project managers and business stakeholders* will learn how to help teams build better, more valuable software for the business.

How the book is organized: A road map

The book is divided into four parts, each addressing different aspects of BDD:

- Part 1 presents the motivations, origins, and general philosophy of BDD and concludes with a quick, practical introduction to what BDD looks like in the real world. This part will help team members and project stakeholders alike get a solid understanding of what BDD is really about.
- Part 2 focuses on collaboration. In it, you will learn how BDD practices can help teams analyze requirements more effectively in order to discover and describe what features will deliver real value to the organization. This section lays the conceptual foundation for the rest of the book and presents a number of important requirements-analysis techniques.
- Part 3 provides more technical coverage of BDD practices. We'll look at techniques for automating acceptance tests in a robust and sustainable way, study a number of BDD tools for different languages and frameworks, and see how BDD helps developers write cleaner, better-designed, higher-quality code. This section is hands-on and practical. The last chapter of part 3 is a little different and takes a look at the broader picture of BDD in the context of project management, product documentation, reporting, and integration into the build process.

Most of the practical examples in the book will use Java-based languages and tools, but we'll also look at examples of BDD tools for JavaScript and TypeScript. The approaches we discuss will be generally applicable to any language.

Because of the broad focus of the book, you may find different sections more or less applicable to your daily work. For example, business analysts might find the material on requirements analysis more relevant than the chapters on coding practices. Table 1 presents a (very) rough guide to the sections various readers might find particularly useful.

Table 1   A rough indicator of the target audience for each section of this book

	Business analyst	Tester	Developer	Project manager
Part 1	☑ ☑ ☑	☑ ☑ ☑	☑ ☑ ☑	☑ ☑ ☑
Part 2	☑ ☑ ☑	☑ ☑ ☑	☑ ☑	☑ ☑ ☑
Part 3 (Chapters 11–15)	☑	☑ ☑ ☑	☑ ☑ ☑	☑
Part 3 (Chapter 16)	☑ ☑ ☑	☑ ☑ ☑	☑ ☑	☑ ☑

Prerequisites

The prerequisites for *BDD in Action* will vary depending on the parts of the book being read:

- *Parts 1 and 2 (high-level BDD)*—These sections require little technical knowledge; they are aimed at all team members and introduce general principles of BDD. A basic understanding of Agile development practices will be helpful.
- *Part 3 (BDD and test automation)*—This section requires programming knowledge. Most of the examples use either Java or JavaScript. The general approach is to illustrate concepts and practices with working code rather than to document any one technology exhaustively. Different technology sections will benefit from a working knowledge of the following technologies:
  - Maven—The Java/JVM code samples use Maven, though only a superficial knowledge (the ability to build a Maven project) is required.
  - HTML/CSS—The sections on UI testing that use Selenium/WebDriver need a basic understanding of how HTML pages are built, what a CSS selector looks like, and, optionally, some familiarity with XPath.
  - Restful web services—The sections on testing web services need some understanding of how web services are implemented, in particular how web service clients are implemented.
  - JavaScript—The section on testing JavaScript and JavaScript applications requires a reasonable understanding of JavaScript programming.
- *Chapter 16 (living documentation)*—This section is general and has no real technical requirements.

About the code

This book contains many source code examples that illustrate the various tools and techniques discussed. Source code in listings or in the text appears in a `fixed-width font like this`. Other related concepts that appear in the text, such as class or variable names, also appear in this font.

Because this book discusses many languages, we've made a special effort to keep all of the listings readable and easy to follow, even if you're not familiar with the language being used. Most of the listings are annotated to make the code easier to follow, and some also have numbered cue balls indicating particular lines of code that are discussed in the text that follows.

Source code and other resources

This book contains many source code examples in a variety of languages. The source code for these examples is available for download on GitHub at https://github.com/bdd-in-action/second-edition, with a separate subdirectory for each chapter. Some examples are discussed across several chapters—in these cases, each chapter contains the version of the source code discussed in that chapter. This site also contains links to the tools and libraries used in the book and other useful related resources.

In addition, you can get executable snippets of code from the liveBook (online) version of this book at https://livebook.manning.com/book/bdd-in-action-second-edition. The code projects don't contain IDE-specific project files, but they're laid out in such a way as to make it easy to import them into an IDE.

liveBook discussion forum

Purchase of *BDD in Action*, second edition, includes free access to liveBook, Manning's online reading platform. Using liveBook's exclusive discussion features, you can attach comments to the book globally or to specific sections or paragraphs. It's a snap to make notes for yourself, ask and answer technical questions, and receive help from the author and other users. To access the forum, go to https://livebook.manning.com/book/bdd-in-action-second-edition/discussion. You can also learn more about Manning's forums and the rules of conduct at https://livebook.manning.com/discussion.

Manning's commitment to our readers is to provide a venue where a meaningful dialogue between individual readers and between readers and the authors can take place. It is not a commitment to any specific amount of participation on the part of the authors, whose contribution to the forum remains voluntary (and unpaid). We suggest you try asking the authors some challenging questions lest their interest stray! The forum and the archives of previous discussions will be accessible from the publisher's website as long as the book is in print.

about the authors

JOHN FERGUSON SMART is an international speaker, consultant, author, and trainer well known in the Agile community for his many books, articles, and presentations, particularly in areas such as BDD, TDD, test automation, software craftsmanship, and team collaboration.

John's main focus is helping organizations and teams deliver more value by combining effective collaboration and technical excellence. John is also the creator and lead developer of the innovative Serenity BDD test automation library and founder of Serenity Dojo (https://www.serenity-dojo.com/), an online training and coaching school that helps testers from all backgrounds become high-performing Agile test automation engineers.

JAN MOLAK is a trainer, speaker, and consultant helping clients around the world improve collaboration and optimize software delivery processes through the introduction of BDD, advanced test automation, and modern software engineering practices.

A contributor to the Screenplay Pattern and a prolific open source developer, Jan is also the author of the Serenity/JS acceptance testing framework, Jenkins Build Monitor, and numerous other tools in the continuous delivery and testing space.

about the cover illustration

The figure on the cover of *BDD in Action*, second edition, is captioned "A Medieval Knight." The illustration by Paolo Mercuri (1804–1884) is taken from a book edited by Camille Bonnard and published in Paris in the mid-1800s.

In those days, it was easy to identify where people lived and what their trade or station in life was just by their dress. Manning celebrates the inventiveness and initiative of the computer business with book covers based on the rich diversity of regional culture centuries ago, brought back to life by pictures from collections such as this one.

Part 1

First steps

Welcome to the world of Behavior-Driven Development (BDD)! Part 1 of this book gives you both a high-level view of the world of BDD and a first taste of what BDD looks like in the field.

In chapters 1 and 2, you'll learn about the motivations and origins of BDD and where it sits with regard to Agile and other software development approaches. You'll discover the broad scope of BDD, learning how it applies at all levels of software development, from high-level requirements discovery and specification to detailed low-level coding. And you'll learn how important it is not only to build the software right, but also to build the right software.

As practitioners, we like to keep things grounded in real-world examples, so in chapter 3 you'll see what BDD looks like in a real project, from discovering the requirements and automating the high-level acceptance criteria to building and verifying the design and implementation, through producing accurate and up-to-date technical and functional documentation.

By the end of part 1, you should have a good grasp of the motivations and overall broad scope of BDD, as well as an idea of what it looks like in practice at different levels of the software development process.

Building software
that makes a difference

This chapter covers

- The problems that Behavior-Driven Development addresses
- General principles and origins of Behavior-Driven Development
- Activities and outcomes seen in a Behavior-Driven Development project
- The pros and cons of Behavior-Driven Development

This book is about building and delivering software that works well and is easy to change and maintain, but more importantly, it's about building software that provides real value to its users. We want to build software well, but we also need to build software that's worth building.

In 2012, the US Air Force decided to ditch a major software project that had already cost over $1 billion. The Expeditionary Combat Support System was designed to modernize and streamline supply chain management in order to save billions of dollars and meet new legislative requirements. But after seven years of development, the system had still "not yielded any significant military capability."[1] The Air Force estimated that an additional $1.1 billion would be required to deliver just a quarter of the original scope and that the solution could not be rolled out until 2020, three years after the legislative deadline of 2017.

This happens a lot in the software industry. According to a number of studies, around half of all software projects fail to deliver in some significant way. The 2011 edition of the Standish Group's annual *CHAOS Report* found that 42% of projects were delivered late, ran over budget, or failed to deliver all of the requested features,[2] and 21% of projects were cancelled entirely. Scott Ambler's annual survey on IT project success rates uses a more flexible definition of success, but still found a 30–50% failure rate, depending on the methodologies used.[3] This corresponds to billions of dollars in wasted effort, writing software that ultimately won't be used or that doesn't solve the business problem it was intended to solve.

What if it didn't have to be this way? What if we could write software in a way that would let us discover and focus our efforts on what really matters? What if we could objectively learn what features will really benefit the organization and learn the most cost-effective way to implement them? What if we could see beyond what the user asks for and build what the user actually needs?

Organizations are discovering how to do just that. Many teams are successfully collaborating to build and deliver more valuable, more effective, and more reliable software. And they're learning to do this faster and more efficiently. In this book, you'll see how. We'll explore a number of methods and techniques, grouped under the general heading of *Behavior-Driven Development* (BDD).

BDD is a collaborative development approach where teams use structured conversations about examples and counterexamples of business rules and expected behavior to build a deep, shared understanding of the features that will really benefit the users and the business as a whole. Very often they express these examples in an executable format that acts as the basis for automated acceptance tests that validate the software's behavior. BDD helps teams focus their efforts on identifying, understanding, and building valuable features that matter to businesses, and it makes sure that these features are well designed and well implemented.

BDD practitioners use conversations around concrete examples of system behavior to help understand how features will provide value to the business. It encourages business analysts, software developers, and testers to collaborate more closely by enabling them to express requirements in a more testable way, in a form that both the development team and business stakeholders can easily understand. BDD tools can help turn

---

[1] Chris Kanaracus, "Air Force scraps massive ERP project after racking Up $1 billion in costs," CIO, November 14, 2012, https://www.computerworld.com/article/2493041/air-force-scraps-massive-erp-project-after-racking-up–1b-in-costs.html.
[2] Whether these figures reflect more on our ability to build and deliver software or on our ability to plan and estimate is a subject of some debate in the Agile development community—see Jim Highsmith's book *Agile Project Management: Creating Innovative Products*, second edition (Addison-Wesley Professional, 2009).
[3] Scott Ambler, "Surveys Exploring the Current State of Information Technology Practices," http://www.ambysoft.com/surveys/.

these requirements into automated tests that help guide the developer, verify the feature, and document what the application does.

BDD isn't a software development methodology in its own right. It's not a replacement for Scrum, XP, Kanban, or whatever methodology you're currently using. As you'll see, BDD incorporates, builds on, and enhances ideas from many of these methodologies. And no matter what methodology you're using, there are ways that BDD can help make your life easier.

1.1 BDD from 50,000 feet

So what does BDD bring to the table? Here's a (slightly oversimplified) perspective. Let's say Chris's company needs a new module for its accounting software. When Chris wants to add a new feature, the process goes something like this (see figure 1.1):

1 Chris tells a business analyst how he would like the feature to work.
2 The business analyst translates Chris's requests into a set of requirements for the developers, describing what the software should do. These requirements are written in English and stored in a Microsoft Word document.
3 The developer translates the requirements into code and unit tests—written in Java, C#, or some other programming language—in order to implement the new feature.

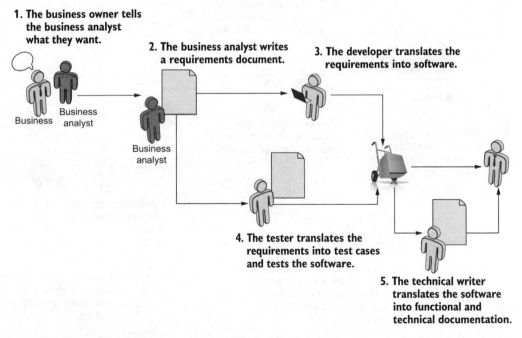

Figure 1.1   The traditional development process provides many opportunities for misunderstandings and miscommunication.

  4 The tester translates the requirements in the Word document into test cases
     and uses them to verify that the new feature meets the requirements.
  5 Documentation engineers then translate the working software and code back
     into plain English technical and functional documentation.

Along the way there are many opportunities for information to get lost in translation,
be misunderstood, or just be ignored. Chances are that the new module itself may not
do exactly what was required and that the documentation won't reflect the initial
requirements that Chris gave the analyst.

Chris's friend Sarah runs another company that's just introduced BDD. In a team
practicing BDD, the business analysts, developers, and testers collaborate to understand and define the requirements (see figure 1.2). They express the requirements in
a common language that helps unite and focus the team's efforts. They can even turn
these requirements into automated acceptance tests that both specify how the software should behave and also demonstrate that the delivered software behaves as it
should. We can see this flow in figure 1.2.

  1 Like Chris, Sarah talks to Belinda, the business analyst, to get a high-level vision
     of what she wants. But she doesn't do so alone: she is joined by a developer and
     a tester who get to hear firsthand what the users really need. To reduce the risk

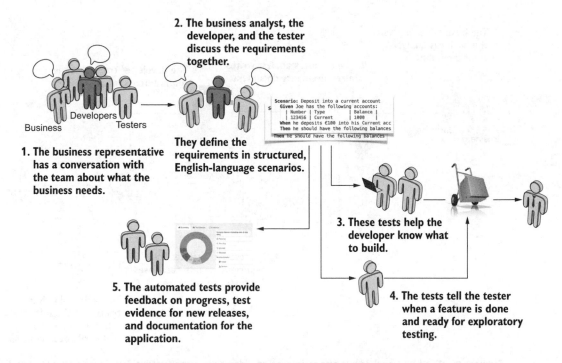

Figure 1.2   **BDD uses conversations around business rules and examples, expressed in a form that can be
easily automated, to reduce lost information and misunderstandings.**

of misunderstandings and hidden assumptions, they talk through examples of what the feature should do and what it shouldn't. They try to articulate the business problem they are trying to solve, the business goal they are aiming for, and what features and capabilities might help achieve this goal.

2   Before work starts on the feature, Belinda gets together with the developer and tester who will be working on it, and they have a conversation about the feature. In these conversations, they discuss the key business goals and outcomes of the feature and work through concrete examples and counterexamples to get a deeper understanding of the requirement. Oftentimes, for more important features, Sarah will participate in this conversation as well.

 After this conversation, team members write up the key examples and counterexamples in a structured, business-readable format that is quite close to plain English. These examples act both as specifications of the features and as the basis for automated acceptance tests.

3   The developers and testers turn these "executable specifications" into automated acceptance tests; these automated tests help guide the development process and determine when a feature is finished.

4   When the automated acceptance tests pass, the team has concrete proof that the feature does what was agreed on in phase 2. The tester might use the results of these tests as the starting point for any manual and exploratory testing that needs to be done.

5   The automated tests also act as product documentation, providing precise and up-to-date examples of how the system works. Sarah can review the test reports to see what features have been delivered and whether they perform the way she expected.

Compared to Chris's scenario, Sarah's team makes heavy use of conversations and examples to reduce the amount of information lost in translation. Every stage beyond step 2 starts with the specifications written in a structured but business-readable style, which are based on concrete examples provided by Sarah. In this way, a great deal of the ambiguity in translating the client's initial requirements into code, reports, and documentation is removed.

We'll discuss all of these points in detail throughout the rest of the book. You'll learn ways to help ensure that your code is of high quality, solid, well tested, and well documented. You'll learn how to write more effective unit tests and more meaningful automated acceptance criteria. You'll also learn how to ensure that the features you deliver solve the right problems and provide real benefit to the users and the business.

1.2   *What problems are you trying to solve?*

Software projects fail for many reasons, but the most significant causes fall into two broad categories:

- Not building the software right
- Not building the right software

Figure 1.3 illustrates this in the form of a graph. The vertical axis represents *what* you're building, and the horizontal axis represents *how* you build it. If you perform poorly on the *how* axis, not writing well-crafted and well-designed software, you'll end up with a buggy, unreliable product that's hard to change and maintain. If you don't do well on the *what* axis, failing to understand what features the business really needs, you'll end up with a product that nobody needs.

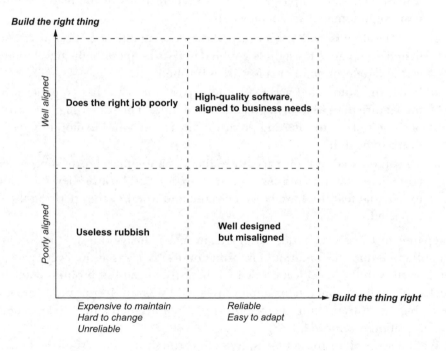

Figure 1.3 Successful projects must both build features well and build the right features.

1.2.1   *Building the software right*

Many projects suffer or fail because of software quality problems. Although internal software quality is mostly invisible to nontechnical stakeholders, the consequences of poor-quality software can be painfully visible. In our experience, applications that are poorly designed, badly written, or lack well-written, automated tests tend to be buggy, hard to maintain, hard to change, and hard to scale.

We've seen too many applications where simple change requests and new features take too long to deliver. Developers spend more and more time fixing bugs rather than working on new features, which makes it harder to deliver new features quickly. It takes longer for new developers to get up to speed and become productive, simply because the code is hard to understand. It also becomes harder and harder to add new features without breaking existing code. The existing technical documentation (if there is any) is inevitably out of date, and teams find themselves incapable of delivering new features quickly because each release requires a lengthy period of manual testing and bug fixes.

Organizations that embrace high-quality technical practices have a different story to tell. We've seen many teams that adopt practices such as Test-Driven Development, Clean Coding, Living Documentation, and Continuous Integration regularly reporting low to near-zero defect rates, as well as code that's much easier to adapt and extend as new requirements emerge and new features are requested. These teams can also add features at a more consistent pace, because the automated tests ensure that existing features won't be broken unknowingly. They implement the features faster and more precisely than other teams because they don't have to struggle with long bug-fixing sessions and unpredictable side effects when they make changes. And the resulting application is easier and cheaper to maintain.

Note that there is no magic formula for building high-quality, easily maintainable software. Software development is a complex field, human factors abound, and techniques such as Test-Driven Development, Clean Coding, and Automated Testing don't automatically guarantee good results. But studies do suggest a strong correlation between lean and Agile practices and project success rates[4] when compared to more traditional approaches. Other studies have found a correlation between Test-Driven Development practices, reduced bug counts,[5] and improved code quality.[6] Although it's certainly possible to write high-quality code without practicing techniques such as Test-Driven Development and Clean Coding, teams that value good development practices do seem to succeed in delivering high-quality code more often.

But building high-quality software isn't in itself enough to guarantee a successful project. The software must also benefit its users and business stakeholders.

1.2.2   Building the right software

Software is never developed in a vacuum. Software projects are part of a broader business strategy, and they need to be aligned with business goals if they're to be beneficial

---

[4] See, for example, Scott Wambler, "2018 IT Project Success Rates Survey Results," http://www.ambysoft.com/surveys/success2018.html.

[5] See, for example, Nachiappan Nagappan, E. Michael Maximilien, Thirumalesh Bhat, and Laurie Williams, "Realizing quality improvement through test driven development: results and experiences of four industrial teams," https://www.microsoft.com/en-us/research/wp-content/uploads/2009/10/Realizing-Quality-Improvement-Through-Test-Driven-Development-Results-and-Experiences-of-Four-Industrial-Teams-nagappan_tdd.pdf.

[6] Rod Hilton, "Quantitatively Evaluating Test-Driven Development by Applying Object-Oriented Quality Metrics to Open Source Projects" (PhD thesis, Regis University, 2009), http://www.rodhilton.com/files/tdd_thesis.pdf.

to the organization. At the end of the day, the software solution you deliver needs to help users achieve their goals more effectively. Any effort that doesn't contribute to this end is wasted.

In practice, there's often a lot of waste. In many projects, time and money are spent building features that are never used or that provide only marginal value to the business. According to the Standish Group's CHAOS studies,[7] on average some 45% of the features delivered into production are never used. Even apparently predictable projects, such as migrating software from a mainframe system onto a more modern platform, have their share of features that need updating or that are no longer necessary. When you don't fully understand the goals that your client is trying to achieve, it's very easy to deliver perfectly functional, well-written features that are of little use to the end user.

On the other hand, many software projects end up delivering little or no real business value. Not only do they deliver features that are of little use to the business, but they fail to even deliver the minimum capabilities that would make the projects viable.

> **The consequences of not building it right and not building the right thing**
>
> The affect of poorly understood requirements and poor code realization isn't just a theoretical concept or a "nice to have;" on the contrary, it's often painfully concrete. In December 2007, the Queensland Health Department kicked off work on a new payroll system for its 85,000 employees. The initial budget for the project was around $6 million, with a delivery date of August 2008.
>
> When the solution was rolled out in 2010, some 18 months late, it was a disaster. Tens of thousands of public servants were underpaid, overpaid, or not paid at all. Since the go-live date, over 1,000 payroll staff have been required to carry out some 200,000 manual processes each fortnight to ensure that staff salaries are paid.
>
> In 2012, an independent review found that the project had cost the state over $416 million since going into production and would cost an additional $837 million to fix. This colossal sum included $220 million just to fix the immediate software problems that were preventing the system from delivering its core capability of paying Queensland Health staff what they were owed each month.

Building the right software is made even trickier by one commonly overlooked fact: early on in a project, you usually don't know what the right features are.[8]

As we will see in the rest of this book, BDD is a very effective way to address both of these problems. And one of the main ways it does so is by tackling one of the principle causes of risk and overrun in software projects: the team not having enough clarity on what they are supposed to be building.

---

[7] The Standish Group's *CHAOS Report 2002* reported a value of 45%, and I've seen more recent internal studies where the figure is around 50%.

[8] See KPMG, "Review of the Queensland Health Payroll System," 2012, http://delimiter.com.au/wp-content/uploads/2012/06/KPMG_audit.pdf.

1.2.3   The knowledge constraint: Dealing with uncertainty

One fact of life in software development is that there will be things you don't know. Changing requirements are a normal part of every software project. Knowledge and understanding about the problem at hand and about how best to solve it increases progressively throughout the project.

In software development, each project is different. There are always new business requirements to cater to, new technological problems to solve, and new opportunities to seize. As a project progresses, market conditions, business strategies, technological constraints, or simply your understanding of the requirements will evolve, and you'll need to change your tack and adjust your course. Each project is a journey of discovery, where the real constraint isn't time, the budget, or even programmer hours, but your lack of knowledge about what you need to build and how you should build it. When reality doesn't go according to plan, you need to adapt to reality, rather than trying to force reality to fit into your plan. "When the terrain disagrees with the map, trust the terrain" (Swiss Army proverb).

Users and stakeholders will usually know what high-level goals they want to achieve and can be coaxed into revealing these goals if you take the time to ask. They'll be able to tell you that they need an online ticketing system or a payroll solution that caters to 85,000 different employees. And you can get a feel for the scope of the application you might need to build early on in the project.

But the details are another matter entirely. Although users are quick to ask for specific technical solutions to their problems, they're not usually the best placed to know what solution would serve them best, or even what solutions exist. Your team's collective understanding of the best way to deliver these capabilities, as well as the optimal feature set for achieving the underlying business goals, will grow as the project progresses.

As illustrated in figure 1.4, the more prescriptive, plan-based requirements-analysis techniques suppose that you can learn almost all there is to know about a project's requirements, as well as the optimal solution design, very quickly in the early phases of the project. By the end of the analysis phase, the specifications are signed-off on and locked down, and all that remains to do is code.

Of course, reality doesn't always work this way. At the start of the project, a development team will often have only a superficial understanding of the business domain and the goals the users need to achieve. In fact, the job of a software engineering team isn't to know how to build a solution; it's to know how to discover the best way to build the solution.

The team's collective understanding will naturally increase over the duration of the project. You become less ignorant over time. Toward the end of the project, a good team will have built up a deep, intimate knowledge of the user's needs and will be able to proactively propose features and implementations that will be better suited to the particular user base. But this learning path is neither linear nor predictable. It's hard to know what you don't know, so it's hard to predict what you'll learn as the project progresses.

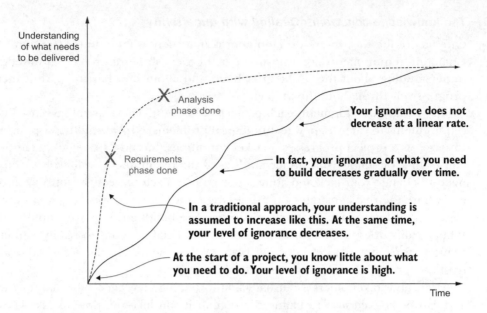

Figure 1.4 At the start of a project, there are many unknowns. You reduce these unknowns as the project progresses, but not in a linear or very predictable way.

For the majority of modern software development projects, the main challenge in managing scope isn't to eliminate uncertainty by defining and locking down requirements as early as possible. The main challenge is to manage this uncertainty in a way that will help you progressively discover and deliver an effective solution that matches up with the underlying business goals behind a project. As you'll see, one important benefit of BDD is that it provides techniques that can help you manage this uncertainty and reduce the risk that comes with it.

1.3   Is BDD right for your projects?

BDD works well with other Agile methodologies such as Scrum, but it can also be used with lean approaches such as Kanban. It is not a separate methodology, but more a collection of practices that helps teams discover and understand business needs more quickly and more effectively and get automated feedback on whether these needs have indeed been met by the features they build. For example, a Scrum team using BDD will work in much the same way as an ordinary Scrum team, but they will apply BDD practices during their backlog refinement sessions to get more clarity on the features they need to build. They will also pay more attention to in-sprint automation and try to write automated tests for the acceptance criteria for the features they deliver during the sprint. A Scrum team practicing BDD will also want to add "passing automated acceptance tests" to the definition of their user stories.

BDD works well for any kind of requirements discovery, both in green fields projects and in ones that are already underway. The examples in this book focus mostly on building new features and new applications (with the exception of chapters 14 and 15, where we look specifically at working with legacy applications). This is by design, to make the domains easier to understand and the examples more engaging. However, BDD is also very effective for existing applications and complex domains. Both authors spend much of their time working in large financial organizations on complex projects. In fact, the techniques you will learn in this book apply to any domain where the requirements are not trivial, where assumptions need to be uncovered, and where complexity and uncertainty lie underneath the surface of each story, which covers almost every project we have ever worked on.

1.4 *What you will learn in this book*

This book gives you both an understanding of the theoretical foundations of BDD, and hands-on knowledge about what you need to do to introduce BDD into your own organization. You will learn the following:

- How to get clarity on real user requirements using collaborative techniques and Agile requirements to discover techniques such as Example Mapping and Feature Mapping
- How to record these requirements in an executable format (*executable specifications*) that can act as automated tests and be integrated into your build process
- How to automate these executable specifications using Java or JavaScript, and using tools such as Cucumber
- How to use these executable specifications to produce living documentation that both verifies and documents the features you deliver

Summary

- The developers of successful projects need to build software that's reliable and bug free (build the software right) and to build features that deliver real value to the business (build the right software).
- BDD is a collaborative development approach where teams use structured conversations about examples and counterexamples of business rules and expected behavior to build a deep, shared understanding of what features will benefit users. Very often they express these examples in an executable format that acts as the basis for automated acceptance tests that validate the software's behavior.
- BDD practitioners use conversations about concrete examples to build a common understanding of what features will deliver real value to the organization.
- These examples form the basis of the acceptance criteria that developers use to determine when a feature is done.

In the next chapter, we'll look at the origins of BDD and learn about the key steps of BDD process in more detail.

Introducing
Behavior-Driven
Development

2

This chapter covers
- The origins of BDD
- Activities and outcomes seen in a BDD project
- The pros and cons of BDD

In this chapter we will dive into what BDD looks like in a little more detail. BDD is a set of software engineering practices designed to help teams build and deliver more valuable, higher-quality software faster. It draws on Agile and lean practices, including in particular, Test-Driven Development (TDD) and Domain-Driven Design (DDD). But most importantly, BDD provides a common language based on simple, structured sentences expressed in English (or in the native language of the stakeholders) that facilitate communication between project team members and business stakeholders. To better understand the motivations and philosophy that drive BDD practices, it's useful to understand where BDD comes from.

2.1 BDD was originally designed to make teaching TDD easier

BDD was originally invented by Daniel Terhorst-North[1] in the early to mid-2000s as an easier way to teach and practice TDD, which was invented by Kent Beck in the early days of Agile.[2] TDD is a remarkably effective technique that uses unit tests to specify, design, and verify application code.

Unit tests and acceptance tests

We will be talking a lot about unit tests and acceptance tests in this chapter, so it is worthwhile clarifying what we mean by these terms.

Unit tests are small tests that describe and verify the behavior of individual components of a system. Unit tests focus on the internal workings of the system; in modern programming languages, a component might be a method or a function.

When we talk about *acceptance tests*, on the other hand, we refer to business-facing tests, tests that end users or business sponsors can use to check that a feature works as intended. We also use the term *executable specifications* for acceptance tests that can be automated and that are written in a business-readable format.

Executable specifications are written using terms and concepts from the business domain. They are designed to be easily understood by business folk and end users and are defined collaboratively by the whole team. Unit tests, on the other hand, are written by developers, for developers. Well-written unit tests describe and document low-level component behavior, much like executable specifications document and describe how users interact with the system.

When TDD practitioners need to implement a feature, they first write a failing test that describes, or specifies, that feature. Next, they write just enough code to make the test pass. Finally, they refactor the code to help ensure that it will be easy to maintain (see figure 2.1). This simple but powerful technique encourages developers to write cleaner, better-designed, easier-to-maintain code[3] and results in substantially lower defect counts.[4]

Despite its advantages, many teams still have difficulty adopting and using TDD effectively. Developers often have trouble knowing where to start or what tests they should write next. Sometimes TDD can lead developers to become too detail focused, losing the broader picture of the business goals they're supposed to implement. Some teams also find that the large numbers of unit tests can become hard to maintain as the project grows in size.

---

[1] Daniel Terhorst-North, "Introducing BDD," http://dannorth.net/introducing-bdd/.

[2] Kent Beck, *Test-Driven Development: By Example* (Addison-Wesley Professional, 2002).

[3] Rod Hilton, "Quantitatively Evaluating Test-Driven Development by Applying Object-Oriented Quality Metrics to Open Source Projects" (PhD thesis, Regis University, 2009), http://www.rodhilton.com/files/tdd_thesis.pdf.

[4] Nachiappan Nagappan, E. Michael Maximilien, Thirumalesh Bhat, and Laurie Williams, "Realizing quality improvement through test driven development: results and experiences of four industrial teams," https://www.microsoft.com/en-us/research/wp-content/uploads/2009/10/Realizing-Quality-Improvement-Through-Test-Driven-Development-Results-and-Experiences-of-Four-Industrial-Teams-nagappan_tdd.pdf.

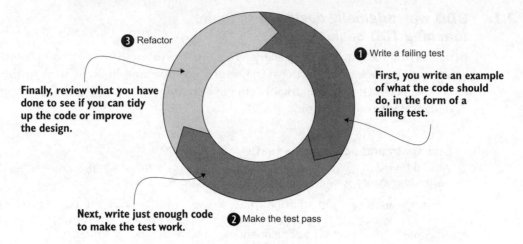

3 Refactor

Finally, review what you have
done to see if you can tidy
up the code or improve
the design.

1 Write a failing test

First, you write an example
of what the code should
do, in the form of a
failing test.

Next, write just enough code
to make the test work.

2 Make the test pass

Figure 2.1   TDD relies on a simple, three-phase cycle.

In fact, many traditional unit tests, written with or without TDD, are tightly coupled to a particular implementation of the code. They focus on the method or function they're testing, rather than on what the code should do in business terms.

For example, suppose Paul is a Java developer working on a new financial trading application in a large bank. He has been asked to implement a new feature to transfer money from one account to another. He creates an Account class with a transfer() method, a deposit() method, and so on. The corresponding unit tests are focused on testing these methods:

```
public class BankAccountTest {
    @Test
    public void testTransfer() {...}
    @Test
    public void testDeposit() {...}
}
```

Tests like this are better than nothing, but they can limit your options. For example, they don't describe what you expect the transfer() and deposit() functions to do, which makes them harder to understand and to fix if they break. They're tightly coupled to the method they test, which means that if you refactor the implementation, you need to rename your test as well. And because they don't say much about what they're actually testing, it's hard to know what other tests (if any) you need to write before you're done.

North observed that a few simple practices, such as naming unit tests as full sentences and using the word "should," can help developers write more meaningful tests, which in turn helps them write higher-quality code more efficiently. When you think in terms of what the class *should* do, instead of what method or function is being tested, it's easier to keep your efforts focused on the underlying business requirements.

For example, Paul could write more descriptive tests along the following lines:

```
public class WhenTransferringInternationalFunds {
    @Test
    public void should_transfer_funds_to_a_local_account() {...}
    @Test
    public void should_transfer_funds_to_a_different_bank() {...}
    ...
    @Test
    public void should_deduct_fees_as_a_separate_transaction() {...}
    ...
}
```

Tests that are written this way read more like specifications than unit tests. They focus on the behavior of the application, using tests simply as a means to express and verify that behavior. Terhorst-North also noted that tests written this way are much easier to maintain because their intent is so clear. The affect of this approach was so significant that he no longer referred to what he was doing as TDD, but as *Behavior*-Driven Development. Nowadays, BDD and TDD are quite distinct, though related, practices.

2.2 BDD also works well for requirements analysis

Describing a system's behavior turns out to be what business analysts do every day. Working with business analyst colleague Chris Matts, Terhorst-North set out to apply what he had learned to the requirements-analysis space. Around this time, Eric Evans introduced the idea of DDD,[5] which promotes the use of a ubiquitous language that businesspeople can understand to describe and model a system. Terhorst-North and Matts's vision was to create a ubiquitous language that business analysts could use to define requirements unambiguously and that could also be easily transformed into automated acceptance tests. To implement this vision, they started expressing the acceptance criteria for user stories in the form of loosely structured examples, known as "scenarios," like this one:

```
Given a customer has a current account
When the customer transfers funds from this account to an overseas account
Then the funds should be deposited in the overseas account
And the transaction fee should be deducted from the current account
```

A business owner can easily understand a scenario written like this. It gives clear and objective goals for each story in terms of what needs to be developed and what needs to be tested.

This notation eventually evolved into a commonly used form often referred to as *Gherkin*. With appropriate tools, scenarios written in this form can be turned into automated acceptance criteria that can be executed automatically whenever required. Terhorst-North wrote the first dedicated BDD test automation library, JBehave, in the

---

[5] Eric Evans, *Domain Driven Design* (Addison-Wesley Professional, 2003).

mid-2000s, and since then many others have emerged for different languages, both at the unit-testing and acceptance-testing levels.

BDD by any other name

Many of the ideas around BDD are not new and have been practiced for many years under a number of different names. Some of the more common terms used for these practices include *Acceptance Test–Driven Development* and *Specification by Example*. To avoid confusion, let's clarify a few of these terms in relation to BDD.

All of these practices belong to the same family: an approach that some practitioners nowadays refer to as *Example-Guided Development*.[a] Concrete examples can greatly aid understanding what a user really needs, and, where possible, automating these examples in the form of tests, before work starts on a feature.

Acceptance Test–Driven Development, or ATDD, is a technique where users collaborate with developers to write automated acceptance criteria for features before they are built. The technique has existed in various forms since at least the late 1990s. In the early days, this was often referred to as *Story Test-Driven Development*. Kent Beck and Martin Fowler mentioned the concept in 2000,[b] though they observed that it was difficult to implement acceptance criteria in the form of conventional unit tests at the start of a project.

But acceptance tests don't have to be written using unit testing tools. Since at least the early 2000s, innovative teams have been asking users to contribute examples of how their software should work, and have been reaping the benefits.[c] Among the more well-known initiatives in this field, Ward Cunningham invented the framework for integrated tests, or Fit, back in 2002, to allow customers to provide examples of acceptance criteria using Excel. Robert C. Martin built on Fit to develop the popular FitNesse tool, which allows users to use a wiki to capture their acceptance criteria.

Specification by Example (sometimes referred to as SBE) describes the set of practices that use examples and conversation to discover and describe requirements. In his seminal book of the same name,[d] Gojko Adzic chose this term as a way to reach out to nontesters: he wanted to emphasize that, despite the use of the word "test" in terms like ATDD, these techniques were actually requirements discovery practices.

Using conversation and examples to specify how you expect a system to behave is a core part of BDD, and we'll discuss it at length in the first half of this book. Over the past decade, these techniques have been converging more than diverging. They have also come a long way beyond simply writing tests first, to embrace the power of collaborative deliberate discovery, domain-driven design, living documentation, and a host of other related practices. When done well, they are virtually indistinguishable from each other.

---

[a] Matt Wynne, "Example-guided development: A useful abstraction for the xDD family?" *Cucumber*, https://cucumber.io/blog/example-guided-development/.

[b] Kent Beck and Martin Fowler, *Planning Extreme Programming* (Addison-Wesley Professional, 2000).

[c] Johan Andersson, Geoff Bache, and Peter Sutton, "XP with Acceptance Test Driven Development: A Rewrite Project for a Resource Optimization System," *Lecture Notes in Computer Science*, vol. 2675, 2003.

[d] Gojko Adzic, *Specification by Example* (Manning, 2011).

2.3 BDD principles and practices

Today BDD is successfully practiced in a large number of organizations of all sizes around the world, in a variety of different ways. In *Specification by Example*, Gojko Adzic provides case studies for over 50 such organizations. In this section, we'll look at a number of general principles or guidelines that BDD practitioners have found useful over the years. Figure 2.2 gives a high-level overview of the way BDD sees the world. BDD practitioners like to start by identifying business goals and looking for features that will help deliver these goals. Collaborating with the user, they use concrete examples to illustrate these features. Wherever possible, these examples are automated in the form of executable specifications, which both validate the software and provide automatically updated technical and functional documentation. BDD principles are also used at the coding level, where they help developers write code that's of higher quality and is better tested, better documented, and easier to use and maintain.

In the following sections, we'll look at how these principles work in more detail.

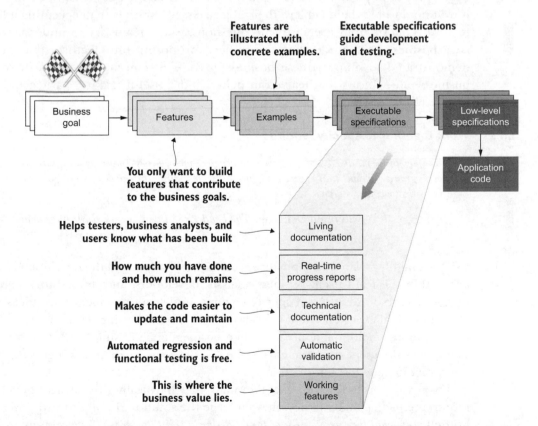

Figure 2.2   The principal activities and outcomes of BDD. Note that these activities occur repeatedly and continuously throughout the process; this isn't a single linear waterfall-style process, but a sequence of activities that you practice for each feature you implement.

2.3.1   *Focus on features that deliver business value*

As you've seen, uncertainty about requirements is a major challenge in many software projects, and heavy upfront specifications don't work particularly well when confronted with a shifting understanding of what features need to be delivered.

A *feature* is a tangible, deliverable piece of functionality that helps the business achieve its business goals. For example, suppose you work in a bank that's implementing an online banking solution. One of the business goals for this project might be "to attract more clients by providing a simple and convenient way for clients to manage their accounts." Some features that might help achieve this goal could be "Transfer funds between a client's accounts," "Transfer funds to another national account," or "Transfer funds to an overseas account."

Rather than attempting to nail down all of the requirements once and for all, teams practicing BDD engage in ongoing conversations with end users and other stakeholders to progressively build a common understanding of what features they should create. Rather than working upfront to design a complete solution for the developers to implement, users explain what they need to get out of the system and how it might help them achieve their objectives. And rather than accepting a list of feature requests from users with no questions asked, teams try to understand the core business goals underlying the project, proposing only features that can be demonstrated to support these business goals. This constant focus on delivering business value means that teams can deliver more useful features earlier and with less wasted effort.

2.3.2   *Work together to specify features*

> *A complex problem, like discovering ways to delight clients, is best solved by a cognitively diverse group of people that is given responsibility for solving the problem, self-organizes, and works together to solve it.*
>
> —Stephen Denning, *The Leader's Guide to Radical Management*
> (Jossey-Bass, 2010)

BDD is a highly collaborative practice, both between users and the development team and within the team itself. Business analysts, developers, and testers work together with end users to define and specify features, and team members draw ideas from their individual experience and know-how. This approach is highly efficient.

In a more traditional approach, when business analysts simply relay their understanding of the users' requirements to the rest of the team, there is a high risk of misinterpretation and lost information.

If you ask users to write up what they want, they'll typically give you a set of detailed requirements that matches how they envisage the solution. In other words, users will not tell you *what they need*; rather, *they'll design a solution for you.* I've seen many business analysts fall into the same trap, simply because they've been trained to write specifications that way. The problem with this approach is twofold: not only will they fail to benefit from the development team's expertise in software design, but they're effectively binding the development team to a particular solution, which may not be the optimal one in business or technical terms. In addition, developers can't use their technical know-how to help deliver a technically superior design, and testers don't get the opportunity to comment on the testability of the specifications until the end of the project.

For example, the "Transfer funds to an overseas account" feature involves many user-experience and technical considerations. How can you display the constantly changing exchange rates to the client? When and how are the fees calculated and shown to the client? For how long can you guarantee a proposed exchange rate? How can you verify that the right exchange rate is being used? All these considerations will influence the design, implementation, and cost of the feature and can change the way the business analysts and business stakeholders originally imagined the solution. When teams practice BDD, on the other hand, team members build up a shared appreciation of the users' needs, as well as a sense of common ownership and engagement in the solution.

2.3.3 *Embrace uncertainty*

A BDD team knows that they won't know everything upfront, no matter how long they spend writing specifications. As we discussed earlier, the biggest thing slowing developers down in a software project is understanding what they need to build.

Rather than attempting to lock down the specifications at the start of the project, BDD practitioners assume that the requirements, or more precisely, their *understanding of* the requirements, will evolve and change throughout the life of the project. They try to get early feedback from users and stakeholders to ensure that they're on track, and change tack accordingly, instead of waiting until the end of the project to see if their assumptions about the business requirements were correct.

Very often, the most effective way to see if users like a feature is to build it and show it to them as early as possible. With this in mind, experienced BDD teams prioritize the features that will deliver value, will improve their understanding of what features the users really need, and will help them understand how best to build and deliver these features.

2.3.4 *Illustrate features with concrete examples*

When a team practicing BDD decides to implement a feature, they work together with users and other stakeholders to define stories and scenarios of what users expect this feature to deliver. In particular, the users help define a set of concrete examples that illustrate key outcomes of the feature (see figure 2.3).

These examples use a common vocabulary and can be readily understood by both end users and members of the development team. They're usually expressed using the Given . . . When . . . Then notation you saw in section 2.2. For instance, a simple

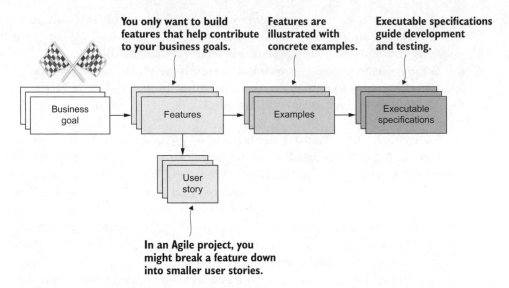

Figure 2.3   Examples play a primary role in BDD, helping everyone understand the requirements more clearly.

example that illustrates the "Transfer funds between a client's accounts" feature might look like this:

```
Scenario: Transferring money to a savings account
    Given Tess has a current account with $1000
    And she has savings account with $2000
    When she transfers $500 from her current account to her savings account
    Then she should have $500 in her current account
    And she should have $2500 in her savings account
```

Examples play a primary role in BDD, simply because they're an extremely effective way of communicating clear, precise, and unambiguous requirements. Specifications written in natural language are, as it turns out, a terribly poor way of communicating requirements, because there's so much space for ambiguity, assumptions, and misunderstandings. Examples are a great way to overcome these limitations and clarify the requirements. Examples are also a great way to explore and expand your knowledge. When a user proposes an example of how a feature should behave, project team members often ask for extra examples to illustrate corner cases, explore edge cases, or clarify assumptions. Testers are particularly good at this, which is why it's so valuable for them to be involved at this stage of the project.

2.3.5   *A Gherkin primer*

Most BDD tools that we'll look at in this book use a format generally known as Gherkin, so before we go any further, it is worth clarifying just what this is. This format is designed to be both easily understandable for business stakeholders and easy to automate using dedicated BDD tools such as Cucumber and SpecFlow. This way, it both documents your requirements and runs your automated tests.

In Gherkin, the requirements related to a particular feature are grouped into a single text file called a *feature file*, which contains a short description of the feature, followed by a number of scenarios, or formalized examples of how a feature works.

```
Feature: Transferring money between accounts
  In order to manage my money more efficiently
  As a bank client
  I want to transfer funds between my accounts whenever I need to
  Scenario: Transferring money to a savings account
    Given Tess has a current account with $1000
    And a savings account with $2000.00
    When she transfers $500 from current to savings
    Then she should have $500 in her current account
    And she should have $2500 in her savings account

  Scenario: Transferring with insufficient funds
    Given Tess has a current account with $1000
    And a savings account with $2000.00
    When she transfers $1500 from current to savings
    Then she should receive an 'insufficient funds' error
    Then she should have $1000 in her current account
    And she should have $2000 in her Savings account
```

As can be seen here, Gherkin requirements are expressed in plain English, but with a specific structure. Each *scenario* is made up of a number of *steps*, where each step starts with one of a small number of keywords (*Given, When, Then, And, But*).

The natural order of a scenario is Given . . . When . . . Then:

- *Given* describes the preconditions for the scenario and prepares the test environment.
- *When* describes the action under test.
- *Then* describes the expected outcomes.

The *And* and *But* keywords can be used to join several Given, When, or Then steps in a more readable way:

```
Given she has a current account with $1000
And she has a savings account with $2000
```

Several related scenarios can often be grouped into a single scenario using a table of examples. For example, the following scenario illustrates how interest is calculated on different types of accounts:

```
Scenario Outline: Earning interest
  Given Tess has a <account-type> account with $<initial-balance>
  And the interest rate for <account-type> accounts is <interest>
  When the monthly interest is calculated
  Then she should have earned $<earnings>
```

```
And she should have $<new-balance> in her <account-type> account
Examples:
  | initial-balance | account-type | interest | earnings | new-balance |
  | 10000           | Current      | 1.0      | 8.33     | 10008.33    |
  | 10000           | Savings      | 3.0      | 25       | 10025       |
  | 10000           | SuperSaver   | 5.0      | 41.67    | 10041.67    |
```

This scenario would be run three times in all, once for each row in the Examples table. The values in each row are inserted into the placeholder variables, which are indicated by the `<...>` notation (`<account-type>`, `<initial-balance>`, etc.). This not only saves typing, but also makes it easier to understand the whole requirement at a glance.

You can also use the following tabular notation within the steps themselves in order to display test data more concisely. For example, the previous money-transfer scenario could have been written like this:

```
Scenario: Transferring money between accounts within the bank
  Given Tess has the following accounts:
    | account | balance |
    | current | 1000    |
    | savings | 2000    |
  When she transfers 500.00 from current to savings
  Then her accounts should look like this:
    | account | balance |
    | current | 500     |
    | savings | 2500    |
```

We'll look at this notation in much more detail in chapter 5.

2.3.6 *Don't write automated tests; write executable specifications*

These stories and examples form the basis of the specifications that developers use to build the system. They act as both acceptance criteria, determining when a feature is done, and as guidelines for developers, giving them a clear picture of what needs to be built.

Acceptance criteria give the team a way to objectively judge whether a feature has been implemented correctly. But checking this manually for each code change would be time-consuming and inefficient. It would also slow down feedback, which would in turn slow down the development process. Wherever feasible, teams turn these acceptance criteria into automated acceptance tests or, more precisely, into *executable specifications.*

An executable specification is an automated test that illustrates and verifies how the application delivers a specific business requirement. These automated tests run as part of the build process and run whenever a change is made to the application. In this way, they serve both as acceptance tests, determining which new features are complete, and as regression tests, ensuring that new changes haven't broken any existing features (see figure 2.4).

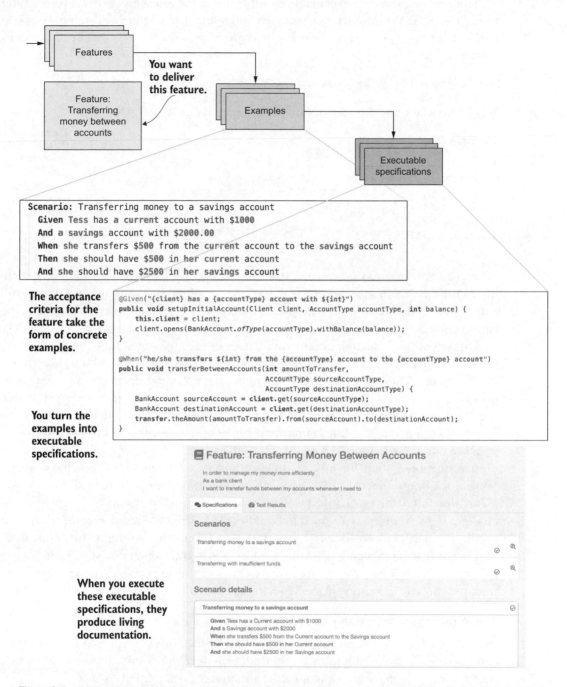

Figure 2.4 Executable specifications are expressed using a common business vocabulary that the whole team can understand. They guide development and testing activities and produce readable reports available to all.

You can automate an executable specification by writing test code corresponding to each step. BDD tools such as Cucumber will match the text in each step of your scenario to the appropriate test code. For example, this is the first step of the scenario in figure 2.4:

```
Given Tess has a current account with $1000
```

You might automate this step in Java using Cucumber with code like this:

```
Client client;

@Given("{client} has a {accountType} account with ${int}")
public void setutAccount(Client client,
                         AccountType accountType,
                         int balance) {
    this.client = client;
    client.opens(BankAccount.ofType(accountType).withBalance(balance));
}
```

The step that this code implements

Call the application code that corresponds to this step.

When Cucumber runs the scenario, it'll execute each step, using basic pattern matching to find the method associated with step 1. Once it knows what method to call, it'll extract variables like `accountType` and `balance` and execute the corresponding application code 2.

Unlike conventional unit or integration tests, or the automated functional tests many QA teams are used to, executable specifications are expressed in something close to natural language. They use precisely the examples that users and development team members proposed and refined earlier on, and the same terms and vocabulary. Executable specifications are about communication as much as they are about validation, and the test reports they generate are easily understandable by everyone involved with the project.

These executable specifications also become a single source of truth, providing reference documentation for how features should be implemented. This makes maintaining the requirements much easier. If specifications are stored in the form of a Word document or on a wiki page, as is done for many traditional projects, any changes to the requirements need to be reflected both in the requirements document and in the acceptance tests and test scripts, which introduces a high risk of inconsistency. For teams practicing BDD, the requirements and executable specifications are the same thing; when the requirements change, the executable specifications are updated directly in a single place. We'll look at this in detail in chapter 9.

2.3.7   *These principles also apply to unit tests*

BDD doesn't stop at the acceptance tests. Many of the core BDD principles and values can also be applied to unit testing, and this helps developers write higher-quality code that's more reliable, more maintainable, and better documented.

Unit tests are small tests that describe and verify the behavior of individual components of a system. Unit tests focus on the internal workings of the system; in modern programming languages, a component might be a method or a function.

The executable specifications we saw in the previous section are written using terms and concepts from the business domain. They are designed to be easily understood by businesspeople and end users. We might call these *customer-facing executable specifications.* Unit tests, on the other hand, are written by developers, for developers. Well-written unit tests describe and document low-level component behavior, much in the same way as executable specifications documents, and describe how users interact with the system.

Developers practicing BDD typically use an *outside-in* approach. When they implement a feature, they start from the acceptance criteria and work down, building whatever is needed to make those acceptance criteria pass. The acceptance criteria define the expected outcomes, and the developer's job is to write the code that produces those outcomes. This is a very efficient, focused way of working. Just as no feature is implemented unless it contributes to an identified business goal, no code is written unless it contributes to making an acceptance test pass, and therefore to implementing a feature.

But it doesn't stop there. Before writing any code, a BDD developer will reason about what this code should actually do and express this in the form of a low-level, or *developer-facing, executable specification.* The developer won't think in terms of writing unit tests for a particular class, but of writing technical specifications describing how the application should behave, such as how it should respond to certain inputs or what it should do in a given situation. These low-level specifications flow naturally from the high-level acceptance criteria and help developers design and document the application code in the context of delivering high-level features (see figure 2.5).

For example, the step definition code in figure 2.5 involves creating a new account:

```
@Given("{client} has a {accountType} account with ${int}")
public void setupAccount(Client client,
                         AccountType accountType,
                         int balance) {
    this.client = client;
    client.opens(BankAccount.ofType(accountType).withBalance(balance));
}
```

Create a new account of a given type and with given initial balance.

This leads the developer to write low-level, developer-facing specifications to design the `Account` class. An example of a developer-facing executable specification written using Junit 5 might look like this:

```
@DisplayName("When creating a new bank account")
class WhenCreatingANewAccount {

    @DisplayName("A new account should have an initial balance")
    @Test
    void newAccountBalance() {
        BankAccount account = BankAccount.ofType(AccountType.Savings)
                                         .withBalance(100);
        assertThat(account.getBalance()).isEqualTo(100.0);
    }
}x
```

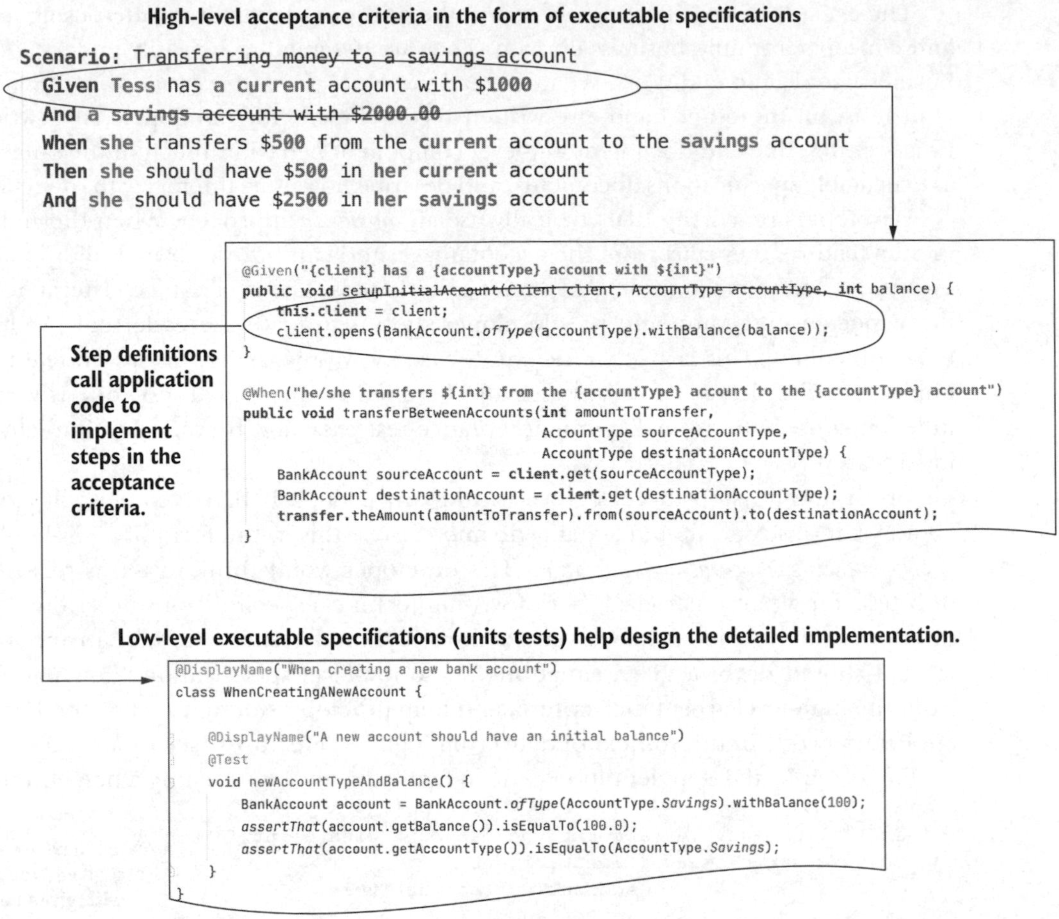

High-level acceptance criteria in the form of executable specifications

Scenario: Transferring money to a savings account
  Given Tess has a current account with $1000
  And a savings account with $2000.00
  When she transfers $500 from the current account to the savings account
  Then she should have $500 in her current account
  And she should have $2500 in her savings account

Step definitions call application code to implement steps in the acceptance criteria.

```
@Given("{client} has a {accountType} account with ${int}")
public void setupInitialAccount(Client client, AccountType accountType, int balance) {
    this.client = client;
    client.opens(BankAccount.ofType(accountType).withBalance(balance));
}

@When("he/she transfers ${int} from the {accountType} account to the {accountType} account")
public void transferBetweenAccounts(int amountToTransfer,
                                    AccountType sourceAccountType,
                                    AccountType destinationAccountType) {
    BankAccount sourceAccount = client.get(sourceAccountType);
    BankAccount destinationAccount = client.get(destinationAccountType);
    transfer.theAmount(amountToTransfer).from(sourceAccount).to(destinationAccount);
}
```

Low-level executable specifications (units tests) help design the detailed implementation.

```
@DisplayName("When creating a new bank account")
class WhenCreatingANewAccount {

    @DisplayName("A new account should have an initial balance")
    @Test
    void newAccountTypeAndBalance() {
        BankAccount account = BankAccount.ofType(AccountType.Savings).withBalance(100);
        assertThat(account.getBalance()).isEqualTo(100.0);
        assertThat(account.getAccountType()).isEqualTo(AccountType.Savings);
    }
}
```

Figure 2.5   Low-level specifications, written as unit tests, flow naturally from the high-level specifications.

Depending on the platform you are working with, you could also write this specification using other unit-testing tools, such as NUnit or Mocha, or more specialized BDD tools such as RSpec.

Executable specifications like this are similar to conventional unit tests, but they're written in a way that both communicates the intent of the code and provides a worked example of how the code should be used. Writing low-level executable specifications this way is a little like writing detailed design documentation, with lots of examples, but using a tool that's easy and even fun for developers.

At a more technical level, this approach encourages a clean, modular design with well-defined interactions (or APIs, if you prefer a more technical term) between the modules. It also results in code that's reliable, accurate, and extremely well tested.

Unit testing the space shuttle

Good developers have known the importance of unit testing for a very long time. The IBM Federal Systems Division team was fully aware of their importance when they wrote the central avionics software for NASA's space shuttle in the late seventies. The approach they took to unit testing, where the unit tests were designed using the requirements and with examples provided by the business, has a surprisingly modern feel to it:

> "During the development activity, specific testing was done to ensure that the mathematical equations and logic paths provided the results expected. These algorithms and logic paths were checked for accuracy and, where possible, compared against results from external sources and against the system design specification (SDS)."[a]

[e] William A. Madden and Kyle Y. Rone, "Design, Development, Integration: Space Shuttle Primary Flight Software System," Communications of the ACM (September 1984).

2.3.8   *Deliver living documentation*

The reports produced by executable specifications aren't simply technical reports for developers but effectively become a form of product documentation for the whole team, expressed in a vocabulary familiar to users. This documentation is always up to date and requires little or no manual maintenance. It's automatically produced from the latest version of the application. Each application feature is described in readable terms and is illustrated by a few key examples. For web applications, this sort of living documentation often also includes screenshots of the application for each feature.

Experienced teams organize this documentation so that it's easy to read and easy for everyone involved in the project to use (see figure 2.6). Developers can consult it to see how existing features work. Testers and business analysts can see how the features they specified have been implemented. Product owners and project managers can use summary views to judge the current state of the project, view progress, and decide what features can be released into production. Users can even use it to see what the application can do and how it works.

Just as automated acceptance criteria provide great documentation for the whole team, low-level executable specifications also provide excellent technical documentation for other developers. This documentation is always up to date, is cheap to maintain, contains working code samples, and expresses the intent behind each specification.

What features have been planned?

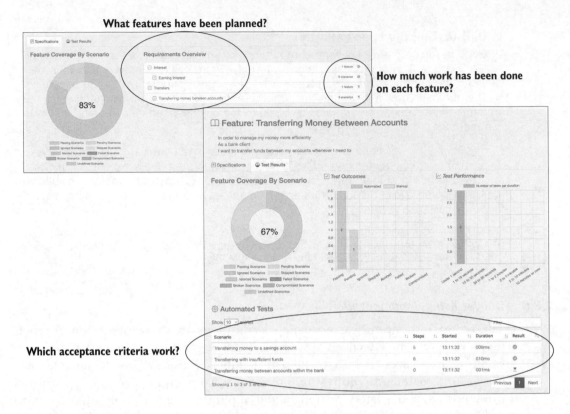

How much work has been done on each feature?

Which acceptance criteria work?

Figure 2.6   Well-organized living documentation can give an overview of the state of a project, as well as describe features in detail.

2.3.9 *Use living documentation to support ongoing maintenance work*

The benefits of living documentation and executable specifications don't stop at the end of the project. A project developed using these practices is also significantly easier and less expensive to maintain.

According to Robert L. Glass (quoting other sources), maintenance represents between 40% and 80% of software costs. Although many teams find that the number of defects drops dramatically when they adopt techniques like BDD, defects can still happen. Ongoing enhancements are also a natural part of any software application.[6]

In many organizations, when a project goes into production, it's handed over to a different team for maintenance work. The developers involved in this maintenance work have often not been involved in the project's development and need to learn the code base from scratch. Useful, relevant, and up-to-date functional and technical documentation makes this task a great deal easier.

---

[6] Robert L. Glass, *Facts and Fallacies of Software Engineering* (Addison-Wesley Professional, 2002).

The automated documentation that comes out of a BDD development process can go a long way toward providing the sort of documentation maintenance teams need in order to be effective. The high-level executable specifications help new developers understand the business goals and flow of the application. Executable specifications at the unit-testing level provide detailed worked examples of how particular features have been implemented.

Maintenance developers working on a BDD project find it easier to know where to start when they need to make a change. Good executable specifications provide a wealth of examples of how to test the application correctly, and maintenance changes will generally involve writing a new executable specification along similar lines or modifying an existing one.

The affect of maintenance changes on existing code is also easier to assess. When a developer makes a change, it may cause existing executable specifications to break, and when this happens, there are usually two possible causes:

- The broken executable specification may no longer reflect the new business requirements. In this case, the executable specification can be updated or (if it's no longer relevant) deleted.
- The code change has broken an existing requirement. This is a bug in the new code that needs to be fixed.

Executable specifications are not a magical solution to the traditional problems of technical documentation. They aren't guaranteed to always be meaningful or relevant; this requires practice and discipline. Other technical, architectural, and functional documentation is often required to complete the picture. But when they're written and organized well, executable specifications provide significant advantages over conventional approaches.

2.4 Benefits of BDD

In the previous sections, we examined what BDD looks like and discussed what it brings to the table. Now let's run through some of the key business benefits that an organization adopting BDD can expect in more detail.

2.4.1 Reduced waste

BDD is all about focusing the development effort on discovering and delivering the features that will provide business value and avoiding those that don't. When a team builds a feature that's not aligned with the business goals underlying the project, the effort is wasted for the business. Similarly, when a team writes a feature that the business needs, but in a way that's not useful to the business, the team will need to rework the feature to fit the bill, resulting in more waste. BDD helps avoid this sort of wasted effort by helping teams focus on features that are aligned with business goals.

BDD also reduces wasted effort by enabling faster, more useful feedback to users. This helps teams make changes sooner rather than later.

2.4.2   *Reduced costs*

The direct consequence of this reduced waste is reduced costs. By focusing on building features with demonstrable business value (building the right software), and not wasting effort on features of little value, you can reduce the cost of delivering a viable product to your users. And by improving the quality of the application code (building the software right), you reduce the number of bugs, and therefore the cost of fixing these bugs, as well as the cost associated with the delays these bugs would cause.

2.4.3   *Easier and safer changes*

BDD makes it considerably easier to change and extend your applications. Living documentation is generated from the executable specifications using terms that stakeholders are familiar with. This makes it much easier for stakeholders to understand what the application actually does. The low-level executable specifications also act as technical documentation for developers, making it easier for them to understand the existing code base and to make their own changes. Last, but certainly not least, BDD practices produce a comprehensive set of automated acceptance and unit tests, which reduces the risk of regressions caused by any new changes to the application.

2.4.4   *Faster releases*

These comprehensive automated tests also speed up the release cycle considerably. Testers are no longer required to carry out long manual testing sessions before each new release. Instead, they can use the automated acceptance tests as a starting point and spend their time more productively and efficiently on exploratory tests and other nontrivial manual tests.

2.5   *Disadvantages and potential challenges of BDD*

While its benefits are significant, introducing BDD into an organization isn't always without its difficulties. In this section, we'll look at a few situations where introducing BDD can be more of a challenge.

2.5.1   *BDD requires high business engagement and collaboration*

BDD practices are based on conversation and feedback. Indeed, these conversations drive and build the team's understanding of the requirements and of how they can deliver business value based on these requirements. If stakeholders are unwilling or unable to engage in conversations and collaboration, or they wait until the end of the project before giving any feedback, it will be hard to draw the full benefits of BDD.

2.5.2   *BDD works best in an Agile or iterative context*

BDD requirements-analysis practices assume that it's difficult, if not impossible, to define the requirements completely upfront and that these will evolve as the team (and the stakeholders) learn more about the project. This approach is naturally more in line with an Agile or iterative project methodology.

2.5.3   *BDD doesn't work well in a silo*

In many larger organizations, a siloed development approach is still the norm. Detailed specifications are written by business analysts and then handed off to development teams that are often offsite or offshore. Similarly, testing is delegated to another, totally separate, QA team. In organizations like this, it's still possible to practice BDD at a coding level, and development teams will still be able to expect significant increases in code quality, better design, more maintainable code, and fewer defects. But the lack of interaction between the business analyst teams and the developers will make it harder to use BDD practices to progressively clarify and understand the real requirements.

Similarly, siloed testing teams can be a challenge. If the QA team waits until the end of the project to intervene, or does so in isolation, they'll miss their chance to contribute to requirements earlier on, which results in wasted effort spent fixing problems that could have been found earlier and fixed more easily. Automating the acceptance criteria is also much more beneficial if the QA team participates in defining, and possibly automating, the scenarios.

2.5.4   *Poorly written tests can lead to higher test-maintenance costs*

Creating automated acceptance tests, particularly for complex web applications, requires a certain skill, and many teams starting to use BDD find this a significant challenge. Indeed, if the tests aren't carefully designed, with the right levels of abstraction and expressiveness, they run the risk of being fragile. And if there are a large number of poorly written tests, they'll certainly be hard to maintain. Plenty of organizations have successfully implemented automated acceptance tests for complex web applications, but it takes know-how and experience to get it right. We'll look at techniques for doing this later on in the book.

Summary

- BDD was originally conceived as a way to teach TDD—a design strategy where developers write low-level specifications describing the expected behavior of their code, in the form of unit tests, before they write the actual code—more easily. This helps them design and implement more precise, higher-quality code.
- Practitioners quickly found that the principles of BDD can also be applied to requirements discovery and business analysis.

- BDD practitioners implement features with a top-down approach, using the acceptance criteria as goals and describing the behavior of each component with unit tests written in the form of executable specifications.
- Executable specifications can be automated using tools like Cucumber or Spec-Flow to produce both automated regression tests and up-to-date functional documentation.
- The main benefits of BDD include focusing efforts on delivering valuable features, reducing wasted effort and costs, making it easier and safer to make changes, and accelerating the release process.

In the next chapter, we'll take a flying tour of what BDD looks like in practice, all the way from requirements analysis to automated unit and acceptance tests and functional test coverage reports.

BDD: The whirlwind tour

3

This chapter covers

- An end-to-end walkthrough of BDD practices in action
- Discovering features and describing them through stories and examples
- Using executable specifications to specify features in detail
- Using low-level BDD to implement features
- Using BDD test results as living documentation and to support ongoing maintenance

In this chapter, we'll look at a concrete example of how BDD might work on a real-world project. As you saw in the previous chapter, BDD involves the development team engaging in conversations with the customer throughout the project, using examples to build up a more concrete and less ambiguous understanding of what the business really needs. You write specifications in an executable form that you can use to define software requirements, drive their implementation, and verify the product you deliver. You can also apply these techniques during more high-level requirements analysis, helping you focus on the capabilities and features of the application that will genuinely add value to the business.

A key part of this practice involves defining scenarios, or concrete examples of how a particular feature or story works. These scenarios will help you to validate and extend your understanding of the problem, and they're also an excellent communication tool. They act as the foundation of the acceptance criteria, which you then integrate into the build process in the form of automated acceptance tests. In conjunction with the automated acceptance tests, these examples guide the development process, helping designers to prepare effective and functional user interface designs and assisting developers to discover the underlying behaviors that they'll need to implement to deliver the required features.

In the rest of this chapter, we'll look at a practical example of this process in action. We'll touch on aspects of the whole development cycle, from business analysis to implementing, testing, and maintaining the code. The aim of this chapter is to give you an idea of the approach and some of the technologies involved, rather than to provide a full working example of any particular technology stack, but we'll go into enough technical detail for you to follow along. In the chapters that follow, we'll look at each of the topics covered in this chapter, and many others, in much more detail.

3.1 *The BDD flow*

A good way to visualize the BDD process is to break it down into the various stages or steps that a requirement goes through in its journey from vague idea to implemented feature. At each stage, teams perform different activities to build up their understanding of what they need to deliver and to be sure that what they do deliver fits the bill.

We can see this flow visualized in figure 3.1. The key phases are outlined here:

1 *Speculate*—Where the team has conversations with businesspeople to identify and understand high-level business goals and identify the key features that will help us deliver these goals.

2 *Illustrate*—Where team members build a deeper understanding of a specific feature, through conversations about concrete examples of business rules and user journeys.

3 *Formulate*—Where team members transform key examples into executable specifications, using a notation that is both readable for businesspeople and that can be executed as automated tests.

4 *Automate*—Where developers and testers turn these executable specifications into automated acceptance tests and use these automated acceptance tests to drive the development process.

5 *Demonstrate*—Where the passing automated acceptance tests act as evidence that a feature has been correctly implemented and as documentation illustrating the current features and how they work. This is where the team verifies that a feature does what was asked of it.

6 *Validate*—Where the team and the business see how the features fare in the real world and whether they deliver the business value they promised.

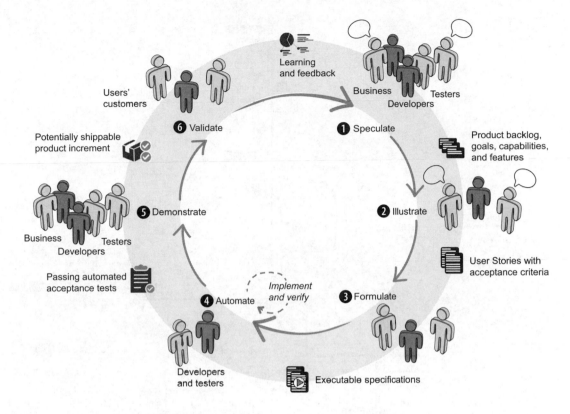

Figure 3.1   Key activities of a BDD team

We will look at each of these phases in detail in the rest of this book. Let's look at this process in the context of a practice example.

3.2   *Speculate: Identifying business value and features*

Tracy works for a large, government public-transport department. She has been asked to lead a small team in building an application that will provide train timetable data and real-time updates about delays, track work, and so on to busy commuters. She has decided to apply BDD practices from start to finish. By following her journey, we will get an idea of how BDD works in real-world projects. Figure 3.2 illustrates the rail network her team will be working with. Let's start by taking a closer look at the project goals.

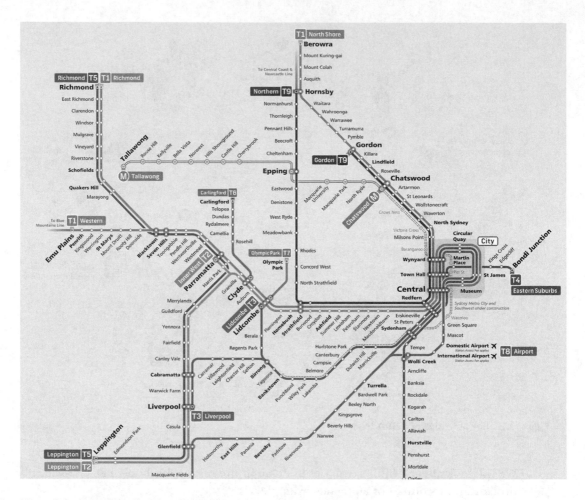

Figure 3.2   Part of the Sydney rail network

3.2.1   *Identifying business objectives*

Can each member of your team articulate the business objectives of your project? Can they state, in a few simple sentences, what business problem they are solving? It is surprising to see for how many teams this is not the case.

A team with a deep, common understanding of their goals will be able to better align their efforts, and also react to change or unexpected hurdles more effectively. For example, if they cannot deliver a particular feature for a technical reason, or they find it would be much more expensive to implement than expected, they can consider alternatives that might achieve the same business outcome.

Teams with a clear vision of the value of their work also tend to be more motivated and engaged. They feel part of the bigger picture. All this goes a long way toward ensuring that the project as a whole meets its objectives.

So, Tracy's first task is to make sure that everyone is clear about the project goals. Early on in the project, she brings the project sponsor and her team members into a large room to discuss these goals. According to the project sponsor, the project goal goes something like this: "We want to build an application that lets commuters plan their journeys online."

Part of the department's mission statement is to make public transport more attractive and more efficient for travelers. Commuters don't like waiting; they want to minimize the unproductive time they have to spend in public transport. And according to customer research, a big pain point for commuters is missing connections. They have trouble knowing what trains they should take and want to avoid standing on platforms for too long.

But the goal doesn't really capture any of these details. It doesn't explain *why* commuters might use the application, and how it might benefit them. So, after a bit of discussion, the team agreed with the business sponsors on the following project vision statement: "The application will help to reduce average travel time for regular commuters by 10% within a year, by allowing them to plan their journeys more effectively."

Now the team has put a number on the goal, which makes it measurable. All commuters have a travel card that they use at the start and end of their trips, so average trip time is something that can be measured fairly easily. This helps the team know what they are aiming for, and also helps the organization know if the application is delivering on its promises.

But this is just the start of the conversation. Next, Tracy and her team need to work with the business sponsors to identify the features that will best deliver on this goal.

3.2.2 *Discovering capabilities and features*

In a more traditional development process, the business hands off a list of requirements to implement. In Agile projects in general, and for teams practicing BDD in particular, team members are much more engaged in the requirements discovery and solution-finding process. Tracy and her team are no exception.

In BDD we call this initial phase the *Speculate* phase, because we are speculating about what features might help the organization achieve their goals. For example, a feature that notifies commuters if their train is late would contribute to the overall goal, because it would give travelers the opportunity to save time by changing their plans accordingly. On the other hand, a feature that lets commuters rate railway stations might not be considered of particularly high value, because it provides little actionable information for a commuter running late.

Many teams find Impact Mapping (see figure 3.3) a useful exercise to discover and prioritize high-level capabilities and features that can help deliver a business goal. Impact mapping helps business and technical people discuss business goals through the prism of four fundamental questions: "*Why* are we doing this (i.e., what are our business goals)?" "*Whose* behavior do we need to change (i.e., who are the key actors)?" "*How* might their behavior change (i.e., what changes in their behavior would help us achieve our business goals)?" and "*What* software features might support this behavior change?" We will look at impact mapping in more detail in the next chapter.

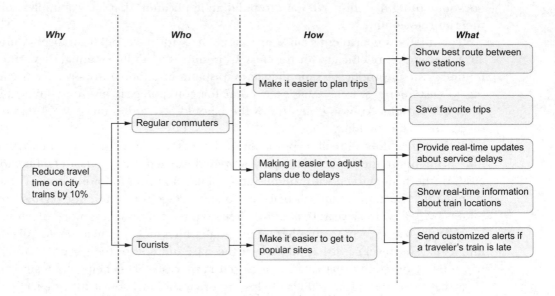

Figure 3.3   An Impact Map identifying high-level capabilities and features

Tracy and her team run an Impact Mapping workshop with businesspeople. This helps them get a deeper understanding of the project. For example, although both tourists and commuters will be using the service, the vast majority of users will be commuters, so features for these users will have more influence on the outcomes they are trying to achieve. They identify two key capabilities that they want to give commuters: the ability to plan their daily commute more easily and the ability to cope with unexpected delays or interruptions.

Finally, they agree on the following essential features that might give commuters these capabilities, which you can see to the right of the Impact Map:

- Shows the optimal route between two stations
- Allows commuters to record their favorite trips
- Provides real-time train timetable information about service delays to travelers
- Shows real-time information about the location of their train
- Notifies commuters if their train is late

Let's look at how you might describe some of these features.

3.2.3   *Describing features*

Once you have a general idea of the features you want to deliver, you need to describe them in more detail. There are many ways to describe a requirement. Agile teams like to write a short outline of the requirement in a format that's small enough to fit on an index card.[1] Teams practicing BDD often use the following format as a guideline:[2]

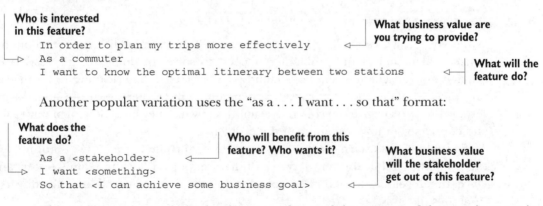

Who needs it?

What business outcomes are you trying to achieve?

```
In order to <achieve a business goal or deliver business value>
As a <stakeholder>
I want <to be able to do something>
```

What must you do to help achieve this outcome?

The order here is important. When you plan features and stories, your principal aim should be to deliver business value. Start out with what business value you intend to provide, then who needs the feature you're proposing, and finally what feature you think will support this outcome.

This helps ensure that each feature actively contributes to achieving a business goal, and so reduces the risk of scope creep. It also acts as a healthy reminder of why you're implementing this feature in the first place. For example, you could say something like this:

Who is interested in this feature?

What business value are you trying to provide?

```
In order to plan my trips more effectively
As a commuter
I want to know the optimal itinerary between two stations
```

What will the feature do?

Another popular variation uses the "as a . . . I want . . . so that" format:

What does the feature do?

Who will benefit from this feature? Who wants it?

```
As a <stakeholder>
I want <something>
So that <I can achieve some business goal>
```

What business value will the stakeholder get out of this feature?

This variation aims to help developers understand the context of the requirement in terms of who will be using a feature and what they expect it to do for them. The stakeholder refers to the person using the feature, or who is interested in its output. The business goal identifies why this feature is needed and what value it's supposed to provide. The equivalent of the feature mentioned earlier might be something like this:

```
As a commuter
I want to know the best way to travel between two stations
So that I can get to my destination quickly
```

---

[1] These index cards can then be used to plan and visualize your progress.

[2] This format was originally proposed by Chris Matts, in the context of Feature Injection, which we'll look at in the next chapter.

Sometimes it is useful to mention how this will be an improvement on the current situation. We can use phrases like "whereas currently" or "unlike currently" to compare and contrast the solution we propose with the current way of working. For example,

```
As a commuter
I want to be able to easily find the optimal route between two stations
So that I can get to my destination quickly
Unlike currently where I need to look up the timetable in a paper booklet
```

All of these are handy conventions, but there's no obligation to choose one format over another, as long as you remember to express the business benefits clearly. For example, some experienced practitioners are happy to use the "in order to . . . as a . . . I want" format for higher-level features, where the emphasis is very much on the business value the system should deliver, but they switch to "as a . . . I want . . . so . . . that" for more detailed User Stories within a feature, when the stories clearly are about delivering value to particular users in the context of that feature.

3.3   *Illustrate: Exploring a feature with examples*

Tracy and her team now have a list of features to deliver, along with a good understanding of how these features will benefit the organization. Now it's time to start exploring them in more detail. And a great way to do this is to ask for some examples.

3.3.1   *Discovering the feature*

When you hear a user asking for a feature, you'll often immediately start to build a conceptual model of the problem you need to solve. In doing so, it's easy to let implicit and unstated assumptions cloud your understanding, leading to an inaccurate mental model and an incorrect implementation further down the line. Asking the stakeholders to give you concrete examples of what they mean is a great way to test and confirm your understanding of the problem.

So, before work starts on the "show the optimal route between two stations" feature, Tracy gets Jill, the rail network domain expert; Tess, the team's tester; and Dave, the developer who will be implementing the feature, together. The conversation goes like this:[3]

> Tracy: Can you give me an example of a commuter traveling between two stations?
>
> Jill: Sure, how about going from Epping to Town Hall?
>
> Tracy: And what would that look like?
>
> Jill: Well, they'd have to take the T9 line. That's a heavily used line, and there are between 8 and 16 trains per hour, depending on the time of day. We'd just need to propose the next scheduled trips on that line.

---

[3] You can follow along with these examples by referring to the map in figure 3.1.

Dave: Is the next train that arrives always the best train to take?

Jill: Not always; if the next train is an all-stops train, and the following is an express, then the following one might be better.

Tess: Will there always be a next train?

Jill: No; they stop around midnight. If the last train has already left for the night, we would need to tell the commuter about the night bus options.

Dave: And are there any days the trains don't run at all?

Jill: Well, I don't think so, but I would have to check with the timetable people; it might happen on certain lines.

Tracy: Could you have a trip where a commuter would have the choice of more than one line?

Jill: Yes, a commuter going from Hornsby to Central could take the T9 or the T1. The trip time will vary from about 37 minutes to around 48 minutes, and trains from any of these lines typically arrive every couple of minutes, so we'd need to give commuters enough information on departure and arrival times for the trains on both lines.

Even in this relatively straightforward example, you can see that there are some subtleties. It's not always a simple matter of proposing the next train; you have to give the commuter details about departure and arrival times for all the scheduled upcoming trains.

Tracy uses a technique called Example Mapping[4] to make the discovery process more visual. She notes these examples and rules using colored Post-Its on a wall: Blue cards represent the business rules, and green cards represent examples and counter-examples of these rules. Pink cards represent questions that they don't have answers for right now. A yellow card at the top of the board reminds them which feature or User Story is being discussed.

BDD teams often use facilitation techniques like this to guide these conversations, to keep them focused, and to record the key examples that come up. Example Mapping is one such technique; Feature Mapping is another. We will look at both of these in much more detail later on in the book.

---

[4] Example Mapping was originally developed by Matt Wynne (see https://cucumber.io/blog/example-mapping -introduction/).

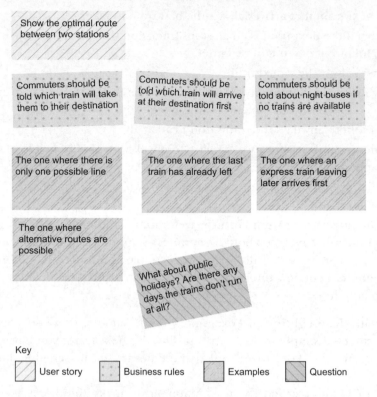

Figure 3.4   **Tracy uses an Example Map to record and organize the business rules and examples.**

3.3.2 *Slicing the feature into User Stories*

Often these conversations uncover uncertainty or complexity, which leads us to split features into smaller chunks. In Scrum, a User Story needs to be small enough to deliver in a single sprint. If a feature will take more than one sprint to build, it is good practice to split it into several stories that can be delivered incrementally over several sprints. This way, the team can get feedback earlier and more often, which in turn reduces the risk of error.

In this case, Tracy and her team decide to split the feature into a number of smaller stories. For instance, the first example card, "The one where there is only one possible line," could be delivered as a User Story in its own right. This simple case will let them build up the initial application architecture without too much domain complexity. We could describe this story as follows:

> *Direct Connections*
>
> As a commuter traveling between two stations on the same line
>
> I want to know what time the next trains for my destination will leave
>
> So that I can spend less time waiting at the station

The next example, "The one where alternative routes are possible," would also justify its own story:

> *Alternative Routes*
>
> As a commuter traveling between two stations on different lines
>
> I want to know what time the fastest train to my destination will leave
>
> So that I can spend less time waiting at the station or for connecting trains

The team agrees that these are enough stories to get started with. Now let's see how they turn these stories and examples into executable specifications.

3.4 Formulate: From examples to executable specifications

Tracy's team now has a set of stories and examples that they want to implement. In this section, we'll see how to take these business-focused examples and rewrite them in the form of executable specifications. You'll see how you can automate these specifications, and how doing so leads to discovering what code you need to write. And you'll see how these executable specifications can be a powerful reporting and living documentation tool.

We can use examples like the ones Tracy and her team recorded as the basis for more formal acceptance criteria. In a nutshell, the acceptance criteria are what will satisfy stakeholders (and QA) that the application does what it's supposed to do.

Conversations like the one with Jill (in section 2.3.1) are a great way to build up your understanding of the problem space, but you can take things a lot further if you use a slightly more structured style. In BDD, the following notation is often used to express examples:[5]

```
Given <a context>
When <something happens>
Then <you expect some outcome>
```

This format helps you think in terms of how users interact with the system and what the outcomes should be. As you'll see in the next section, they're also easy to convert into automated acceptance tests using tools like Cucumber. But because you may want to automate these tests later on, their format is a little less flexible. As you'll see, words like *Given*, *When*, and *Then* have special meanings for these tools, so it's best to think of them as special keywords.

In BDD parlance we call these formalized examples *scenarios*. Let's see what scenarios Tracy's team come up with for the Direct Connections story:

---

[5] As we mentioned in chapter 1, the Given . . . When . . . Then syntax shown here is often referred to as the Gherkin format. Gherkin is the syntax used by Cucumber and related tools, which is what we will use for this example. We'll look at all this in great detail in chapter 5.

Direct Connections

The one where there is only one possible line

As a commuter traveling between two stations on the same line

I want to know what time the next trains for my destination will leave

So that I can spend less time waiting at the station

Tracy gets together with Jill and Tess to work through some concrete examples and to express these using the Given . . . When . . . Then notation:

> Tess: Can we start with a simple example? Say, Travis the traveler wants to take a trip that only involves a single line?
>
> Jill: Sure; he could take the 8:02 from Hornsby to Chatswood, which is a direct trip.

Tess writes this up as follows:

**What is the context or
background for this example?**

```
Scenario: Display the next train going to the requested destination
   Given the next train leaves Hornsby at 8:02
   When Travis wants to travel from Hornsby to Chatswood at 8:00
   Then he should be told to take the 8:02 train
```

**What action are
you describing?**

**What is the
expected
outcome?**

When Jill reads this aloud, she notices a glitch. "That's not quite right," she says. "There are two lines that depart from Hornsby, and an 8:02 train from Hornsby could go in one of two directions. You need to know which line Travis is taking, and in which direction."

Tess refines the scenario accordingly:

```
Scenario: Display the next train going to the requested destination
   Given the T1 train to Chatswood leaves Hornsby at 8:02
   When Travis wants to travel from Hornsby to Chatswood at 8:00
   Then he should be told to take the 8:02 train
```

**Now we include both the
line name and the direction.**

Jill reads the new scenario. She's still not happy. "That's not very realistic. Travis only has two minutes to buy a ticket and get to the right platform. He really needs to be told about the next few trains, not just the next one."

"Would it be safer just to show the next two trains?" asks Tess. Jill thinks so, so Tess refines the scenario a bit more:

```
Scenario: Display the next train going to the requested destination
   Given the T1 train to Chatswood leaves Hornsby at 8:02, 8:15, 8:21
   When Travis wants to travel from Hornsby to Chatswood at 8:00
   Then he should be told about the trains at: 8:02, 8:15
```

**Identifies several train times to make
the example more representative**

**Now we need to tell Travis
about the next two trains.**

The simple act of working together to write out scenarios like these is a great way to improve our understanding of the problem we are solving, flush out hidden assumptions, and reduce risk. Many teams find that these conversations alone significantly reduce defects and improve the quality of the delivered features.

But one of the most powerful things about BDD is the idea that these examples can somehow become executable, so that they become simultaneously automated acceptance tests and business-readable specifications. In the next section, we will see how we can transform these acceptance criteria into executable specifications using Java, Cucumber, Maven, and Git.

3.5   Automate: From executable specifications to automated tests

There are many specialized BDD tools that you can use to automate your acceptance criteria. Popular choices include tools like Cucumber (for Java, JavaScript, Ruby, and many other languages), SpecFlow (for .NET), and Behave (for Python). While not indispensable, these tools do make it easier to express the automated tests in a structured form similar to the Given . . . When . . . Then expressions used in the previous section. This makes it easier for product owners and testers to understand and identify the automated acceptance criteria, which in turn can help increase their confidence in the automated tests and in the automated acceptance testing approach in general.

3.5.1   Setting up a project with Maven and Cucumber

Throughout the rest of this book, we'll illustrate examples using several different BDD tools. In this chapter, we'll see how to write executable specifications using Cucumber and Java,[6] and the project will be built and run using Maven. Maven (http://maven.apache.org/) is a widely used build tool in the Java world. The test reports will be generated using Serenity BDD,[7] an open source library that makes it easier to organize and report on BDD test results.

The source code for this chapter is available on GitHub[8] and on the Manning website. We will walk through the full process, following along with Tess and Dave as they implement the automated acceptance tests in Cucumber, and use these tests to drive their development process. If you want to follow along, you'll need a development environment with the following software installed:

- A Java JDK (the sample code was developed using OpenJava 12.0.2, but it should work fine with JDK 1.8 or higher)
- Maven 3.6.x or higher
- Git (if you want to see the sample solution in action and follow along, you will also need to set up a GitHub account)

---

[6] If Java isn't your cup of tea, don't worry; the code samples are designed to be readable by anyone with some programming background.
[7] See the Serenity BDD site (http://serenity-bdd.info) for more details about this library.
[8] The source for this chapter is available on GitHub (https://github.com/bdd-in-action/second-edition).

The first thing Tess and Dave do is create a new Maven project using the Serenity Cucumber Starter template project on GitHub[9] (see figure 3.5). GitHub template projects are a convenient way to create skeleton projects using a specific set of libraries. If you have a GitHub account, you can click the Use This Template button to create a new repository in your own account with a copy of the template project. And if you don't have a GitHub account, you can click the Code menu to download a zip file containing the source code for the template project. This particular project template contains a skeleton project structure with recent versions of Cucumber and Serenity BDD.

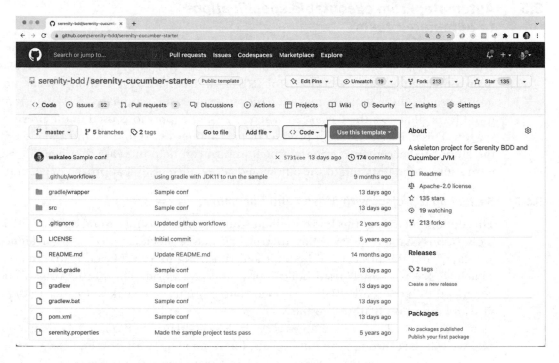

Figure 3.5   The Serenity Cucumber Starter template project on GitHub

Tess clicks the Use This Template button to create a new GitHub repository, which she calls train_timetables (see figure 3.6). This creates a new skeleton project in her own account, that she can clone to her local machine:

```
C:\Users\tess\projects>git clone
> https://github.com/bdd-in-action-second-edition/train-timetables.git
Cloning into 'train-timetables'...
remote: Enumerating objects: 43, done.
```

---

[9] See https://github.com/serenity-bdd/serenity-cucumber-starter.

```
remote: Counting objects: 100% (43/43), done.
remote: Compressing objects: 100% (35/35), done.
Receiving objects:  32% (14/43)sed 23 (delta 1), pack-reused
0 receiving objects:  30% (13/43)
Receiving objects: 100% (43/43), 65.71 KiB | 1.29 MiB/s, done.
```

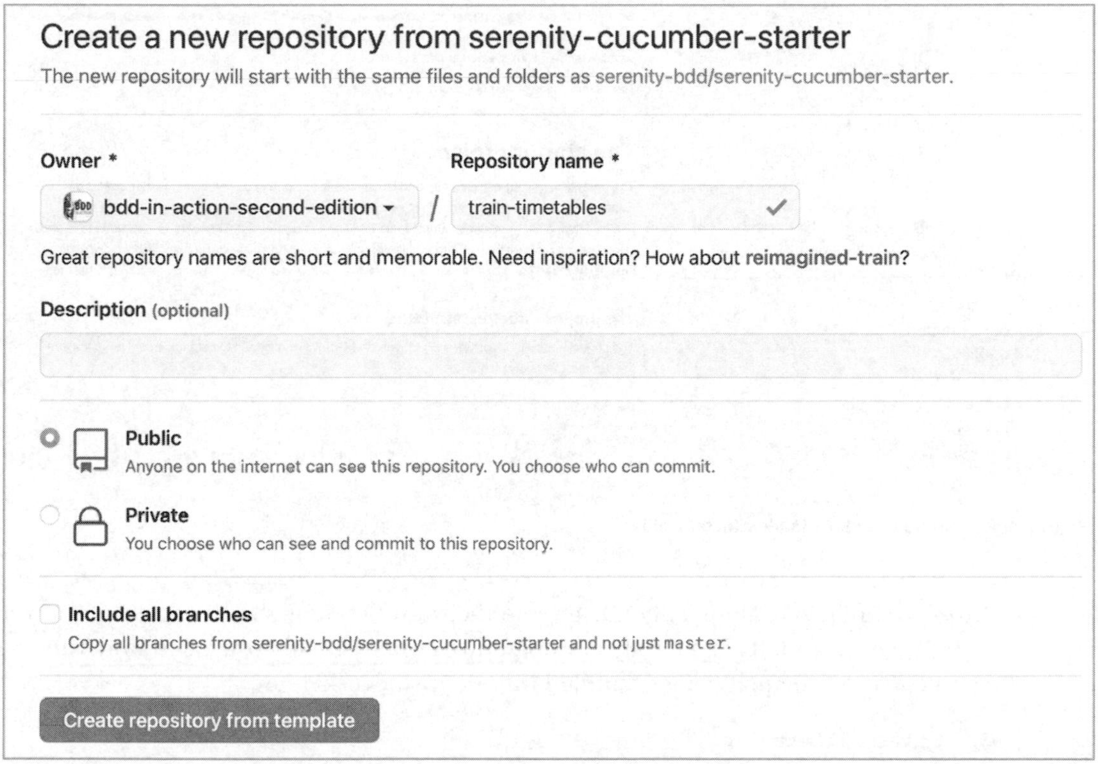

Create a new repository from serenity-cucumber-starter

The new repository will start with the same files and folders as serenity-bdd/serenity-cucumber-starter.

Owner *   **Repository name ***

  🔵 bdd-in-action-second-edition ▾   /   train-timetables   ✓

Great repository names are short and memorable. Need inspiration? How about **reimagined-train**?

Description (optional)

[   ]

🔵 📖 **Public**
      Anyone on the internet can see this repository. You choose who can commit.

⚪ 🔒 **Private**
      You choose who can see and commit to this repository.

☐ **Include all branches**
   Copy all branches from serenity-bdd/serenity-cucumber-starter and not just `master`.

[Create repository from template]

Figure 3.6   Creating a new repository from the Template project

Next, Tess imports the template project into her IDE (see figure 3.7). This starter project contains a standard directory structure along with a few sample test classes. The most important files and directories include

- *src*—The main directory containing the application source code.
- *src/main/java*—The source code for your application goes here.
- *src/test/java*—This is where the Java classes for your tests go.
- *src/test/resources*—This is where other files needed for the test suite, such as Cucumber feature files, are placed.
- *pom.xml*—The Maven build script.
- *build.gradle*—The equivalent Gradle build script.

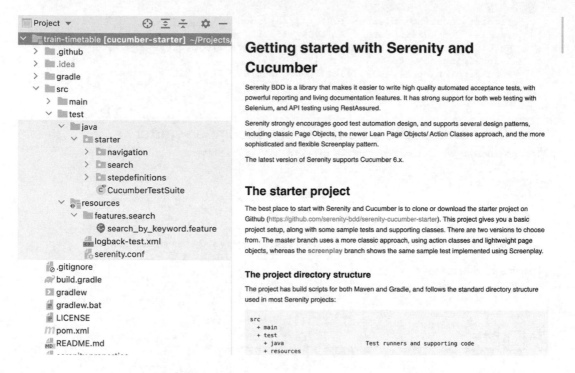

Figure 3.7 The new project loaded into IntelliJ

If you are following along at home, go into the train-timetables folder and run the mvn verify command. This should download any dependencies you need and run the simple feature file that comes bundled with the project skeleton:

```
$ cd train-timetables
$ mvn verify
[INFO] Scanning for projects...
…
[INFO] -------------------------------------------------------
[INFO]  T E S T S
[INFO] -------------------------------------------------------
…
[INFO] ------------------------------------------------------------------
[INFO] BUILD SUCCESS
[INFO] ------------------------------------------------------------------
[INFO] Total time:  14.320 s
[INFO] Finished at: 2021-10-09T07:54:04+01:00
[INFO] ------------------------------------------------------------------
```

The last piece of housekeeping work Tess needs to do is to make the project her own. She renames the starter package to something more related to her organization and project and deletes the sample code and sample feature file. The project she ends up with looks like the one in figure 3.8.

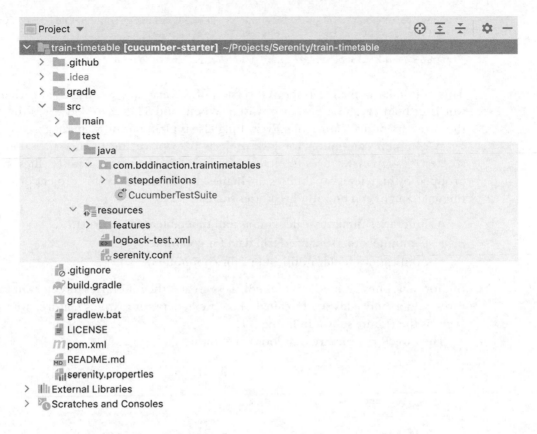

Figure 3.8   The tailored project structure ready to start work

Now that they have a project skeleton up and running, Tess and Dave move on to more interesting work: implementing the scenarios they discovered earlier on in a form that Cucumber can execute.

3.5.2   *Recording the executable specifications in Cucumber*

In Cucumber, we record scenarios like the ones we wrote earlier in special files called *feature files*. These files have a ".feature" suffix and are designed to contain, as the name suggests, all of the scenarios that describe the behavior of a particular feature. Tess records the scenario that she defined with Jill in the previous question, as follows.

Listing 3.1   An acceptance criteria expressed in Cucumber

```
Feature: Show next departing trains

    As a commuter traveling between two stations on the same line
    I want to know what time the next trains for my destination will leave
    So that I can spend less time waiting at the station
```

```
Scenario: Next train going to the requested destination on the same line
   Given the T1 train to Chatswood leaves Hornsby at 8:02, 8:15, 8:21
   When Travis wants to travel from Hornsby to Chatswood at 8:00
   Then he should be told about the trains at: 8:02, 8:15
```

This is little more than a structured version of the example we discussed earlier. The words in bold (Feature, Scenario, Given, When, and Then) are keywords that mark the structure of the feature file. Everything else is plain business language.

A common convention for Java projects is to place the feature files under the src/test/resources/features directory. Within this directory, feature files can be grouped by high-level capabilities or themes. For example, as this project progresses, the team might end up with directories such as

- itineraries (itinerary calculations and timetable information)
- commuters (personalized trip data for commuters)
- notifications (delay notifications for commuters)

But for now, one feature file is enough. Tess creates the itineraries directory in the features folder and adds a file called show_next_departing_trains.feature, where she records the feature shown in listing 3.1.

The directory structure now looks like this:

```
|____src
| |____test
| | |____resources
| | | |____features
| | | | |____itineraries
| | | | | |____show_next_departing_trains.feature
```

This now counts as an executable specification. Though there is no code behind the scenario to make it test anything, you can still execute it. When you execute it, the tests will fail (because there is no code to implement them), but Serenity BDD will still generate a report presenting the scenarios that are awaiting implementation. If you want to try this out, go into the train-timetables directory and run the following command:

```
$ mvn clean verify
```

This will produce a big ugly error message like the one in figure 3.9, but it will also generate a set of reports in the target/site/serenity directory.[10]

If you open the index.html file in this directory and click on the only test in the Test table at the bottom of the screen, you should see something like figure 3.10.

---

[10] If you're not a regular Maven user, Maven will first download the libraries it needs to work with; this may take some time, but you'll only need to do it once.

```
[INFO] ------------------------------------------------
[INFO]
[INFO] SERENITY REPORTS
[INFO]    - Full Report: file:///Users/john/Projects/Serenity/train-timetable/target/site/serenity/index.html
[INFO]
[INFO] --- maven-failsafe-plugin:3.0.0-M5:verify (default) @ cucumber-starter ---
[INFO] ------------------------------------------------
[INFO] BUILD FAILURE
[INFO] ------------------------------------------------
[INFO] Total time:  5.173 s
[INFO] Finished at: 2022-11-22T22:49:31Z
[INFO] ------------------------------------------------
[ERROR] Failed to execute goal org.apache.maven.plugins:maven-failsafe-plugin:3.0.0-M5:verify (default) on project cucumber-starter: There are test failures.
[ERROR]
[ERROR] Please refer to /Users/john/Projects/Serenity/train-timetable/target/failsafe-reports for the individual test results.
[ERROR] Please refer to dump files (if any exist) [date].dump, [date]-jvmRun[N].dump and [date].dumpstream.
[ERROR] -> [Help 1]
[ERROR]
[ERROR] To see the full stack trace of the errors, re-run Maven with the -e switch.
[ERROR] Re-run Maven using the -X switch to enable full debug logging.
[ERROR]
[ERROR] For more information about the errors and possible solutions, please read the following articles:
[ERROR] [Help 1] http://cwiki.apache.org/confluence/display/MAVEN/MojoFailureException
```

Figure 3.9   Running the executable specification without any underlying test code will result in error.

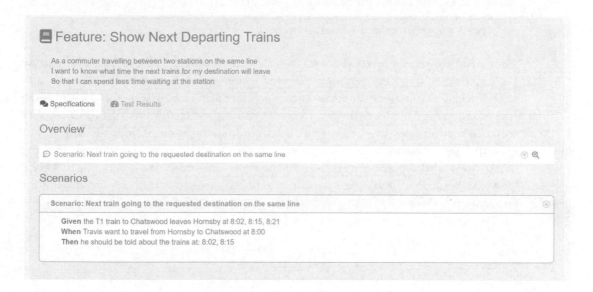

Figure 3.10   The Pending Cucumber feature in the acceptance test reports

At this point, the scenario is no longer a simple text document; it's now an *executable specification*. It can be run as part of the automated build process to automatically determine whether a particular feature has been completed.

The language used in these scenarios is very close to the terms that Jill used in the conversations with the team. And when the scenarios appear in the test reports, the use of this familiar language makes it easier for testers, end users, and other nondevelopers to understand what features are being tested and how they're being tested.

3.5.3   *Automating the executable specifications*

Now it is time to turn this executable specification into an automated test. First Tess double-checks the test runner class that came with the skeleton project. It is configured to run all of the feature files under the features directory, and looks like this:

```
@RunWith(CucumberWithSerenity.class)
@CucumberOptions(features="src/test/resources/features/",
                 glue="manning.bddinaction"
)
public class AcceptanceTestSuite {}
```

At a future date, she may add some more options to this runner class, but for now it will do just fine.

Next, she and Dave write some test automation code that will be called whenever their scenario is executed. Remember (from listing 3.1), their scenario looks like this:

```
Scenario: Next train going to the requested destination on the same line
    Given the T1 train to Central leaves Hornsby at 08:02, 08:15, 08:21
    When Travis wants to travel from Hornsby to Chatswood at 08:00
    Then he should be told about the trains at: 08:02, 08:15
```

They need to write a method for each one of these Given, When, and Then steps. Cucumber uses special annotations (named rather appropriately @Given, @When, and @Then) to know which method to run for each scenario step. These annotations use a special notation called Cucumber Expressions to identify the bits of the Cucumber scenario that represent test data (e.g., the train line and stations, and the times). For example, the annotation for the first Given step needs to pass in the train line, the departure and destination stations, and the departure time. We often call this code *glue code*, because it binds the text in the scenario steps to actual test automation or application code.

The initial code that Tess and Dave write for this step looks something like this:

```
@Given("the {line} train to {station} leaves {station} at {times}")
public void theTrainLeavesAt(String line,
                             String to,
                             String from,
                             List<LocalTime> departureTimes) {}
```

Tess places these methods in a class called DepartingTrainsStepDefinitions, which she places in a steps package right underneath the test runner class, as follows.

> **Listing 3.2   A basic Cucumber scenario implementation**

```
package com.bddinaction.traintimetables.stepdefinitions;

import io.cucumber.java.ParameterType;
import io.cucumber.java.en.Given;
```

```
import io.cucumber.java.en.Then;
import io.cucumber.java.en.When;

public class DepartingTrainsStepDefinitions {

    @Given("the {} train to {} leaves {} at {}")
    public void theTrainLeavesAt(String line,
                                 String to,
                                 String from,
                                 String departureTimes) {}

    @When("Travis want to travel from {} to {} at {}")
    public void travel(String from, String to, String departureTime) {}

    @Then("he should be told about the trains at: {}")
    public void shouldBeToldAboutTheTrainsAt(String expectedTimes) {}
}
```

For teams practicing BDD, code like this is the gateway to production code. It tells you precisely what your underlying code needs to do to satisfy the business requirements. From here, we can start to think not only about what our production code should do, but also how best to test it.

And this is what Tess and Dave do next. Let's follow their progress, as they turn these empty methods into fully fledged automated acceptance tests, and then use these tests to drive out the production code.

3.5.4   *Implementing the glue code*

BDD practitioners like to start with the outcome they need to obtain and work backward, so Tess and Dave start with the @Then step, which expresses the outcome they expect. They imagine a service to implement the timetable logic. They aren't too sure what this service should look like just yet, but they do know that it needs to give them a list of proposed departure times. And writing the glue code gives them the perfect opportunity to experiment with different API designs and see what they like best.

DEFINING THE EXPECTATIONS IN THE @THEN METHOD

Tess starts by updating the @Then method to describe the outcome she expects:

We introduce a custom Cucumber Expression called {times} to represent a list of expected times.

```
    @Then("he should be told about the trains at: {times}")
    public void shouldBeToldAboutTheTrainsAt(List<LocalTime> expected) {
      assertThat(proposedDepartures).isEqualTo(expected);
    }

    @ParameterType(".*")
    public LocalTime time(String timeValue) {
      return LocalTime.parse(timeValue, DateTimeFormatter.ofPattern("H:mm"));
    }
```

We define the {time} and {times} Cucumber Expressions to parse string values and convert them to either a single date or a list of dates, respectively.

```
@ParameterType(".*")
public List<LocalTime> times(String timeValue) {
    return stream(timeValue.split(","))
            .map(String::trim)
            .map(this::time)
            .collect(Collectors.toList());
}
```

> We define the {time} and {times} Cucumber Expressions to parse string values and convert them to either a single date or a list of dates, respectively.

Naturally, this code doesn't compile. They need to declare the proposedDepartures variable and figure out where the proposed train will come from. But this will come in good time.

Writing the executable specifications before writing the code is a great way to discover and flesh out the technical design you need in order to deliver the business goals. It helps you discover what domain classes would make sense, what services you might need, and how the services need to interact with each other. It also helps you think about how to make your code easy to test. And code that is easy to test is easy to maintain.

DISCOVERING THE SERVICE CLASS API IN THE @WHEN METHOD

In this case, Tess imagines a simple method called findNextDepartures() to find the next departure times from a given station. When she adds this code to the step definition method, the result looks something like this:

> In the When step we add a {time} expression to describe the expected departure time.

```
List<LocalTime> proposedDepartures;

@When("Travis want to travel from {} to {} at {time}")
public void travel(String from, String to, LocalTime departureTime) {
    proposedDepartures = itineraryService.findNextDepartures(departureTime,
                                                              from, to);
}

@ParameterType(".*")
public LocalTime time(String timeValue) {
    return LocalTime.parse(timeValue);
}
```

> Finding the next departure times

> Our {time} Cucumber Expression converts a string parameter into a Java Time object.

"But where does the itineraryService come from?" Dave wonders. "We'll need to define it earlier on." He adds the following line at the top of the class to create the service:

```
ItineraryService itineraryService = new ItineraryService();
```

Next, he creates the ItineraryService class itself, along with an empty implementation of the findNextDepartures() method:

```
public class ItineraryService {
  public List<LocalTime> findNextDepartures(LocalTime departureTime,
                                            String from, String to) {
```

```
        return null;
    }
}
```

"The `itineraryService` will also need to know about the timetable details we mention in the Given step," points out Tess. "That's a pretty separate concern, so it probably should go in its own class."

"I agree," says Dave. "But let's not get sidetracked by that just yet; the timetable logic could be pretty hairy. Let's just create a `TimeTable` interface to model how our itinerary service needs to interact with the timetable service."

This is a typical BDD approach, often referred to as *outside-in*. As we implement a layer, we will discover other things it needs to function, other services it needs to call. We have a choice: we can either build these things straight away, or we can put them to one side, model them as an interface or a dummy class, and come back to them later. If the first approach works for simpler problems, for more complex code it is generally much more efficient to stay focused on the work at hand.

To get this acceptance criteria to pass, our heroes now need to implement the `findNextDepartures()` method. But to make this scenario work, they need to change gears, and go from acceptance testing to unit testing. As you'll see, acceptance testing is used to demonstrate the high-level, end-to-end behavior of an application, and unit testing is used to build up the components that implement this behavior.

GOING FROM ACCEPTANCE TESTS TO UNIT TESTS

Acceptance tests often use a full or near-full application stack, whereas unit tests concentrate on individual components in isolation. Unit tests make it easier to focus on getting a particular class working and identifying what other services or components it needs. Unit tests also make it easier to detect and isolate errors or regressions. You'll typically write many small unit tests in order to get an acceptance criterion to pass (see figure 3.11). At the unit testing level, teams practicing BDD often use TDD to drive out the actual implementation.

As we saw in the previous chapter, TDD is deceptively simple. You write a test that describes how you expect your application to behave. Naturally, it will fail, because you haven't written any code. Now, you write just enough code to make this test pass. And once your test passes, you look at your code and think about how you could tidy it up, refactor it to improve the design, or simply make it easier to read and understand when you come back to it down the track.

Both BDD and TDD are examples of example-driven development. In both approaches, we use concrete examples to illustrate, discuss, and understand the behavior we want to implement. The main difference is that TDD tends to be a developer-centric activity and operates at the detailed level of classes, methods, and APIs. BDD, as we have seen, is team centric and looks at the bigger picture of business goals, features, and scenarios.

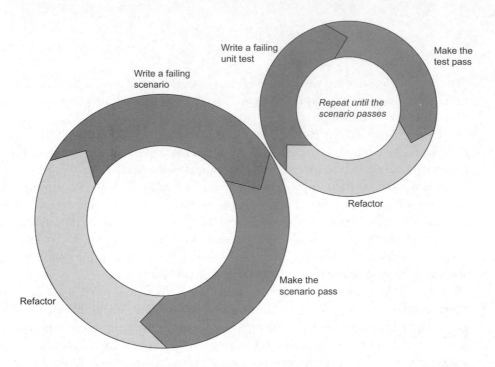

Figure 3.11 You'll typically need to write many low-level, TDD-style unit tests to get an automated acceptance criterion to pass.

WRITING A SIMPLE TDD TEST CASE

Let's get back to Tess and Dave. They will be writing their unit tests using JUnit 5, a common unit testing library for Java. We'll look at some more BDD-specific unit testing tools later on in the book. As we will see, modern unit testing libraries often include good support for BDD-style testing. Tess and Dave start with a unit test that illustrates a very basic use case of the findNextDepartures() method, as follows.

Listing 3.3   A simple BDD-style unit test

```
package manning.bddinaction.itineraries;

import org.junit.jupiter.api.DisplayName;
import org.junit.jupiter.api.Test;
import java.time.LocalTime;
import java.util.List;

import static org.assertj.core.api.Assertions.assertThat;

@DisplayName("When finding the next train departure times")
class WhenFindingNextDepatureTimes {
```

```
@Test
@DisplayName("we should get the first train after the requested time")
void tripWithOneScheduledTime() {

    // Given
    ItineraryService itineraryService = new ItineraryService();

    // When
    List<LocalTime> proposedDepartures
        = itineraryService.findNextDepartures(LocalTime.of(8:25),
                                              "Hornsby",
                                              "Central");

    // Then
    assertThat(proposedDepartures)
        .containsExactly(LocalTime.of(8:30));
    }
}
```

Create a new itinerary service.

Look up the departure times from Hornsby to Central after 8:25.

Check that the service returns at the expected time of 8:30.

"I'm not too happy with this test," says Tess. "I can see that we want to find the next train from Hornsby to Central after 8:25. It doesn't make it very clear why the answer is 8:30. Are we relying on test data that might change? Where does this time come from?"

"That's a good point," says Dave. "We need to include a timetable and set up some test data. We don't know exactly what the `TimeTable` API should look like, but we could wrap this in a method that creates a timetable that will always return a certain list of departure times." Dave refactors the unit test to look like this:

```
private LocalTime at(String time) {
return LocalTime.parse(time, DateTimeFormatter.ofPattern("H:mm"));
}

private TimeTable departures(LocalTime... departures) {
    return null;
}

    @Test
@DisplayName("should the first after the departure time")
void tripWithOneScheduledTime() {

    // Given
    timeTable = departures(at("8:10"), at("8:20"), at("8:30"));
    itineraries = new ItineraryService(timeTable);

    // When
    List<LocalTime> proposedDepartures
        = itineraries.findNextDepartures(at("8:25"),"Hornsby","Central");

    // Then
    assertThat(proposedDepartures).containsExactly(at("8:30"));
    }
```

A utility method to create a LocalDate

This method will return a properly configured TimeTable, once we know how the TimeTable class works.

Look up the departure times from Hornsby to Central after 8:25.

Create a timetable with trains that depart at specified times.

Create an itinerary service that uses this timetable.

Check that the service returns at the expected time of 8:30.

"We could guess at what methods the `TimeTable` class needs, but it might be easier just to start to implement the `findNextDepartures()` method and see what information we need the timetable to provide," suggests Tess.

After some experimenting, Tess and Dave agree that the main job of this method is to find out which lines go between the two stations (this is something the timetable should know) and to find the next two trains to arrive after the specified time, as follows.

Listing 3.4   The `ItineraryService` class

```java
package manning.bddinaction.itineraries;

import manning.bddinaction.timetables.TimeTable;

import java.time.LocalTime;
import java.util.List;
import java.util.stream.Collectors;

public class ItineraryService {
    private TimeTable timeTable;

    public ItineraryService(TimeTable timeTable) {
        this.timeTable = timeTable;
    }

    public List<LocalTime> findNextDepartures(LocalTime departureTime,
                                              String from,
                                              String to) {

        var lines = timeTable.findLinesThrough(from, to);

        return lines.stream()
                .flatMap(line -> timeTable.getDepartures(line)
                                          .stream())
                .filter(trainTime -> !trainTime.isBefore(departureTime))
                .sorted()
                .limit(2)
                .collect(Collectors.toList());
    }
}
```

Annotations:
- Asks the timetable for the lines going through the departure and destination stations
- Asks the timetable for the list of departure times on these lines
- Shows the earlier trains first
- Keeps only the departure times that are not before the requested departure time
- Returns these as a list of LocalTime objects
- Only keeps the first two departure times

Finally, they implement a dummy version of the timetable in their test, one that just returns a hard-coded list of times. The actual logic of the `TimeTable` class will eventually be much more complex than this, but from the point of view of the itinerary service, all it needs to know is that the timetable will send back the right departure times when it asks for them.

This is a good example of the outside-in development style commonly practiced in BDD teams. In writing this class, Tess and Dave have discovered two things they need from the `TimeTable` class: it needs to tell them which train lines go through any two stations and also what time trains leave a given station on each line. They have precisely identified the methods they need and what these methods should do.

Based on this implementation, the `TimeTable` interface needs to include at least these methods:

```
public interface TimeTable {
    List<String> findLinesThrough(String from, String to);
    List<LocalTime> getDepartures(String lineName, String from);
}
```

It might have more later on, but from the point of view of the itinerary service, these will be enough.

Now that they have defined the `TimeTable` interface, they can return to the original test and complete the `departures()` method so that it returns the departure times we ask it to:

```
private TimeTable departures(LocalTime... departures) {
    return new TimeTable() {
        @Override
        public List<String> findLinesThrough(String from,
                                             String to) {
            return List.of("T1");
        }

        @Override
        public List<LocalTime> getDepartures(String line, String from) {
            return List.of(departures);
        }
    };
}
```

Success! With this dummy implementation, their first unit test passes. "Great!" says Tess. "What else does this class need to do?"

The pair continue to explore the behavior of the itinerary service and add a few more tests to illustrate different facets of this behavior. For example, they want to add scenarios where multiple scheduled times are returned to make sure that only the first two are returned, and they want to check the edge case where there are no more trains, as in the following listing.

Listing 3.5 The completed `WhenFindingNextDepatureTimes` class

```
package manning.bddinaction.itineraries;

import manning.bddinaction.timetables.TimeTable;
import org.junit.jupiter.api.DisplayName;
import org.junit.jupiter.api.Test;

import java.time.LocalTime;
import java.time.format.DateTimeFormatter;
import java.util.List;
```

```
import static org.assertj.core.api.Assertions.assertThat;

@DisplayName("When finding the next departure times")
class WhenFindingNextDepatureTimes {

    private LocalTime at(String time) {
        return LocalTime.parse(time, DateTimeFormatter.ofPattern("H:mm"));
    }

    private static TimeTable departures(LocalTime... departures) {
        return new TimeTable() {

            @Override
            public List<String> findLinesThrough(String departingFrom,
                                                 String goingTo) {
                return List.of("T1");
            }

            @Override
            public List<LocalTime> getDepartures(String line,
                                                 String from) {
                return List.of(departures);
            }
        };
    }

    TimeTable timeTable;
    ItineraryService itineraries;

    @Test
    @DisplayName("should the first after the departure time")
    void tripWithOneScheduledTime() {

        timeTable = departures(at("8:10"), at("8:20"), at("8:30"));
        itineraries = new ItineraryService(timeTable);

        List<LocalTime> proposedDepartures
            = itineraries.findNextDepartures(at("8:25"),
                                             "Hornsby","Central");

        assertThat(proposedDepartures).containsExactly(at("8:30"));

    }

    @Test
    @DisplayName("should propose the next 2 trains")
    void tripWithSeveralScheduledTimes() {

        timeTable
          = departures(at("8:10"), at("8:20"), at("8:30"), at("8:45"));
        itineraries = new ItineraryService(timeTable);

        List<LocalTime> proposedDepartures
          = itineraries.findNextDepartures(at("8:05"),"Hornsby","Central");
```

Creates a dummy timetable for testing purposes

A fake timetable that returns a hard-coded set of departure times

Calls the ItineraryService to find the next departure times

Checks with the expected departure times

A slightly more sophisticated test that checks that we return no more than two times

```
        assertThat(proposedDepartures)
          .containsExactly(at("8:10"), at("8:20"));
    }
```

> **An edge-case test to check that no times are returned after the last departure time**

```
    @Test
    @DisplayName("No trains should be returned if none are available").
    void anAfterHoursTrip() {

        timeTable = departures(at("8:10"), at("8:20"), at("8:30"));
        itineraries = new ItineraryService(timeTable);

        List<LocalTime> proposedDepartures
                = itineraries.findNextDepartures(at("8:50"),
                "Hornsby", "Central");

        assertThat(proposedDepartures).isEmpty();
    }
}
```

AUTOMATING THE PRECONDITIONS IN THE @GIVEN METHOD

With the itinerary service complete, the When step is now operational. It is time to move on to the Given step:

Given the T1 train to Central leaves Hornsby at 8:02, 8:15, 8:21

This step needs to prepare the TimeTable that the itinerary service will use. While they could use a dummy timetable, like the one we saw in the previous unit test, BDD scenarios like this generally want to verify that all the system components work together as they should.

"It looks like we need to prepare the actual timetable data in this step. What would that look like?" wonders Tess.

"How about we create a CanScheduleServices interface with a scheduleService method to represent this ability? We could add also add it to the TimeTable interface, but it feels like a separate concern," suggests Dave. "Something like this":

```
public interface CanScheduleServices{
    void scheduleService(String line,
                         List<LocalTime> departingAt,
                         String departure,
                         String destination);
}
```

Tess refactors the glue code for the Given step to use this method:

```
    InMemoryTimeTable timeTable = new InMemoryTimeTable();
    ItineraryService itineraryService = new ItineraryService(timeTable);

    @Given("the {} train to {}  leaves {}  at {times}")
    public void theTrainLeavesAt(String line,
                                 String from,
                                 String to,
                            List<LocalTime> departureTimes) {
```

```
        List<LocalTime> departureTimes = localTimesFrom(departingAt);
        timeTable.scheduleService(line, departureTimes, from, to);
    }
```

Schedules the departure time for a specific line

IMPLEMENTING THE SERVICE

"Now we just need to write a class that implements both the TimeTable interface and
the CanScheduleService interface," Tess says. Once again, the pair use a test-first strategy to imagine and implement a TimeTable class. They decide to start with a simple
implementation called InMemoryTimeTable. They start off with an empty implementation like this one:

```
public class InMemoryTimeTable implements TimeTable, CanScheduleServices {

    @Override
    public void scheduleService(String line,
                                List<LocalTime> departingAt,
                                String departure,
                                String destination) {}

    @Override
    public List<String> findLinesThrough(String from, String to) {
        return null;
    }

    @Override
    public List<LocalTime> getDepartures(String lineName, String from) {
        return null;
    }
}
```

Thanks to the modular design they have chosen, it will be easy to evolve this implementation later on, or even replace it with a totally different one. The first test focuses
on scheduling services, and looks like this:

```
@DisplayName("When scheduling train services")
class WhenRecordingTrainSchedules {

    // Given
    InMemoryTimeTable timeTable = new InMemoryTimeTable();

    @Test
    @DisplayName("We can schedule a trip with a single scheduled time")
    void tripWithOneScheduledTime() {
        // When
        timeTable.scheduleService("T1", LocalTimes.at("09:15"),
                                  "Hornsby",
                                  "Central");
        // Then
        assertThat(timeTable.getDepartures("T1", "Hornsby")).
            .hasSize(1);
    }
}
```

Creates a new timetable

Schedules a service with a single departure time

Checks the scheduled departure times

This test leads the pair to add some data structure to the `InMemoryTimeTable` class. They decide to store the scheduled trips in a map, indexed by line name:

```
public class InMemoryTimeTable implements TimeTable, CanScheduleServices {
    private Map<String, ScheduledService> schedules = new HashMap<>();

    @Override
    public void scheduleService(String line,
                                List<LocalTime> departingAt,
                                String from,
                                String to) {
        schedules.put(line,
                new ScheduledService(from, to, departingAt));
    }
}
```

Stores scheduled services in a map indexed by line name

Records the scheduled service

They also decide to represent scheduled services as a domain class, like this one:

```
public class ScheduledService {
    private final String departure;
    private final String destination;
    private final List<LocalTime> departureTimes;

    public ScheduledService(String from, String to, List<LocalTime> at) {
        this.departure = from;
        this.destination = to;
        this.departureTimes = at;
    }
    ...
}
```

This is enough to make the code pass. And it is simple enough, so they decide that no refactoring is necessary yet.

Now that they are happy with the code, they continue to explore the timetable behavior, checking what happens when you schedule several departure times and when you add more than one line. Each time they repeat the cycle, writing a small test, making it fail, and then reviewing their code to look for potential improvements. After a few more passing tests, they are satisfied that line scheduling works correctly.

IMPLEMENTING THE TIMETABLE SERVICE

"So, we're done, right?" says Dave. "Not so fast," says Tess. "We almost forgot about the `TimeTable` interface methods."

Tess is right. This is enough for the given step to work, but not for the scenario as a whole. Their next job is to write a test that explores the `findLinesThrough()` and `getDepartures()` methods. "Let's start with the simple case of finding a line that goes through two stations," proposes Dave:

```
@Test
@DisplayName("When querying train services")
class WhenQueryingTrainServices {
```

```
    // Given
    InMemoryTimeTable timeTable = new InMemoryTimeTable();

    @Test
    @DisplayName("We can ask which lines go through any two stations")
    void queryLinesThroughStations() {
        // When
        timeTable.scheduleService("T1",
                                   LocalTimes.at("09:15"),
                                   "Hornsby", "Central");
        // Then
        assertThat(timeTable.findLinesThrough("Hornsby",
                                   "Central")).hasSize(1);

    }
}
```

Their initial implementation of the findLinesThrough() method looks like this:

```
    @Override
    public List<String> findLinesThrough(String from, String to) {
        schedules.entrySet()
                .stream()
            .filter(line -> (line.getValue().getDeparture().equals(from)
                        && line.getValue().getDestination().equals(to)))
                .map(Map.Entry::getKey)
                .collect(Collectors.toList());
        }
```

REFACTORING THE COMPLETED CODE

This makes the test pass, but Dave isn't convinced. "It's not the most readable code in the world," he comments. "Let's see if we can refactor it to make it a bit easier to follow."

"Maybe we could tidy up the filtering logic," suggests Tess. "What we are trying to do is to find the line or lines that go through the two stations we provide, in the right direction."

"What if we wrote just that?" says Dave. He tinkers with the code and comes up with a couple of new methods that allow him to refactor the linesGoThrough() method into something a little more readable:

Finds the names of all the scheduled lines

```
private Set<String> lineNames() { return  schedules.keySet(); }    ←

private boolean lineGoesThrough(String line, String from, String to){   ←
    return schedules.getOrDefault(line, ScheduledService.NO_SERVICE)
                .goesBetween(from,to);
}
```

A convenience method to check whether a given scheduled line goes between two stations

```
@Override
public List<String> findLinesThrough(String from, String to) {
    return lineNames().stream()
                    .filter(line  -> lineGoesThrough(line, from, to))
                    .collect(Collectors.toList());
}
```

This also leads him to refactor the `ScheduledService` class:

```
public class ScheduledService {
  private final String from;
  private final String to;
  private final List<LocalTime> departureTimes;

  public static ScheduledService NO_SERVICE
                  = new ScheduledService("","", Lists.emptyList());

  public ScheduledService(String from, String to, List<LocalTime> at) {…}

  public List<LocalTime> getDepartureTimes() {
    return departureTimes;
  }

  public boolean goesBetween(String from, String to) {
    return this.from.equals(from) && this.to.equals(to);
  }
}
```

A constant value representing a service with no departure times

A convenience method to make it easier to check that a given service goes between two stations

Once they make this one pass, they add a new test that illustrates how to get the departure times of a given line:

```
@Test
@DisplayName("Each line can have a number of departure times")
void trainLinesHaveMoreThanOneDepartureTime() {
  // When
  timeTable.scheduleService("T1",
            LocalTimes.at("09:15","09:45"),
            "Hornsby",
            "Central");
  // Then
  assertThat(timeTable.getDepartures ( "T1", "Hornsby")).hasSize(2);
}
```

And so on. After half a dozen small tests like this, they end up with the `InMemoryTimeTable` class, as in the following listing. You can also see the full test classes on GitHub.

Listing 3.6 The completed `InMemoryTimeTable` class

```
package manning.bddinaction.timetables;

import java.time.LocalTime;
import java.util.*;
import java.util.stream.Collectors;

public class InMemoryTimeTable implements TimeTable, CanScheduleServices {

  private Map<String, ScheduledService> schedules = new HashMap<>();

  @Override
  public void scheduleService(String line,
```

```
                            List<LocalTime> departingAt,
                            String from,
                            String to) {
    schedules.put(line,
                new ScheduledService(from, to, departingAt));
}

private Set<String> lineNames() { return  schedules.keySet(); }

private boolean lineGoesThrough(String line, String from, String to) {
  return schedules.getOrDefault(line, ScheduledService.NO_SERVICE)
                    .goesBetween(from,to);
}
@Override
public List<String> findLinesThrough(String from, String to) {
  return lineNames().stream()
                  .filter(line  -> lineGoesThrough(line, from,to))
                  .collect(Collectors.toList());
}

@Override
public List<LocalTime> getDepartures(String lineName, String from) {
    if (!schedules.containsKey(lineName)) {
      throw new UnknownLineException("No line found: " + lineName);
    }
    return schedules.get(lineName).getDepartureTimes();
  }
}
```

3.6   *Demonstrate: Tests as living documentation*

Once a feature has been implemented, you should be able to run your tests and see passing acceptance criteria among pending ones (see figure 3.12). When you're applying practices like BDD, this result does more than simply tell you that your application satisfies the business requirements. A passing acceptance test is also a concrete measure of progress. An implemented test either passes or fails. Ideally, if all of the acceptance criteria for a feature have been automated and run successfully, you can say that this feature is finished and ready for production.

More than just evaluating the quality of your application, the state of the tests gives a clear indication of where it's at in the development progression. The proportion of passing tests compared to the total number of specified acceptance criteria gives a good picture of how much work has been done so far and how much remains. In addition, by tracking the number of completed automated acceptance tests against the number of pending tests, you can get an idea of the progress you're making over time.

When you write tests in this narrative style, another benefit emerges: each automated acceptance test becomes a documented, worked example of how the system can be used to solve a particular business requirement. And when the tests are web tests, the worked examples will even be illustrated with screenshots taken along the way.

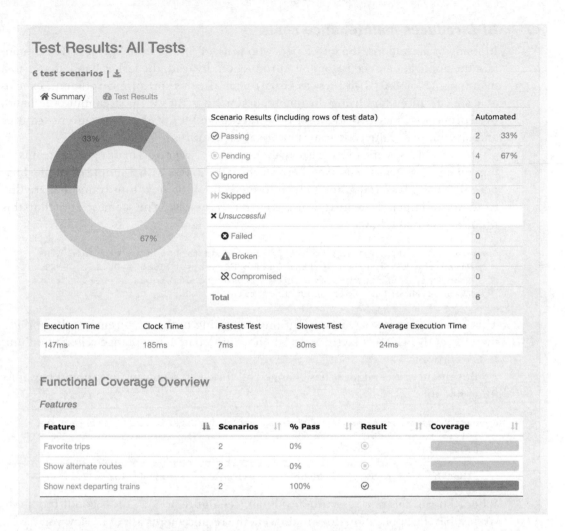

Figure 3.12   The passing test should now appear in the test reports.

But what about the testers? Automated acceptance testing and QA

Automatically deploying your application into production when the automated acceptance tests pass requires a great deal of discipline and the utmost confidence in the quality and comprehensiveness of your automated tests. This is a worthy goal, and a number of organizations do manage this, but for most, things are not quite that simple.

In typical enterprise environments, the testers will probably still want to do at least some exploratory testing before releasing the application to production. But if the automated test results are clear and visible, they can save the QA team days or weeks of time that would normally be spent on regression or basic mechanical testing and let them focus on more interesting testing activities. This, in turn, can speed up the release cycle significantly.

3.7   *BDD reduces maintenance costs*

In many organizations, the developers who worked on the initial project don't maintain the application once it goes into production. Instead, the task is handed over to a maintenance or BAU (Business as Usual) team. In this sort of environment, executable specifications and living documentation are a great way to streamline the handover process, as they provide a set of worked examples of the application's features and illustrations of the code that supports these features.

Executable specifications also make it much easier for maintenance teams to implement changes or bug fixes. Let's see how this works with a simple example. Suppose that users have requested to be informed about the next four trains that are due to arrive, and not just the next two, as is currently the case. The scenario related to this requirement is as follows:

```
Scenario: Next train going to the requested destination on the same line
    Given the T1 train to Central leaves Hornsby at 08:02, 08:15, 08:21
    When Travis wants to travel from Hornsby to Chatswood at 08:00
    Then he should be told about the trains at: 08:02, 08:15
```

This scenario expresses your current understanding of the requirement: the application currently behaves like this, and you have automated acceptance criteria and unit tests to prove it.

But the new user request has changed all this. The scenario now should be something like this:

```
Scenario: Next train going to the requested destination on the same line
    Given the T1 train to Chatswood leaves Hornsby at 08:02, 08:15, 08:21,
➥  8:34, 8:45
    When Travis wants to travel from Hornsby to Chatswood at 08:00
    Then he should be told about the trains at: 08:02, 08:15, 08:21, 08:34
```

When you run this new scenario, it will fail (see figure 3.13). This is good! It demonstrates that the application doesn't do what the requirements ask of it. Now you have a starting point for implementing this modification.

From here, you can use the unit tests to isolate the code that needs to be changed. You'll update the "should propose the next 2 trains" unit test to reflect the new acceptance criterion:

```
@Test
@DisplayName("should propose the next 4 trains")
void tripWithSeveralScheduledTimes() {

    timeTable
      = departures(
          at("8:10"),at("8:20"),at("8:30"),at("8:45"),at("8:45"));   ⟵   The pretend service
    itineraries = new ItineraryService(timeTable);                        now returns
                                                                           more trips.
    List<LocalTime> proposedDepartures
      = itineraries.findNextDepartures(at("8:05"), "Hornsby", "Central");
```

```
assertThat(proposedDepartures)
    .containsExactly(at("8:10"), at("8:20"), at("8:30"),at("8:45")); ⟵
}
```

**You now expect the itinerary
service to return four times.**

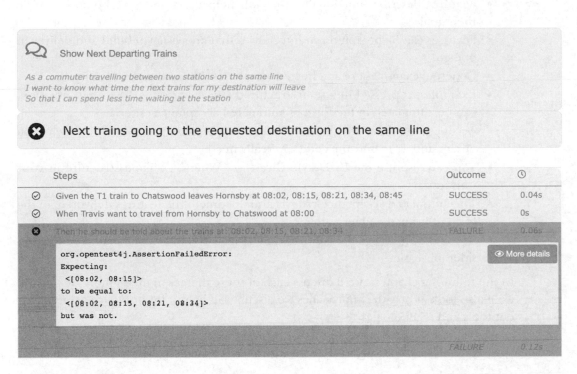

Figure 3.13 A failing acceptance criterion illustrates a difference between what the requirements ask for and what the application currently does.

This, in turn, helps you isolate the code that needs to change in the `ItineraryService` class. From here, you'll be in a much better position to update the code correctly.

For larger changes, more work will obviously be involved. But the principle remains the same for modifications of any size. If the change request is a modification of an existing feature, you need to update the automated acceptance criteria to reflect the new requirement. If the change is a bug fix that your current acceptance criteria didn't catch, then you need to first write new automated acceptance criteria to reproduce the bug, then fix the bug, and finally use the acceptance criteria to demonstrate that the bug has been resolved. And if the change is big enough to make existing acceptance criteria redundant, you can delete the old acceptance criteria and write new ones.

Summary

- Understanding the underlying business objectives of a project lets you discover features and stories that can deliver these business objectives.
- Features describe functionality that will help users and stakeholders achieve their goals.
- Features can be broken down into stories that are easier to build and deliver in one go.
- Concrete examples are an effective way to describe and discuss features.
- Examples, expressed in a semi-structured Given . . . When . . . Then notation, can be automated in the form of automated acceptance criteria.
- Acceptance criteria drive the low-level implementation work and help you design and write only the code you really need.
- You can also use the BDD-style Given . . . When . . . Then structure in your unit tests.
- The automated acceptance criteria also document the features delivered, in the form of living documentation.
- Automated acceptance criteria and BDD-style unit tests make maintenance considerably easier.

In the following chapters, we'll discuss each of these themes in much more detail, and we'll also look at how the approaches we discuss can be put into practice using different tools and technologies.

Part 2

What do I want? Defining requirements using BDD

BDD principles are applicable at all levels of software development, from requirements discovery and definition to low-level coding and regression testing. Part 2 of this book focuses on the first aspect of BDD: how you can use BDD to discover and describe the features you need to build. Part 2 is written for the whole team.

In chapter 4, we'll look the role BDD plays in higher-level requirements. You'll see how important it is to consider and understand the business motivation and value behind the software you're asked to deliver. You'll learn how to discuss the relative value of proposed features and use these discussions to determine what features to build and, more importantly, what features not to build. This is at the heart of building the right software.

In chapters 5 and 6, we'll go into more detail. You'll learn how BDD teams collaborate to discover, describe, and define the features they need to deliver. You'll discover how to explore the scope and detailed requirements of a feature using conversation and concrete examples, and you'll learn how these conversations can change your understanding of the features you're trying to define.

Finally, in chapter 7, you'll learn how to formalize the examples we discussed in chapter 6 in a clear, unambiguous form that we'll refer to as executable specifications. This too is a collaborative process; as you'll see, the act of expressing the examples in a more rigorous form helps eliminate ambiguities and assumptions around the requirements, and it also paves the way for automation.

At the end of part 2, you should have a solid understanding of why and how BDD teams collaborate to discover and define the features they need to deliver, and you'll be able to express the acceptance criteria around these features in the form of executable specifications.

Speculate: From business goals to prioritized features

4

This chapter covers

- What happens during the Speculate phase
- BDD and business agility
- Describing a project vision and business goals
- Visualizing assumptions and prioritizing features with Impact Mapping
- Building an Epic Landscape with Pirate Canvases

Before you can implement a software solution, and before you can even judge what features you should implement, you need to understand the problem you're solving and how you can help. Who will be using the system, and what benefits will they expect from it? How will your system help users do their jobs or provide value to your stakeholders?

How can you know if a particular feature will really benefit the organization as you suppose it should? Are you building software that will have a measurable, positive impact for your client's business? Will your project make a difference? Sometimes a particular feature, or even a particular application, shouldn't be implemented because it will clearly not deliver the business benefits expected of it.

These are the sort of questions we ask during the Speculate phase. In this chapter you'll learn how to gain a deeper understanding of high-level needs of the business, an essential cornerstone of effective BDD practices. You'll learn about how BDD fits into strategic project planning and high-level requirements discovery, and you'll learn how to discuss and describe high-level business vision and goals, as well as about two techniques, Impact Mapping and Pirate Canvases, that can help you identify the key deliverables that might deliver on these goals. In the next chapter, we will look at BDD and Product Backlog Refinement activities, where we break these deliverable features into more manageable User Stories. And in chapter 5, we see how to identify and explore the acceptance criteria of these stories in the Illustrate phase.

> ### When BDD meets business agility
>
> The Speculate phase is where BDD meets business agility. According to the Agile Business Consortium (https://www.agilebusiness.org/), business agility is the ability of an organization to
>
> - Adapt quickly to market changes—internally and externally
> - Respond rapidly and flexibly to customer demands
> - Adapt and lead change in a productive and cost-effective way without compromising quality
> - Continuously be at a competitive advantage
>
> Business agility is concerned with the adoption of the evolution of values, behaviors, and capabilities. These enable businesses and individuals to be more adaptive, creative, and resilient when dealing with complexity, uncertainty, and change, leading to improved well-being and better outcomes.
>
> BDD practices are a cornerstone of business agility, and leveraging business agility is a prerequisite for getting the most value out of your BDD adoption. BDD gives teams the techniques and tools teams need to collaborate both at a strategic and at a team level, and executable specifications and living documentation both help to provide faster and more accurate feedback about features as they are delivered. BDD at its heart is about delivering value; it's no use writing great executable specifications if they don't solve a problem that is useful to the business.

4.1   The Speculate phase

The Speculate phase involves several different activities, performed at different points in the project life cycle (see figure 4.1). The most important of these are Strategic Planning and Product Backlog Refinement.

During Strategic Planning, you define key business goals and identify the high-level features that might help achieve these goals. These high-level features are then refined and prioritized during Product Backlog Refinement sessions and are then ready for teams to pick them up and start work on them.

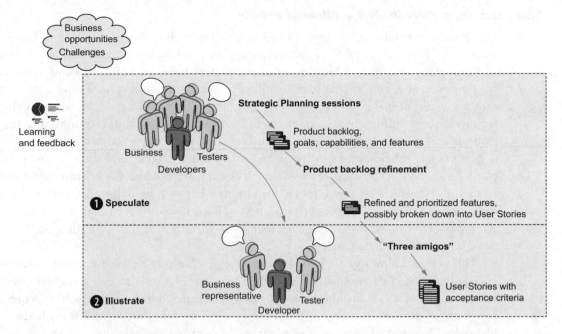

Figure 4.1   The Speculate phase helps teams, and organizations as a whole, identify and prioritize the deliverables that matter most.

4.1.1   *Strategic Planning in a BDD project*

Strategic Planning is where you transform strategic business opportunities or challenges into a prioritized collection of deliverable features. The high-level features that come out of these discussions make up the product backlog for the team or teams building them:

- Strategic Planning happens not just once, but repeatedly throughout the life of a project.
- Activities involve both high-level executives and stakeholders, as well as members of the teams who will build and deliver the features.
- During Strategic Planning, business stakeholders, supported by delivery team members, identify and articulate the most important business problems that need solving and the most promising opportunities to explore.
- Teams use collaboration practices such as Pirate Canvases and Impact Mapping to identify business value and opportunities, to understand what features might deliver this value, and to highlight assumptions and risks.

Let's look at each of these points in more detail.

4.1.2   Strategic Planning is a continuous activity

For many organizations, Strategic Planning involves high-level stakeholders and executives who spend a lot of time and effort agreeing on business goals and objectives and mapping out detailed, long-term plans anywhere between 12 months and 5 years.

However, it is generally difficult to plan in much detail beyond a time frame of around three months. As we discussed in chapter 1, you'll rarely understand the requirements completely or correctly at the start of a project, and requirements and assumptions often change during the life of a project. It's unproductive to try to draw detailed specifications in the initial phases of a project, when you know relatively little about it; this just sets you up for rework later, when the requirements, or your understanding of them, inevitably change. Instead, you should try to build a deep understanding of the business context behind the project so that you can react appropriately to change and remain focused on delivering the value that the business expects from the project.

This is why, for an Agile organization, Strategic Planning and requirements discovery is an ongoing process that occurs both at the start of a project and at regular intervals throughout the life of the project or product under development. As the project progresses, you look at changes in market conditions, take on board lessons learned from already released features, and adapt your priorities accordingly.

The frequency of these activities varies from project to project and from organization to organization. Many shops find that two- to three-month cycles work well. For teams practicing SAFe, this cadence aligns nicely with PI (program increment) planning activities (https://www.scaledagileframework.com/program-increment).

Other teams, such as those following XSCALE practices (https://xscalealliance.org), work with a more frequent cadence. Some shops find that weekly strategic meetings, involving both team delegates and senior stakeholders, allow for smoother coordination and alignment between teams. Smaller, more regular meetings make it easier to adjust and reprioritize features as new information is discovered.

> ### Agile organizations are learning organizations
> The key to better business outcomes is not faster coding; it is faster learning. You need to be able to both learn more quickly and react to what you learn more quickly. Smaller feedback cycles are the lifeblood of agility, both at a team and at an organizational level.

4.1.3   Strategic Planning involves both stakeholders and team members

Traditionally this sort of high-level planning is the reserve of senior stakeholders, executives, domain experts, and senior architects. The requirements that come out of these discussions are written up as functional specifications and handed down to development teams, who have limited opportunities to provide input or feedback.

And from the perspective of the development teams, requirements discovery starts with a backlog of User Stories or epics.

Agile organizations take a much more collaborative approach to requirements discovery. Discussions about high-level planning still involve senior stakeholders, but they also involve members of the teams who will actually be building the solutions.

When team members (or team representatives, for larger organizations) actively participate in Strategic Planning activities, teams build up a much deeper understanding of the business vision and the goals they are trying to achieve. They can also provide valuable feedback about the feasibility of the proposed ideas. In addition, this deeper understanding allows them to be more creative in finding the best way to achieve these goals.

Involving team members in high-level requirements discussions may seem odd at first. But the best teams I have worked with are the ones in which the team members have built up a deep, practical domain knowledge as well as an understanding of the technical constraints they will need to work with. Developers and testers might not have the business domain knowledge to contribute very much initially, but they will learn. And exposing them to real-world user needs and concerns is a great way to reduce misunderstandings and incorrect assumptions that can cause problems later in the project.

4.1.4 *Identifying hypotheses and assumptions rather than features*

The reason we call this phase Speculate is that the word "speculate" reminds us that the value of any new feature is not guaranteed in advance. We tend to think of requirements as rigid dictates that are set in stone by the business, with little scope for change. We tend to assume that business folk know what they want, and that what they ask for is indeed what they need. But often we assume too much.

In fact, any new feature is more like a bet. We are wagering development time and effort, in the hope that the feature will be worth building. We are betting that the feature we build will return enough business value to compensate for the effort we spend building it.

Another way to think about this is in terms of hypotheses. Back in 2011, Jeffery L. Taylor coined the expression "Hypothesis-Driven Development,"[1] which is a key concept in DevOps and the lean start-up methodology today. In Hypothesis-Driven Development, development is viewed not as a list of features to implement, but rather as a series of small experiments to validate or invalidate a hypothesis about the project's problem domain. These experiments help us progressively and incrementally increase our understanding of a problem domain.

---

[1] Jeffrey L. Taylor, "Hypothesis-Driven Development," January 13, 2011, https://www.drdobbs.com/architecture-and-design/hypothesis-driven-development/229000656.

A hypothesis can be described as a simple phrase describing the belief or assumption and how you intend to verify it. One popular format goes like this:

We believe <some capability>

will result in <some outcome>.

We will know this to be true when <some measurable result is observed>.

For example, if you work for an online bookstore, you might come up with a hypothesis like this one: "We believe that if we show products related to a customer's previous purchases on the home page, we will increase engagement and sales. We will know this to be true when we see a 5% increase in sales of related products."

Hypotheses like these are designed to be proved or disproved, which is why we associate them with success criteria or metrics. Thinking in terms of hypotheses encourages us to figure out the simplest way to prove or disprove each hypothesis. For example, you could implement a simple version of the "related products" feature by showing other books from authors that a customer has already purchased and see how your customers react.

When a feature is deployed, you collect the corresponding metrics during the validate phase. These metrics are fed into the next Speculate phase (see figure 4.2).

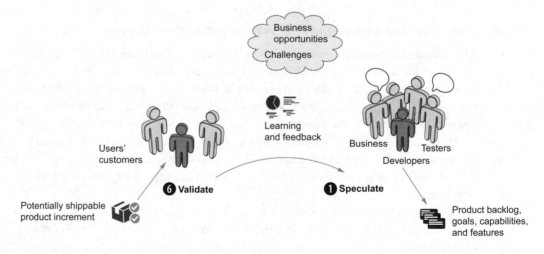

Figure 4.2   The Speculate and Validate phases act as feedback loops where hypotheses and assumptions about features can be validated once they have been delivered.

Building features with the goal in mind also helps you think about the metrics you will need to use to validate the product. Because the team has already understood and agreed on the hypothesis goal (in this case, increasing sales of related products by 5%), and identified the metric (sales of related products), you can now prove or disprove the initial hypothesis and validate whether the new feature delivered the expected results.

Depending on the results, you might decide to continue to develop and enhance a feature, adjust the approach with another experiment, or even abandon the feature entirely. Focusing on a continuous experimentation cycle and on regularly validating your understanding of both the problem domain and the solution helps you deliver more valuable software.

In the following sections, we will look at some of the practices that can help us understand business goals and identify and prioritize hypotheses. But before we look at techniques such as Pirate Canvases and Impact Mapping that can help us do this, we need to look at how we can describe business visions and goals more effectively.

4.2 Describing business vision and goals

Let's start by introducing the client you'll work with throughout the rest of the book: Flying High Airlines. Flying High Airlines is a large commercial airline that runs both international and domestic flights. Flying High has been under pressure due to increasing costs and competition from low-cost carriers, so management has recently launched a new and improved version of their Frequent Flyer program to try to retain existing customers and attract new ones. This new program will offer many compelling reasons to join; like all Frequent Flyer programs, members will accumulate points when they fly, but members will also benefit from many exclusive privileges, such as access to lounges and faster boarding lines, and they'll be able to easily spend their accumulated miles on flights and on other purchases for themselves or their family members.

As part of this initiative, management wants a new website where Frequent Flyer members can see their current status in real time, redeem points, and book flights. The existing system just sends out paper account statements to members each month to tell them how many points they've accumulated. In addition, the Flying High call center is currently overloaded with calls, as Frequent Flyer members can only benefit from their member privileges and use their accumulated points if they book over the phone. Management hopes that being able to book directly online instead of over the phone will encourage Frequent Flyer members to book more often with Flying High. In this chapter, and throughout the rest of the book, we'll use examples from this project to illustrate the concepts and techniques we discuss.

4.2.1 Vision, goals, capabilities, and features

A team practicing BDD collaborates with business stakeholders to articulate and understand a business's vision and goals. They try to identify capabilities that might allow users and other stakeholders to achieve these goals, and software features that might enable these capabilities. And they use conversations about real-world examples and counterexamples to better understand how these features should work. The relationship between these concepts is illustrated, along with a few examples from our Frequent Flyer project, in figure 4.3.

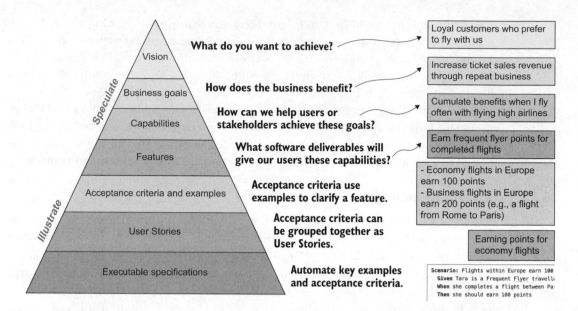

Figure 4.3   All features, and ultimately all code, should map back to business goals and the project vision.

At the highest level is the project vision, a short statement that provides a high-level guiding direction for the project. This statement helps ensure that all the team members understand the principal aims and assumptions of the project. For the Flying High Frequent Flyer website, the vision could be to build a loyal base of customers who actively prefer to fly with us.

More specifically, any project aims to support a number of business goals. Business goals are executive-level concepts that generally involve increasing revenue, protecting revenue, or reducing costs (this is where the "business value" comes from). For the Flying High Frequent Flyer website, one of the primary business goals might be "Earn more ticket sales revenue through repeat business from Frequent Flyer members."

As a software developer, your job is to design and build capabilities that help the business realize these goals. A capability gives your users the ability to achieve some goal or fulfill some task, regardless of implementation. Liz Keogh says that a good way to spot a capability is that it can be prefixed with the words "to be able to." For example, Flying High Frequent Flyer members need the capability to be able to cumulate benefits when they fly with us, or to be able to book flights and benefit from their member privileges while doing so.

Capabilities don't imply a particular implementation. They don't even need to be done using software, though software might make them more efficient. For example, "the ability to book a flight" could be provided online or manually, over the telephone.

You design and implement *features* to deliver these capabilities. Features are what you actually build, and they're what deliver the value. Unlike capabilities, features generally represent pieces of deliverable software functionality. Some features that might help us deliver the capability to book flights might be "Earn points for each completed flight" and "Book flights online using Frequent Flyer points."

A feature is often too big to deliver in one go, so the delivery team typically slices the feature up into more manageable chunks, which we call *User Stories*. A User Story delivers a subset of the examples that illustrate a feature. You can automate these examples in the form of executable specifications in order to speed up feedback and benefit from automated regression tests. We will look at slicing features into User Stories to make them easier to deliver in chapter 5.

As the project progresses, teams need to learn more about the features they decide to deliver. To build up a more detailed understanding about a feature, you can use concrete examples of what the system should do in different situations. These examples illustrate the key acceptance criteria of a feature.

This isn't done upfront, but shortly before work starts on a feature, as part of the *Illustrate* phase. We will discuss describing features with examples and acceptance criteria during the Illustrate phase in much more detail in chapter 5.

In the rest of the chapter, we will see how you can use two practical techniques, Impact Mapping and Pirate Canvases, to discover and discuss the capabilities and features you need to build. But first, let's talk a little more about project visions and business goals.

4.2.2 *What do you want to achieve? Start with a vision*

Suppose I was to ask you to buy me a new power drill for some DIY jobs I need to do around the house. I'm not sure how much a power drill costs these days, but I certainly don't want to spend more than I have to. A red one would be nice, as it would go with my red toolbox.

Being an obliging sort of person, you drive down to the local hardware store and look at the range of power drills on display. But without a bit more background, you'd be hard-pressed to make me happy. If I'm trying to assemble a large bed with a lot of screws, a small and inexpensive cordless electric drill, or maybe even a cordless screwdriver, should suffice, and a heavier model would just be cumbersome. On the other hand, if I'm going to install some new shelves on a brick wall in my garage, I'll need a more powerful hammer drill, as well as a set of masonry drill bits and some screw anchors. If the garage has no power outlets, the drill will have to be of the more expensive cordless variety.

To get things done effectively, you need a clear understanding both of what you're trying to achieve and of the ultimate goal or purpose of your work. Studies have demonstrated that team collaboration improves significantly when members share a clearly identifiable goal.[2] This is equally true for software development. If you are to

---

[2] Panagiotis Mitkidis, Jesper Sørensen, Kristoffer L. Nielbo, Marc Andersen, and Pierre Lienard, "Collective-Goal Ascription Increases Cooperation in Humans," *PLoS ONE*, vol. 8, no. 5, May 2013, http://www.plosone .org/article/info%3Adoi%2F10.1371%2Fjournal.pone.0064776.

deliver effective solutions for the problems your clients face, you need to understand the underlying business goals.

4.2.3   *The vision statement*

One useful way to express what a project is supposed to achieve is to write a *vision statement*, which outlines the expected outcomes and objectives of the project in a few concise and compelling phrases. It gives the team an understanding of what they're trying to achieve, helping to motivate them and focus their efforts on the essential value proposition of the product. It provides a beacon for all to see, helping teams align their direction and concentrate their efforts on building features that actively contribute to the project's goals.

> **TIP** The vision statement should be simple, clear, and concise—short enough to read and assimilate in a few minutes. It should also be intimately familiar to the whole team. Indeed, in the midst of an iteration, when requirements are changing quickly and frequently, it's all too easy for teams to get sidetracked by minor details, and the vision statement can remind them about the broader goals of the project.

A good vision statement will focus on the project's objectives, not on how it will deliver these objectives. It won't go into detail about what technology should be used, what time frame the project delivery should respect, or what platform it should run on. Rather, it presents the project objectives in the context of the problem the project is trying to address.

Most traditional projects generally have a vision of some sort. Executive managers usually know, at least in the back of their minds, what they expect out of a project in terms of business value, or they wouldn't have approved it. By the nature of their jobs, executives usually have a very keen understanding of how a project is expected to contribute to the bottom line. Despite this, they may not have articulated the expected outcomes in a way that can be easily shared with the development team.

Larger organizations typically require some sort of formal documentation that explains the business case and scope of a project, and this document will usually contain a vision statement of sorts. But these are often dry, rigid documents, written to respect the local project management process requirements, and they're relegated to a project management office once the project has been signed off on. They're the realm of project managers and project management offices (PMOs). In many cases, these documents never make it to the development team, which effectively renders them useless as vision statements in the Agile sense. Indeed, how can a shared vision be useful if not everyone can see it?

4.2.4   *Using vision statement templates*

A project vision statement need not be a long and wordy document. It can be a succinct paragraph that sums up the focus of the project in one or two sentences. In his book *Crossing the Chasm: Marketing and Selling High-Tech Products to Mainstream Customers*

(Harper Business, 2002), Geoffrey A. Moore proposes the following template for a good product vision statement, which I've often heard mentioned in Agile circles:

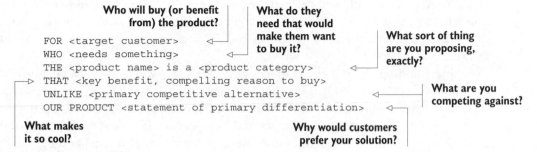

For example, the vision statement for Flying High's Frequent Flyer program might go something like this:

```
FOR travelers
WHO want to be rewarded for traveling with Flying High Airlines
THE Flying High Frequent Flyer program IS A loyalty program
THAT lets members easily and conveniently view and manage their accumulated
  points in real time, and spend their points for real purchases with
  unequaled ease.
UNLIKE other airline Frequent Flyer programs,
OUR PRODUCT lets members use their points easily for any sort of online or
  brick-and-mortar purchase.
```

This short text sums up who your target audience is, what they want, how your product will give it to them, and how your product distinguishes itself from its competitors. Of course, there's no obligation to follow this (or any other) template to the letter, but it does provide a good summary of the sort of things that you should consider including in your vision statement.

Writing a viable vision statement can be a tricky exercise, but it pays off over the life of the project. One effective approach to writing a good vision statement is to think in terms of designing a product flyer. In a nutshell, what does your product do? How will the product benefit your organization? Who is your target audience, and why would they buy your product rather than that of a competitor? What are its three or four principal selling points? Discuss these questions with all the key project players, including users, stakeholders, and the development team. Then try to formulate a vision statement using Moore's template. If your project team is big enough, you can split up into several cross-functional groups and compare results, refining the statement until everyone agrees.

4.2.5 *How will it benefit the business? Identify the business goals*

Once you have a clear idea of the project vision, you need to define the underlying business goals that drive the project and contribute to realizing this vision. A business goal succinctly defines how the project will benefit the organization or how it will align with the organization's strategies or vocation.

All projects have business goals; otherwise, management wouldn't have approved them in the first place. But not all projects have clearly defined and visible business goals. And projects with well-defined and well-communicated business goals have a much better chance of success than those that don't. A recent university study found that teams with a clear common understanding of their goal cooperated better and worked more effectively.[3]

Understanding these goals is even more important when unforeseen problems arise, when technical challenges make implementing a particular solution harder than initially thought, or when the team realizes they've misunderstood the requirements and need to do things differently. If developers are expected to respond appropriately to these sort of challenges, they need to have a solid understanding of what business value is expected from the system.

At the end of the day, businesspeople want the software being built to help them achieve their business goals. If the software delivers in this regard, the business will consider it a success, even if the scope and implementation vary considerably from what was originally imagined. But if the software fails to meet the underlying business goals, then it will rightly be considered a failure, even if it meets the requirements provided by the customers down to the letter.

4.2.6   *Writing good business goals*

Business goals are high-level statements that focus on business value or opportunity, statements that executives would be able to relate to and discuss. For example, one of the more important business goals for the Frequent Flyer program discussed earlier might be the following:

> Increase ticket sales by 5%.

A statement like this has the merit of clarifying the "why" of the project: why exactly are you building this software? But like the project vision, business goals are often very poorly communicated. Many development teams have only a vague notion of the business goals they're trying to deliver. And yet, understanding these goals is essential to making correct scope, design, and implementation choices during the project.

You can also write goals using the following "In order to . . . as . . . I want to . . ." format:

```
In order to increase ticket sales by 5% over the next year
As the Flying High Sales Manager
I want to encourage travelers to fly with Flying High rather than with a
    rival company
```

This is a variation on the more traditional "As a . . . I want . . . so that . . ." form used in many project teams for story cards. This form puts the goal first ("In order to . . .") as

---

[3]   Mitkidis et al., "Collective Goal Ascription."

opposed to the more traditional User Story format, where the stakeholder is placed in the primary position. Putting the goal first places the emphasis on the expected outcome, which should be of obvious value to the business. When the stakeholder comes first, the last section ("so that . . .") tends to be eclipsed, and you may find yourself proposing high-level capabilities and then struggling to justify them with a solid business goal. This is a very versatile format, and you'll use it to describe requirements at various levels of abstraction throughout the book.

Whatever format you prefer, a good business goal should be precise. Some business managers use the SMART acronym. Business goals should be

- Specific
- Measurable
- Achievable
- Relevant
- Time-bound

First and foremost, a goal should tell readers specifically what you're trying to do ("encourage travelers to fly with Flying High"). But it should also describe why you want to do this and outline the business benefits you're trying to achieve by doing so ("increase ticket sales").

A goal should also be measurable. A measurable goal will give you a clearer idea of business expectations and also help you determine whether it been achieved once the work is done. You can make a goal measurable by introducing notions of quantity and time (e.g., "Increase ticket sales by 5% over the next year").

Quantifying a goal in this way will also make it much easier to determine how best to approach the problem, or whether the goal is even achievable in the first place. Increasing sales by 200% in six months would be quite a different proposition than increasing by 5% over the next year. Knowing the time frame (six months) also makes the goal more tangible and focused. In all of these cases, precise figures help manage expectations and ensure that everyone is on the same page.

But possibly the most important attribute of a good goal is its relevance. A goal is relevant if it will make a positive contribution to the organization in the current context within the specified time frame, and if it is aligned with the overall strategy of the organization. Relevant goals are goals that will make a difference to the business.

4.2.7   Show me the money: Business goals and revenue

Let's take a closer look at the business goals behind the Frequent Flyer program. A more complete list of goals might include the following:

- Increase ticket sales revenue by 5% over the next year by encouraging travelers to fly with Flying High rather than with a rival company.
- Increase the customer base by 10% within a year by building a positive image of the Frequent Flyer program.

- Avoid losing existing customers to the new rival Hot Shots Frequent Flyer program.
- Reduce hotline costs by enabling Frequent Flyer members to purchase flights with their points directly online, unlike the current program, where travelers need to call to make a booking.

Notice that the preceding goals all seem to boil down to earning more money, either by increasing revenue or by reducing costs. The goals of most commercial organizations are, by definition, ultimately financial in nature. In fact, almost all business goals can be grouped into one of the four following categories:

- Increasing revenue
- Reducing costs
- Protecting revenue
- Avoiding future costs

For example, "Increasing ticket sales revenue by 5%" (the first of the goals previously listed) is clearly about increasing revenue by selling more tickets. The second, "Increase the customer base by 10% within a year," is similar, though the connection with generating revenue is slightly more indirect. "Avoid losing existing customers" is an example of protecting revenue, whereas the fourth, "Reduce hotline costs," is clearly about reducing costs.

   An example of avoiding future costs might be implementing certain reports that will be required by new compliance legislation due to take effect next year. In this case, you're investing effort now in order to avoid fines for noncompliance in the future; the feature itself doesn't add any direct business value, but it avoids the future cost of fines.

Business goals in a public service organization: Transport for NSW

Transport for NSW, the government agency responsible for public transport in New South Wales, Australia, recently implemented a project to provide Google Maps with real-time scheduling information for trains and buses, as is done in many large cities around the world. Travelers can use Google Maps not only to find public transport options between two locations, but also to find out when the next bus or train is scheduled to arrive, based on real-time data coming from the buses and trains.

There's no profit motivation here; the aim is to allow public transport passengers to be able to use the public transport network more efficiently and reduce the time passengers need to wait for public transport. The motivation behind this may be increasing customer satisfaction. Happier passengers are more likely to use this service instead of any alternatives. A secondary goal could be to save people time, freeing them up for more productive work, which in turn benefits the local economy. This project will generate no increased revenue for the government agency implementing the project.

This rule still holds true for government or nonprofit organizations, but in a slightly modified form. Public services, for example, are not as interested in generating revenue as they are in providing valuable services to the public. This type of organization also typically has an externally defined budget; the service is responsible for how taxpayer dollars are spent, so cost plays a critical role in business goals. In general, the business goals for projects in nonprofit organizations tend to fall into the following categories:

- Improving service
- Reducing costs
- Avoiding future costs

4.2.8   *Popping the "why stack": Digging out the business goals*

If you want to build software that delivers real value to your customers, understanding the core business goals of a project is essential. And for a team practicing BDD, a deep understanding of business goals, needs, and concerns, shared across the whole team, is especially important. With a deep shared understanding of the customer needs, teams are better able to

- Propose a broader range of possible implementation solutions
- Write executable specifications that business folk can understand and relate to, allowing better feedback and communication
- Adapt to changing circumstances more effectively; if one solution doesn't work so well, or is too expensive, they can try out a different approach that will still deliver the same business goals

All of this comes much easier when team members participate as much as possible in the requirements discovery process, rather than getting the information secondhand.

Unfortunately, neither business sponsors nor end users typically express their needs in terms of pure business value. Instead, they talk in terms of concrete features or solutions that they have in mind. In addition, stakeholders are rarely capable of providing all the requirements up front, even if they do know them ahead of time.

Objective-driven management

Don't tell people how to do things, tell them what to do and let them surprise you with their results.

—George S. Patton

General George S. Patton was a highly successful American general known for his achievements in the European theater during the Second World War and for his unconventional and dynamic leadership style. Patton was once asked at a press conference how he was able to get such outstanding competence and devoted loyalty from his staff. "I never tell people how to do things," replied Patton. "I tell them what to do but not how. If you give people responsibility, they will surprise you with their ingenuity and reliability."

Stakeholders in large organizations have often been trained to believe that they must provide a detailed list of all their requirements at the start of a project. In many projects, once the requirements have been signed off on, change-control processes hinder any modifications, corrections, or additions that users might want to make. A dissuasive change-control process tends to result in very large sets of requirements full of everything the stakeholder can possibly think of, with many features being included just because they "might come in handy" someday. And this culture has been inherited by many organizations today even when they introduce agile practices.

It would be easy to take the feature requests that come out of such a process at face value. After all, shouldn't the users know better than anyone else what they want? Why not just note down what they want, and then do it? There are two very good reasons why this would be a bad idea.

First, the people who produce these requirements—the business sponsors, the end users, and so forth—are typically not well versed in the technologies that will be used to deliver the solution. The features they request may not be optimal from a technical viewpoint (there may be better ways of getting the job done), from a usability perspective (they are not UX experts), or from a financial one (you may be able to get the job done faster and cheaper using a different approach). The development team has a professional responsibility to propose the most appropriate solution for a given problem. But if the business goals are not clearly expressed and understood, you'll be hard-pressed to suggest potentially more appropriate solutions.

But there's a second reason that's arguably even more important than the first: if you don't know why you need to deliver a feature in a particular way, you'll have no way of knowing whether this feature is still useful or relevant when change happens. Any software project is an exercise in ongoing learning. Things inevitably change along the way, including assumptions and even the team's understanding of how a particular feature might benefit the business. A requirement that's expressed in the form of a detailed technical solution is embedded in a fabric of assumptions and preconceptions. You can be sure that some of these assumptions will turn out to be incorrect, or will change along the way, but it's hard to predict which ones will be wrong. When changes do happen, you need to be able to reassess the relevance of the features that you're building, but if you don't know why the business wants a feature, this will be much more difficult.

You usually need to drill down a little to discover what the business really needs. One of the best ways to do this is to repeatedly ask "why" until you get to a viable business goal. As a rule of thumb, five why-style questions are usually enough to identify the underlying business value (see figure 4.4).

Let's look at an example. Sam is a sales manager with Flying High Airlines. He comes to Bianca, a business analyst, with a request: "We need to integrate our Frequent Flyer with an affiliate program with major credit card vendors."

"Sure," says Bianca. "Can you walk me through this feature? Why is this something our users or stakeholders would value?"

Figure 4.4   It's always important to understand why you're undertaking a project.

Sam replies: "We've made a deal with a credit card company and propose a special Flying High credit card to our members, and they earn points when they spend money. We just need to make sure the points get credited to their account."

Bianca hasn't identified where the value is coming from to her satisfaction, so she asks another question: "Can you spell out for me how this will benefit our users or stakeholders?"

"Well, our members will appreciate that they get benefits not just when they fly, but also when they shop," says Sam.

At this point, Bianca still isn't sure she's identified the real value proposition behind this new feature, so she follows up with another question: "So, if I understand correctly, we want to increase the number of Frequent Flyer members by giving them rewards and privileges, and this will hopefully increase the sale of tickets?"

Sam explains: "Not exactly. We sell Frequent Flyer points in bulk to the banks that issue the credit cards. The banks want people to spend money with their cards, so they can earn a commission on the sales. Card holders also get other benefits, such as extra checked baggage, and we charge the bank for this too."

"Gotcha," says Bianca. "So the main business benefit here is from the sale of Frequent Flyer points, not from ticket sales. And how will this feature help us realize the business benefit?"

"We have negotiated a deal with our banking partner, but we can't actually issue the cards or sell any Frequent Flyer points until our software system integrates with theirs."

By asking these questions, Bianca now has a clear mapping back to a measurable business goal: generate revenue from selling Frequent Flyer points and other member benefits to the banks, who then pass on these benefits to their customers.

This process, sometimes known as "popping the why stack," is a powerful analysis tool, and BDD teams use it often to get a better understanding of a new feature request. Discovering and crystalizing the value proposition behind the features that users ask for not only helps you understand why they're asking for these features but also puts you in a position to evaluate their relative value and to adapt them to changing circumstances.

BDD is a deeply collaborative process. We have seen the value of identifying and articulating business vision and goals so that the whole team can have a deeper understanding of what they are trying to achieve. Now we will look at how to identify the capabilities and features that might help us realize those goals. We will look at two techniques that are particularly useful in a BDD context: Impact Mapping and Pirate Canvases. We will learn about a third technique, Feature Mapping, in the next chapter. High-level Feature Mapping is often used during the Speculate phase, though it is more commonly encountered during the Illustrate phase.

4.3   *Impact Mapping*

Impact Mapping[4] is a simple and convenient approach to building up an initial picture of what you're trying to achieve in a project. Impact maps are visual and intuitive, fast to draw, and accessible for both business and technical folk. They help create a picture of the relationship between the business goals behind a project, the actors who will be affected by the project, and the features that will enable the project to deliver the expected results. And they help document these goals and highlight any assumptions that underlie them.

This makes Impact Maps a great way both to kick off the initial requirements-analysis process and to get a high-level view of what you're trying to achieve. They can also help define or adjust project milestones as the project progresses. You can see an example of an Impact Map for our Frequent Flyer project in figure 4.5. But more interesting than the map itself is how we create it.

An Impact Map is a mind map built during a conversation, or series of conversations, between stakeholders and members of the development team. Unlike traditional requirements analysis approaches, where teams are presented with a list of preestablished features or User Stories that they need to build, Impact Mapping starts by identifying the business goals and the problem that needs solving.

---

[4] Impact Mapping is the brainchild of Gojko Adzik, who describes it in his book of the same name (Provoking Thoughts, 2012).

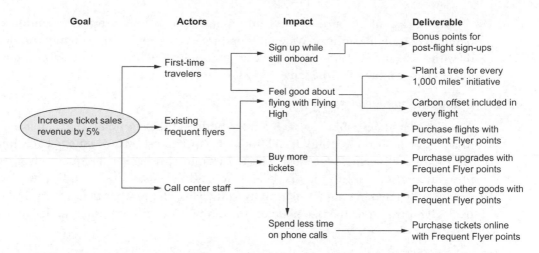

Figure 4.5 **What can you do to encourage or allow the stakeholders to modify their behavior to help achieve the business goal?**

The conversation centers around five different but related questions:

- *Pain point*—Why are we doing this? What business problem are we solving, and how can we measure it?
- *Goal*—What are we going to do about it? What do we aim to improve, and by how much?
- *Actor*—Who are the key people who interact with our system, and whose behavior could help or hinder our goals?
- *Impact*—How can we help, encourage, or empower these actors to help us achieve our goals? What changes in behavior do we want to see?
- *Deliverables*—What application features might support these changes in behavior? What can we do as a delivery team to help achieve the impact we are looking for?

Let's look at each of these questions in more detail.

4.3.1   *Identify the pain point*

The first question you need to ask is *why* you're building the software in the first place. What problem are you solving? And, just as importantly, how will you know if you have made a difference? Understanding the pain point[5] we want to address helps to give context and background to the business goals we describe in the next step.

---

[5] Impact Mapping conventionally starts with the business goal. In his blog entry, "Impact Mapping for Business Outcomes," November 17, 2017 (https://elabor8.com.au/impact-mapping-for-business-outcomes), Daniel Schrader proposes the idea of starting with the pain point to help identify the business goals and associated metrics.

In the case of our airline, the pain point might be low customer retention compared to competing airlines. We want to improve our sales by encouraging travelers to fly with us again. A good metric for this pain point might be the overall number of ticket sales compared to the same period in previous years.

4.3.2   Define the business goal

A business goal describes how we intend to address the pain point. What are we trying to achieve? How do we think it will improve things, and by how much? Each Impact Map starts with a single business goal. For example, using our Frequent Flyer example, you might start with the first goal, "Increase ticket sales revenue by 5% over the next year by encouraging travelers to fly with Flying High rather than with a rival company." This would be the first node in your Impact Map, as illustrated in figure 4.6.

Goal

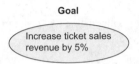

Figure 4.6   An Impact Map starts with the business goal you want to achieve.

4.3.3   Who will benefit? Defining the actors

The next question we ask is *who*. Who are the actors who will interact with our application? Who are the stakeholders impacted by the project? Who will benefit from the outcomes? If you're selling something, who are your customers? Who will be in a position to cause or influence the outcome you're trying to achieve? Who can prevent your project from being a success?

As you've seen, all projects ultimately aim to benefit the organization in some way. But organizations are made up of people, and it will be people within this organization (or people who interact with this organization) who will be affected by the outcomes of your project. These people are the *stakeholders* or *actors*.

Note that even when the overall effect of a project is designed to be beneficial for the organization, the impact of the project on an individual basis may be negative. For example, adding additional steps in a mortgage application process may be perceived as being cumbersome and annoying for the banker selling the mortgage and for the client applying for a house loan. But the net effect of reducing the risk of bad loans may be considered beneficial enough for the bank as a whole to outweigh these disadvantages. It's important to be aware of these negative impacts and to try to minimize them where possible.

Many different types of stakeholders will be interested in the outcomes of your work. Future users of your product are probably the most obvious example; their daily work will be impacted by your project, for better or for worse. For the Frequent Flyer website, this category of stakeholder will include current and future Frequent Flyer members. It may also include call center staff, who will have to answer questions from Frequent Flyer members about the new program and be able to view a client's current status and miles. They may also need to perform more complicated tasks that are not supported on the Frequent Flyer website, such as transferring Frequent Flyer miles between family members or crediting earned miles manually.

Note that future users may not always be directly interested in the business goals. A Frequent Flyer member has no particular reason to want to see an increase in Flying High ticket sales. Sometimes what the user wants and asks for will have little or no bearing on the original business objectives. When you think about what features you need to deliver to achieve the business goals, you need to think in terms of how you can encourage these stakeholders to behave in a way that helps you achieve the goals (see figure 4.7). For example, you want to provide features that encourage users to book flights with Flying High rather than with a competitor in order to increase ticket sales revenue.

Figure 4.7   An example of a wasteful feature. The ultimate purpose of any new feature is to deliver value to the organization. If it's not doing this in some way, it is probably waste.

Another category of stakeholder includes people who won't use the application themselves, but who are directly affected by, or interested in, the outcomes of the project. For example, Bill is the director of sales at Flying High Airlines and is therefore responsible for ticket sales. An increase in ticket sales revenue of 5% will help him meet his own goals of increasing sales revenue in general. In addition, his budget is paying for the new Frequent Flyer members' website, so understanding and quantifying this business goal will give Bill a way to justify the cost of the project in terms of ROI (return on investment). With this information, Bill can see how much the project is likely to earn in increased revenue, and therefore have a clearer idea of how much he's willing to spend to achieve these increased earnings.

Other stakeholders will not be directly affected by the project but will want to have a say in how the project is implemented and may have the power to block the project if they aren't contented. Regulators, those who work in security, and system administrators are good examples of this sort of role.

The actual role of the various stakeholders in achieving business goals and delivering business value is often overlooked. If users don't use the application in the expected way, the software may not realize the benefits you expected. Looking at things from another angle, a very effective way to identify the features that are most likely to support the business goals and provide real value is to think in terms of changing stakeholder behavior. How can you encourage users to behave in a way that supports the business goals?

For the Frequent Flyer project, you could identify several significant stakeholders who might have an influence on the "increase sales" business goal. For the sake of simplicity, let's focus on three: first-time travelers, existing Frequent Flyer members, and call center staff. In an Impact Map, we attach these actors to the business goal, as you can see in figure 4.8.

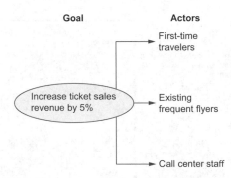

Figure 4.8   **The second layer of an Impact Map investigates who will benefit from, or who can help achieve, the business goal. It should also include anyone who might be in a position to *prevent* this goal from happening.**

4.3.4   *How should their behavior change? Defining the impacts*

The next question to ask is *how*. How can stakeholders and users contribute to achieving the business goals? How could their behavior or activities change to better meet our business goals and address the pain points? For example, if they are users, how could you make it easier for them to do their job? If they are customers, how can we encourage them to prefer our products to that of the competition? Alternatively, how might they or their behavior prevent or hinder these goals from being met and cause the project to fail?

Here, you're thinking about the impact you want to have on user behavior. You are considering how the system might make it easier for stakeholders to contribute to the business goals, or how you can influence their behavior and encourage them to do so in other ways. You're expressing things from the point of view of the stakeholder, which emphasizes that you're trying to write software that will change the way people do things, preferably in a positive way for the business.

In the case of our Frequent Flyer program, we could try to increase ticket sales revenue by encouraging existing Frequent Flyer members to buy more tickets or get new customers to join the program so that they might fly with us again. First-time flyers might be encouraged to sign up for our Frequent Flyer program while still onboard.

For both new and existing members, we could increase the likelihood that they fly with us by making them feel that choosing Flying High is the right thing to do.

Telephone sales are time-consuming and costly. Reducing the time taken to sell a ticket over the phone could also contribute to increasing sales revenue by reducing the number of call center staff required. You could illustrate these concepts in the Impact Map, as shown in figure 4.9.

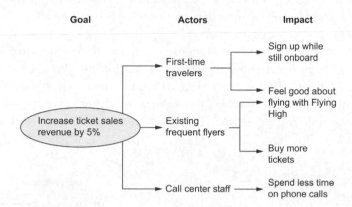

Figure 4.9   **How can these stakeholders help achieve these goals?**

4.3.5   *What should we do about it? Defining the deliverables*

The last type of question you need to ask is *what*. What can your application do to support the impacts you've listed in the previous three stages? Are there other ways to achieve these results without using software? In the context of building an application, the "what" corresponds to high-level deliverables. We want to give our users the capability to do something they couldn't previously do, or to do something they could do more easily. These capabilities often, but not always, map to software features. Depending on the size of the project, these might correspond to epics or high-level features, or even whole program initiatives.

In our example, you might encourage Frequent Flyer members to buy more tickets by making it easier to redeem miles on flights or on other products or by allowing them to use their points to upgrade flights when they check in.

Airlines are receiving a lot of heat due to aviation's environmental impact. You might make travelers feel better about flying with Flying High, compared to competing airlines, by offsetting their carbon emissions free of charge, or by engaging in environmentally friendly programs such as through reforestation or tree planting. And you might reduce the number of telephone bookings by determining what sort of bookings are being done over the phone and making online purchases for these tickets easier.

Deliverables can also represent nonsoftware initiatives or activities. For example, one way to encourage first-time flyers to sign up with the Frequent Flyer program might be to propose double Frequent Flyer points on the flight they just completed, on the condition that they sign up within 24 hours.

Impact mapping helps you visualize how features and deliverables contribute to a business goal. It also helps underline any assumptions you may be making. For example, here you're assuming that social media integration will be enough for Frequent Flyer members to proudly post about all their trips. Impact Mapping encourages you to not only sketch out these relationships and assumptions, but to also define metrics that you can use when the feature goes live to test whether your assumption was correct. In this case, you might keep track of the number of Facebook and Twitter posts that are generated by Frequent Flyer members in order to learn how effective your new social media integration strategy really is.

It's important to remember that Impact Maps are not plans; they're iterative, living documents that can help you visualize assumptions and relationships between capabilities and business goals. Whenever you deliver something into production, you should be able to validate certain assumptions, and you may prove others wrong. Based on this feedback, you'll be able to update your Impact Map and your short-term plans accordingly (see figure 4.10).

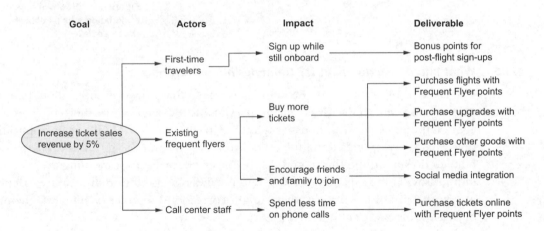

Figure 4.10   What deliverables can help make this impact?

4.3.6   *Reverse Impact Mapping*

Impact Maps make great high-level discovery tools at the start of a project. But they can also be used very effectively in the other direction, though for a slightly different purpose. Suppose, for example, that you already have a set of proposed features: a product backlog in an Agile project, a set of use cases, or even a set of high-level requirements in a more traditional requirements-specification document. Suppose, while you're at it, that the requested features come from different stakeholders, who are each convinced that "their" feature should be done first.

In this case, Impact Maps make a great conversation starter. I've found the following strategy effective: get your stakeholders together, put the requested features on a whiteboard, and identify who they'll benefit and how they'll benefit them, working back to the underlying business goals. Eventually you'll end up with a graph that shows a number of goals, with a relatively clear illustration of which features map to which goals. This visual representation of all the goals and the supporting features is an excellent starting point for a discussion of the relative merit of each goal, and of each feature, and makes it much easier to prioritize the different features more objectively.

If you're interested in learning more about Impact Mapping, look at the Impact Mapping website (http://impactmapping.org) and read the book *Impact Mapping* by Gojko Adzic (Provoking Thoughts, 2012).

4.4 Pirate Canvases

Pirate Canvases are another way for high-level stakeholders to think about the big picture. Pirate Canvases take a breadth-first approach to product design that combines elements from Impact Mapping, pirate metrics from the world of start-ups and marketing, and Goldratt's theory of constraints.[6]

A Pirate Canvas encourages conversations not just about immediately obvious deliverables, but about the broader ecosystem of products and services. Peter Merel[7] calls this Ecosystem Thinking. It considers how we might motivate various actors in the ecosystem to behave in a way that is mutually beneficial, that works not only for our own benefit, but for their benefit as well. And this can lead to surprisingly fruitful discussions that reveal previously unrecognized but urgent priorities and indeed whole new business opportunities. But before we can look at Pirate Canvases, we need to look at Pirate Metrics.

4.4.1 Pirate Metrics

Back in 2007, angel investor Dave McClure identified five key metrics that businesses in general, and start-ups in particular, need to focus on to be successful. The metrics in question are Acquisition, Activation, Retention, Referral, and Return, or AARRR (see figure 4.11).

Acquisition refers to how we pull actors into our ecosystem of products and services. Often this will involve proposing some small but real benefit for potential users that they can use for free, which will attract them to our services in the first place.

But in most cases users are not the only actors in our ecosystem. A cafe needs to grab the interest of coffee lovers, but also needs to build sustainable relationships with coffee suppliers and baristas. A bank needs to consider customers, but also investors, financial service providers (whose products the bank might supply), accounting software providers, regulators, and many others.

Activation is getting actors to engage with our products or services. People see the value in using your system. This might be getting them to try a sample product, start a

---

[6] Eliyahu M. Goldratt, *Theory of Constraints* (North River Press, 1999).
[7] Peter Merel is the creator of the Pirate Canvas technique.

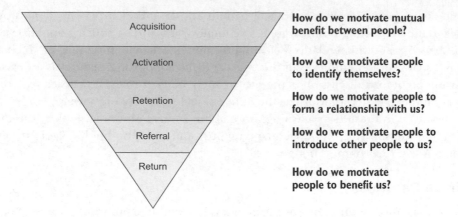

Figure 4.11   What can you do to encourage or allow the stakeholders to modify their behavior to help achieve the business goal?

free trial, watch a video, or register for a newsletter. When we are looking at a broader ecosystem rather than a simple sales pipeline, activation is inducing users to identify themselves so that we can potentially bill someone (the users or some other actor) for their behavior.

Retention is all about how we get people to form a relationship with us. How do get users coming back for more? How do we get them to stay in our ecosystem? For example, how many visitors to our site are return visitors? How often do they revisit our site?

Referral is how we encourage people to introduce other people to us. This is another important, potentially viral, way to drive growth. Do our users recommend our services to others? How can we motivate them to do so? This could take the form of positive reviews or comments, or may involve a more deliberate refer-a-friend program.

Finally, *Return* is about how we get people to deliver us with tangible benefits. How much value does each user generate for the organization? How much do they contribute to the organizational goals? We might measure revenue in a sales organization, or something else, such as risk reduction in a compliance or regulatory government department. We might even look to measure learning in a change initiative.

But to be effective, Pirate Metrics should correspond to concrete values that we can measure and that make sense for our particular domain. Very often, we can identify a small number of critical numbers that we can use to track each metric. Understanding what these numbers are can help us know what we need to do to make an impact.

For example, if we were looking at the Frequent Flyer program we discussed earlier, we could use the following:

- Acquisition could be measured by counting the number of visitors to our Frequent Flyer website.
- Activation might correspond to the number of users who sign up for the Frequent Flyer card.

- Retention might measure the number of users who sign up to the Frequent Flyer program and come back to check out the latest special deals.
- Referral could keep track of the number of likes or shares on social media, or the number of positive reviews on travel websites.
- Return could be measured by things like ticket sales from Frequent Flyer members, or maybe the impact in the overall ticket sales.

Each metric measures a constraint, or bottleneck, on the road to a growing business. It is important to keep track of all of these metrics so that you can know where the next most important problem to solve lies.

For example, if our users can't find the Frequent Flyer website, we may be facing a bottleneck in the Acquisition phase. We could launch an extensive marketing campaign to make customers more aware of the Frequent Flyer brand. But if our users don't see any value in our product, and don't spend very much time on the site, we might have an Activation bottleneck, and spending more money on marketing will be wasteful. Alternatively, if we notice that users are spending time on the site and even registering for the Frequent Flyer card, but that very few users return to the site, we may have a problem with retention. While all of these metrics are interesting, in general we should try to focus on optimizing only one of them at a time.

4.4.2 *From Pirate Metrics to Pirate Canvases*

Pirate Canvases build on and extend the concept of Pirate Metrics. A Pirate Canvas looks at these metrics not just in the context of existing products or sales pipelines, but also as a way to discuss the constraints to the growth of an ecosystem more broadly.

For existing products and services, a Pirate Canvas helps us structure our conversations about how we can remove bottlenecks and improve our results. But we can also use these metrics to discover areas of opportunity, where we might build or integrate new products and services to fill previously unknown market gaps. A Pirate Canvas is a great way to highlight our assumptions about the market impact of potential new products or services. And this in turn helps us discuss how we can test these assumptions, and which ones we should work on first.

4.4.3 *Discovering what sucks*

As with Impact Mapping, a Pirate Canvas starts with a pain point. But rather than focusing on a specific release goal, Pirate Canvases take a breadth-first approach to identifying the most important goals to work on. This can help us discover and prioritize release goals from a number of different areas. Peter Merel, originator of the Pirate Canvas idea, doesn't talk about pain points. He likes to ask, "What sucks?"

Let's look at an example. Flying High management has noticed that their share of the lucrative business travel market is not as big as they would like. They would like to see how they can increase their revenue share from this market. But to break into this competitive market, they need to offer something that sets Flying High apart from other airlines. More than just offering champagne and nuts to business travelers, they want to offer something new. The question is what.

They could start with a very high-level question such as "What sucks about business traveling with Flying High?" But Carrie, our Agile coach, prefers to start with something even more general: "What sucks about business travel?" Broader questions lead to broader thinking and more innovative ideas; they help teams consider what unique solution they might be able to bring to the table.

We start this discussion by looking at the five Pirate Metrics. In the previous section, we saw how these metrics might apply to the Frequent Flyer program. But Pirate Canvases generally look beyond individual features or even applications and consider the broader ecosystem in which the company operates. Participants are encouraged to think about problems and opportunities across the whole ecosystem in which their products and services operate.

During a Pirate Canvas workshop, participants discuss each of these metrics in turn, flushing out things that stink about each area, and using the five why's technique we saw earlier to get to the root cause of the problem.

Let's watch as the Flying High team considers what stinks for business travelers, and how that might affect each of these metrics. Carrie is facilitating the Pirate Canvas session. First, she draws five columns on a whiteboard, corresponding to each of the five Pirate Metrics (see figure 4.12). "Remember, Acquisition is about bringing business travelers into our ecosystem, so what sucks about acquiring business travelers?" she asks.

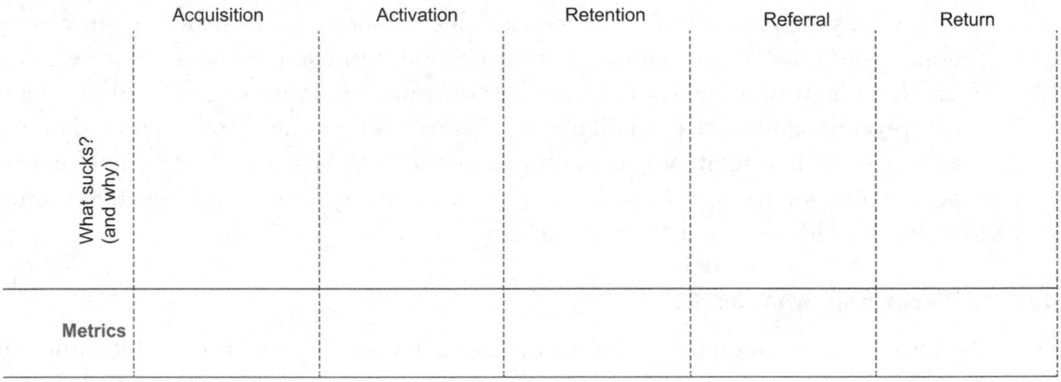

Figure 4.12   The top half of a Pirate Canvas identifies key bottlenecks and impediments, grouped by Pirate Metric.

Sam, from sales, has some thoughts. "First, there just isn't that much interest in our business offerings. According to our analytics, only 5% of the booking inquiries on our site come from business users. Business users just aren't coming to our site."

"And why do you think that is?" asks Carrie.

"Well, they have no particular reason to come to our site," says Mark from marketing. "We are better known as a low-cost airline for tourist destinations."

"Well, business travelers don't really want to go to any travel site," points out Sam. "They don't even want to travel, when it comes to it. Travel time is considered waste for most business travelers."

"If they don't want to travel, what do they want?" asks Carrie.

"They want to be able to do deals. *What* they would really like is more time and opportunities to do business," Sam answers.

"Aha! So what sucks here is that business travelers can't do business on their flights?" asks Carrie.

"Exactly."

Carrie notes down these points on Post-Its and puts them on the board under the Acquisition column (see figure 4.13). "So we acquire a business traveler when they come to our site because they want the opportunity to do more business, not just to travel. But how could we quantify this? What dial do we need to move to improve things?"

"The simplest metric would be to measure the number of visits from business travelers," says Mark. "We can get this data from our web analytics."

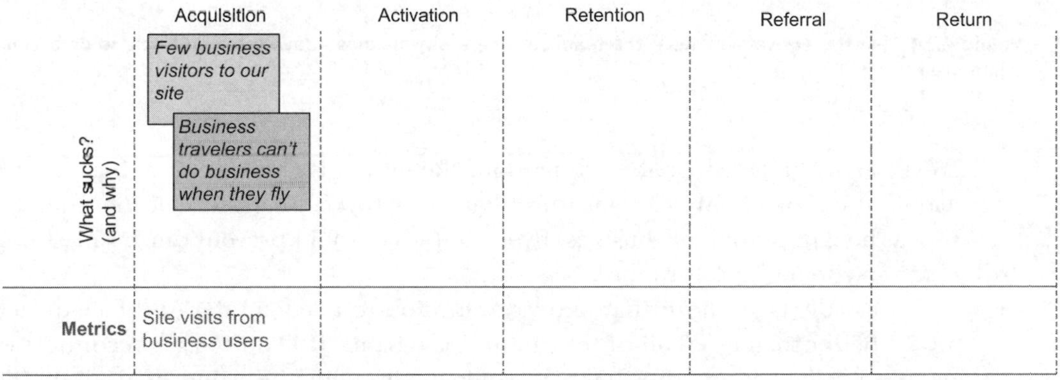

	Acquisition	Activation	Retention	Referral	Return
What sucks? (and why)	Few business visitors to our site / Business travelers can't do business when they fly				
Metrics	Site visits from business users				

Figure 4.13 Carrie notes the key impediments in the Acquisition phase and how to measure progress.

Next, Carrie wants to talk about activation. "What does activation mean for us in this context? Remember, this is where the customer has an 'aha' moment and sees value in our services."

"Well, if acquisition is about attracting business flyers who want more business opportunities, activation must be making them want to fly with us in order to take advantage of new business opportunities, whatever they might be," says Mark.

Sam continues: "In our case, that might correspond to the number of productive business conversations our business travelers are having."

"And what sucks about acquisition?" asks Carrie.

"Currently, it is hard to do business on a flight. Assuming we have the Activation phase sorted, the travelers might know who else is on the flight, but it is still impractical to talk to anyone other than the person next to you, let alone make a sales pitch," points out Mark. Carrie records these points on pink cards and puts them in the Activation column (see figure 4.14).

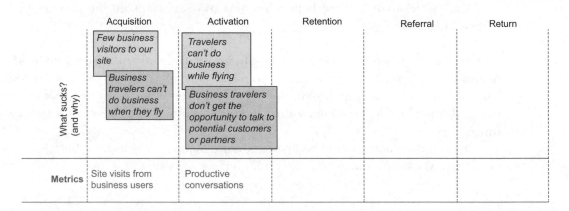

Figure 4.14   For the Activation phase, the team considers why business travelers aren't able to do business while flying.

Next Carrie wants to talk about retention. "Retention is getting repeat business from acquired customers. We can measure that easily by keeping track of the number of repeat bookings from our business flyers. But what would prevent our business travelers from coming back for more?"

"It usually takes more than one conversation to make a sale. And face-to-face is always better than by email or telephone," says Sam. "If I can't easily reconnect with people I talked to on the flight, it would really limit the value of these in-flight opportunities."

"So the problem is that our business travelers can't use their flights to leverage and maintain their business relationships," Carrie resumes. She notes these ideas in the Retention column on the board.

"And what about referral?" asks Carrie. "Remember, referral is how our customers do our marketing work for us and encourage others to join our ecosystem."

"As it stands, there's no way for business flyers to do this," points out Mark. "They have no incentive to invite their business contacts to fly with us."

"Great," says Carrie. "The last metric is return. We could just measure sales revenue from business flyers. Or we could think a bit more broadly. What if we looked at things differently? What if we could figure out how to help our ecosystem grow, and benefit from that growth?"

"Good thinking," says Mike. "There are plenty of small companies and start-ups that might miss out on opportunities if they can't send their employees to events or customer visits, but their travel budget is limited. Maybe we could have some kind of start-up accelerator concept, where start-ups give us equity in exchange for free or discounted business flights. We could give them both the travel capabilities they need to grow and get them on flights with other travelers whom they might want to do business with."

"OK, let's note that as 'No way to benefit from the deals flyers make,' and see where your start-up idea takes us," says Carrie. "We could measure this by tracking the market value of the equity we get."

The Pirate Canvas now looks like the one in figure 4.15. The team has identified the key problems they face; now it is time to look at some possible solutions to these problems.

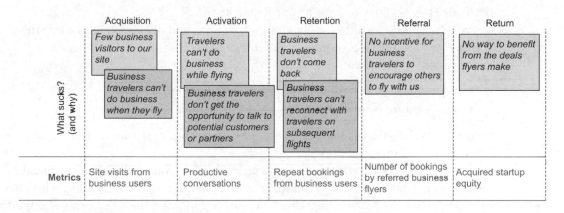

Figure 4.15   The Pirate Canvas now describes the key impediments at each stage.

4.4.4   *Building the Epic Landscape*

A Pirate Canvas does not just aim to highlight problems. More importantly, it helps teams have more effective conversations about the impact they want to make, and about what high-level deliverables they need to deliver to make this impact. These high-level deliverables are often referred to as *Epics*, and we call this breadth-first vision of the epics that we want to deliver an *Epic Landscape*—a broad picture of the capabilities we need to deliver, in the context of the business problems we are trying to solve.

FIND AN ACTION PLAN FOR EACH METRIC

The next step of a Pirate Canvas workshop is to come up with an action plan for each Pirate Metric category. The team makes the pain points and metrics, and converts them into tangible, measurable goals. Then, starting with these goals, they follow a similar approach to that used with Impact Mapping to identify actors, impacts, and deliverables. These deliverables in turn become the epics in the Epic Landscape.

As we saw in earlier in this chapter, Impact Mapping can produce a large number of capabilities and deliverables that could contribute to any given goal. Pirate Canvases do things a little differently. A Pirate Canvas is a breadth-first approach, and a forest of impacts and deliverables will make it harder to focus on the high-impact deliverables. So while we may discover many potential impacts and deliverables, we discuss each one in turn and only keep the most valuable ones.

Let's see this process in action. Carrie starts with the Acquisition column. "Let's turn the acquisition pain point into a goal. We aren't getting enough interest from business customers, and we want to fix this. How much of an increase in site visits do we need? How would you know if your fix worked?"

"We have very few visitors at the moment, so we would need to at least triple the visits from business travelers to make a difference," says Sam.

Carrie notes this down:

- *Why*—Increase site visits from business travelers by 300%
- *Who*—Business travelers

"And what actions do we need to take to encourage business travelers to use our site for booking their business trips?"

"I know," says Mark. "What we need is a big 'fly business with us' marketing campaign."

Carrie cuts him short. "Let's not worry about *what* just yet. How should their behavior change? We need that nailed down before we can worry about what we should do to make it happen."

"We want them to change their behavior so that they come looking for business opportunities on our business flights," says Mark.

"And how could we do that?" asks Carrie.

"We really need to give them a reason to come to our site. Give them some small thing for free, that is valuable to them," replies Sam.

"What if we could help them make their trips more productive?" wonders Mark. "For example, suppose we enabled an online community of business travelers who could know what sort of potential customers or partners would be flying on their flight?"

She lists these points vertically in the Acquisition column, as shown in figure 4.16. Putting them up on the board makes it easier for the team to visualize and challenge the assumptions they are making. This is what happens next.

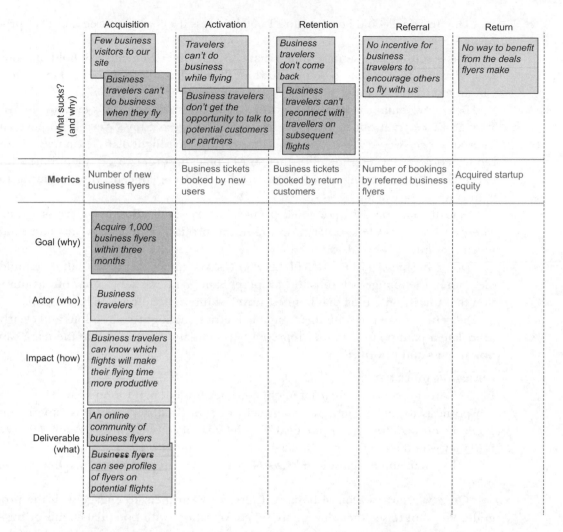

Figure 4.16 **The bottom part of a Pirate Canvas describes how we could address the pain points in the top section.**

"You're making a pretty big assumption in the *how*," points out Dave, the developer. "How do we know that is something business travelers would really want to do?"

"We could test the concept easily with a survey of some of our business contacts," says Sam. "But come to think of it, that's not the riskiest assumption. That *why* feels like a vanity metric. Are site visits really the best way to measure acquisition? Wouldn't it be more accurate to measure the number of people who join the business flyers community?"

"Sure, we can do that," says Carrie. "But we will also need to revise the goal, actors, and impact, to make sure they are still good."

"The new goal could be to acquire 1,000 business flyers within three months," proposes Mark.

"Makes sense," says Carrie. "And in that case, the other elements still hold. But our riskiest assumption seems to be that business flyers will result in more bookings. How can we test that assumption?"

"Before we build a new social network for business travelers, let's test our theory. Why don't we try it out on our own sales staff?" suggests Sam. "We can propose an internal service where a few willing executives share their flight plans. That way we can see if people are willing to adjust their travel plans in order to get some time with executives they are trying to influence. We can trial the concept without having to write any software at all."

"And if that goes well, we could propose a very simple Business Flyer program, where business travelers can sign up to see the profiles of other travelers and send meeting requests," says Mark.

"Doing business on the actual flights won't be very practical just yet, but they could meet up in the lounge beforehand," proposes Sam. "This way we can test our assumption that this is something that business travelers more broadly would find useful."

Deliverables like this, with their tangible metrics, highlight assumptions and clearly articulate a pain point, and they represent a potential release goal that the team can now discuss and prioritize.

FINDING THE OTHER METRICS

In a real-world scenario, the team might consider this enough for one day. They have a hypothesis to validate and an experiment to run. Feedback from this experiment would be enough for one release goal. For the sake of completeness, though, let's see how they would continue their discussion about the other metrics.

"OK, what about activation?" says Carrie. "What impact would we like to see here?"

"Once we start to acquire business flyers, we want them to engage with the program. We want to see them having useful conversations with potential clients or business partners, and building new connections," says Mark. "If they get value out of the program, they will come back for more."

"Let's put a number on that," says Carrie.

"I would like to see 30% of business bookings lead to productive conversations," says Sam. "We could measure that by an online survey after each flight. Maybe we could gamify it so that the business flyers rate the conversations after the flight, and business flyers get points when the other person rates the conversation well."

"So this is about the business travelers," says Carrie. "How should their behavior change?"

"They have more and more useful conversations during their trip," says Mark. We could do this in lots of ways. Maybe we can rearrange the business cabins so that it is easier to talk with different people. We could have name tags given out in the lobby, and maybe even have areas where people can hold discussions or pitch their product or idea, a bit like a mini conference."

Carrie notes all this down (see figure 4.17):

- *Why*—Thirty percent of flight bookings lead to productive conversations.
- *Who*—Business flyers.
- *How*—Business flyers engage easily in conversations with potential clients or business partners.
- *What*—Conversation-friendly business cabin, mini conferences in the lounge.

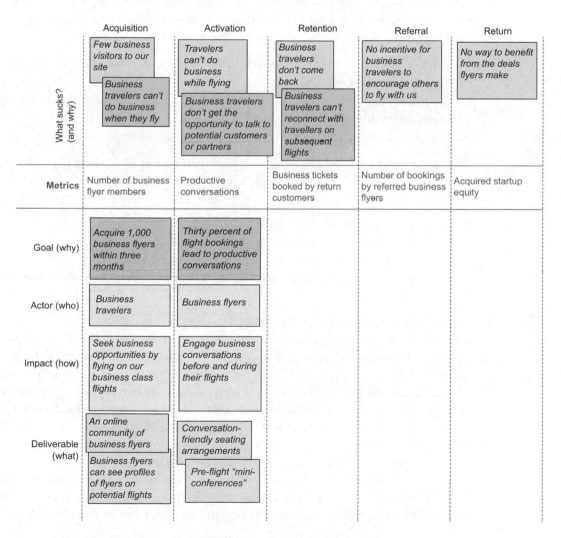

Figure 4.17   The activation bottleneck focuses on engaging business flyers.

Notice how these deliverables don't necessarily involve software. A Pirate Canvas encourages us to look beyond software solutions and at how we could improve the broader ecosystem.

The retention side of things does involve some software deliverables. "This is all about enticing our business travelers to come back for more. As a goal, we want 80% of our business travelers rebooking," says Mark.

"We need business travelers to follow up with the connections they make," says Sam. "Maybe the points they earn for highly rated conversations can go toward Frequent Flyer points that they can spend on new flight bookings."

"And maybe a social media application could help the business flyers build relationships and coordinate subsequent flights with people they have met," continues Mark.

Carrie records these details on the board (see figure 4.17):

- *Why*—Eighty percent of new business flyers book again within three months.
- *Who*—Business flyers.
- *How*—Business flyers connect with their new contacts and organize follow-up meetings for subsequent flights.
- *What*—Business Flyer points program and social media app.

The team continues this exercise for the other two columns, coming up with one or more potential deliverables for each Pirate Metric. They discover several key deliverables:

- Integration with other social media platforms so that business flyers can invite their own contacts to join the program
- A feature where new business flyers can invite contacts from their address book to the program, where each earn bonus Frequent Flyer points when the new contact signs up

You can see the completed Pirate Canvas in figure 4.18.

A Pirate Canvas isn't limited to one actor, one impact, or one deliverable per metric. Just like with Impact Mapping, we may discover many paths to delivering the goal we are after. The role of the Pirate Canvas is to map out the various possible deliverables that we could work on so that we can understand how they contribute to resolving our pain points. Laying them out side-by-side, in the context of the business goals they aim to support, is a great way to help teams prioritize and know where they should spend their efforts next.

A Pirate Canvas views each stage of the canvas as a potential bottleneck or constraint on the path toward growth. It is a living document: as our understanding of the bottlenecks evolves, and as we implement and deliver solutions that remove constraints, the dynamics will change, and the priorities will need to be reevaluated.

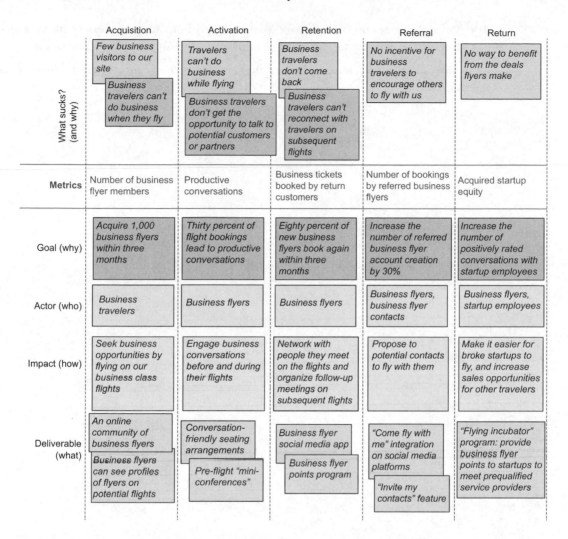

Figure 4.18 **A completed Pirate Canvas shows an Epic Landscape, high-level deliverables in the context of the bottlenecks they aim to eliminate.**

Summary

- Strategic requirements discovery is an ongoing process that happens regularly throughout the project and involves both senior stakeholders and delivery team members.
- Identifying and understanding the fundamental business goals behind the applications you build makes it much easier to design and build valuable features.
- Impact Mapping enables you to visualize the relationships between stakeholders, capabilities, features, and business goals.

- Pirate Metrics combine Impact Mapping and help stakeholders to build a picture of the Epic Landscape and to know which goals they should focus on first.

In the next chapter, we look at how to describe features in more detail and how to slice them into User Stories.

Describing and prioritizing features

This chapter covers

- BDD and Product Backlog refinement
- Describing and organizing features
- Breaking features into User Stories
- Using Real Options to determine the best time to commit to building a particular feature
- Using Deliberate Discovery to reduce the impact of what you don't know

A surprising number of the benefits of BDD come from simply having a conversation with the business, using examples to challenge assumptions and build a common understanding of the problem space. One of the principal benefits of BDD is to encourage and structure this kind of conversation. In the previous chapter you learned how important it is to understand why you're building a piece of software and what its ultimate purpose will be in business terms. We looked at how you can clarify *what* you want to achieve and *how* you expect this to benefit the business (the business goals), and also at *who* will benefit or be affected by the project (the stakeholders) and *what* you need to deliver at a high level to achieve the business goals (the capabilities). We also learned about Impact Mapping and Pirate Canvases—two powerful techniques that can help us understand business needs and identify features that might deliver these needs.

Now it's time to describe *how* you can provide these capabilities. In this chapter we look at the next step, which is to discuss and describe the deliverables you discovered through Impact Mapping or on a Pirate Canvas. We will learn how to break down high-level features or Epics into User Stories, how to describe these features, and how to prioritize them using Deliberate Discovery and Real Options, and how what we learn during this process can help us plan for upcoming sprints and releases.

Some of the key topics we will explore include these:

- Features and User Stories. In BDD terms, a feature is a piece of software functionality that helps users or other stakeholders achieve some business goal. A feature is not a User Story, but it can be described by one or several User Stories. A User Story is a way of breaking the feature down into more manageable chunks to make them easier to implement and deliver.
- Managing uncertainty plays a major role in BDD practices. When they've identified areas of uncertainty, experienced BDD practitioners avoid committing to a definitive solution too early, keeping their options open until they know enough to be able to deliver the most appropriate solution for the problem at hand. This approach is known as Real Options.
- Deliberate Discovery tries to reduce project risk by managing uncertainty and ignorance proactively wherever possible.

But let's start off by looking at the role that BDD plays in the traditional Agile activity of Product Backlog Refinement.

5.1   *BDD and Product Backlog Refinement*

We saw in the previous chapter how BDD teams identify strategic business goals, capabilities, and high-level features using techniques such as Pirate Canvases and Impact Mapping during the Speculate phase. Another important part of the Speculate phase is detailing features in the Product Backlog to the point that they are ready to be picked up by individual teams and refined during the Illustrate phase (see figure 5.1).

This activity is often known as Product Backlog Refinement and is a common Agile practice. The term comes from Scrum. A *Product Backlog* is essentially the list of things that need to be done in a project, a bit like a high-level to-do list for the team. For a team practicing BDD, the Product Backlog will contain the features identified during the discovery activities we learned about in the previous chapter, such as Impact Mapping and Pirate Canvases.

According to the Scrum guide, "Product Backlog Refinement is the act of adding detail, estimates, and order to items in the Product Backlog. This is an ongoing process in which the Product Owner and the Development Team collaborate on the details of Product Backlog items" (https://www.scrumguides.org).

During Product Backlog Refinement, features are estimated at a high level, and key examples and acceptance criteria are identified. Larger features might be broken

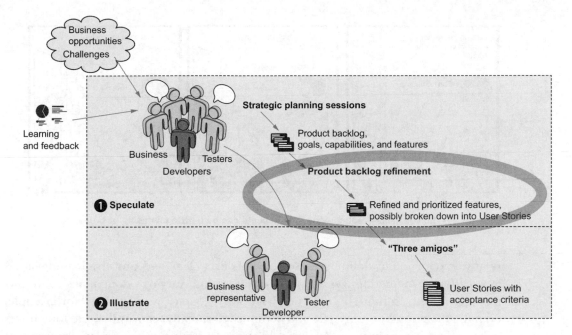

Figure 5.1 The vocabulary around Agile requirements can be a little confusing at times.

down into smaller features or stories to make them easier to discuss and plan, and upcoming release and iteration goals are discussed and defined.

Product Backlog Refinement activities happen on a regular basis during the life of a project: some teams have weekly Product Backlog Refinement sessions; others run a regular session shortly before the end of each sprint. But other Product Backlog Refinement activities, such as research and preparation for requirements discovery sessions, can also happen in smaller groups.

For a team practicing BDD, items in the Product Backlog are the high-level features or Epics that emerged from the strategic discovery sessions that we discussed in chapter 4. They might use techniques such as high-level Feature Mapping (which you will learn about in chapter 6) to get a better understanding of the features being discussed.

Product Backlog Refinement activities don't always involve all team members. In larger projects involving multiple teams, Product Backlog Refinement sessions can involve delegates from the various teams.

During Product Backlog Refinement, a team takes features and breaks them down into User Stories. Let's take a more in-depth look at what we mean by these terms.

5.2 What is a feature?

In Agile projects, developers use lots of different words to describe what they want to build (see figure 5.2): Epics, capabilities, themes, requirements, features, use cases, User Stories, tasks. Confusing? Guilty as charged. The Agile community has done a

Figure 5.2   The vocabulary around Agile requirements can be a little confusing at times.

relatively poor job of defining these concepts in a clear and universally understood way. Different methodologies and different teams use varying—sometimes contradictory—terms. And although the terms "User Story," "Epic," and "theme," for example, do have a long tradition in Agile and Scrum circles, many teams still waste long hours debating what terminology they should use or whether a particular requirement should be called a story, a feature, an Epic, or something else entirely.

How did we get ourselves into this predicament? All we really want to do is describe what we think our users need. We want to express ourselves in a way that business stakeholders can understand so that they can validate our understanding, contribute, and provide feedback as early as possible. We want to be able to describe what our users need in a way that makes it easier to build and deliver software that meets these needs.

The terms we use are intended to simplify discussion around user requirements. In essence, we're trying to do two things:

- Deliver tangible, visible value to the business at regular intervals
- Get regular feedback so we know if we're going in the right direction

The way we describe and organize the requirements should support these goals. The various ways different teams organize and structure stories, Epics, features, and so forth are simply ways to decompose higher-level requirements into manageable sizes, describe them in terms that users can understand, and allow them to provide feedback at each level. There are many perfectly legitimate ways to do this, and what works best for your team will depend on the size and complexity of your project and on the background and culture of your organization and team members.

For the sake of simplicity and consistency, let's step through the vocabulary we'll use throughout the rest of this book. We'll mainly deal with four terms: *capabilities, features, User Stories,* and *examples* (see figure 5.3).

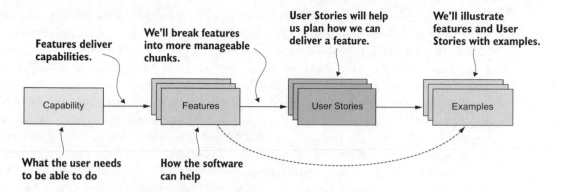

Figure 5.3   Features deliver capabilities to stakeholders. We'll use User Stories to plan how we'll deliver a feature. We'll use examples to illustrate features and User Stories.

I introduced these concepts briefly in chapter 3, but here's a quick refresher:

- *Capabilities* give users or stakeholders the ability to realize some business goal or perform some useful task. A capability represents the ability to do something; it doesn't depend on a particular implementation. For example, "the ability to book a flight" is a capability.
- *Features* represent software functionality that you build to support these capabilities. "Book a flight online" is a feature.
- When you build and deliver these features, you can use User Stories to break down the work into more manageable chunks and to plan and organize your work.
- You can use examples to understand how the features will help your users and to guide your work on the User Stories. You can use examples to understand both features and individual User Stories.

> **What about Epics?**
>
> In Scrum and other Agile methodologies, an *Epic* generally refers to a large User Story that can't be delivered in a single iteration. An Epic should deliver a capability (though there may be times when an Epic can contribute to more than one capability).
>
> A feature also delivers or supports a capability in some way, and may take more than one iteration to deliver, so there is some overlap in the terms. Some teams use the term Epic to refer to features in the sense that we are using them in this chapter, and this is fine. Others consider an Epic larger than a feature, so an Epic may contain many features. And this is fine too.

5.2.1   *Features deliver capabilities*

As developers, we build features so that end users, and stakeholders in general, can achieve their goals. Users need our software to give them the capabilities that will help them contribute to these business goals.

Features are what we deliver to users to support these capabilities. A feature is a tangible piece of functionality that will be valuable for users and that relates closely to what the users actually ask for, which may or may not be deliverable in a single iteration. A feature can be delivered relatively independently of other features and be tested by end users in isolation. Features are often used to plan and document releases.

Features are expressed in business terms and in a language that management can understand. If you were writing a user manual, a feature would probably have its own section or subsection. In the past, when off-the-shelf software was packaged in boxes, features were what appeared on the side of the package.

Let's look at an example. Flying High Airlines is very proud of its recently introduced Frequent Flyer program. Belonging to the Flying High Frequent Flyer club lets members earn points that they can spend on flights, upgrades, and so forth, and it's designed to encourage travelers to book with Flying High rather than a competitor. But management has noticed a high rate of lapsed memberships, which they suspect is due to the cumbersome renewal process. Currently, members need to call Flying High or return a renewal form by nonelectronic mail to renew.

Suppose you have identified the capability "Enable members to renew their membership more easily." Some useful features supporting this capability on the Flying High customer site might be "Allow members to renew their membership online" and "Notify members when their membership is due for renewal." To support these capabilities, you could define features such as "Renew membership online" or "Notify members that their membership is due for renewal by email" (see figure 5.4).

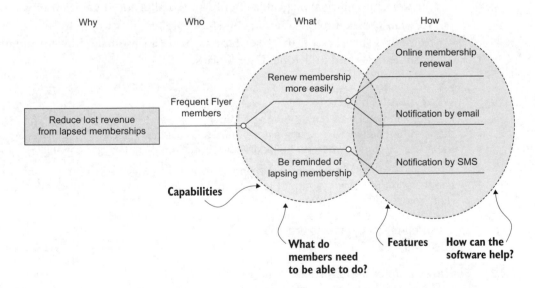

Figure 5.4 As illustrated in this Impact Map, features provide users or stakeholders with the capability to do something useful.

Let's focus on the online renewal feature. You could describe this using the "in order to . . . as a . . . I want" format, like this:

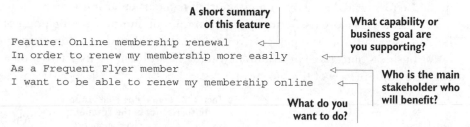

```
Feature: Online membership renewal
In order to renew my membership more easily
As a Frequent Flyer member
I want to be able to renew my membership online
```

A short summary of this feature

What capability or business goal are you supporting?

Who is the main stakeholder who will benefit?

What do you want to do?

You used this format in the previous chapter to describe capabilities, but it works equally well for requirements at any level. You start off with a short summary or title of the feature to give some context. This is the text proposed in the Impact Map in figure 5.4, in the "How" section. In fact, until you actually schedule, design, and implement this feature, this short overview is usually enough to work with. You only really need to flesh out the details when you're fairly sure you want to (and are ready to) start working on the feature.

At that point, you can try to formulate what the feature is about in more detail. First you outline what business goal you think this feature will support. This helps remind you why you're building this feature in the first place, and ties back nicely to the capability in the impact graph. It also allows you to do a sanity check on your requirement. You can ask yourself questions such as "Will the feature I'm proposing really help us achieve this business goal? If not, what business goal is it supporting? Based on what I know now, is it still worth building this feature?" Both your understanding of the requirements and the business context behind the project may have changed since you first envisaged the feature (see figure 5.5), and you might need to reevaluate how important the feature really is.

Next, you identify which users you think this feature will affect, or which stakeholders will benefit. This helps you look at things from the point of view of the people who will be using the feature or who expect to benefit from its outcomes.

Figure 5.5 Sometimes features become less important as we learn more about them.

Finally, you describe the feature itself and what it's meant to do. Here, you focus on describing what the software does in business terms; you don't want to get too hung up on the technical details or commit yourself to a particular implementation just yet.

Sometimes it's more useful to consider a requirement not from the point of view of the end user, but from the perspective of the stakeholder who's ultimately interested in this business outcome. For example, you might find it more useful to look at things from the point of view of the business:

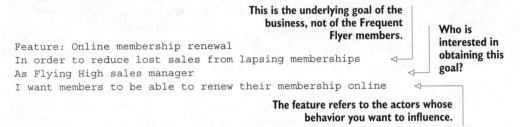

This highlights an interesting point. It's really the Flying High sales manager who wants members to renew so that they'll continue to book flights on Flying High planes. In this case, the real stakeholder you need to satisfy is the sales manager, not the members. Maybe the members aren't always that motivated to renew. Maybe you need to find ways to entice them into renewing their memberships.

The format we've been using here is popular among BDD practitioners because it focuses on the business value or capability that the feature is meant to deliver. But many teams also use the more traditional "as a . . . I want . . . so that" format:

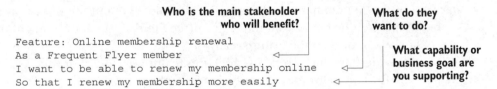

If you're new to all this, the "in order to . . . as a . . . I want" format will help you stay focused on the business goals, but both forms are valid, and they convey essentially the same information. Experienced practitioners will be able to produce high-quality and meaningful definitions in both formats.

Ultimately, there's no right or wrong way to describe a feature, and no standard canonical format that you must use, though it's nice to agree on a consistent format within a team or project.

EXERCISE 5.1 Look at the Impact Map in figure 5.6. You want to give call center staff the capability to sell tickets more quickly over the phone. Define some features that would help support this capability.

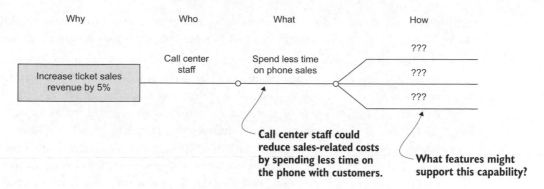

Figure 5.6 **What features would support this capability?**

5.2.2 *Features can be broken down into more manageable chunks*

When you describe a feature, you need to think in terms of functionality that delivers some useful capability to the end user. When you build and deliver a feature, you often need to break the feature down into smaller, more manageable pieces. You may or may not be able to deliver the whole feature in one iteration.

You can break features down further as you explore the best way to deliver a particular capability, using what's effectively a form of functional decomposition. In an Agile project, when you've broken the features down into chunks small enough to build within a single iteration, you can call the chunks User Stories. As you can see in figure 5.7, it's common to need more than one level of decomposition to get from a real-world feature to a reasonably sized User Story.

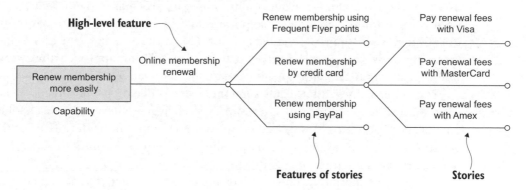

Figure 5.7 **Breaking down features into smaller features or User Stories makes them easier to organize and deliver.**

Knowing when the decomposed chunks are no longer features is a little subjective and varies from project to project. As we discussed earlier, a feature is something users can test and use in isolation. A feature can deliver business value in itself; once a feature is completed, you could theoretically deploy it into production immediately, without having to wait for any other features to be finished first. Let's look at some examples:

- "Online membership renewal" would certainly qualify as a feature. If you were to deploy this feature into production by itself, it would still be of significant business value. But could you provide business value faster by incrementally delivering smaller parts of this feature rather than waiting for it to be completely finished? This is generally a question for the business stakeholders.
- "Renew membership by credit card" would not be a feature in itself unless it included the entire renewal process. Even if it did, you'd still have to ask the project sponsor if they would be happy to deploy this feature into production without the other payment methods.
- "Pay renewal fees with Visa" and other similar features are often considered too low level to be delivered in isolation, especially if they represent only a small amount of work. Paying by Visa, for example, is just one aspect of "Renew membership by credit card," and would be of little business value in isolation, so you'd represent these in the form of User Stories rather than features.
- On the other hand, if you were working in a FinTech start-up, and accepting payments for each different type of card represented a large amount of work, you might see them as features in their own right. In that case, you might roll out "Accept payments via PayPal" in a first release and "Accept payments via Visa" in a subsequent release.

There are two main strategies when it comes to decomposing features. The one used here involves decomposing a feature into a number of smaller business processes or tasks ("Renew by credit card," "Pay with MasterCard," etc.). You express tasks in terms of business goals and try to avoid committing to a particular implementation solution until you know more about what solution would be most appropriate. When you use this strategy, visual approaches such as Impact Mapping also make it easier to keep the larger business goals in perspective. This is generally the approach that works best when practicing BDD (and Agile in general, for that matter).

The other strategy that teams sometimes use is deciding what needs to be built early on and coming up with User Stories to deliver whatever technical solution is envisaged. This approach is risky and involves much more upfront work, with the dangers that entails. For example, figure 5.8 shows a different decomposition of the membership renewal online feature into a number of User Stories.

In this decomposition, you've already imagined or designed a particular sequence of screens to implement this feature and have created User Stories based on these screens. The problem is that you can lose focus on the real business goals when you commit early to a given solution, and you can miss the opportunity to provide a more appropriate solution. In figure 5.7, for example, the ability to renew memberships using Frequent Flyer points has been forgotten in all the excitement around implementing a PayPal-based solution.

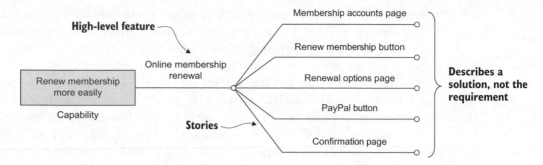

Figure 5.8   It's dangerous to decompose features with a particular solution in mind.

5.2.3   *A feature can be described by one or more User Stories*

User stories are the bread and butter of Agile projects, and they've been around, in slightly differing forms, since the origins of Agile. A User Story is a short description of something a user or stakeholder would like to achieve, expressed in language that the business can understand. For example, the following User Story describes a requirement around forcing users to enter at least a moderately complex password when they register to be a Frequent Flyer member. For this story, you can use a format very similar to the ones used for features earlier on:

```
Story: Providing a secure password when registering
In order to avoid hackers compromising member accounts
As the systems administrator
I want new members to provide a secure password when they register
```

This is the same format that you used for features.

User stories are traditionally represented on story cards like the one in figure 5.9, which also includes other details, such as a priority and a rough estimate of size in some agreed metric (estimates are often in hours, or they may use the more abstract notion of "story points"). You can also use similar cards to represent features.

#120 Providing a secure password when registering
In order to avoid hackers compromising member
accounts
As the systems administrator
I want new members to provide a secure password
when they register
Priority: HIGH
ESTIMATE: 4

Figure 5.9   A typical User Story card format

On the flip side of the card, you can put an initial list of acceptance criteria in simple bullet points (see figure 5.10). These acceptance criteria clarify the scope and boundaries of the story or feature. They help remove ambiguities, clarify assumptions, and build up the team's common understanding of the story or feature. They also act as a starting point for the tests. But the aim of these acceptance criteria isn't to be definitive or exhaustive. It's unreasonable to expect the product owner or stakeholders to think of a definitive list of the acceptance criteria when the stories are being discovered. You just want enough information to be able to move forward. You'll have plenty of time to refine, expand, and complete them, and to add any additional requirements documentation that the team might need, when it comes to implementing the story, and even later on when you learn more about the requirements.

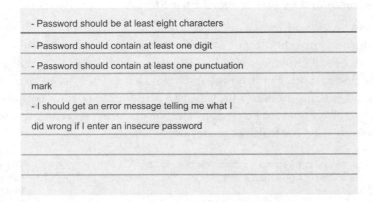

Figure 5.10   You can put an initial list of acceptance criteria on the back of the story card.

As you can see in figure 5.9, these User Stories look a lot like features, but they tend to be a little lower level. A User Story doesn't have to be deliverable in isolation but can focus on one particular aspect of a feature. User stories can help you plan and organize how you'll build a feature. Although you may not deliver a User Story into production by itself, you can and should show implemented stories to end users and other stakeholders to make sure that you're on the right track and to learn more about the best way to implement the subsequent stories.

You can use User Stories to break down the features we discussed in the previous section. For example, figure 5.11 builds on figure 5.4, continuing the investigation of what features might help you reduce lost revenue from lapsed Frequent Flyer memberships.

One of the features you discovered for this requirement was "Email notification of lapsing membership." This is a fairly large piece of work, so you could break it down into stories like the following:

- Send notification emails to members whose membership will finish within a month.
- Configure notification message texts.
- Open a renewal page from the notification email.

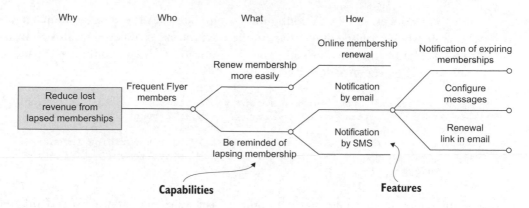

Figure 5.11   You can break large features down into smaller, more manageable ones.

Although each of these stories adds business value in its own way, they aren't designed to be deployed into production independently. But they do provide great opportunities for getting useful feedback from stakeholders.

For example, suppose you're working on the following story:

```
Story: Send notification emails to members whose membership will finish
➥ within a month
In order to increase retention rates for our Frequent Flyer program
As a sales manager
I want members to be notified a month before their memberships finish
```

When you show the implementation of this story to the Flying High sales manager, the conversation goes something like this:

> You: And this is how the email notification works. When their membership is about to expire, they receive an email that looks like this.
>
> John the sales manager: Looks good. And what about the follow-up email?
>
> You: Is there a follow-up email?
>
> John: Of course. Bill from marketing wants a follow-up email that will include a discount offer of some kind to encourage ex-members to come back.
>
> You: And is the discount always the same?
>
> John: No, Bill needs to be able to change it depending on his latest marketing strategy. We talked about configuring the messages last time.

The value of this sort of feedback is huge. You've just discovered a new story for a requirement that had been overlooked or initially misunderstood: "Send follow-up notification emails to ex-members whose membership has just lapsed."

In addition, you now have a clearer understanding of what's expected regarding the "Configure notification message texts" story, which we'll look at next. Originally this was conceived of as a configurable template that the development team could change when required and deliver in the next release. But based on this conversation, you now know that the marketing people want to be able to configure the message at any time. You can now describe this next story as follows:

```
Story: Include a configurable incentive in the follow-up notifications
In order to increase retention rates for our Frequent Flyer program
As a sales manager
I want to be able to include a configurable text describing incentives to
➥ rejoin such as discount offers or bonus points in the notification
➥ message
```

This example illustrates another point. User stories allow you to put off defining detailed requirements until as late as possible. As time goes on, you'll learn more and more about the system you're delivering. This is what the ongoing conversations promoted by BDD are designed to facilitate. If you specify the details of a User Story too early, you may miss some important fact that you'll learn later on. If you specified the details of the "Configure notification message texts" story first, you'd implement a piece of functionality with little business value, and it wouldn't correspond to the stakeholders' expectations at all.

But you can't procrastinate forever. If you address it too late, you won't have time to talk to stakeholders and understand the detailed requirements before the feature is due. This is what we call the *last responsible moment*. This concept is also heavily used in an approach called Real Options, which we'll look at in more detail later in this chapter.

> **EXERCISE 5.2**   Develop the features you defined in the previous exercise and break them down into stories of different sizes until you get to stories that you think are of a manageable size. Describe some of them in more detail using the "in order to . . . as a . . . I want" format.

5.2.4   *A feature is not a User Story*

In many projects, the features we've been discussing would be represented as high-level User Stories, and some teams don't find it necessary to break the features down into smaller stories. This is fine and will work well on smaller projects.

But there are some advantages to keeping a distinction between the two. Remember,

- A feature is a piece of functionality that you deliver to end users or to other stakeholders to support a capability that they need in order to achieve their business goals.
- A User Story is a planning tool that helps you flesh out the details of what you need to deliver for a particular feature.

You can define features quite a bit ahead of time, but you want to start creating stories for a feature in the Illustrate phase, which generally happens shortly before a new sprint starts or before work starts on implementing a feature.

It's important to remember that User Stories are essentially planning artifacts. They're a great way to organize the work you need to do to deliver a feature, but the end user doesn't really care how you organize things to get the feature out the door, as long as it gets delivered. Future developers are more interested in what the application currently does than how you went about building it.

Once the feature has been implemented, the User Stories can be discarded. The description of the features is generally more effective at describing what the application does. The examples and rules you use to illustrate the features do a great job of illustrating how the software actually works, as do the automated acceptance criteria that you'll write later on in this book.

5.2.5 *Release features and product features*

As we have seen, a capability is something that allows users to achieve some business goal or that helps them to achieve a goal more easily. And from a BDD perspective, a feature is a piece of functionality that supports a capability. We might call this a product feature. If you were building software back when software came in boxes, such a feature would be important enough to appear on the side of the product box.

But in many scaled Agile methodologies such as XSCALE (https://xscalealliance .org), LeSS (https://less.works), and SAFe (https://www.scaledagileframework.com), the word "feature" is used slightly differently. In these frameworks, features describe new or modified functionality that we want to release, not system behavior in absolute terms. Let's call these (for the sake of clarity) Release Features. A *release feature* is a piece of functionality that enables or supports some business goal and that can be used for release planning. In fact, it is the smallest slice of functionality that you can deliver in isolation and still show some tangible business benefit. Release features are not necessarily small enough to be built and delivered in a single iteration, so they are often sliced into User Stories to make them easier to manage. A good way to think of a release feature is that it might appear in a bullet-point list in your release notes.

The difference of usage is subtle but important to be aware of, as it has implications for the way we organize and maintain our BDD-executable specifications and living documentation. A product feature may improve over the life of the product, as new release features are delivered. In fact, a release feature can describe an improvement to an existing product feature or an entirely new one.

Let's look at a real-world example of this distinction. Suppose that you are working for a FinTech startup, trying to develop a new online banking application for business customers. One thing customers want to be able to do is to set up direct debits. You might express the underlying business goal like this: "We believe that if clients can pay their bills via direct debit with our app, they will be more likely to open an account with us rather than with our competitors who do not have this capability."

Direct debits is a capability you want to add to your product. You could implement the ability to arrange direct debits in a number of ways; in an extreme case, the mobile app could send a message to a call center where someone could set up the direct debit manually. But this wouldn't be very efficient nor very scalable.

It turns out that implementing direct debits depends on the currency used for the account. For example, the implementation of direct debits for Euro accounts is quite different to direct debits for USD or British Pounds, and both are nontrivial pieces of work—neither could be delivered in a single iteration. "Direct debit for Euro accounts" and "direct debit for USD accounts" would be different deliverable features. When the team is ready to work on a deliverable feature, they define detailed acceptance criteria and break it down into User Stories.

Because it is useful in its own right, and because they can learn from the customer feedback, you decide to include the "direct debit for Euro" deliverable feature in the next release. A number of deliverable features make up a release. These might come from the same Epic, or there might be features from several Epics in a release.

But from the point of view of the product as a whole, direct debits is a coherent, well-contained piece of functionality. It is a single product feature. If you were writing a user manual, or a specifications document, you would have a chapter or section for direct debits. At most you might have a section to describe different fields you need for different currency accounts. From a BDD perspective, it would make sense to have all your direct debit examples in the same place. And if you are using Cucumber, you would have all the direct debit scenarios in a single feature file.

5.2.6   *Not everything fits into a hierarchy*

In real-world projects, not all requirements fit into the sort of neat hierarchical structures we've been talking about. Although this will work for many User Stories, you'll sometimes come across a story that supports several features. For example, the "providing a secure password when registering" story we discussed might relate to two features:

- Join the Frequent Flyer program online
- Keep client data safe

In that situation, you might say that the "join the Frequent Flyer program online" feature is a logical parent for this User Story, but it's clearly also related to the cross-functional feature, "keep client data safe." This often happens when multiple stakeholders are involved. In this case, the business stakeholder wants travelers to be able to join the Frequent Flyer program, and the security stakeholder wants the feature to be delivered safely. There may be other stakeholders as well, such as compliance, legal, operations, and so forth.

Tags are a good way to handle this sort of situation. Many requirements-management and reporting tools let you use tags to organize your requirements, in addition to enabling a more conventional parent–child relationship. This way, you can present a relatively structured view of the main requirements hierarchy, but also keep track of any looser relationships. We'll look at using tags as part of the living documentation in part 3 of this book.

5.3   *Real Options: Don't make commitments before you have to*

Software development is a journey of discovery. There are always things we don't know at the start of a project, that we discover along the way. And in software development, it's essential to know what you don't know, and to proactively manage for your ignorance in your decisions. Two important BDD concepts can help us do just that: Real Options and Deliberate Discovery.

In the mid-2000s, Chris Matts identified a fundamental principle underlying many Agile practices: putting off decisions until the "last responsible moment," an idea that comes from lean software development. He called this principle *Real Options*. Understanding this principle changes the way you think about many Agile practices and opens the door to a few new ones.

In finance, an *option* gives you the possibility, but not the obligation, to purchase a product sometime in the future at today's price. For example, imagine that there's a high probability that you'll need to purchase a large quantity of steel in the next three months, and that the price of steel is currently on the rise. You don't want to buy the steel now, because you aren't completely sure that you'll need it; you expect to know for sure sometime in the next two months. But if you wait another few months, the price of steel might have gone up, which means that you'll lose money. To get out of this conundrum, you can buy an option to purchase the steel sometime within the next three months, at today's price. If the price of steel goes up, you can still buy at today's price. And if the price goes down, or if you don't need the steel, you can choose not to use the option. You need to pay for this option, but it only costs a fraction of the total price of the steel. It's worthwhile because it allows you to not commit yourself to buying the steel until you're sure you need it.

This principle also applies in day-to-day life. When you buy a plane ticket, you're actually buying an option to travel: the ticket places you under no obligation to travel. But the price you pay for this option varies. Imagine your favorite airline is offering tickets for $600 to go from Sydney to Wellington, but these cheaper tickets are nonrefundable if you decide not to travel. You're not sure that you'll be able to make the trip, so you opt for a more expensive $800 ticket, which has a $25 cancellation fee.

Let's look at the math here. The option to cancel the flight costs you an extra $200. If you're likely to travel, this might be a lot to pay for an option you're unlikely to use, so you might prefer the cheaper ticket. But if you think that there's a 50% chance you won't be able to fly, you may be happy to pay the extra $200. If you cancel, you'll only lose $225 (the extra $200, plus the $25 cancellation fee), whereas if you cancel after opting for the cheaper flight, you'll lose $600.

Real Options is an application of these principles to software development invented by Chris Matts (see figure 5.12).[1] Chris summarizes the principles of Real Options in three simple points:

- Options have value.
- Options expire.
- Never commit early unless you know why.

Figure 5.12   **Real Options lets you reduce risk by leaving your options open.**

Let's look at each of these principles in a little more detail.

5.3.1   *Options have value*

Options have value because they allow you to put off committing to a particular solution before you have enough knowledge to determine what solution is best. In the finance industry, the value of an option can be calculated precisely. This isn't the case in software development, but, in general, the less you know about the optimal

---

[1] Chris Matts and Olav Maassen, "'Real Options' Underlie Agile Practices," InfoQ (2007), http://www.infoq .com/articles/real-options-enhance-agility.

solution for a particular problem, the more value there is in being able to keep your options open.

Options also have a price. The price in software development is the effort involved in incorporating this flexibility. This price might involve discussing the possible options upfront, adding layers of abstraction to allow a different implementation to be switched in more easily, making certain parts of the application configurable, and so forth.

For example, suppose that you're building a new website for a dynamic young start-up. The founders have no clear idea of the volume of users they expect; they know it will start small, but they're very ambitious and expect millions by the end of the year.

You have three options here. You could build the application with no particular regard to scalability and make it more scalable if and when the need arises, using the YAGNI (you ain't gonna need it) principle. This is fine if the application never scales. But if it does, the refactoring work will be extensive.

Alternatively, you could invest in a highly scalable architecture from the get-go. This would avoid rework, but it would be wasted effort if volume remains low.

A third possibility is to buy an option to scale up later. You wouldn't implement a fully scalable architecture immediately, but you could spend a little time upfront to see what would be needed to make the initial implementation easily scalable in the future if required. If you don't need to scale, you've only invested a little upfront design time, and if you do, you'll be able to do so at reduced costs.

5.3.2   Options expire

You can't keep an option open forever. In software development, an option expires (i.e., you can no longer use it) when you no longer have time to implement it before the related feature is due to be delivered. For example, in figure 5.13, you have the

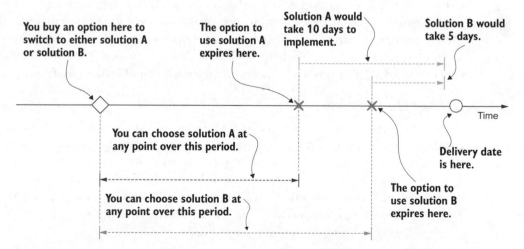

Figure 5.13   Real Options expire. Once you pass an option's expiry date, you can no longer exercise this option.

choice between two implementations (solution A and solution B). At this point, you don't know which solution is best, so you add a layer of code to make it possible to switch to either solution A or B at a later date.

If you decide on solution A, it will take 10 days to integrate. Implementing solution B, on the other hand, would only take 5 days. In practical terms, this means that if you decide to implement solution A, you must do so at least 10 days before the delivery date, which is when your option on solution A expires. If you delay any further, you won't be able to exercise this option. You have a bit more time to opt for solution B, as this option expires only 5 days before the delivery date.

Unlike financial options, you sometimes have the power to push back expiry dates. For example, if you can find a way to integrate solution A more quickly, you can leave that option open longer.

5.3.3 *Never commit early unless you know why*

The third principle of Real Options is simply to defer committing to a particular solution (exercise the option) until you know enough about why you're choosing that solution. Real Options give you the possibility to put off making a decision, but the aim is not to systematically delay until the last possible (or responsible) moment. With Real Options, you only delay until you have enough information to act. When you have enough information, you implement your chosen solution as quickly as possible. For example, you may delay your decision because solution A is being developed by another team, and you want to wait to see if this library will work well in your situation. In this case, you can wait until the option for solution A expires, but no longer. If the library takes longer than this to develop, you'll be forced to exclude solution A from your list of options.

But you may choose to act sooner if you can. For example, if your team can build either solution A or solution B, but you don't know which is the most appropriate, you might choose to build experimental versions of both solutions concurrently. If you obtain enough information to act before the options expire, it makes sense to act sooner rather than later. To help you learn enough to make sensible design and implementation decisions, you can use an approach called Deliberate Discovery.

5.4 *Deliberate Discovery*

Deliberate Discovery is the flip side of Real Options, and the two principles go hand-in-hand. Originally proposed by Dan North[2] and developed by Liz Keogh and other members of the London BDD community, Deliberate Discovery is an approach to software development that encourages us to acknowledge and embrace our own ignorance, and the fact that we will learn things as the project progresses, so that we might be better prepared to respond to changes and surprises when they occur.

---

[2] Dan North, "Introducing Deliberate Discovery," August 30, 2010, http://dannorth.net/2010/08/30/introducing -deliberate-discovery.

In software development, ignorance is the constraint. You know a lot more about the best way to build a particular solution after you've finished building it, but by then it's too late to take advantage of your knowledge. You can use the principles of Real Options to put off choosing a particular implementation, or implementing a particular feature or story, until you know enough to make a reasonable decision. But if you're aware that you don't know what the best solution is, you can proactively investigate your options in order to make a reasonable decision sooner rather than later. Uncertainty represents risk, and where possible you should hunt out and reduce uncertainty. This is where Deliberate Discovery steps in.

Deliberate Discovery starts with the assumption that there are things you don't know. This might be something bad that you couldn't possibly have anticipated and that will pop up and cause you problems at some point during the project. Or it might be an opportunity to innovate: "If only we'd known about that technology earlier, we could have built this feature in half the time."

Real Options help you keep your options open until you have enough information to act; Deliberate Discovery helps you get this information. If you actively try to increase your knowledge in a specific area, you can both reduce the risk of uncertainty and make decisions faster; remember, as soon as you know enough to commit to a particular solution, you can choose to exercise your option or not.

But Deliberate Discovery also has broader applications. For example, suppose you've decided to implement a particular feature and have broken it down into a number of stories. Some of these stories may seem straightforward, and others may not be so simple.

The natural tendency is to implement the simplest stories first, and there are good reasons why you might do this. But reducing your ignorance should be high on your priority list. Wherever possible, identify the stories that involve the most uncertainty, and tackle these ones first. Then review the remaining stories, keeping in mind what you've learned and considering the feedback the stakeholders give you. This simple approach can go a long way in helping you increase your knowledge and understanding in areas that matter.

5.5 Release and sprint planning with BDD

Real Options and Deliberate Discovery show us that planning in too much detail, too far ahead of the actual work, is wasteful. It is more effective to first plan broadly at a high level, and to drill down into planning individual Epics and features when we are sure that we will need them.

Let's recap to see how the various activities in the Speculate and Illustrate phases can help teams plan and deliver new features. Figure 5.14 gives an overview of this process.[3]

---

[3] In XSCALE, this layout is known as a 3D-Kanban, which we will address in a later chapter.

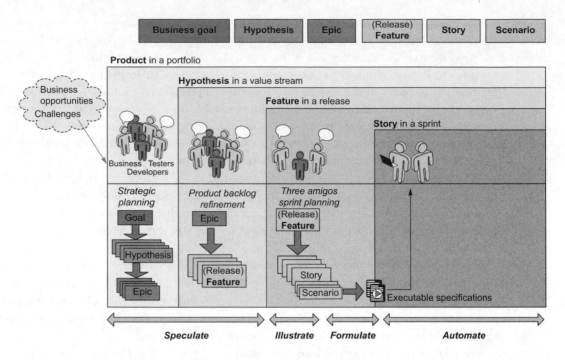

Figure 5.14   BDD and release planning

During *strategic planning activities,* you discover and describe the business goals and the capabilities that support them, and you use techniques like Impact Mapping and Pirate Canvases to identify hypotheses that we want to validate and deliverables that might prove or disprove these hypotheses. We call these deliverables Epics or Product Backlog items, and they go into the Product Backlog. During strategic planning, teams also prioritize Epics in order to plan upcoming releases.

During Product Backlog refinement, teams break down the Epics scheduled for the next release into features. Depending on the size of the project, this can happen at either a team level (for smaller projects) or across multiple teams (for larger ones). These features go into individual team backlogs.

During the Illustrate phase, which we will look at in the next chapter, a team takes a feature from their backlog, identifies and clarifies key functional and nonfunctional acceptance criteria (which we call *scenarios*), and breaks the feature down into User Stories. And during the formulate phase (which we will look at from chapter 6 and on) we will see how to turn these scenarios into executable specifications that act as the basis for the development work done during each sprint or iteration.

It's important to remember that the diagram in figure 5.14 isn't a rigid process but more a framework for discovering and validating business hypotheses. Feedback cycles exist at all levels; for example, if a hypothesis is invalidated during Product Backlog Refinement, then the teams are free to correct their goals and priorities immediately.

Summary

- Describing and organizing features, and illustrating them with examples, are important aspects of BDD.
- A capability enables some business goal, regardless of implementation.
- A feature is a piece of deliverable software functionality that provides users with a capability.
- You can break large features down into smaller features to make them easier to organize and deliver.
- Agile projects use User Stories to plan and deliver features, and features to plan and deliver releases.
- The principle of Real Options recommends that you shouldn't commit to a particular solution until you have enough information to be confident that it's the most appropriate one.
- Deliberate Discovery points out that one of the biggest risks in any software project is your own ignorance, and that you should actively aim to identify and reduce uncertainty wherever you can.

One of the principal benefits of BDD is to encourage and structure business conversations. But there's also a great deal to gain by automating these examples, in the form of automated acceptance criteria. In the next chapter, you will learn about practical techniques you can use to facilitate these conversations.

Illustrating features with examples

This chapter covers

- Requirements discovery workshops and the Three Amigos
- Using tables to represent examples
- Example Mapping
- Feature Mapping
- The OOPSI model

Before work starts on a feature or story, Agile teams come together to talk through the requirements. Some teams have these conversations during Backlog Refinement or Sprint Planning sessions, while others have dedicated requirements discovery workshops. The aim of these conversations is to understand, define, and agree on the acceptance criteria of the features (or User Stories) that the team intends to work on.

Teams that practice BDD have conversations about concrete examples and counterexamples of business rules to come up with these acceptance criteria. In terms of the BDD cycle we saw in chapter 1, these conversations are common during the Illustrate phase, the second part of the requirements discovery process that starts with the Speculate activities we saw in the previous chapters.

While this makes perfect sense in theory, many teams find that having these conversations is not as easy as it might seem. People don't always ask the right questions, they get side-tracked, and the sessions can drag on without seeming to go anywhere. As a result, many teams find it a challenge to run these sessions as often as they should or find that they aren't anywhere near as productive as they would like them to be.

In this chapter we will follow our Frequent Flyer team as they use conversations and examples to break high-level features down into smaller User Stories with well-defined acceptance criteria. We will see our team use three popular and effective techniques to facilitate these conversations: working with tables, Example Mapping, and Feature Mapping. All three of these techniques are intuitive and easy to explain to nontechnical stakeholders and are a great way to get them engaged and talking about their requirements.

A surprising number of BDD's benefits come from simply having a conversation with customers or business stakeholders, using examples to challenge assumptions and build a common understanding of the problem space. One of the principal benefits of BDD is to encourage and structure this kind of conversation. But there's also a great deal to gain by automating these examples, in the form of automated acceptance criteria. But before we look at any of these techniques, we need to talk about when and with whom these conversations take place.

6.1   The Three Amigos and other requirements discovery workshops

Conversations about requirements can take many forms. For example, some teams find value in large requirements discovery workshops early in the project, where the whole team, including business stakeholders, is involved. These workshops are a great way to get communication happening sooner rather than later to give the team a shared understanding of the features they're building and to produce a set of high-quality examples. On the downside, they can be hard to organize and are expensive in terms of people's hours.

Other teams like to discuss stories and acceptance criteria during Backlog Refinement or Sprint Planning sessions. This can be a good way to get an overview of the scope of work to be done, but sometimes there is not enough time to cover all the stories in enough detail.

One popular approach used by many teams is known as the "Three Amigos." In this approach, a small number of team members with different perspectives—often a developer, a tester, and a business analyst or product owner—get together to discuss a feature and draw the examples before any actual implementation starts. For this to work well, all three need to be reasonably familiar with the problem space, but the dynamic interaction of each role is often very productive. The tester, with great attention to detail and a focus on validation, will propose obscure edge cases and often point out scenarios that the other team members have missed. The developer will point out technical considerations, and the business analyst or product owner will be able to judge the relevance and relative value of the different scenarios. In addition, the developer will gradually obtain a much deeper understanding of the business requirements than would normally happen in a more traditional project, and this understanding becomes more and more useful as the project progresses.

Sometimes in this approach, the three will even sit around a computer and write an initial draft of the automated scenarios together. This helps reduce the risk of information loss later and can work well in mature teams with a well-established set of executable specifications or for practitioners who are very fluent in both Gherkin and the business domain. However, writing Given . . . When . . . Then scenarios directly in the requirements discovery session can be time-consuming and distract team members from the bigger picture. For this reason, many teams prefer to use more breadth-first practices such as Feature Mapping and Example Mapping during the requirements discovery sessions (in the Illustrate phase) and leave the Given . . . When . . . Then to a smaller group in the Formulate phase (see figure 6.1).

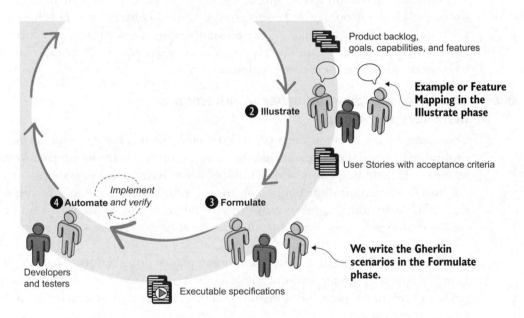

Figure 6.1   Example and Feature Mapping typically happen during the Illustrate phase.

In some teams, the business analyst prefers to do the bulk of the scenario writing, referring to stakeholders if they have any questions, before passing them to the development team to implement. Experienced practitioners generally don't recommend this approach, as it fails to build a shared understanding as effectively as the previous strategies. Executable specifications, such as Given . . . When . . . Then scenarios, should be considered an output of the conversations, not an input.

6.2 Illustrating features with examples

Examples are at the heart of BDD. In conversations with users and stakeholders, BDD practitioners use concrete examples to develop their understanding of features and User Stories of all sizes, but also to flush out and clarify areas of uncertainty (see figure 6.2). These examples, expressed in language that businesses can understand, illustrate how the software should behave in very precise and unambiguous terms.

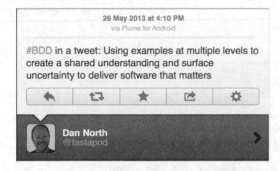

26 May 2013 at 4:10 PM
via Plume for Android

#BDD in a tweet: Using examples at multiple levels to create a shared understanding and surface uncertainty to deliver software that matters

Dan North
@tastapod

Figure 6.2   The essence of BDD, according to its inventor Dan North

According to David Kolb's experimental learning theories, effective learning is a four-stage process.[1] In Kolb's model, we all start learning from concrete experiences of some real-world situations or events (*experience*). When we observe and think about an experience (*reflection*), we analyze and generalize that example, forming a mental model that represents our current understanding of the problem space (*conceptualize*). Finally, we can test this mental model against other real-world experiences to verify or invalidate all or part of our understanding (*test*).

BDD uses a very similar approach (see figure 6.3), where examples and conversations with users, stakeholders, and domain experts drive the learning process. You discuss concrete examples of how an application should behave and reflect on these examples to build up a shared understanding of the requirements. Then you look for additional examples to confirm or extend your understanding.

Let's see how this works in practice. The story card and the initial acceptance criteria jotted down on the back (or in some dedicated field if you are using software to track your backlog) make a great place to start a conversation that will discover these examples. To see what such a conversation might look like, let's revisit the "secure password" User Story we discussed in chapter 5. Bianca (the business analyst), Terri (the tester), and David (the developer), who work on the Frequent Flyer project, are discussing the requirements. The story goes like this:

```
Story: Providing a secure password when registering for the Frequent Flyer program
In order to avoid hackers compromising member accounts
As the systems administrator
I want new members to provide a secure password when they register
```

---

[1] David A. Kolb, *Experiential Learning: Experience as a Source of Learning and Development* (Prentice Hall, 1984).

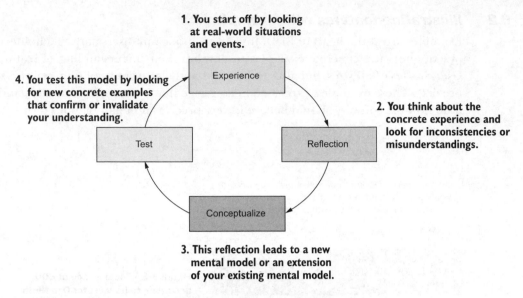

1. You start off by looking at real-world situations and events.

4. You test this model by looking for new concrete examples that confirm or invalidate your understanding.

2. You think about the concrete experience and look for inconsistencies or misunderstandings.

3. This reflection leads to a new mental model or an extension of your existing mental model.

Figure 6.3   David Kolb's experimental learning theories apply well to BDD.

Bianca has already prepared an initial set of acceptance criteria:

- The password should be at least eight characters.
- The password should contain at least one digit.
- The password should contain at least one punctuation mark.
- I should get an error message telling me what I did wrong if I enter an insecure password.

These acceptance criteria are a good start, but there are still some potential ambiguities. Can you have all lowercase characters, or do you need a mixture of uppercase and lowercase? Does the position of the number in the password matter? How detailed should the error message be? To clear things up, the team talks to Sid, the systems administrator.

The power of examples

In BDD, we use examples to try to clarify questions like these, because we rarely think of everything. You can use a few key examples as the basis for your formal acceptance criteria (we'll discuss how to express acceptance criteria in a more structured way in the next chapter). Not all of the examples that you'll discover in these conversations will make it into the scenarios—many will simply be useful to guide the conversation and expand your understanding of the problem space.

This sort of conversation is more productive if you use some simple strategies. Remember, the aim of this exercise is to build a mental model of the requirements and to illustrate this mental model with a number of key examples. Think of the problem

> space for the story as a set of jigsaw puzzle pieces. When you ask for an example, you're really asking for clarification of your understanding of the requirements. This is like picking up a piece of the jigsaw and placing it where you think it should go. If it fits, you've confirmed your understanding and expanded your mental model. If it doesn't, then you've flushed out an incorrect assumption and can move forward on a more solid basis.

Sid is an expert in system security and knows a great deal about what makes a secure password. Sid is very concerned about this problem, as in his experience most users naturally use passwords that are very easy to hack. The conversation with Sid goes along the following lines:

Bianca: I'd like to make sure I've understood what you need for the "secure password" story. The first acceptance criteria we defined is about password length. A password should be rejected if it has less than eight characters?

Sid: Yes, that's right. Passwords need to be at least eight characters to make it harder for hacking algorithms to guess them.

Bianca: So "secret" would be rejected because it has only six characters?

Sid: Correct.

Bianca: What about "password"? Would that be acceptable?

Sid: No, we also said that we need at least one digit.

Bianca: So we did. So "password1" would be OK?

Sid: No, actually that's still really easy to hack. It's a word from a dictionary: the digit at the end wouldn't slow down a hacking algorithm for very long. Random letters and punctuation marks make it a bit harder.

Bianca: OK, so would "password1!" be OK? It has a number and an exclamation mark, and it has more than eight characters.

Sid: No, like I said, using words from a dictionary like "password" is really bad. Even with numbers and punctuation, a hacking algorithm would solve that pretty much instantaneously.

Notice what has just happened here. Bianca is deliberately testing her assumption that the initial acceptance criteria represent all the constraints that make a secure password. At each step, she used a different example to verify her understanding of the various rules. Now she has found another requirement that she wasn't aware of before: dictionary words should be avoided. She decides to push this further:

Bianca: How about "SeagullHedgehog"?

Sid: That would be better.

Bianca: But there are no numbers or punctuation marks in it.

Sid: Sure, that would make it better. But it's still a random sequence of words, which would be pretty hard to crack.

Bianca: How about "SeagullHedgehogCatapult"?

Sid: Pretty much uncrackable.

To keep track of these cases, Terri the tester has been noting a simple table of examples to use for her tests. Here's what she has so far:

Password	Secure
secret	No
password	No
password1	No
SeagullHedgehog	Yes
SeagullHedgehogCatapult	Yes

Bianca decides to check another of her assumptions:

Bianca: OK, how about "aBcdEfg1"?

Sid: That one would actually be pretty easy for a machine to crack—it's just a sequence of alphabetically ordered letters and a number. Sequences are easy to crack, and just adding a single number at the end doesn't add much complexity.

Bianca: What about "qwertY12"?

Sid: That's just a sequence of keys on the keyboard. Most hacking algorithms know about that trick, so it would be very easy to guess.

Bianca: Oh. OK, how about "dJeZDip1"?

Sid: That would be a bit short, but OK.

Now the team has a new requirement: alphabetical sequences of letters and spatial sequences of keys on the keyboard are both a no-no. But David has noticed something interesting:

David: Sid, rather than just saying if a password I give you is secure or not, you seem to be grading them by how hard they are to hack—is that intentional?

Sid: Well, I wasn't thinking of it like that, but yes, of course: the whole point of a secure password is so that it doesn't get hacked, and the passwords most people use are pretty easy to hack.[2] There are a lot of studies and a lot of algorithms out there that measure password strength.[3] And many sites provide feedback on

---

[2] See, for example, Dan Goodin, "Anatomy of a hack: Even your 'complicated' password is easy to crack." *Wired*, May 20, 2013, http://www.wired.co.uk/news/archive/2013-05/28/password-cracking.

[3] For anyone interested in this field, there's an interesting article on password strength by Dan Wheeler, "zxcvbn: Realistic password strength estimation," https://tech.dropbox.com/2012/04/zxcvbn-realistic-password-strength-estimation.

the strength of the passwords you enter. In those terms, we need passwords to be of at least medium strength.

Sid brings up a screen similar to the one in figure 6.4.

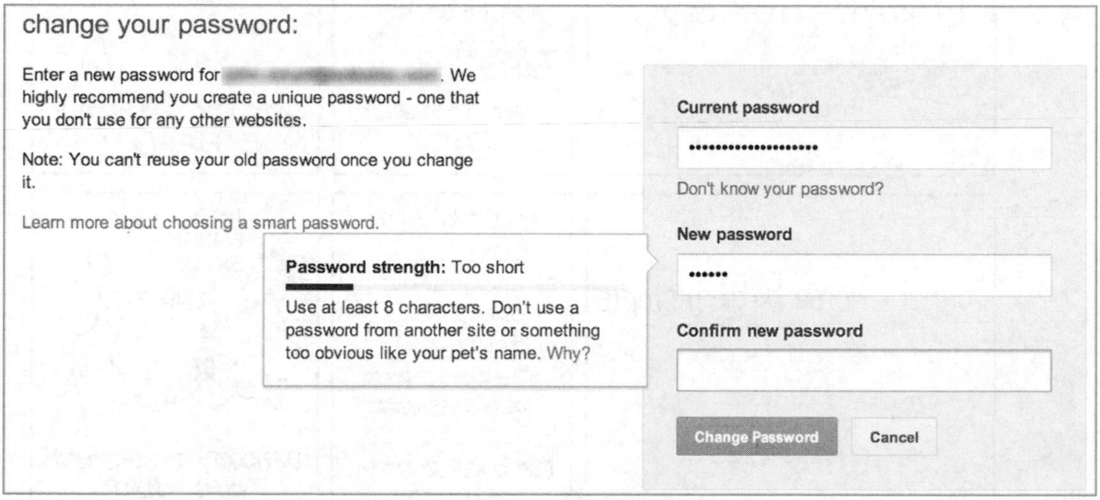

change your password:

Enter a new password for ▓▓▓▓▓▓▓▓▓▓▓▓▓▓▓. We highly recommend you create a unique password - one that you don't use for any other websites.

Note: You can't reuse your old password once you change it.

Learn more about choosing a smart password.

Password strength: Too short

Use at least 8 characters. Don't use a password from another site or something too obvious like your pet's name. Why?

Current password

••••••••••••••••••••

Don't know your password?

New password

••••••

Confirm new password

Change Password   Cancel

Figure 6.4   A password security meter helps users provide more secure passwords by measuring how easy a password would be to crack.

Bianca: Sid, I think we've been focusing on the detailed rules for password validation too much. Working through these examples seems to indicate that the rules are less clear-cut than we initially thought. And the rules we're describing focus on one particular solution to the problem we're trying to solve: the real value in this story comes from ensuring that users have a strong password, not enforcing a particular set of rules. If we reason in terms of password strength rather than specific rules, maybe we could rephrase the acceptance criteria like this:

- The password should be at least of medium strength to be accepted.
- I should be informed of the strength of my proposed password.
- If the password is too weak, I should be informed why.

Sid: Yes, that sounds fine. But how do we know what qualifies as a medium-strength password (see figure 6.5.)?

David: It looks to me like we have a few options here. We can either write our own password-strength algorithm or use an existing one. There are pros and cons to each approach, but using an existing library would probably be faster to implement.

Bianca: Let's keep our options open; we don't know enough about what will suit us best to commit to a particular solution just yet, so let's do what we can to learn

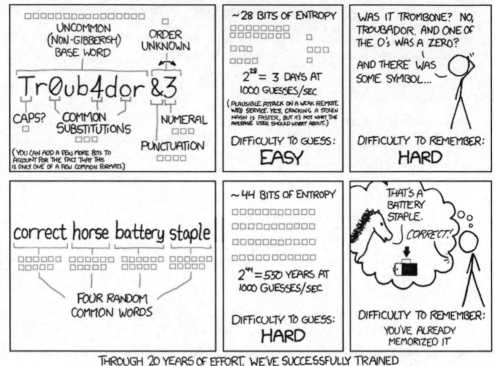

Figure 6.5   Password strength is not as simple as it seems (courtesy of xkcd.com).

more. We'll see if we can find a good existing library and experiment with it, but we should integrate it in a way that we can easily switch to another library or our own custom solution later on if we aren't happy with the one we find.

David: Sid, I should be able to build a version of this using a couple of possible libraries by Thursday that you can play around with. Based on your feedback, we can fine-tune the solution we pick or try out another one.

Terri: We can use this table of sample passwords as a starting point for the acceptance criteria. We may refine it or add new examples later as we learn more about what we can do.

Password	Strength	Acceptable
secret	Weak	No
password	Weak	No
password1	Weak	No

Password	Strength	Acceptable
aBcdEfg1	Weak	No
qwertY12	Weak	No
dJeZDip1	Medium	Yes
SeagullHedgehog	Strong	Yes
SeagullHedgehogCatapult	Very strong	Yes

The team has now gone from having what appeared to be a clear and simple set of requirements to discovering that the real requirements are not quite so obvious. What initially appeared to be business rules requested by the user turned out to be just one possible solution to the underlying business problem of ensuring that members have secure passwords. The team identified several possible approaches but deferred choosing a specific option until they knew more about what solution they would use. And they identified a strategy that the team could use to get useful feedback from the business; this will help them select the most appropriate solution.

6.3   *Using tables to describe more complex requirements*

Tables like the ones we saw in the previous section can be a good way to discuss more complex requirements. Business rules that involve processing or transforming data are common in many industries, and this kind of data is often easy to represent and discuss in tabular form.

For example, suppose Flying High Airlines has launched a special offer: when new Frequent Flyer members join the program, flights that they have completed over the past 90 days count towards their Frequent Flyer points:

```
Story: Loading previous Frequent Flyer flights
As a new Frequent Flyer
I want my previous flights to be associated with my account
So that I can get more Frequent Flyer benefits sooner
```

Flying High Airlines can find all the flight records for past flights for each person, so when a member signs up, this new feature needs to identify the eligible flights and credit their Frequent Flyer points accordingly.

To understand the finer points of this requirement, Bianca, Terri, and David go to talk with Fred, the Frequent Flyer program manager.

Bianca: So our application needs to identify all the recent flights for a given person and credit them to their new Frequent Flyer account. How far back should we go?

Fred: We need to include any flights in the 90 days preceding the sign-up date.

To keep track of the discussion, Bianca sketches a simple table that shows a recent flight that is eligible to be included in the special offer and a counterexample of a flight that is too old:

Flight Date	Eligible
60 days ago	Yes
100 days ago	No

The team also agrees that the 90-day period starts at midnight. To make sure this piece of knowledge is not lost, they add it as a note underneath the table. But Terri isn't sure they have covered all the angles just yet.

Terri: Are *all* flights in the past 90 days eligible? Are there never any exceptions?

Fred: Sure, there are plenty of exceptions, but they are pretty obvious. For example, only Flying High flights are eligible, not flights on partner or codeshare flights.

David: And how do we distinguish between Flying High flights and the other ones?

Fred: Flying High flights have a flight number that starts with "FH."

This is news to the team. Oftentimes, business rules that seem obvious to users or business folk are less obvious to development team members. Bianca adjusts her table to include some examples of eligible and ineligible flight numbers:

Flight Number	Flight Date	Eligible	Reason
FH-99	60 days ago	Yes	
FH-87	100 days ago	No	Too old
OH-101	60 days ago	No	Not a Flying High flight

These examples succinctly illustrate the new rules they have learned. But Terri isn't done yet.

Terri: OK, let's focus on Flying High flights. Are there any Flying High flights that we might need to handle, that are not eligible even if they are in the correct time period?

Fred: Well, if the flight was cancelled, it wouldn't count.

Bianca: What about flights that are booked but haven't happened yet?

Fred: No, you need to have completed a flight for it to count.

With these new rules, Bianca can add two more examples to her table. But if she wants them to make sense, she also needs to add a new column to indicate the status of the flight:

Flight Number	Flight Date	Status	Eligible	Reason
FH-99	60 days ago	COMPLETED	Yes	
FH-87	100 days ago	COMPLETED	No	Too old
OH-101	60 days ago	COMPLETED	No	Not a Flying High flight
FH-99	60 days ago	CANCELLED	No	Must be completed
FH-99	In 5 days time	CONFIRMED	No	Must have taken place

Once again, these examples illustrate the new rules the team has discovered. In the next chapter, we will see how we can turn tables like this into an executable format that not only serve to illustrate a requirement but can also demonstrate that our application behaves correctly.

Tables are simple, intuitive, and easy to use. They work wonders for problems that can be described in terms of clearly defined inputs and outputs. And collaborating around a set of tabular examples can be as simple as writing on a whiteboard or opening a spreadsheet. But sometimes simply listing examples is not enough, and a tabular, data-centric approach is a little too rigid. For more complex requirements, or ones with more uncertainty, we need a little more structure to guide our conversations. In the following sections, we will look at two other techniques that can help us facilitate these conversations: Example Mapping and Feature Mapping.

6.4 Example Mapping

Example Mapping[4] is a simple, low-tech way for teams to identify key examples and counterexamples that will eventually become automated scenarios in the executable specifications. It is a fast, breadth-first approach that is quick to explain, easy to learn, and surprisingly effective at channeling conversations in the right direction.

During an Example Mapping session, teams identify the key business rules or constraints associated with a feature and list examples and counterexamples for these rules. Example Maps use colored index cards that you arrange on a large table or sticky notes that you post on a wall or whiteboard. Distributed teams can use remote whiteboarding tools such as Miro (https://miro.com) or MURAL (https://mural.co), or even Excel or PowerPoint over Skype.

The cards represent and record four key concepts that are illustrated in table 6.1.

---

[4] Example Mapping was first created by Matt Wynne (https://cucumber.io/blog/example-mapping-introduction/).

Table 6.1   The different types of cards used during Example Mapping

Card	Description	Color	Example
User Story	The feature or User Story under discussion	Yellow	Loading previous Frequent Flyer Flights
Business rule	Constraints or known acceptance criteria related to the User Story	Blue	Only Flying High flights are eligible
Example	Concrete examples and counterexamples of the business rule	Green	The one where the flight was booked with a partner airline
Question	Uncertainty or assumptions that cannot be answered or confirmed during the session	Pink	What about codeshare flights?

6.4.1   *Example Mapping starts with a User Story*

An Example Mapping session starts with the product owner (or business analyst) present-ing the User Story under discussion. Remember, the User Story is not a requirements specification, but more a description of a problem that needs solving. The User Story goes on a yellow index card at the top of the board. For example, figure 6.6 is a User Story from the Frequent Flyer application that we introduced in the previous chapters.

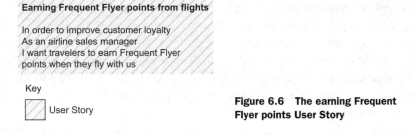

Earning Frequent Flyer points from flights

In order to improve customer loyalty
As an airline sales manager
I want travelers to earn Frequent Flyer
points when they fly with us

Key

☐ User Story

Figure 6.6   The earning Frequent Flyer points User Story

The team discusses the User Story, asks questions, and tries to identify the key business rules or constraints related to the story. The business analyst or product owner may have already noted some of these in the form of acceptance criteria before the session. For this story, the product owner has already noted the following acceptance criteria:

- Flights within Europe earn 100 points.
- Flights outside Europe earn 1 point per 10 km flown.
- Business flights earn an extra 50%.

The team starts by writing these acceptance criteria as business rules on blue cards underneath the User Story (see figure 6.7).

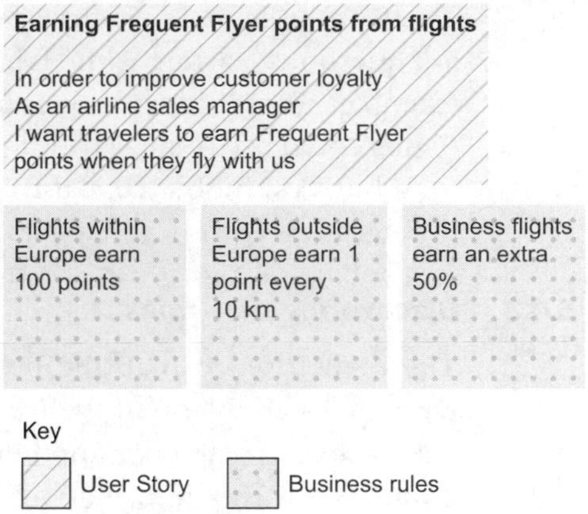

6.4.2 *Finding rules and examples*

Next, the team discuss the rules and asks for an example of each. Examples are often described using a short phrase that starts with the words "The one where . . ." This notation, originally described by Daniel Terhorst-North, is known as the "*Friends* episode notation," from the 90s TV series of the same name. According to Terthorst-North, the very first example used was "the one where Joey gets his head stuck in a turkey." For instance, we could illustrate the first two rules with examples such as "the one where Tara flies economy from Paris to Berlin" and "the one where Tara flies economy from London to New York."

You can add as much detail as you need to the example cards, but it is generally better to keep them lightweight and succinct. For example, if the outcome isn't obvious, you can note it on the card using an arrow (see figure 6.8). You can also use bullet points to indicate examples where several inputs or steps are involved.

Earning Frequent Flyer points from flights

In order to improve customer loyalty
As an airline sales manager
I want travelers to earn Frequent Flyer points when they fly with us

Flights within Europe earn 100 points

Flights outside Europe earn 1 point every 10 km

Business flights earn an extra 50%

Key

User Story   Business rules

Figure 6.7 Rules are represented by blue cards.

Earning Frequent Flyer points from flights

In order to improve customer loyalty
As an airline sales manager
I want travelers to earn Frequent Flyer points when they fly with us

Flights within Europe earn 100 points

Flights outside Europe earn 1 point every 10 km

Business flights earn an extra 50%

The one where Tara flies economy from Paris to Berlin

The one where Tara flies economy from London to New York

Betty flies business from Paris to Berlin => 150 pts

Key

User Story   Business rules   Examples

Figure 6.8 Examples are represented by green cards.

The team uses these examples to ask questions and look for counterexamples. They ask questions starting with "What if . . . ?" "Is this always the case?" or "Are there any examples where this rule does not apply?" For example, the third rule about business flights could use some clarification: is it always the case that a traveler earns 150 points for a business flight? To clarify this point, we could add another example where Betty flies business class from Paris to Hong Kong.

6.4.3   *Discovering new rules*

These questions can also lead to new rules being discovered. For example, do these point rules apply for all flights? Or for all customers? These questions lead the product owner to remember another rule: Silver Frequent Flyer members earn 25% more points. With this information, the team can add a new rule and a corresponding example (figure 6.9).

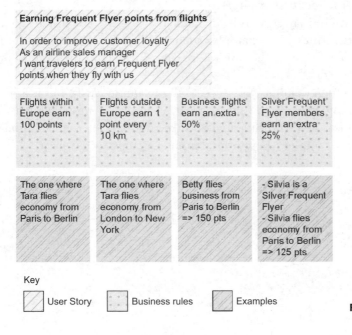

Earning Frequent Flyer points from flights

In order to improve customer loyalty
As an airline sales manager
I want travelers to earn Frequent Flyer
points when they fly with us

| Flights within Europe earn 100 points | Flights outside Europe earn 1 point every 10 km | Business flights earn an extra 50% | Silver Frequent Flyer members earn an extra 25% |
| The one where Tara flies economy from Paris to Berlin | The one where Tara flies economy from London to New York | Betty flies business from Paris to Berlin => 150 pts | - Silvia is a Silver Frequent Flyer
- Silvia flies economy from Paris to Berlin => 125 pts |

Key

☐ User Story   ☐ Business rules   ☐ Examples

Figure 6.9   Discovering new rules

Sometimes these new rules might be out of scope of the original story. This can help clarify the scope of the story and slice the story into manageable chunks. For example, the team might decide to leave Frequent Flyer status for a separate story and focus only on regular customers to start with.

6.4.4   *Surfacing uncertainty*

Questions that can't be answered immediately are noted as pink cards. For example, in this case, one question might be about the scope of "flights within Europe"—does this include only countries within the European Union (EU) or also cover countries such as Norway, which are within the European Economic Area (EEA), or is there some other definition? Question cards can be added anywhere on the map; sometimes it makes sense to add them near the example or rule that triggered them, whereas other times they are simply grouped to one side of the map (figure 6.10).

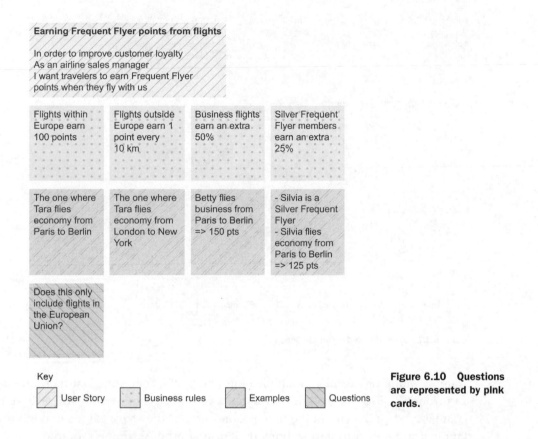

Earning Frequent Flyer points from flights

In order to improve customer loyalty
As an airline sales manager
I want travelers to earn Frequent Flyer
points when they fly with us

Flights within Europe earn 100 points

Flights outside Europe earn 1 point every 10 km

Business flights earn an extra 50%

Silver Frequent Flyer members earn an extra 25%

The one where Tara flies economy from Paris to Berlin

The one where Tara flies economy from London to New York

Betty flies business from Paris to Berlin => 150 pts

- Silvia is a Silver Frequent Flyer
- Silvia flies economy from Paris to Berlin => 125 pts

Does this only include flights in the European Union?

Key

User Story   Business rules   Examples   Questions

Figure 6.10   Questions are represented by pink cards.

Other questions might need the product owner to consult with other stakeholders, or the team might need to do some research or experimentation. For example, Frequent Flyer members can purchase flights with the points they earn; should they also earn points on flights that they purchase with their points? In this case, the product owner will need to check with the marketing team.

Question cards help keep the conversation flowing. If you come across something you don't know, don't get bogged down discussing it; simply note down the question and move on! The full Example Map looks like the one shown in figure 6.11.

6.4.5   *Facilitating an Example Mapping session*

It is often useful to have someone to facilitate Example Mapping sessions, especially when you are new to the technique. It can be easy to get caught up in the conversation and forget to record the rules and examples.

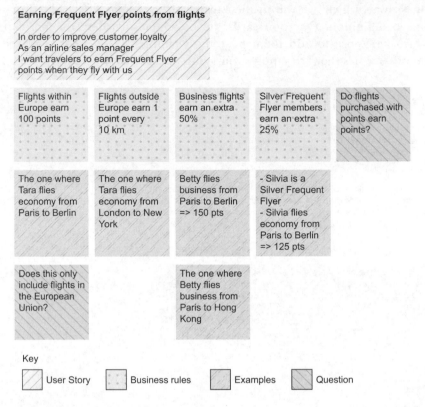

Figure 6.11   A completed Example Map

Example Mapping sessions should be quite short; 25–30 minutes is usually enough to get through a story. One useful technique is to timebox the session and to have team members vote at the end of the timebox on whether they have gained enough understanding of the story to start working on it or if another session is required.

Example Mapping is an excellent technique for discovering and discussing key business rules, examples, and counterexamples at a relatively superficial level. It is very much a breadth-first approach, and it can help teams cover a lot of ground in a small amount of time, without getting into the finer details of each example. Teams go on to look at the details of each example in the Formulate phase, when they turn key examples into Given . . . When . . . Then scenarios.

But when it comes to requirements discovery, Example Mapping is not the only tool at our disposal. For more complex requirements, such as ones that involve workflows, user journeys, or data transformation, many teams find another technique more useful. This technique is known as Feature Mapping, and it is what we will learn about in the next section.

6.5   *Feature Mapping*

Like Example Mapping, Feature Mapping is a simple, low-tech way for teams to discover, explore, and deeply understand the features their customers need. In a Feature Mapping session, teams work through concrete examples of how a feature should work, breaking these examples down into steps and tangible business outcomes. For many domains, mapping out these examples in more detail helps team members discover edge cases, flush out assumptions, and spot uncertainty.

As with Example Mapping, teams practicing Feature Mapping use colored index cards or sticky notes, or online collaboration tools like Miro or MURAL, to represent key concepts. These key concepts are outlined in table 6.2.

Table 6.2   The various types of cards used in Feature Mapping

Card	Description	Color	Example
User story	The feature or User Story under discussion. Feature Mapping works well for both high-level requirements (at the feature or epic level) and for more detailed ones.	Yellow	Canceling an existing booking
Business rule	Constraints or known acceptance criteria related to the User Story.	Blue	Bookings made with points can only be refunded in points
Example	Concrete examples and counterexamples of the business rule.	Green	The one where Fiona cancels a booking made with Frequent Flyer points
Step	Each example is broken up into steps, which go on yellow cards. Steps can represent tasks or actions a user performs, but also preconditions or input values.	Yellow	Tara books a flight from London to New York for 500 points · Tara chooses to cancel her flight
Consequence	The last step or steps of an example represent the expected outcome or result. We often mark consequence cards with an arrow at the top.	Mauve	=>Tara's account is credited with 500 Frequent Flyer points
Question	Uncertainty or assumptions that cannot be answered or confirmed during the session.	Pink	What if Tara books with points and cash?

Don't worry if this seems a lot to take in at first. Not all cards are used in every Feature Map, and the context makes the purpose of the cards quite clear. The colors are just conventions to make the map easier to understand at a glance. In practice, it is common for teams to make do with whatever colors they have on hand. Now that we have seen what each card means, let's see how they work in practice.

6.5.1   *Feature Mapping begins with an example*

Feature Mapping can start with either a feature or a User Story. In this case we start with a fairly large feature; we want travelers to be able to modify their bookings quickly and easily through the online booking system without having to talk with anyone in a call center (figure 6.12).

Figure 6.12   **Modifying an existing booking User Story**

A good way to start any requirements discovery workshop is with a story. The product owner walks the team through a concrete, end-to-end example of how a user would use this feature. In this case, the story might go something like this:

> Tara (a traveler) has booked a flight from London to New York that leaves on Monday. But something has come up, and now she has to push her trip back by a couple of days. She views her booking online and decides to modify it to fly on the following Wednesday. The ticket is in the same price category so there is no extra charge.

Stories like this make it easier for participants to relate to the user and think about what they are really trying to achieve. They are deliberately not exhaustive because they aim to provoke questions. What happens if the ticket is not in the same price category? What happens if all the flights are full? These questions play an important role in the workshop, helping participants to probe the requirement and flush out ambiguities or assumptions.

These stories can be either told on the spot or prepared ahead of time by the product owner or the business analyst. Many teams find that it is easier to prepare them in advance to save time for the team and to help ensure that the story is detailed and precise.

6.5.2   *Examples are broken into steps*

In Feature Mapping, we can start by listing the business rules we know about and then working through examples for each of these, just as we do in Example Mapping. Alternatively, we can start with a concrete example and use the steps and outcomes to explore the known business rules and constraints and discover new ones. This second approach often works well with requirements that involve user journeys, as it helps people focus on the bigger picture and not get bogged down in the details of specific rules.

Steps are a key part of Feature Mapping. Steps cards can represent preconditions or input data, steps in the user journey, actions a user takes, or different points in a workflow. While examples make great conversation starters, breaking examples down into steps can take the conversation even further. Steps help us spot important variations and edge cases and identify different user journeys or flows of information through the system.

Let's start with the example where Tara changes flights to another date. We could break this example into four steps, which we record on yellow cards next to the green example card (figure 6.13).

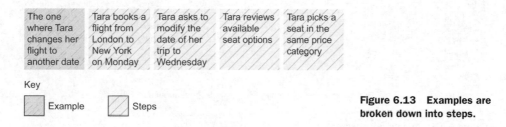

Figure 6.13   Examples are broken down into steps.

But the example doesn't finish there. In a Feature Map, an example always has a goal or outcome that we want to achieve. Or, as we call them in Feature Mapping terms, every example leads to at least one *consequence*. The consequence for this example would be that Tara's booking is updated to the new date at no additional cost. The mapped example would now look like figure 6.14.

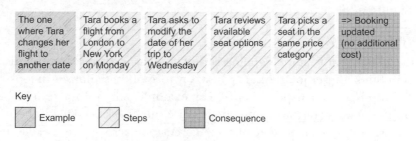

Figure 6.14   Every example leads to a consequence.

6.5.3   *Look for variations and new rules*

Using this example as a starting point, the team now looks for alternative flows and outcomes. They query each step, asking questions such as "What else could happen here? Why is this detail significant? What other outcomes might we expect?"

Some questions will lead to new business rules and examples. For example, in this case the new seat is in the same price category as the original one, so there is no additional cost, but what if the new seat is more expensive? Or what if it is cheaper? This could lead to another example: "The one where the new flight is more expensive." We could explain the context of this new example with a rule card: "Traveler pays the price difference for more expensive flights." The Feature Map would now look something like figure 6.15.

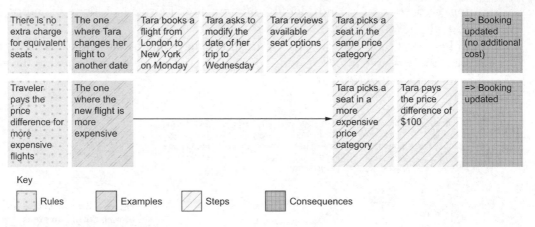

Figure 6.15   Adding new examples

The arrow in the second row is used to indicate that the steps in this part of the example are the same as those in the previous row.

Other variations might lead to additional or different consequences. For example, if Tara opts for a seat on a cheaper flight, she needs to receive a refund for the difference. We can highlight this need by including an additional consequence card, as shown in figure 6.16.

6.5.4   *Look for alternate flows*

One of the things that Feature Mapping is very good at is discovering and discussing variations in flows or user journeys. The best way to spot these flows is to look at each step as "What else could happen here?" For example, when Tara reviews her seat options on the new day of travel, one question we might ask is "What if there are no available seats?" In this case, to keep our regular customers happy, we need to propose either a refund or, for Frequent Flyer members, a credit of an equivalent number of Frequent Flyer points. This leads to a new row in our feature map that describes the case of Tara, who is not a Frequent Flyer member (figure 6.17).

For the second variation we can introduce a new persona, Fiona, who is a Frequent Flyer member. When she tries to change her flight to a day with no available flights, she is proposed either a refund or a Frequent Flyer points credit (figure 6.18).

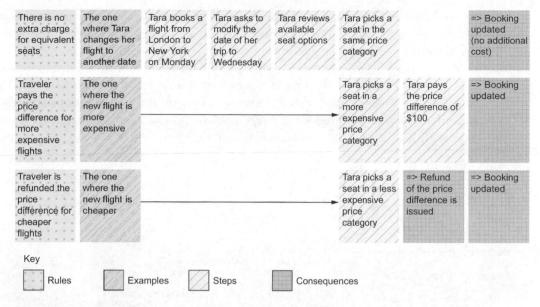

Figure 6.16   Scenarios can have more than one consequence.

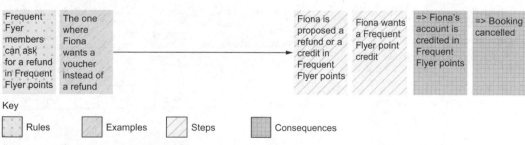

Figure 6.17   The one where Tara wants a refund

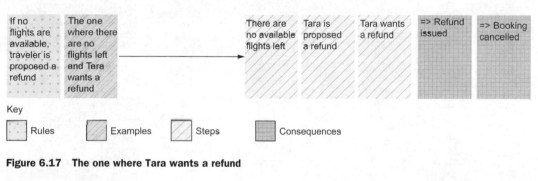

Figure 6.18   The one where Fiona wants a voucher

6.5.5   Grouping related flows and recording uncertainty

For larger Feature Maps, some teams find it useful to group business rules by themes or higher-level functionality. For example, the flows we have discovered so far for the "modify an existing booking" feature could be grouped into two categories: the traveler successfully modifies their booking, or there are no available seats, so the traveler gets a refund.

We can visually group flows by using blue rule cards, often with the text underlined to emphasize that this is the title of a group of related rules. As with Example Mapping, we sometimes want to record uncertainty or assumptions. Questions are written on pink cards and serve the same purpose as they do in Example Mapping. Both of these additional cards can be seen in action in figure 6.19.

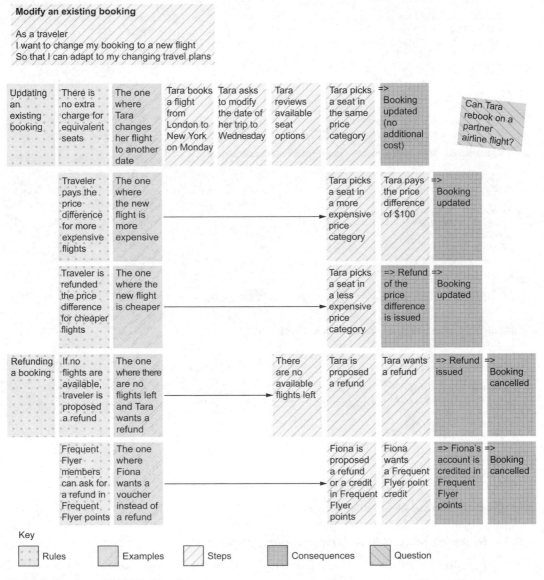

Figure 6.19   A completed feature map

Feature Mapping works well for many different domains. For a front-end application, team members might explore the different ways users will interact with the application to achieve their business goals. For back-end applications, they may look at how data should flow through a system, or what different types of inputs need to be catered to.

Feature Maps are not just for small, focused User Stories. They can also be used very effectively at a high level, to discuss larger features or user journeys. This can help business stakeholders see and discuss the main flows or outcomes that a large feature or epic needs to achieve. Each card might even contain more detailed business rules that can be explored later in more detail using Example Mapping or a table of examples.

As we will see in the next chapter, Feature Maps are also easy to convert into high-quality, highly readable acceptance criteria. This makes them a good choice for teams new to BDD or for teams discovering a new or complex domain.

6.6   *OOPSI*

Another useful collaborative discovery practice from the BDD family is the OOPSI model. OOPSI is short for "Outcome, Outputs, Process, Scenarios, Inputs" and was created by Jenny Martin and Pete Buckney (http://mng.bz/m2X4). Like Feature Mapping and Example Mapping, OOPSI is a great way to get teams to collaborate during Three Amigos sessions, before they turn their examples into more formal Gherkin scenarios.

In section 6.5, we saw how in Feature Mapping we focus on the flows and user journeys to understand business rules and identify key scenarios, working toward the consequences, or outcomes, at the end of each flow.

OOPSI does things the other way round: we start by identifying the highest value outcomes and then work backward to identify the highest value outputs that will contribute to those outcomes, and then find examples and scenarios that illustrate and clarify what needs to be done.

A Three Amigos session following the OOPSI model typically involves five steps:

1 Outcome
2 Outputs
3 Process
4 Scenarios
5 Inputs

Let's walk through what each stage means, in the context of our Frequent Flyer application.

6.6.1   *Outcomes*

The outcome refers to the problem we need to solve and generally corresponds to the feature or User Story being discussed in the Three Amigos session. For example, suppose we need to allow Frequent Flyer members to book flights with their Frequent Flyer points. The User Story might look like the one in figure 6.20.

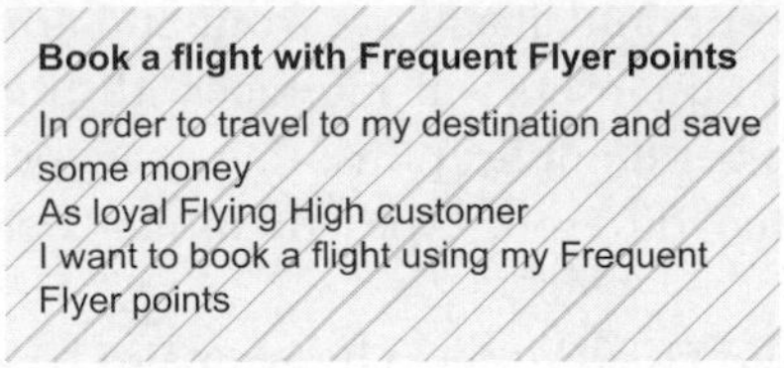

Book a flight with Frequent Flyer points

In order to travel to my destination and save
some money
As loyal Flying High customer
I want to book a flight using my Frequent
Flyer points

**Figure 6.20   The outcome typically
corresponds to the feature or User
Story we want to deliver.**

6.6.2   Outputs

The value of any feature comes from the impact it can make and the outputs it produces. With the OOPSI model, we start by thinking about the concrete outputs produced by the feature.

The outputs will include both what we expect to happen when everything goes smoothly as well as what should happen when something goes wrong. For example, some of the outcomes for the story in figure 6.21 might include

- The new ticket should be issued.
- A "ticket purchased" message is published.
- A confirmation email should be sent to the frequent flyer.
- The frequent flyer's point balance should be updated.
- If the frequent flyer doesn't have enough points, an appropriate error message should be displayed.

Email
confirmation
sent to customer

New ticket issued

Frequent Flyer
points balance
updated

"Sorry, you don't
have enough
points for this
flight"

"Ticket Purchase"
message
published

**Figure 6.21   Outcomes
describe what is tangible.**

Discussing the outputs of a feature is a great way to get a deeper understanding of the underlying requirement, particularly when we illustrate each output with some concrete examples. Does the customer get a confirmation email when they book? What does it look like, and what information does it provide?

6.6.3   Process

The next step is to define the process that gets you to your outcomes. This part is very similar to what we do in Feature Mapping, where we define the steps that lead to various consequences. We typically start with the most important output first, though in many cases the same process will lead to a number of related outputs. For example, the process for booking a flight using Frequent Flyer points could look like the one in figure 6.22.

Figure 6.22 The process maps out the steps that lead to the outputs we want.

6.6.4 Scenarios

A simple process like this leaves out a lot of edge cases and subtle variations. The next step helps us identify these.

In the Scenarios step, the team comes up with various scenarios that illustrate different flows through the process. In OOPSI, the word "scenarios" can refer to both business rules or constraints, or to examples of edge cases that need to be considered. For example, there are only a limited number of seats on a flight that can be purchased with Frequent Flyer points, so when a traveler chooses a flight, we need to check that there are still enough eligible seats available. This appears implicitly in the process diagram in figure 6.22, but by noting it down as a scenario, we can explore how this might happen and what we should do when it does. We can see some possible scenarios in figure 6.23.

Figure 6.23 Scenarios illustrate different flows through the process, as well as applicable business rules.

6.6.5 Inputs

Some of the scenarios we find in the previous step will be self-explanatory, but often adding some concrete examples or data can make things a lot clearer. In the OOPSI model, we call these concrete examples and data the *inputs*.

Tables are often a convenient format for representing our inputs. For example, the fourth scenario in figure 6.23 is a business rule: "Flights can be purchased at a rate of 10 Frequent Flyer points per dollar." We can provide some examples of this business rule and how it works in conjunction with the other scenarios we discovered, in a tabular format (table 6.3).

Figure 6.24 shows the whole OOPSI model, starting from the Outcome and Outputs steps and working back to the Scenarios and Inputs steps.

Table 6.3   Examples of flight purchase rules in a tabular format

Point Balance	Flight	Cost	Available FF Seats	Purchase successful	Cost in Points	New Point Balance
5,000	London to Paris	$450	Yes	Yes	4,500	500
5,000	London to Athens	$650	Yes	No		5,000
5,000	London to Paris	$450	No	No		5,000

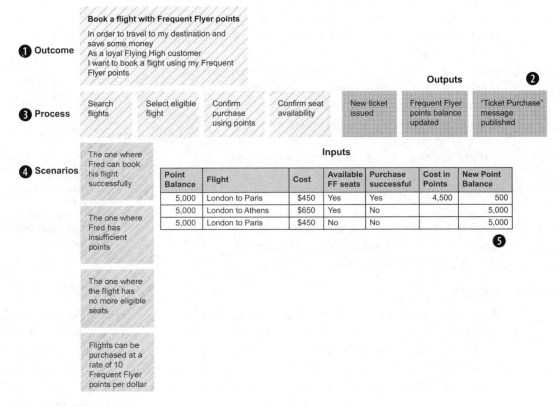

Figure 6.24   A complete OOPSI model from outcomes and outputs to scenarios and inputs

Summary

- You can use conversations about concrete examples and business rules to build a deeper understanding of user needs.
- You can use tables quite effectively to describe variations of inputs and expected outcomes and have conversations about different edge-cases that might occur.

- Example Mapping is a visual technique that uses colored cards to represent business rules and examples. Example Mapping is a great way to rapidly enumerate and better understand business rules.
- Like Example Mapping, Feature Mapping also uses colored cards to represent rules and examples. Unlike Example Mapping, Feature Mapping breaks examples down into steps and outcomes and is very effective when exploring user journeys in more detail.
- The OOPSI model is another approach that starts by identifying key outputs of a feature and works backward to identify the overall process as well as the rules and examples of edge cases and variations.

In the next chapter, you'll learn how to express clear, precise examples in a structured format and how to turn these examples into executable specifications that can be read by tools like Cucumber and SpecFlow.

From examples to
executable specifications

7

This chapter covers
- Turning concrete examples into executable scenarios
- Writing basic scenarios
- Using data tables to drive scenarios
- Writing more advanced scenarios using more Gherkin keywords
- Organizing scenarios

In the last chapter, you saw how conversations with the stakeholders around business rules and concrete examples are a very effective way to build up a common understanding of a problem space. In this chapter, you'll learn how to express these examples clearly and precisely in a way that will allow you to transform them into executable specifications and living documentation (see figure 7.1).

The aim of this chapter is to help developers, business analysts, testers, and other interested team members get a solid shared understanding of how to read and write executable specifications in a way that makes it easy to automate them. BDD has a number of well-defined practices to achieve this shared understanding:

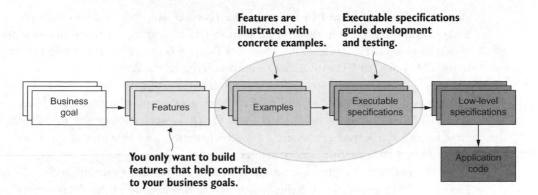

Figure 7.1   In this chapter we'll take examples we used to discuss and illustrate features in previous chapters and turn them into executable specifications.

- BDD practitioners express concrete examples as executable scenarios, using a semi-structured Given . . . When . . . Then format that's easy for both stakeholders and team members to read.
- This format can be automated using BDD tools such as Cucumber or SpecFlow.
- Tables can be used to combine several similar examples more concisely in a single scenario, or to express test data or expected results in a more succinct way.
- Experienced BDD practitioners take care to write their scenario steps well, providing enough detail for the scenario to be meaningful, but not so much that the essential business goals of the scenario are hard to find.
- Scenarios are organized in feature files and can be annotated with tags to indicate cross-functional concerns and to coordinate test execution.

It's important for everyone to be comfortable with the notation and structures used for these scenarios; that way, team members can focus on discussing the requirements and not be distracted by the form that you use to express them. As in any language, there are common patterns and structures that recur (idioms, so to speak), and those can help you express your ideas more fluently.

In the next chapter, you'll see how to automate these examples in Java using Cucumber. If you want to experiment with the examples we discuss in this chapter, you can download the source code from GitHub (https://github.com/bdd-in-action/second-edition/) or the Manning website.

In the rest of the chapter, we'll pick up where we left off in chapter 5 and use some of the examples we discovered using tables, Example Mapping, and Feature Mapping.

7.1   Turning concrete examples into executable scenarios

One of the core concepts behind BDD is the idea that you can express significant concrete examples in a form that's both readable for stakeholders and executable as part of your automated test suite. You'll write executable specifications in the native language of your users and produce test results that report success or failure not in terms of classes and methods, but in terms of the features that the stakeholders requested. Stakeholders will be able to see their own words appear in the living documentation, which does wonders in increasing their confidence that you've understood their problems. This is what BDD tools like Cucumber bring to the table.

When you automate your acceptance criteria using this sort of BDD tool, you express your examples in a slightly more structured form, often referred to as scenarios. Dan North defined a canonical form for these scenarios in the mid-2000s, built around a simple Given . . . When . . . Then structure, and this format has been widely adopted by BDD practitioners ever since.

In the previous chapter, we explored business rules and examples for the "Earning Frequent Flyer points from flights" story. You can see some of the rules and examples in the Example Map in figure 7.2.

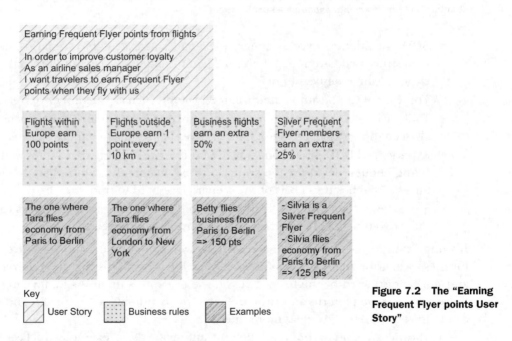

Figure 7.2   The "Earning Frequent Flyer points User Story"

The first business rule we considered in this map is "Flights within Europe earn 100 points." The example we found was "The one where Tara flies economy from Paris to Berlin." You could write this example as shown:[1]

```
Feature: Earning Frequent Flyer points from flights

Scenario: Flights within Europe earn 100 points
   Given Tara is a Frequent Flyer traveler
   When she completes a flight between Paris and Berlin
   Then she should earn 100 points
```

[1] You can find this feature in the earning_points_from_flights.feature file, which you can get in the sample project in the src/test/resources/features/frequent_flyer/earning_points folder.

Although the example is a little more stylized than a free-text paragraph, you're still speaking the language of the stakeholders. With a little practice, stakeholders quickly become comfortable enough with the format to be able to propose and discuss examples like this one.

This approach works equally well when the native language of the stakeholders is not English; you can write scenarios like this in any language. For example, here's the equivalent of this scenario in French:

```
#language: fr
Fonctionnalité: Gagner des points Frequent Flyer en completant des vols

    Scénario: Les vols en Europe valent 100 points
        Etant donné que Tara est un member du programme Frequent Flyer
        Quand elle complete un vol entre Paris and Berlin
        Alors elle devrait gagner 100 points
```

Scenarios like this are not only readable for nontechnical folk; they are also executable. BDD tools like Cucumber and SpecFlow can read and execute these scenarios to verify your application's behavior and generate meaningful test reports. These test reports are a central part of the living documentation that will help you understand and maintain the application (see figure 7.3).

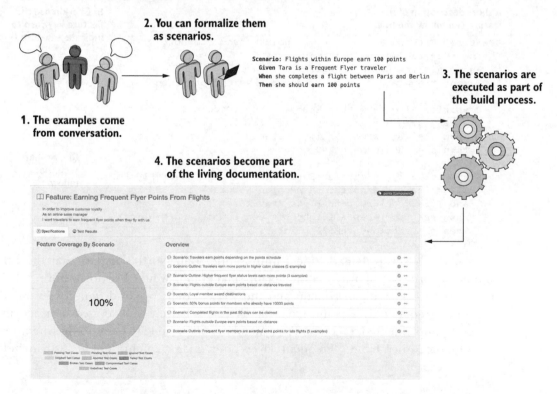

Figure 7.3 When examples are expressed as scenarios, they can be automated and used to generate living documentation.

We'll look at how you can take advantage of this sort of automation in chapter 8. But first, you need to learn how to write effective scenarios in this format using tools like Cucumber.

7.2 Writing executable scenarios

Scenarios written in this format will make up the core of your executable specifications. But to make them truly executable, you need to integrate them into your projects.

In this section, you'll see how to do this using Gherkin. Gherkin is the language used by Cucumber and the vast majority of Cucumber-based BDD tools, including SpecFlow (for .NET), Behave (for Python), and many others. Another older Java-based tool, JBehave, also uses a very similar format.

Scenarios are stored in simple text files and grouped by feature. These files are called, logically enough, *feature files*.

7.2.1 A feature file has a title and a description

At the top of a feature file is a section where you can include the description of the corresponding feature. A typical example is shown here:

A short description of the feature can follow the title.

In Gherkin use the Feature keyword to indicate a feature title.

```
Feature: Earning Frequent Flyer points from flights
  In order to improve customer loyalty
  As an airline sales manager
  I want travelers to earn frequent flyer points when they fly with us

  Scenario: Flights within Europe earn 100 points
    Given Tara is a Frequent Flyer traveler
    When she completes a flight between Paris and Berlin
    Then she should earn 100 points

  Scenario: Flights outside Europe earn 1 point every 10 km
    Given the distance from London to New York is 5500 km
    And Tara is a Frequent Flyer traveler
    When she completes a flight between London and New York
    Then she should earn 550 points
```

One or more scenarios follow.

The Feature keyword marks the feature's title. Dan North suggests that the title should describe an activity that a user or stakeholder would like to perform.[2] This makes the work easier to contain and the scope easier to nail down. For example, "Earning Frequent Flyer points from flights" is a relatively well-defined user activity; when it's implemented, Frequent Flyer members will be able to earn points when they fly. On the other hand, "Frequent Flyer point management" might also include

---

[2] See Dan North's article, "What's in a story," for some interesting tips on writing well-pitched stories and scenarios: http://dannorth.net/whats-in-a-story/.

rewarding Frequent Flyer members points when they make purchases with partner companies, letting members view their current point status, and so forth.

In addition to the title, it's a good idea to include a short description of your feature so that readers can understand the underlying business objectives and background behind the scenarios that the file contains. Any text between this title and the first scenario is treated as a feature description.

If you store feature descriptions electronically, using Agile software management tools or even an issue tracking system such as JIRA, you can configure reporting tools such as Serenity BDD to fetch this information from these systems and display it in the test reports (you'll see how to do this in chapter 16).

7.2.2 Describing the scenarios

After the feature title and description, a feature file describes a set of examples of behavior, which we call scenarios. Each scenario starts with the `Scenario` keyword and a descriptive title:

```
Scenario: <a title>
```

The title is important. As with most things in BDD, good communication is essential. The scenario title should summarize what is special about this example in a short, declarative sentence, a bit like a subtitle for a book. You can see some examples in figure 7.4.

Scenario titles play a key role in reporting, making the living documentation reports easier to read and navigate. Having a succinct list of scenario titles makes it easier to understand what a particular feature is supposed to do, without having to study the details of the Given . . . When . . . Then text. It also makes it easier to isolate issues when tests break.

Another good practice suggested by Matt Wynne[3] is to summarize the Given and When sections of the scenario in the title and avoid including any expected outcomes. Because scenarios are based on real business examples, the context and events are usually relatively stable, but the expected outcomes may change as the organization changes and evolves the way it does business.

Gherkin also lets you complement the scenario title with a description, as shown in this example:

```
Scenario: Flights outside Europe earn points based on distance traveled

Normal flights earn 1 point every 10 km                    ←————    Anything after the
                                                                    scenario title and
    Given the distance from London to New York is 5500 km           before the first
    And Tara is a Frequent Flyer traveler                           Given is considered
    When she completes a flight between London and New York         a description.
    Then she should earn 550 points
```

---

[3] See Matt Wynne and Aslak Hellesøy, *The Cucumber Book* (Pragmatic Bookshelf, 2012).

Feature: Earning Frequent Flyer Points From Flights

`Points (component)`

In order to improve customer loyalty
As an airline sales manager
I want travellers to earn frequent flyer points when they fly with us

Specifications   Test Results

Scenarios

Flights within europe earn 100 points

Flights outside europe earn 1 point every 10 km

Business flights earn an extra 50%

Silver frequent flyer members earn an extra 25%

Scenario details

Flights within Europe earn 100 points

Given Tara is a Frequent Flyer traveller
When she completes a flight between Paris and Berlin
Then she should earn 100 points

Flights outside Europe earn 1 point every 10 km

Given the distance from London to New York is 5500 km
And Tara is a Frequent Flyer traveller

Figure 7.4   A Cucumber report rendered using Serenity BDD, showing how scenario titles act as subheadings in the living documentation reports.

This is a great way to add extra details about business rules or calculations, as the additional text will appear as part of the living documentation.

7.2.3   *The Given . . . When . . . Then structure*

The meat of each scenario is made up of three parts: an initial state or context, an action or event, and an expected result. As you saw in chapters 1 and 2, these are expressed using the following structure:

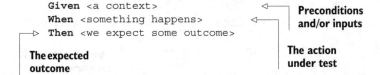

```
Given <a context>
When  <something happens>
Then  <we expect some outcome>
```

Preconditions and/or inputs

The action under test

The expected outcome

This is a simple yet surprisingly versatile format. It helps you cleanly define the context of a test, what action is being tested, and what the expected outcome should be. It also helps you focus on what the requirement aims to achieve, rather than on how it will do so. Let's look at each of these steps in more detail.

GIVEN SETS THE STAGE

The `Given` step describes the preconditions for your test. It sets up any test data your test needs and generally puts the application in the correct pretest state. Typically, this includes things such as creating any required test data, or, for a web application, logging on and navigating to the right page. Sometimes a `Given` step may be purely informative, to provide some context or background, even if no action is required in the test implementation.

You should be careful to only include the preconditions that are directly related to the scenario. Too many `Given`s can make it harder for a reader to know precisely what's required for the scenario to work and can make the scenarios harder to maintain. But preconditions that should be present in the `Given` steps, but aren't, are effectively assumptions that can lead to misunderstandings later on.

For example, suppose we want to automate the scenario we discovered in chapter 6, where a traveler modifies the date of their booking (see figure 7.5).

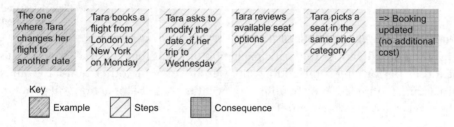

Figure 7.5   A Feature Map showing a traveler changing their booking

We could write this scenario as shown:

```
Scenario: Change a flight to another date
  Given Tara has booked the following flight:
    | Departure | Destination | Date       | Class   |
    | London    | New York    | 13-01-2020 | Economy |
  When Tara updates the flight date to 15-01-2020
  Then there should be no additional charge
  And the booking should be updated to the following:
    | Departure | Destination | Date       | Class   |
    | London    | New York    | 15-01-2020 | Economy |
```

However, we are missing some context about who Tara is. If this feature is only applicable for Frequent Flyer members (non-Frequent Flyer members might be charged a fee to change a booking), then it would be important to mention this fact in the `Given` steps:

```
Scenario: Change a flight to another date
  Given Tara is a Frequent Flyer traveler
  And Tara has booked the following flight:
```

```
                  | Departure | Destination | Date       | Class   |
                  | London    | New York    | 13-01-2020 | Economy |
          …
```

Other preconditions might not be so useful. For example, suppose that, to change her booking, Tara first needs to log on to the Frequent Flyer application. We could include this as one of the given steps. However, it is not directly related to the business logic in the scenario. Furthermore, if Tara is a frequent flyer, then we can safely assume that she needs to log on to be able to change her flights, so the second given shown in the scenario should not be included:

```
Scenario: Change a flight to another date
  Given Tara is a Frequent Flyer traveler
  And Tara has logged on to the Frequent Flyer app using tara@email.com
  And Tara has booked the following flight:
      | Departure | Destination | Date       | Class   |
      | London    | New York    | 13-01-2020 | Economy |
```

This detail is important to the business logic in the scenario.

This step is an implementation detail that is not directly related to the scenario outcome.

WHEN CONTAINS THE ACTION UNDER TEST

The When step describes the principal action or event that you want to test. This could be a user performing some action on a website, or some other non-UI event, such as processing a transaction or handling an event message. This action will generate some observed outcome, which you'll verify in the Then step.

THEN DESCRIBES THE EXPECTED OUTCOMES

The Then step compares the observed outcome or state of the system with what you expect. The outcome should tie back to the business value you expect to get out of the story or feature this scenario belongs to.

7.2.4   *Ands and buts*

Any of the previous steps can be extended using and. Gherkin also allows you to use the synonym but. You've seen this before:

```
Scenario: Flights outside Europe earn points based on distance traveled
  Given the distance from London to New York is 5500 km
  And Tara is a Frequent Flyer traveler
  When she completes a flight between London and New York
  Then she should earn 550 points
```

And is equivalent to Given.

Technically, the BDD tools consider any step with And or But to be the same as the previous step that wasn't And or But. The main goal is to make the scenarios read more easily.

It's often a good habit to keep Given . . . When . . . Then clauses concise and focused. If you're tempted to place two conditions in the same step, consider splitting them into two separate steps. This will make the scenario easier to read and give developers more freedom to reuse steps between scenarios.

For example, suppose travelers can earn bonus points if they fly during special bonus-flyer periods. One way to express this might be the following:

```
Scenario: Earning extra points in a bonus flyer period

  European flights earn 50 extra points during bonus flyer periods

    Given Tara is a Frequent Flyer traveler
    When she flies from London to Paris in a 'Bonus Flyer' period
    Then she should earn 100 points and 50 bonus points
```
A composite Then step

Alternatively, you could split the `Given` and `Then` steps into smaller ones:

```
Scenario: Earning extra points in a bonus flyer period

  European flights earn 50 extra points during bonus flyer periods

    Given Tara is a Frequent Flyer traveler
    When she flies from London to Paris in a 'Bonus Flyer' period
    Then she should earn 100 points
    And she should earn 50 bonus points
```
This step can be reused.
So can this one.

Although it's slightly longer, this second version has several advantages. Each step is focused on a particular aspect of the problem—if something breaks, or the requirements change, it will be easier to see what needs to be changed. In addition, reuse is easier. Steps 1 and 2 are also used in some of the other scenarios you've seen, so you can simplify writing and maintaining the tests by reusing them.

7.2.5   Comments

You may also occasionally want to place comments in your feature files, such as to note some technical detail about how the scenario should be implemented.

You can insert a comment, or comment out a line, by placing the hash character (#) at the start of a line:

A comment line in Gherkin starts with the # character. It can be used to comment out any line.

```
# This feature is really important for the Marketing team
Feature: Earning Frequent Flyer points from flights
  In order to improve customer loyalty
  As an airline sales manager
  I want travelers to earn frequent flyer points when they fly with us

  Scenario: Flights within Europe earn 100 points
    # Given Tara is a Frequent Flyer traveler
    When she completes a flight between Paris and Berlin
    Then she should earn 100 points
```
It's often used to comment out steps.

Comments can appear anywhere in the scenario, though they're often used to leave a technical note for other developers or to temporarily comment out a step.

Unlike the narrative and descriptive texts you saw earlier, comments are not part of the living documentation. They don't appear in the reports and are therefore of limited communication value for the stakeholders. For this reason, other than for temporarily commenting out a step, comments should be used with moderation.

7.3 Using tables in scenarios

Scenarios are like application code: you should write with the intention of making readability and maintenance easy. If you're using your scenarios as living documentation, they'll likely long outlast the development project, and it's important to make sure that they're easy to understand and update in the future.

One way *not* to do this is to include a lot of duplicated text in your scenarios. In programming, duplication is one of the worst enemies of maintainable code, and the same applies to scenarios. But if you only use the Given . . . When . . . Then notation we've discussed so far, it's sometimes hard to avoid overly wordy scenarios peppered with duplicated text. In the following section, we'll look at how you can use tables in different ways to avoid duplication, improve readability, and make maintenance easier.

7.3.1 Using tables in individual steps

Suppose you're working on a feature that allows Frequent Flyer members to transfer points to other members. For example, suppose Danielle and Martin are Frequent Flyer members in the same family. Both Danielle and Martin have accumulated a lot of points over the year. They want to go on holidays using their points, but neither of them has enough points to buy the tickets outright in a single booking. Martin needs to be able to transfer some of his points to Danielle so that she can purchase the flights for both of them with her points.

You could express this scenario as follows:

```
Scenario: Transfer points between family members
Given Danielle and Martin are family members
And Danielle's account has 100000 points and 800 status points      A lot of
And Martin's account has 50000 points and 50 status points          duplication here
When Martin transfers 40000 points to Danielle
Then Martin should have 10000 points and 50 status points           Here too
And Danielle should have 140000 points and 800 status points
```

The problem is that there's a lot of repetition and clutter in this scenario, and the meaning gets lost in all the words. A much better way to write this scenario would be to express the data in a more concise tabular format, like this:

```
Scenario: Transfer points between family members
     Given Danielle and Martin are family members
```

```
    And they have the following accounts:
        | owner     | points  | status points |
        | Danielle  | 100000  | 800           |
        | Martin    | 50000   | 50            |
    When Martin transfers 40000 points to Danielle
        | owner     | points  | status points |
        | Danielle  | 140000  | 800           |
        | Martin    | 10000   | 50            |
```

Provide a table of data for the Given step.

Data for the Then step

The tables start directly after the Given and Then steps, with the values separated by pipes (|). The headers at the top of each column are useful in this case.

Tables like this are a concise and effective way to represent sets of similar data, such as the user accounts shown here. Tables can also be used to represent a single record, rather than a collection of records, by organizing the field names vertically in the first column and then placing the corresponding values in the second column. You can see an example of this approach here, where we represent the account details of one particular user:

```
Given Daniel is a Frequent Flyer with the following details:
    | Home City     | London |
    | Points        | 100000 |
    | Status Points | 50     |
```

You can even use data tables to represent a simple list of values, as shown here:

```
Then Tara should be able to upgrade to one of the following cabin classes:
| Premium Economy |
| Business        |
| First           |
```

Embedding tabular data is a great way to express preconditions and expected outcomes in a clear and concise way. But there's another equally useful way to use tabular data in your scenarios: tables of examples.

7.3.2 Using tables of examples

Previously, we saw how Bianca and her team used a table to better understand how past flights could be counted toward the Frequent Flyer points of a new joiner. The table looked like this:

Flight Number	Flight Date	Status	Eligible	Reason
FH-99	60 days ago	COMPLETED	Yes	
FH-87	100 days ago	COMPLETED	No	Too old
OH-101	60 days ago	COMPLETED	No	Not a Flying High flight
FH-99	60 days ago	CANCELLED	No	Must be completed
FH-99	In 5 days time	CONFIRMED	No	Must have taken place

You could write examples illustrating these rules as separate scenarios, as shown in the following listing.

Listing 7.1   Scenarios for calculating the eligibility of past flights
---

```
Feature: Earning points from past flights

  As a Flying High Frequent Flyer program manager
  I want new members to be credited with points from their recent flights
  So that more people will join the program

Scenario: Eligible flight
  Given Todd has just joined the Frequent Flyer program
  And Todd asks for the following flight to be credited to his account:
    | Flight Number | Flight Date | Status    |
    | FH-99         | 60 days ago | COMPLETED |
  Then the flight should be considered Eligible

Scenario: Old flight
  Given Todd has just joined the Frequent Flyer program
  And Todd asks for the following flight to be credited to his account:
    | Flight Number | Flight Date  | Status    |
    | FH-87         | 100 days ago | COMPLETED |
  Then the flight should be considered Ineligible

Scenario: Not a Flying High flight
  Given Todd has just joined the Frequent Flyer program
  And Todd asks for the following flight to be credited to his account:
    | Flight Number | Flight Date | Status    |
    | OH-101        | 60 days ago | COMPLETED |
  Then the flight should be considered Ineligible

Scenario: Flights must be completed
  Given Todd has just joined the Frequent Flyer program
  And Todd asks for the following flight to be credited to his account:
    | Flight Number | Flight Date | Status   |
    | FH-99         | 60 days ago | CANCELED |
  Then the flight should be considered Ineligible

Scenario: Flights must have taken place
  Given Todd has just joined the Frequent Flyer program
  And Todd asks for the following flight to be credited to his account:
    | Flight Number | Flight Date    | Status    |
    | FH-99         | In 5 days time | CONFIRMED |
  Then the flight should be considered Ineligible
```

This is starting to get quite wordy. Having a lot of similar scenarios to describe a set of related business rules is a poor practice; the duplication makes the scenarios harder to maintain. In addition, after the first couple of almost-identical scenarios, readers are likely to just skim over the subsequent ones and miss important details, making them a poor communication tool.

When you're writing scenarios in BDD, a good rule of thumb is "less is more." You can often describe behavior more concisely and more effectively using a single scenario and a table of examples that summarizes the different cases. To do this in Cucumber we need to use the `Scenario Outline` keyword instead of a conventional `Scenario`. A `Scenario Outline` (or `Scenario Template`) uses the conventional Given . . . When . . . Then steps but includes placeholders for variables that will be defined in a table of examples.

Once we have defined the template structure, we use the `Examples` (or `Scenarios`) keyword to list the examples that illustrate the business rule we want to describe. For example, you could express the scenarios in listing 7.1 more succinctly using an example table like in the following listing.

Listing 7.2 Scenarios expressed as a scenario outline

When we use tables we need to use the Scenario Outline keyword.

Express the rule in more generic terms. Data from the example table is passed into the steps.

```
Scenario Outline: Eligible flights in the past 90 days can be claimed.
    Given Todd has just joined the Frequent Flyer program
    And Todd asks for the following flight to be credited to his account:.
        | Flight Number  | Flight Date | Status   |
        | <Flight>       | < Date>     | <Status> |
    Then the flight should be considered <Eligibility>
Examples:
    | Flight  | Date      | Status    | Eligibility | Reason            |
    | FH-99   | -60 days  | COMPLETED | Eligible    |                   |
    | FH-87   | -100 days | COMPLETED | Ineligible  | Too old           |
    | OH-101  | -60 days  | COMPLETED | Ineligible  | Different airline |
    | FH-99   | -60 days  | CANCELLED | Ineligible  | Must be completed |
    | FH-99   | +5 days   | CONFIRMED | Ineligible  | Hasn't taken place|
```

The Examples keyword indicates the start of a table of examples.

Summarize the different cases using a few well-chosen examples. The scenario will be checked for each row of data in the table.

This is effectively five scenarios wrapped into one—the scenario will be run five times, each time with the values from one row in the example table. Data from the table is passed into each step via the field names in angle brackets: `<Flight>`, `<Date>`, and so forth. You've reduced four wordy scenarios into a single concise scenario and a table of examples!

When you use a table of sample data like this, the scenario will be checked once for each row in the table, making this the equivalent of five separate scenarios. But presenting data in tabular form can make it easier to spot patterns and get a more holistic view of the problem. It also makes it easy to describe and explore boundary conditions and edge cases (which is what you did in the preceding examples), and it produces excellent living documentation (see figure 7.6).

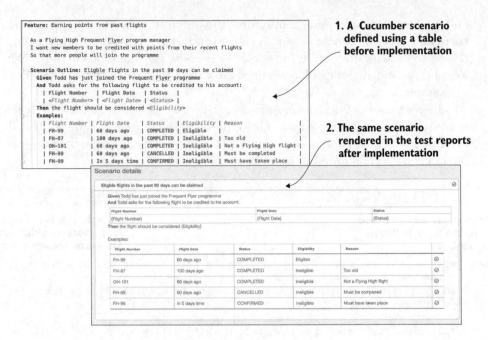

Figure 7.6 Tabular data also produces great living documentation.

7.3.3 *Pending scenarios*

Sometimes we might want to record a feature in your acceptance test suite before it has been fleshed out in detail, as a placeholder for future work. You can do this by simply recording the feature and scenario titles, without filling in the detailed steps.

```
Feature: Booking flights with Frequent Flyer points

  As a Frequent Flyer program manager
  I want members to be able to book flights with their points for themselves
  and their families
  So that they will want to earn more points


  Scenario: Booking an individual flight using points
  Scenario: Booking an individual flight using money and points
  Scenario: Booking a flight for more than one passenger
```

This feature will now figure in your living documentation, as a reminder of work that has yet to be done. The scenarios will be reported as *pending*, meaning they have been recorded but not yet implemented (see figure 7.7).

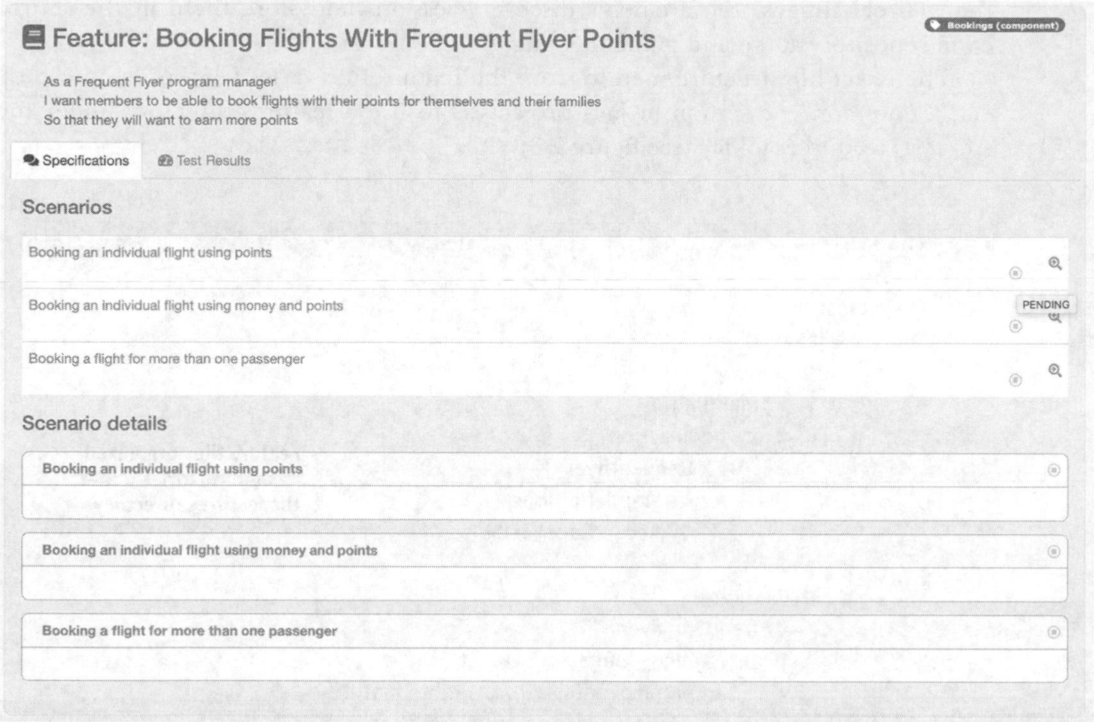

Figure 7.7 **Unimplemented scenarios are marked as pending in the reports.**

7.4 *Organizing your scenarios using feature files and tags*

In real-world projects, scenarios can become quite numerous, and it's important to keep them well organized. You may also need to be able to identify and group scenarios in different ways; for example, you might want to distinguish UI-related scenarios from batch-processing scenarios or identify the scenarios related to cross-functional concerns. In this section, you'll learn how to organize and group your scenarios to make them easier to understand and maintain.

7.4.1 *The scenarios go in a feature file*

The role of a scenario is to illustrate a feature, and you place all the scenarios that describe a particular feature in a single file, usually with a name that summarizes the feature (e.g., earning_points_from_flights.feature). We call these files *feature files*, and they conventionally use the .feature suffix. They can be read and edited in a simple text editor, though plug-ins also exist for most modern IDEs. During the rest of the chapter, we'll refer to these files as feature files, regardless of the file suffix used.

As you saw in chapter 2, these scenarios are part of the project's source code, and they'll be placed under version control. Many teams write the feature files shortly after the "Three Amigos" requirements discovery sessions and store them in the source code repository at the end of the meetings.

The exact file structure used to store the feature files varies from project to project; a common convention in Java projects is to use a features directory under the src/test/resources folder (see figure 7.8).

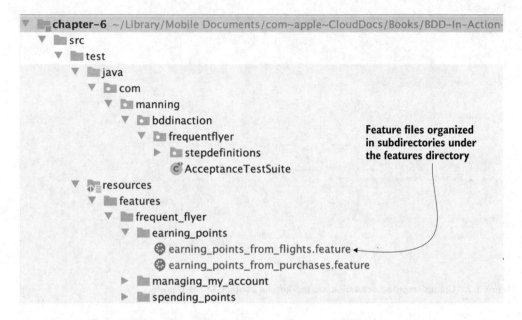

Figure 7.8   Feature files are stored in plain-text files as part of the project source code (this example is from a Cucumber project in Java).

Some teams have separate feature files for each User Story. This is generally a bad idea.[4] Remember, stories are transitory planning artifacts that can be disregarded at the end of an iteration, but features are valuable units of functionality that stakeholders can understand and relate to. Organizing scenarios in terms of features rather than stories makes it easier to generate meaningful living documentation. It can be useful to associate scenarios with the corresponding stories for planning and reporting purposes during an iteration, but the primary association should be between a scenario and the feature it illustrates.

7.4.2   *A feature file can contain one or more scenarios*

As discussed in chapter 5, you use concrete examples to illustrate each feature. Any example you decide to automate will be represented by a single scenario in the

---

[4] There's nothing wrong with using tags or some other metadata to relate a scenario to a story for planning and reporting purposes.

corresponding feature file. As a result, the feature file will contain all the examples that illustrate its expected behavior. These examples illustrate not only the simple cases but also alternative paths and edge cases that flesh out how the feature behaves in different situations.

7.4.3 Organizing the feature files

When you start to get a large number of feature files in your project, it's important to keep them organized in a way that makes them easy to find and browse. A good way to do this is to place them into subdirectories, as illustrated in figure 7.8. Of course, you'll need to decide what directory structure makes the most sense for your team. There are a few ways you can do this.

7.4.4 Using a flat directory structure

It is perfectly possible to keep all your feature files in the same directory (e.g., under src/test/resources/features for a Java project). However, for anything other than a small project with only a few feature files, this can quickly become confusing.

7.4.5 Organizing feature files by stories or product increments

Some teams like to have a separate feature file for each User Story. While this seems like a logical approach on the surface, in practice it is not ideal. A User Story is a planning artifact, designed to help organize the work of the team to get a feature into the hands of the users. A feature, on the other hand, is a distinct piece of functionality, that might take several User Stories to complete. And sometimes a new User Story may change or replace the scenarios defined for a previous User Story, which makes it hard to know where a particular scenario should go.

Other teams group their features around product releases; they have a directory for each iteration or release, and all the features related to that release are stored in that directory. However, this approach isn't ideal either. Very often, the development of a feature can be split across several iterations, which either makes it hard to know where the feature file should live or introduces unnecessary duplication with multiple feature files containing scenarios that are actually related to the same feature.

But there is also a more fundamental problem with both of these approaches. They confuse *project delivery* with *product documentation*. Feature files, and the scenarios they contain, are intended to be product documentation; they describe what the application does, what business rules it applies, and what user behavior it supports. This functionality will evolve and grow with each new iteration or release, but there is not always a clean relationship between a feature and a release, particularly as the application evolves. In other words, you wouldn't organize a user manual or a requirement specification document with one chapter per release, so you probably shouldn't organize your feature files this way either.

7.4.6 *Organizing feature files by functionality and capability*

Generally speaking, a better way to organize your feature files is in terms of business capabilities. Feature files are living documentation; they help us understand what the application does, so it makes sense to organize your feature files in a way that describes the app.

If you've organized your features in terms of capabilities, as described in chapters 3 and 4, it's very natural to create a directory for each capability. And for larger projects, you might first organize your features in terms of higher-level functionalities, and then group features within these functional areas in terms of more fine-grained capabilities. You can see an example here:

```
+ features
    + frequent_flyers
        + account
            + register.feature
            + change_password.feature
            + view_flight_history.feature
        + book_a_flight
            + book_with_points.feature
            + book_with_points_and_cash.feature
        + earn_points
            + earn_points_from_flights.feature
            + earn_points_from_hotel_stays.feature
            + earn_points_from_car_rentals.feature
```

As you can see in this example, the top-level directories give an overview of what the application does, a bit like sections in a requirements document. And if you want to know more about a particular functional area, you can drill down into the corresponding directory to see what specific capabilities are supported. As you'll see later, the Serenity BDD reporting tool (www.serenity-bdd.info) can be configured to use this directory structure to group executable requirements by features, capabilities, tags, and so forth.

7.4.7 *Annotating your scenarios with tags*

You've seen how you can organize your feature files into subdirectories that mirror your requirements' structure. But often it's nice to have other ways to categorize your scenarios, such as by technical component or module, or by some cross-cutting business rule that may apply to many features. Fortunately, this is quite easy to do. Gherkin lets you add *tags* to features, scenarios, and even example tables. Tags can be used to filter reports and test execution, and to provide extra context when you look at a feature or scenario.

For example, we could indicate that a feature is related to the Frequent Flyer module with a tag like this:

```
@frequentflyer
Feature: Earning Frequent Flyer points from flights

  Scenario: Travelers earn points based on the distance traveled
    ...
```

We could highlight that the first scenario is particularly important by adding a tag at the scenario level:

```
@frequentflyer
Feature: Earning Frequent Flyer points from flights

  @important
  Scenario: Travellers earn points based on the distance traveled
    ...
```

Tags are also a great way to categorize scenarios by other cross-functional concerns, to identify related parts of the system, and to help organize test execution. For example, you might want to flag all of the web tests, or mark certain tests as being slow, so that they can be grouped together during the automated build process. In the following example, the scenario is flagged as a UI test (as well as being important):

```
@frequentflyer
Feature: Earning Frequent Flyer points from flights

  @important @ui
  Scenario: Travelers earn points based on the distance traveled
    ...
```

This way, when executing the tests, you can configure a filter to only run the tests with a particular tag (or without a particular tag; you'll see how to do this in chapter 8).

Tags can be made up of any nonblank characters, and this fact is used by some reporting tools to provide more advanced integration with other tools. For example, many projects store details about features or User Stories in issue-tracking software such as Atlassian's JIRA. Many teams use tags to relate a feature or an individual scenario back to the corresponding issue, both for information and so that reporting tools can use this data to create a link back to the corresponding issue. For example, the second scenario is as illustrated here:

```
@frequentflyer
Feature: Earning Frequent Flyer points from flights

  @important
  Scenario: Travelers earn points based on the distance traveled
    ...

  @issue:FF-123
  Scenario: Travellers extra points in Business class
    ...
```

Serenity BDD and Serenity/JS in particular use a simple tagging convention to make it easier to group scenarios by tags:

```
@<tag-type>:<tag-name>
```

For example, imagine that project stakeholders want to see how various components in a system behave and how well they are tested. The following feature defines two scenarios that related to two different components in the system: the *authentication* component and the *accounts* component:

```
Feature: Signing up to the Frequent Flyer program

  @component:authentication
  Scenario: Users can sign up online

  @component:accounts
  Scenario: Users can request credits for flights completed in the past three
            months
```

Using this convention, you can configure Serenity BDD to include test results grouped by these components. This gives a succinct overview of test coverage for each component (see figure 7.9). More importantly, from a BDD perspective, this overview also gives you a place to go for documentation about a particular component.

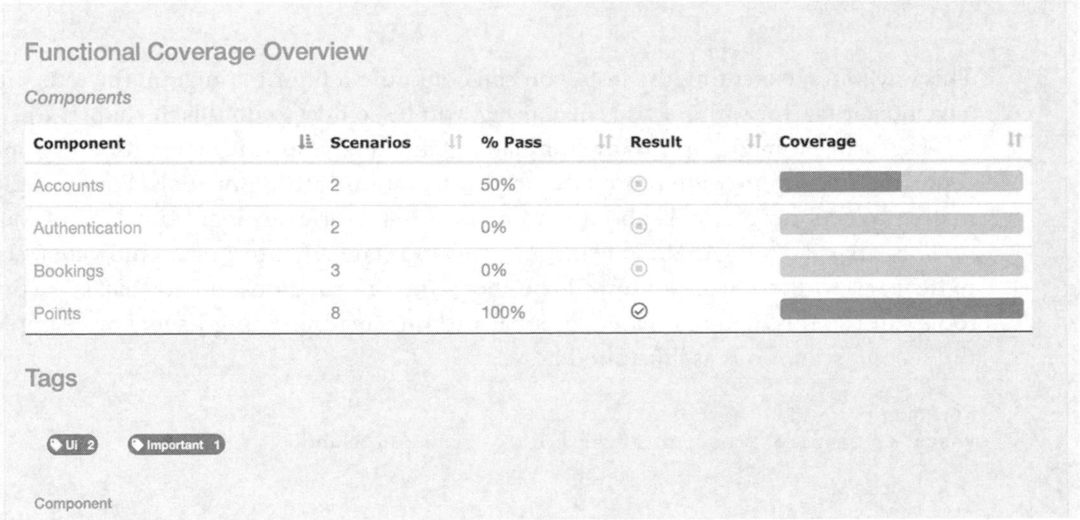

Functional Coverage Overview

Components

Component	Scenarios	% Pass	Result	Coverage
Accounts	2	50%	◉	
Authentication	2	0%	◉	
Bookings	3	0%	◉	
Points	8	100%	⊘	

Tags

🏷 Ui 2   🏷 Important 1

Component

Figure 7.9   Using tags to organize the test reports

BDD tools also let you write *hooks*—methods that will be executed before or after a scenario with a specific tag is executed. This is a great way to set up a test environment for certain types of tests, or to clean up afterward. You'll learn more about how to do this in chapter 8.

You can also use tags as a powerful reporting tool (see figure 7.9). For example, Serenity BDD reports on tags, allowing you to filter test results by tag or tag type, which provides an alternative to the folder-based requirements hierarchy and can help to focus attention on functionality or components that really matter to businesspeople.

7.4.8 *Provide background and context to avoid duplication*

Another common way that duplication slips into scenarios is when several scenarios start off with the same steps. For example, Frequent Flyer members can log on to the Frequent Flyer website to consult their points and status, book flights, and so forth. The following Gherkin scenarios relate to logging on to this site:

```
Feature: Logging on to the 'My Flying High' website
  Frequent Flyer members can register on the 'My Flying High' website
  using their Frequent Flyer number and a password that they provide

  Scenario: Logging on successfully
    Given Martin is a Frequent Flyer member
    And Martin has registered online with a password of 'secret'
    When Martin logs on with password 'secret'
    Then he should be given access to the site

  Scenario: Logging on with an incorrect password
    Given Martin is a Frequent Flyer member
    And Martin has registered online with a password of 'secret'
    When Martin logs on with password 'wrong'
    Then he should be informed that his password was incorrect

  Scenario: Logging on with an expired account
    Given Martin is a Frequent Flyer member
    And Martin has registered online with a password of 'secret'
    But the account has expired
    When Martin logs on with password 'secret'
    Then he should be informed that his account has expired
    And he should be invited to renew his account
```

Note the duplicated steps.

These scenarios contain a lot of repetition, which makes them harder to read and to maintain. In addition, if you ever need to change one of the duplicated steps, you'll need to do so in several places.

You can avoid having to repeat the first two steps by using the `Background` keyword, as shown here:

```
Feature: Logging on to the 'My Flying High' website
  Frequent Flyer members can register on the 'My Flying High' website
  using their Frequent Flyer number and a password that they provide

  Background: Martin is registered on the site
    Given Martin is a Frequent Flyer member
    And Martin has registered online with a password of 'secret'

  Scenario: Logging on successfully
    When Martin logs on with password 'secret'
    Then he should be given access to the site
```

These steps will be run before each scenario.

The scenarios are more focused.

```
Scenario: Logging on with an incorrect password
  When Martin logs on with password 'wrong'
  Then he should be informed that his password was incorrect

Scenario: Logging on with an expired account
  Given the account has expired
  When Martin logs on with password 'secret'
  Then he should be informed that his account has expired
  And he should be invited to renew his account
```

The Background keyword lets you specify steps that will be run before each scenario in the feature. You can use this to avoid duplicating steps in each scenario, which also helps focus attention on the important bits of each scenario.

7.5   *Rules and examples*

Cucumber 6 introduced some new keywords that let you define the business rules for a feature more clearly and group examples and counterexamples for each business rule (see listing 7.3). The Rule keyword represents a single business rule, in the context of a feature. Underneath the Rule you group one or more scenarios that illustrate this rule.

The Example keyword is used to indicate a concrete example or counterexample of a Rule. The Example keyword is actually a synonym of the Scenario keyword we have seen up until now; you can use them interchangeably.

Listing 7.3   Using the Cucumber 6 Rule and Example keywords

```
Feature: Transferring points between members

  As a Frequent Flyer Member
  I want to transfer points that I don't need to members of my family
  So that the points don't go to waste

  Background:
    Given the following Frequent Flyer members
        | Name  | Surname | Family Code |
        | Sarah | Sparrow | FAM-101     |
        | Steve | Sparrow | FAM-101     |
        | Fred  | Falcon  | FAM-202     |

  Rule: Frequent Flyer members in the same family can transfer points
    Example: Transfer points between existing members
      Given the following Frequent Flyer account balances:
          | owner | points | status-points |
          | Sarah | 100000 | 800           |
          | Steve | 50000  | 50            |
      When Sarah transfers 40000 points to Steve
      Then the accounts should be as follows:
          | owner | points | status-points |
          | Sarah | 60000  | 800           |
          | Steve | 90000  | 50            |
```

```
Example: Transfer points between non-family members
  Given the following Frequent FLyer account balances:
    | owner | points | status-points |
    | Sarah | 100000 | 800           |
    | Fred  | 20000  | 50            |
  When Sarah tries to transfer 10000 points to Fred
  Then the transfer should not be allowed

Rule: Members cannot transfer more points than they have
  Example: Steve tries to transfer more points than he has
    Given the following Frequent Flyer account balances:
      | owner | points | status-points |
      | Sarah | 100000 | 800           |
      | Steve | 50000  | 50            |
    When Steve tries to transfer 100000 points to Sarah
    Then the transfer should not be allowed
```

7.6   Expressive scenarios: Patterns and anti-patterns

Now that you've seen the mechanics of writing scenarios in Gherkin, it's time to take things to the next level. In this section we'll go beyond just seeing how scenarios are structured and written and look at what goes into a good scenario.

7.6.1   The art of good Gherkin

As we have seen, scenarios are intended to document and illustrate a feature with a mixture of free-text description and executable examples, all written in a language businesspeople can understand. They act both as a description of a business need, and as documentation of the feature that supports this need (see figure 7.10). Let's unpack this.

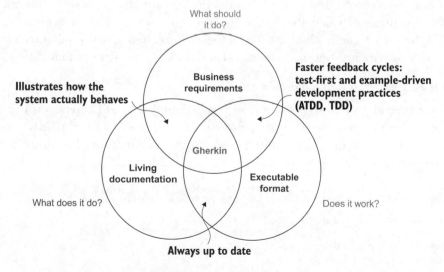

Figure 7.10   Gherkin scenarios are simultaneously requirements specifications, executable tests, and living documentation.

Gherkin scenarios are first and foremost a way to discuss and record business requirements. But they are written in an executable format, which means they can be readily turned into automated tests and run as part of your normal build process. This leads to faster feedback cycles and opens the way to test-first development practices, such as ATDD and TDD.

One of the problems with traditional requirements documents is that they quickly become out of date. But when they are written in an executable format, and can be tested against the running application, they act as *living documentation*. We know they reflect not only what the software should do, but also what it does. And when they are executed with every build, we can be confident that they do indeed reflect the current behavior of the application.

But writing good Gherkin scenarios is not an easy task. It takes practice and collaboration to get it right. Like good prose, writing scenarios that are clean and easy to read is hard. Very often, the easier a Gherkin scenario is to understand, the more effort the authors have put in to make it so.

And poorly written Gherkin scenarios are, unfortunately, very easy to find in the wild. Many existing Cucumber test suites were (and still are) written by people who have not been exposed to BDD practices, or who have assumed that Cucumber is a traditional test-scripting tool and not the collaboration and documentation tool that it is.

Poorly written Gherkin is not just hard on the eyes. It is bad for your project too! Dodgy Gherkin scenarios are more fragile, harder to understand, and more expensive to maintain than scenarios written in the spirit of living documentation and executable specifications. If they fail, it is harder to know what went wrong, which reduces confidence in the test suite as a whole.

They also tend to be much harder to extend and update. One team I worked with reported gains of 80% in the time taken to write and automate new scenarios when they refactored their old Cucumber test scripts using a more declarative approach. In the rest of this section, we will look at some of the traps to avoid, and you will learn some tips on how to make sure your scenarios stay clean, readable, and easy to maintain.

7.6.2   *What bad Gherkin looks like*

If good Gherkin is like something written by Hemingway, bad Gherkin is like one of those trashy novels you pick up on the way to the beach, or the poorly translated instruction manual that came with your washing machine. Consider for example the scenario in the following listing.

Listing 7.4   A poorly written Gherkin scenario

```
Scenario: End-to-end hotel booking test
  Given I login to the Travel Booking App
  Then I am on the Home Page
  And I click the New Trip tab
  And I click on the Hotels dropdown menu item
  Then I am on the Hotel Search page
```

```
When I Enter "Paris" into the city field
And I set price range to "Any"
And I set check-in date to "04-04-2019"
And I enter number of nights to "2"
And I set distance to "10"
When I hit "search" button
Then the hotels listed are:
   | Hotel Name | Distance | Availability | Price | Pool | Gym |
   | Ritz       | 3.2      | Yes          | 400   | Y    | Y   |
   | Savoy      | 6.9      | Yes          | 500   | N    | Y   |
When I select "Ritz" from the list
And I select "Pay with points"
And check that I have enough points
And I click "Pay"
Then verify the message that appears
And verify that the price is correct
And I click on logout
```

There are many things wrong here. The scenario is long and dense, a monotonous sequence of low-level UI interactions that make it hard to see what it is really trying to test. If the buttons or fields change, the scenario would break even if the business logic is still valid. Furthermore, there is no clear goal or outcome; the scenario seems to be exercising many different business rules. If this scenario failed, it would be quite hard to know exactly what was broken.

As often is the case, it is easy to criticize but more difficult to articulate how to do things better. In the rest of this section, we will go through some key characteristics that well-written Gherkin scenarios tend to share, and that can hopefully help you improve your own scenarios as well.

7.6.3   *Good scenarios are declarative, not imperative*

In grammar, the imperative mode is what you use when you are telling someone what to do. "Take your dirty clothes off the floor and put them in the laundry basket; then clean up those toys," for example. A declarative style, on the other hand, focuses on the outcome you are trying to achieve, or what you would like to happen, rather than giving instructions on what to do: "Your room needs to be tidy by dinner time."

Or, imagine you arrived at a restaurant with your partner. If you were in an imperative mood, you might say to the server who greets you, "I would like to walk across the room to the second table from the right just by the window and sit down, and for you to bring us two menus." Alternatively, in a more declarative style, you could say, "A table for two by the window, please."

In programming languages, an imperative style focuses on how we perform a task. For example, if we wanted to find the average age from a list of ages, an imperative style would add up the ages and divide them by the number of ages in the list:[5]

---

[5] These examples are written in Kotlin, a JVM language that supports both an imperative and a declarative style of programming.

```
val ages = listOf(20,40,50,15,80);
var totalAges = 0
for (age in ages) {
    totalAges = totalAges + age
}
val averageAge = totalAges / ages.size
```

In a declarative style of programming (which is often associated with functional programming languages), you focus more on *what* you want to achieve than *how* you will achieve it. To find the average age, you would simply declare that you want the average of the list of ages:

```
val ages = listOf(20,40,50,15,80);
val averageAge = ages.average();
```

In Gherkin, when we say that a scenario is written in an imperative style, we mean that it reads like a list of low-level instructions. Rather than describing business rules and expected outcomes, imperative scenarios focus on how the user interacts with the application at a very granular level. Rather than describing *what* the user wants to do, they focus on the *how*. They talk about what buttons to click, what fields to fill in, or what system calls to make.

The scenario in listing 7.4 is a typical example of an imperative style. The following steps are just a long list of detailed instructions on how to interact with the application:

```
When I Enter "Paris" into the city field
And I set price range to "Any"
And I set check-in date to "04-04-2019"
And I enter number of nights to "2"
And I set distance to "10"
When I hit "search" button
```

Why is this so bad? With all these clicks and selects, it's hard to see what the steps are doing as a whole. The focus on detail makes it harder to give feedback on the overall flow or business logic. In addition, this makes the scenario more unwieldy and more work to maintain. The Gherkin scenario is tightly coupled to the screens that implement it: if any of the user interface details change, the scenario will need updating, even if the underlying business logic has not changed.

> **TIP** Good scenarios model business behavior, not system interactions. They describe the tasks a user is trying to accomplish, not the clicks and selects that the user needs to do to perform these tasks. If you follow the techniques we learned in the previous chapters, which focus on describing business behavior and goals, writing good-quality scenarios comes much more naturally.

Gherkin scenarios are intended to illustrate examples of business rules and of how the application is expected to behave in certain circumstances. They describe what the application should do, before a feature is implemented. For example, the previous steps might be part of the following business rule: "When a user searches for hotels in a given location, the system should show all the hotels that have availability on the requested dates and that are no more than the requested distance from the city center."

A more declarative equivalent of the steps shown earlier might be

```
When I look for a hotel with:
    | City  | Check-in Date | Nights | Distance from center |
    | Paris | 04-04-2019    | 2      | 10 km                |
```

Or even

```
When I look for a hotel within 10 km of Paris for 2 nights on 04-04-2019
```

Notice how we focus on what the user is trying to do and leave the step implementation to worry about how it does so. It's like the manager telling her team what tasks need to be done and leaving the team to decide what they need to do to make it happen. Scenarios written in this style tend to be more flexible and easier to read and to maintain.

Imperative-style Gherkin is a bit like a manager who micromanages her team, not just telling them what task they need to complete, but giving them detailed, prescriptive instructions on how to do so. It's a lot of extra work for the manager, and the team members don't have much freedom to decide for themselves the best way to complete each task.

A declarative style is more like when a manager explains what the end goal is; it's up to her people to come up with the best way of accomplishing it. In Gherkin, a declarative style gives us more flexibility when it comes to automating the scenario. For example, the hotel search step could interact with a web page, with a web service, or even with the system domain model. From the point of view of the scenario, how the step is implemented should make no difference to the validity of the business rule.

7.6.4   Good scenarios do one thing, and one thing well

In the previous section we transformed a group of six low-level interaction steps into a more business-centric one that captures what the user is really trying to do:

```
When I look for a hotel within 10 km of Paris for 2 nights on 04-04-2019
```

However, when we bring these smaller steps together, we come to realize that the business logic here is actually quite involved. We are simultaneously searching by distance and checking hotel availability, which are really two separate concerns. It is not necessarily a bad thing to illustrate such an example; we will need to get there eventually. But it might make it harder to read if this is the first scenario in the feature.

Features tend to be easier to understand if the scenarios start out with simple cases and build up progressively to more complex ones. Our scenario would be easier to follow if we were to start with a single concern first, such as searching by distance:

```
When I look for a hotel within 10 km of Paris
```

Once we have established that this case works correctly, we can explore more complex scenarios involving locations and availability dates.

> **TIP** Good scenarios focus on testing a single business rule. If a business rule is complex, or if a scenario gets too big and hard to read, a good trick is to break the scenario into smaller, more focused ones that test a specific aspect of the rule.

Scenarios in general are easier to understand, easier to maintain, and easier to troubleshoot if they focus on a single business rule. The scenario in listing 7.4 does not focus on a single rule, which is one of the reasons it is hard to follow. Instead of concentrating on what happens when a user searches for a hotel with various criteria, the scenario proceeds to book a room, start the payment process (presumably to check the correct total price), and then log out of the application:

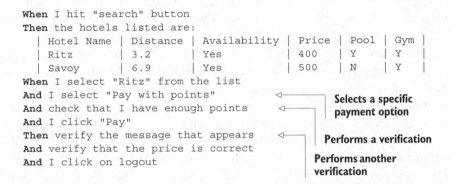

```
When I hit "search" button
Then the hotels listed are:
   | Hotel Name | Distance | Availability | Price | Pool | Gym |
   | Ritz       | 3.2      | Yes          | 400   | Y    | Y   |
   | Savoy      | 6.9      | Yes          | 500   | N    | Y   |
When I select "Ritz" from the list
And I select "Pay with points"            ◁
And check that I have enough points       ◁ ──┐  Selects a specific
And I click "Pay"                                payment option
Then verify the message that appears      ◁
And verify that the price is correct      ──┐  Performs a verification
And I click on logout
                                          Performs another
                                          verification
```

This is typical of manual or so-called "end-to-end" test scripts. It tries to cram as many checks as it can into a single scenario. But reading the scenario raises far more questions than it answers. What other payment options could I have, and how would they alter the outcome of the scenario? How many points do I need to pay, and what is the relationship between points and the price? What is the message that should appear, and why is it significant? And so on.

A more readable approach would be to focus on a single rule at a time. For example, the following scenario focuses on looking for hotels by distance:

```
Scenario: Search for available hotels by distance
   Given the following hotels:
      | Hotel Name | Location | Distance from center |
      | Ritz       | Paris    | 3.2                  |
      | Savoy      | Paris    | 6.9                  |
      | Hilton     | Paris    | 12.5                 |
   When I search for a hotel within 10 km of Paris
```

```
Then I should be presented with the following hotels:
   | Hotel Name | Location | Distance from center |
   | Ritz       | Paris    | 3.2                  |
   | Savoy      | Paris    | 6.9                  |
```

Other scenarios would explore business rules around room availability, payment options, and so forth.

It can be useful to have a few examples of complete user journeys in your scenarios. However, these will typically be high level examples of flows, which do not go into the details of each step. An example of this type of high-level scenario is shown:

```
Scenario: Booking a business trip
   Given Bindi needs to make a business trip to Paris
   When she books a flight and a hotel on the corporate booking system
   Then the trip should be placed in her calendar
   And her corporate credit card should be charged
```

The majority of the scenarios will focus on exploring examples and variations of specific business rules.

7.6.5   *Good scenarios have meaningful actors*

Did you notice how we switched from the first person ("I") to the third person ("Bindi") in that last scenario? This was quite intentional, and generally makes for more readable scenarios.

If you have ever worked in a team practicing User Experience (UX) design, you will probably have come across the term *persona*. In UX, a persona is a detailed, illustrated example of a typical user of your system. There are usually several personas for a given product. For an online travel planner, you might have Jill, the regional director, who travels every week and is frustrated at how long it takes her to plan relatively simple trips (figure 7.11). Or, for an online banking application, you might have Elsa, the young executive who is always on the go, and who needs to see the information she wants fast. And you might have Sam, the stay-at-home dad who consults his accounts on his laptop, keeps a close eye on his expenses, and who wants to see all the details of everything that goes on in his account.

Designers spend a lot of effort in writing realistic personas. They aren't simply generic user roles; they are rich descriptions, including goals, abilities, and background information. For the online banking application, the descriptions of Elsa and Sam could also include details about jobs, income, and spending habits.

Designers, and development teams in general, use personas to build applications that will respond better to the needs of real-world users. If you can imagine the person who will be using your feature, it is easier to get a feel for what might be useful for them.

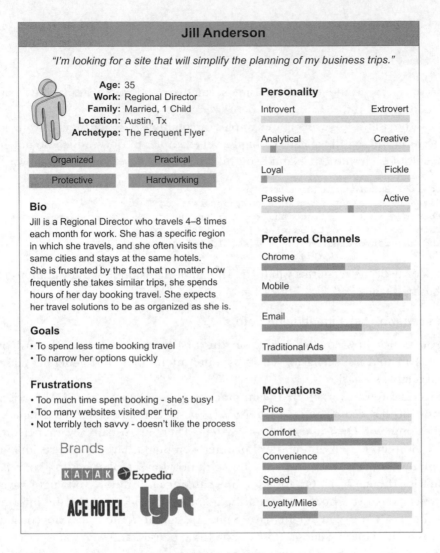

Figure 7.11   Jill's persona poster[6]

PERSONAS IN USER STORIES

This is where User Stories come into the picture. Many teams write User Stories with faceless, generic users, giving bland titles like "The User" or "The Customer."

> As a user
>
> I want to see my account details
>
> So that I can know how much money I have in my account

---

[6] Design and content courtesy of Xtensio (https://xtensio.com)

The first line of this story tells us very little and gives us no clues as to the finer points of what the user might be looking for. But when we introduce personas into these conversations, the User Stories become much more interesting. Suppose we present this story from the point of view of Elsa:

> Elsa, the young executive on the go
>
> Wants to view her account balance at a glance
>
> So that she can quickly know whether she needs to transfer money from her savings account

This story gives us many more hints about the sort of design Elsa might like. There are many ways to view a user's account details, but Elsa would surely prefer to see the figures of her primary accounts in a prominent font on the home page, rather than three clicks away and in the top-left corner of the screen.

USING PERSONAS IN SCENARIOS

Personas work well for acceptance criteria as well. They help us look at scenarios more critically, to assess whether they would really deliver value to our users.

Take the following scenario, for example:

```
Scenario: Account home page
  Given I have a savings account
  When I open my accounts home page
  Then I should see details about my account
```

This feels a tad vague. We don't describe what specific account details would be relevant, which leaves a lot to the imagination. But while having options to explore is a good thing, a design process needs constraints and guidelines to produce good results.

Now suppose we consider this scenario from the point of view of Sam. Sam watches his expenses like a hawk. So, he will want to know *which* details. From Sam's perspective, Sam is really interested in knowing how much money he has left to spend, and he knows that often the current balance of an account doesn't always reflect the actual amount available.

Taking this into consideration, we could write a scenario like this:

```
Scenario: Account owners should be able to see their balance at a glance
  Given Sam has the following accounts:
    | Type    | Number | Current Balance | Pending Transaction |
    | Current | 123456 | $530.00         | $-200.00            |
    | Savings | 234567 | $2500           |                     |
  When he views his account summary
  Then he should see the balance and pending transactions for each
  account:
    | Type    | Current Balance | Pending Transactions | Available |
    | Current | $530.00         | $-200.00             | $330.00   |
    | Savings | $2500           |                      | $2500.00  |
```

Notice how much richer this second example is? Not only does it give more details about what information is relevant and useful, but it directly addresses Sam's goals and concerns.

> **Soap opera personas**
>
> Personas are clearly a powerful tool. However, many teams don't work with personas in this sense. Many teams do not have a dedicated UX activity, or the time to invest in detailed user research. If you are in this category, do not be troubled! This won't stop you from making effective use of actors. If you don't have any full-blown personas handy, Agile coach Andy Palmer recommends using the idea of soap opera personas.[a] Rather than spending a lot of time upfront defining your personas, you simply introduce them on the go, as you write the stories.
>
> The idea comes from TV soap operas. When you watch a new series on Netflix, you don't get a detailed presentation of each new character. At best, you might get a short introduction from a narrator or a snarky comment from the main character: "This is my brother-in-law, Bill. He hates my guts."
>
> Instead, you start with simple characters, like "Carrie, the compliance officer" or "Barry, the small business owner." As the stories develop, we will learn more about Carrie and Barry. For example, Barry has a business account and is domiciled in Bermuda, which will subject him to extra attention from the compliance office. Or we might discover scenarios that don't fit any of our existing scenarios, such as Sandra the senior analyst, who needs to review cases that Carrie is not qualified to handle.
>
> ───────────────────────
>
> [a.] Andy Palmer, "Soap Opera Personas," March 8, 2014, http://andypalmer.com/2014/03/soap-opera-personas/

7.6.6   *Good scenarios focus on the essential and hide the incidental*

Gherkin scenarios are all about communication—communication between business-people and the development team, and communication between members of the development team. Each scenario has a message, a story to tell. However, when a scenario describes each step in detail, it is easy to lose track of the actual message. And this makes it harder to have conversations or give useful feedback about the business.

For example, the first five lines of the scenario in listing 7.4 read as follows:

```
Given I login to the Travel Booking App
Then I am on the Home Page
And I click the New Trip tab
And I click on the Hotels dropdown menu item
Then I am on the Hotel Search page
```

If our scenario is about searching for hotels based on availability and distance from the town center, we can assume that we know how to log on to the application. So, the first step can safely be assumed and implemented behind the scenes.

The following four steps describe the navigation from the home page to the Hotel Search page. But the subject of this scenario is not about navigation (which could change; what if the user has a bookmark that takes her directly to the search page? Would this change the business logic?). The subject of this scenario is about how you search for a hotel, once you are on the Hotel Search page. All these steps could be resumed in a single step that would bring the application to the desired state, such as the following:

```
Given Bindi needs to make a business trip to Paris
```

But irrelevant and overly detailed steps are not the only place we find incidental detail. For example, the Then step in listing 7.4 describes the hotels that Bindi should see:

```
Then the hotels listed are:
  | Hotel Name | Distance | Availability | Price | Pool | Gym |
  | Ritz       | 3.2      | Yes          | 400   | Y    | Y   |
  | Savoy      | 6.9      | Yes          | 500   | Y    | Y   |
```

This step contains a lot of information, much of which is not relevant to the scenario we are looking at. For the purposes of this scenario (which focus on searching by distance), we really don't need details about hotel facilities such as pool and gym. Nor is the price relevant, as we are not interested in payment for this scenario. The availability is important but could be assumed to be true for all hotels for the purpose of this scenario.

Once we remove all this, we are left with a much more concise and focused table that resumes the essential information that the reader needs to know:

```
Then the hotels listed are:
  | Hotel Name | Distance |
  | Ritz       | 3.2      |
  | Savoy      | 6.9      |
```

We are still missing some important information: Where do these hotels come from? Why these hotels in particular? Real-world Gherkin scenarios often fall into the trap of relying on production or production-like data.

Good Gherkin scenarios show a logical progression from the first Given statement to the final When, and this includes describing and setting up any initial data that the scenario needs to work. In this instance, we could describe the known hotels before Bindi performs her search, with a step like the following:

```
Given the following hotels have available rooms:
  | Hotel Name | Location | Distance from center |
  | Ritz       | Paris    | 3.2                  |
  | Savoy      | Paris    | 6.9                  |
  | Hilton     | Paris    | 12.5                 |
```

TIP Well-written scenarios describe both behavior and data. When a scenario uses data to illustrate behavior (such as in these search-related scenarios), it should describe the initial state and the final state and manage or set up the test data to ensure that the system is in the expected initial state.

Using the techniques we have seen so far, the first half of our original scenario could be rewritten as follows:

```
Scenario: Search for available hotels by distance
  Given Bindi needs to make a business trip to Paris
  And the following hotels have available rooms:
    | Hotel Name | Location | Distance from center |
    | Ritz       | Paris    | 3.2                  |
    | Savoy      | Paris    | 6.9                  |
    | Hilton     | Paris    | 12.5                 |
  When Bindi searches for a hotel within 10 km of Paris
  Then she should be presented with the following hotels:
    | Hotel Name | Location | Distance from center |
    | Ritz       | Paris    | 3.2                  |
    | Savoy      | Paris    | 6.9                  |
```

Incidental detail often slips into example tables as well. For example, the following scenario describes how new Frequent Flyer members can earn points from flights that they took in the three previous months:

```
Scenario Outline: Earning Frequent Flyer points for past flights
  Given Terry joined the Frequent Flyer program on 20-01-2019
  When he asks for this flight to count towards his Frequent Flyer
points:
    | Booking Reference | <Booking> |
    | Flight Number     | <Number>  |
    | Flight Date       | <Date>    |
    | Airline           | <Airline> |
    | Departure         | <From>    |
    | Destination       | <To>      |
  Then the flight should be credited: <Credit>
Examples:
  | Booking | Number | Date       | Airline     | From   | To     | Credit |
  | DDSF245 | FH-101 | 20-12-2018 | Flying High | London | Paris  | Yes    |
  | SFGG345 | FH-201 | 21-10-2018 | Flying High | London | Oslo   | Yes    |
  | DDSF245 | FH-092 | 20-11-2018 | Flying High | London | Paris  | Yes    |
  | SFGG345 | FH-999 | 25-05-2018 | Flying High | London | Berlin | No     |
  | KEGR264 | OA-102 | 20-12-2018 | Other Air   | Paris  | Madrid | No     |
```

This scenario has a lot of unnecessary incidental information, which makes it harder to discern the actual business logic. There are many rows of data, but it is not immediately obvious why some are credited and some are not. The scenario is also missing a few details that would make it easier to digest.

Generally, a table should only include information that is directly relevant to the business rule being described. For example, the booking reference has no direct affect on whether a flight will be credited or not, so this information could be hidden in the implementation details.

One useful rule of thumb is to question the value of any column whose values are identical or have no clear influence on the outcome of the scenario. For example, in the table, the departure and destination cities have no bearing on whether a flight should count toward the new member's Frequent Flyer points. This information will be important when it comes to knowing how many points were earned, but that is not the topic of this scenario.

Although the flight number might seem like an incidental detail, we've decided to keep it as people working for Flying High Airlines are intimately familiar with them. When removing incidental detail from a scenario it's important to remember that we need to remove enough of it so that the scenario is focused on the things we want to highlight, but not too much, so that it doesn't become overly generic and vague.

We can also add extra information in a table, or in the scenario itself, to give a few more clues about the examples. In the following version, we have added a Notes column to give readers some clues about the business rule being applied for each example.

```
Scenario Outline: Earning Frequent Flyer points for past flights
Users can request credits for Frequent Flyer flights completed in the past
⇨ three months
  Given Terry joined the Frequent Flyer program on 20-01-2019
  When Terry requests credit for flight <Number> on <Date> with <Airline>
  Then the flight should be credited: <Credited>
  Examples:
```

Number	Date	Airline	Credited	Notes
FH-101	01-02-2019	Flying High	Yes	
FH-999	20-10-2018	Flying High	No	Flight too old
OA-102	01-02-2019	Other Air	No	Not with Flying High

The story of the fish seller

Eliminating the incidental is a bit like the old joke about the fish seller.[a] A fish seller in a busy marketplace has just painted a new sign. It reads: "Fresh fish sold here."

A friend passing by notices the sign, and points out, "Would you sell rotten fish?" So the fish seller changes the sign to "Fish sold here."

Another friend in the vicinity sees the new sign and says, "Why do you bother saying 'sold'? No one expects you to give them away." So he updates the sign once more, to "Fish here."

Later in the day, another friend comes by. He reads the sign and asks, "Why say 'here'? Where else would they be?" So the seller replaces his sign with a single word: "Fish."

Finally, another friend passes by and sees the sign. He says, quite logically, "But everyone can see you sell fish!" So the last remaining word on the sign disappears.

[a.] This story dates back to at least 1890, when it was printed in the *New Haven Register*.

7.6.7   *Gherkin scenarios are not test scripts*

A common practice for teams new to BDD is to transform traditional test scripts or manual test cases into Gherkin scenarios. This is generally not a good idea.

Manual testing works very differently than automated testing. In a manual test script, you often try to do as much testing as possible in a single pass, because it takes time to set up the environment and step through the screens. You want to make the most of the time on each screen to test as much as you can.

But this isn't a good strategy for automated acceptance tests or BDD scenarios. Well-designed automated acceptance tests run much more quickly than a manual test, but to be useful they need to give precise feedback when something goes wrong. BDD scenarios explore business rules using examples and counterexamples, in a language that businesspeople can understand and give useful feedback on. Long test scripts that focus on a single flow make it much harder to have these conversations and make it easier to miss important edge cases or variations.

It is easy to spot manual test scripts that have been automated. They often have test-script style names like "End-to-end Hotel Booking Test" or "TC1–Hotel Booking–positive test case." Or they are written in the imperative style ("Check that I have enough points" or "Verify the message that appears"), as if they are instructions to a human tester. Test script scenarios also tend to be made up of long lists of low-level or UI interactions, with a mixture of Given, When, and Then statements in no particular order. They often describe what the tester should do ("Verify the message that appears") but without describing the actual expected outcome.

> **TIP**   A scenario with words like "verify" or "check" is often a test script in disguise. Well-written scenarios describe the outcomes they want to achieve in unambiguous terms rather than giving general instructions to a tester.

For example, in listing 7.4, we see the following steps:

```
When I select "Ritz" from the list
And I select "Pay with points"
And check that I have enough points
```

These steps would work as instructions for a human tester, who could interpret them sensibly. However, for an automated acceptance test, "Check that I have enough points" is far too vague. A better approach would be to have a separate scenario to explore the business rules around paying with points, such as in the following example:

```
Scenario: Travelers can pay for a hotel booking using points
Frequent Flyers can book rooms using points at a rate of $1 per point
  Given the following hotels have available rooms:
     | Hotel Name | Location | Nightly cost |
     | Ritz       | New York | 500          |
  And Bindi has a balance of 1200 points
  When she books 2 nights at the Ritz
```

```
Then she should be charged a remaining balance of $0
And she should have 200 remaining points
```

Having a separate scenario means we can explore different aspects and counterexamples of a specific business rule, which is much harder to do with an end-to-end test script. For example, we could use a scenario outline to explore different ways a traveler can pay with a combination of cash and points:

```
Scenario Outline: Travelers can pay using cash and points
Points are consumed before cash
    Given the following hotels have available rooms:
        | Hotel Name | Location | Nightly cost |
        | Ritz       | New York | 500          |
    And Bindi has a balance of <Available Points> points
    When she books 2 nights at the Ritz
    Then she should be charged a remaining balance of $<Cash cost>
    And she should have <Remaining Points> points remaining
    Examples:
        | Available Points | Cash cost | Remaining Points |
        | 1200             | 0         | 200              |
        | 800              | 200       | 0                |
        | 0                | 1000      | 0                |
```

Good Gherkin scenarios are very effective at describing business rules and behavior and exploring what can happen at different stages in a user journey. Together, scenarios written this way give a much more complete picture of the user journey than a single, end-to-end test script.

7.6.8 *Good scenarios are independent*

As we have seen, long-winded scenarios like the one in listing 7.4 are far from ideal. Scenarios with many steps, particularly UI tests, tend to be slower and more brittle than short, focused ones. A brittle test is one that is prone to failing randomly, for no apparent reason. Long-running web tests are particularly subject to this type of failure; modern asynchronous applications can sometimes be tricky to automate in a reliable manner, and web tests can sometimes also fail due to system load or network issues.

Sometimes long end-to-end tests are written not as a single scenario with lots of steps, but as a sequence of related scenarios, where each scenario follows on from the previous one. An example of this approach is shown in the following listing.

Listing 7.5   A sequence of scenarios

```
Scenario: Step 1 - User navigates to the booking page
    Given I log in to the Corporate Booking App
    When I click on the "Hotels" button
    Then I should see the Hotel search page

Scenario: Step 2 - User looks for a hotel by location
    Given I Enter "Paris" into the city field
```

We expect this scenario to take the user to the Hotel search page.

Once on the search page, the user starts entering search criteria.

```
    And I set price range to "Any"
    And I set check-in date to "04-04-2019"
    And I enter number of nights to "2"
    And I click on OK
    Then I should see the relevant hotels
```

> Once a list of matching hotels has been found, select a hotel.

```
Scenario: Step 3 - User pays with points and cash
    Given I select the Ritz hotel
    And I click on Pay with Points and Cash
    Then I should see a dialog asking how many points I want to spend
...
```

> More scenarios perform other related actions.

The first scenario takes the user to the Hotel search page, and the second searches for a hotel in a given location. The second scenario will only work if the first one completed successfully. Likewise, the third scenario will only work if the second was successful. Other similar scenarios would follow to complete the user journey.

A series of related scenarios is certainly easier to read than a single scenario with a large number of steps, but the result can be just as fragile. If one scenario fails, the following ones will be compromised, making it harder to get a clear picture of the health of the application.

Teams working with data processing or messaging applications often have similar problems when they try to simulate a flow of production-like data through many stages of processing. The testing infrastructure can be hard to set up and maintain, steps are often slow to run, and if one step fails, the following scenarios will also be compromised.

Nevertheless, businesspeople often find this format useful when it comes to describing a complete user journey. Many teams like to have a few end-to-end scenarios to give the bigger picture, before using more focused scenarios to explore specific business rules at each stage of the process.

> **TIP** It's important to remember that even if the scenarios live together in the same feature file, each scenario should be independent. Each scenario should be able to work in isolation: a scenario should not rely on a previous one running to set up data or to put the system into a particular state.

A better approach is to organize a series of independent scenarios that illustrate each step of a user journey. Each scenario is responsible for putting the test environment into the correct initial state and verifying that it completes this step of the process correctly. If one step fails, the others can still be executed, which makes it easier to troubleshoot issues. An example of this approach is shown in the following listing.

Listing 7.6   A series of related-but-independent scenarios

```
Scenario: A traveler can look for a hotel by location and price
    Given Bindi needs to travel to New York for business
```

```
And the following hotels have available rooms:
   | Hotel Name | Location   | Nightly cost | In policy |
   | Ritz       | Paris      | 400          | Yes       |
   | Hilton     | New York   | 600          | Yes       |
   | Conrad     | New York   | 800          | No        |
When she looks for hotels in New York
Then she should be shown the following hotels:
   | Hotel Name | Location   | Nightly cost | In policy |
   | Hilton     | New York   | 600          | Yes       |
   | Conrad     | New York   | 800          | No        |
```

```
Scenario: A traveler books a hotel using their corporate credit card
   Given Bindi is looking for hotels in New York
   When she books a room in the New York Hilton with her corporate card
   Then the booking should be placed on hold
   And the travel plan should be submitted to Logistics for approval
```

```
Scenario: Each trip needs to be approved by a logistics officer
   Given Bindi has booked the following trip:
      | Destination | Date       | Nights | Hotel  | Flight  |
      | New York    | 15-05-2020 | 3      | Hilton | FH-101  |
   And Logan is a logistics officer
   When Logan reviews his list of tasks
   Then Logan should see the following trips in his inbox:
      | Destination | Date            | Bookings      | Status           |
      | New York    | 15-18 May, 2020 | Flight, Hotel | Pending Approved |
```

> **Logan, a logistics officer, needs to approve Bindi's travel plans.**

```
Scenario: Travelers can see their approved upcoming trips
   Given Bindi has booked the following trip:
      | Destination | Date       | Nights | Hotel  | Flight  |
      | New York    | 15-05-2020 | 3      | Hilton | FH-101  |
   And the trip has been approved by logistics
   When she reviews her upcoming trips
   Then her upcoming trips should include:
      | Destination | Date            | Bookings      | Status    |
      | New York    | 15-18 May, 2020 | Flight, Hotel | Approved  |
```

Each scenario in listing 7.5 illustrates part of the story of a business traveler booking a trip in a corporate travel system. Each scenario semantically builds on the previous ones; you read them in sequence to get the full picture. But each scenario is independent and responsible for setting up its own test data. So, if one scenario fails, the others will still work correctly.

There is another more subtle advantage to this approach. Each of these scenarios is the starting point for a conversation about what else could happen. For example, in the third scenario, Bindi gets her trip approved. But what if the trip was not approved? This could lead to another complete feature file that explores the approval process in more detail.

7.7   *But where are all the details?*

You will notice how all the scenarios we have been looking at are very business focused and high level. This is one of the things that makes them easier to maintain than more granular scenarios. Sometimes, though, readers also like to know what a user needs to do in more detail to perform a particular task. In the following chapters you'll see how to write high-level tests at this level that are both very maintainable and that still provide all the nitty-gritty low-level details for anyone who needs them.

Summary

- You can turn examples into executable specifications by writing them as scenarios using variations on the Given . . . When . . . Then format.
- The executed scenarios are organized in feature files.
- You can make scenarios more concise and more expressive by using embedded data tables and table-driven scenarios.
- Scenarios can be completed with background information and tags.

Hopefully you've now learned enough to be able to write your own feature definitions, illustrated with concise, expressive scenarios. In the next chapter, you'll see how to automate and implement this process using different languages and environments.

Part 3

How do I build it?
Coding the BDD way

In the chapters in part 2, you learned about the importance of conversation and collaboration in the BDD process. You also learned that you need to work with team members to define acceptance criteria in a clear and unambiguous format that can be automated using tools such as Cucumber.

In part 3, we look under the hood to see how you can do this automation. While part 2 should be understood by the whole team, part 3 gets a bit more technical and will be of more interest to testers and developers.

In chapter 8, you'll learn about tools that you can use to automate the executable specifications we defined in part 2. Automation is an important part of BDD; it forms the basis of the automated acceptance criteria that verify the features being delivered and of the living documentation that illustrates and documents these features.

As with any code base, the maintenance of automated acceptance tests can be costly if they're not written well. In chapter 9, you'll learn how to structure and organize your automated acceptance criteria to make them easier to understand and to maintain.

In chapters 10 and 11, you'll learn about writing automated acceptance criteria for web applications, including why and when you should implement your acceptance criteria as web tests. Many teams struggle in this area, so we'll look at how to write high-quality automated web tests using Selenium Web-Driver in some detail. And in chapter 12, you'll learn about the Screenplay

Pattern, a powerful technique to make your automation code more flexible and more scalable.

Automated acceptance tests aren't just for web testing. In chapter 13, we'll look at techniques for implementing automated acceptance tests for pure business rules and other requirements that don't need to be verified through the UI.

In chapter 14, we'll focus on introducing automated acceptance tests to an existing software system. You'll learn how Journey Mapping can help you identify and visualize high-value workflows and test scenarios, and how using a layered architecture can help you design scalable test automation frameworks. To help you gain a better understanding of non-Java test automation stacks, we'll discuss examples written in TypeScript and using Serenity/JS.

In chapter 15, we'll continue to explore the idea of layering the architecture of our test automation system and ways to reflect business vocabulary in our code. We'll also look at how Serenity/JS APIs can help you make your test automation code portable across test integration tools and easy to share and reuse across projects and teams.

Communication and feedback are essential parts of the BDD process, and living documentation is an important part of the communication process. In chapter 16, you'll see how to produce high-quality living documentation out of your automated acceptance criteria. We'll introduce concepts such as feature readiness and feature coverage, which you use to keep tabs on project progress and overall product quality. We'll also see how well-written BDD unit tests serve as effective technical documentation.

From executable specifications to automated acceptance tests

This chapter covers

- The basic principles of automating your scenario steps
- The responsibilities of a step definition method
- Implementing step definitions using Cucumber in Java and TypeScript
- Setting up virtual environments for your tests

Over the previous few chapters, you've seen how the BDD life cycle takes acceptance criteria and turns them into executable specifications. Acceptance criteria start as brief notes you write on the back of your story cards that help define when a story or feature is complete. During Three Amigos sessions or other requirements discovery workshops, these notes are fleshed out into more complete examples and counterexamples that illustrate business rules and objectives. And as we saw in the previous chapter, you can write more complete versions of these acceptance criteria in the form of Gherkin scenarios, using the Given . . . When . . . Then notation.[1]

---

[1] The Gherkin language is not the only way we can write executable specifications, but it is one of the most frequently used, so we will focus our examples on automating scenarios in this format in the next few chapters.

A lot of the value in BDD comes from the conversations about these scenarios. This is why collaborating to write these scenarios is so important. Not all scenarios need to be automated; some may be too tricky to automate cost-effectively and can be left to manual testing. Others may only be of marginal interest to the business and might be better off implemented as unit or integration tests. Still others may be experimental and might not be understood well enough to define clear scenarios; in this case, it could be worthwhile to do some initial prototyping to get a better feel for what's really needed.[2]

But when a scenario can be automated, when it makes sense to do so, and when it's done well, automating the scenario brings its own set of undeniable benefits:

- *Testers spend less time on repetitive regression testing.* When acceptance criteria and the corresponding scenarios are written in close collaboration with testers, automated versions of these scenarios give testers more confidence in new releases. The testers can understand and relate more easily to what the automated tests are verifying, because they took part in defining them. In addition, the application that the testers receive for testing will have already passed a broad range of simpler test cases, letting the testers focus on more complex or exploratory testing.

- *New versions can be released faster and more reliably.* Because less manual testing is required, new releases can be pushed out more efficiently. New versions are less likely to introduce regressions. Comprehensive automated testing is essential if you're trying to implement continuous integration, continuous delivery, or continuous deployment.

- *The automated scenarios give a more accurate vision of the current state of the project.* You can use them to build a progress dashboard that describes which features have been delivered and how they've been tested, based on the results of the automated scenarios.

Continuous integration, continuous delivery, and continuous deployment

Continuous integration is a practice that involves automatically building and testing a project whenever a new code change is committed to the source code repository. Continuous integration is a valuable feedback mechanism, alerting developers to potential integration issues or regressions as early as possible. But to be really effective, continuous integration strongly relies on a robust and comprehensive set of automated tests.

Continuous delivery is an extension of continuous integration, where every build is a potential release. Whenever a developer puts new code into the source code repository, a build server compiles a new release candidate version. If this release candidate

---

[2] Highly experimental start-up applications might fall into this category. If the business needs to get market feedback to discover what features they really need, it will be hard to formalize scenarios with very much detail.

passes a series of automated quality checks (unit tests, automated acceptance tests, automated performance tests, code quality metrics, etc.), it can be pushed into production as soon as business stakeholders give their go-ahead.

Continuous deployment is similar to continuous delivery, but there's no manual approval stage. Any release candidate that passes the automated quality checks will automatically be deployed into production. The deployment process itself is often automated using tools like Chef, Puppet, or Octopus Deploy.

Both continuous delivery and continuous deployment encourage a much more streamlined, efficient deployment process. And both require a very high degree of confidence in the application's automated test suites.

In chapter 6 you saw how to express scenarios using the Given . . . When . . . Then notation. In this chapter, you'll learn how to write the test code that automates these scenarios (see figure 8.1).

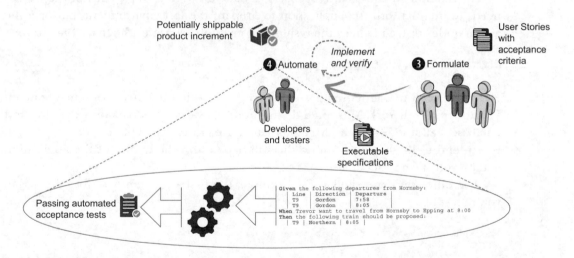

Figure 8.1   In this chapter we'll look at how to turn executable specifications into automated acceptance tests.

When you automate these scenarios, they become *executable specifications*, but these will be reported as *pending*, or incomplete, until you write the underlying code that actually exercises the application and verifies the outcomes. Once this happens, you can talk of *automated acceptance tests*.

In chapter 3, you saw how to set up a simple Cucumber project using Java and Maven, how to write features and scenarios in feature files, and how to implement basic automation code ("glue code") for these scenarios. In this chapter, we will look at how tools like Cucumber allow us to convert executable specifications into automated acceptance tests in much more detail. But before we do this, we need to discuss some general principles that will apply no matter what tool you choose.

8.1   Introduction to automating scenarios

Before we look at specific tools, let's go through the basics. In chapter 7, you saw how to describe requirements in terms of plain-text scenarios like the following:

```
Scenario: Flights outside Europe earn points based on distance traveled
    Given the distance from London to New York is 5500 km
    And Tara is a Frequent Flyer traveler
    When she completes a flight between London and New York
    Then she should earn 550 points
```

The scenario title

The scenario steps

This scenario is just loosely structured text. It explains what requirement you're trying to illustrate and how you intend to demonstrate that your application fulfills this requirement. But how you actually perform each step will depend on your application and on how you decide to interact with it.

For example, the preceding scenario is made up of four steps. Each of these steps needs to interact with the application to prepare the test environment, perform the action under test, and check the results. For example, consider the first `Given` step:

```
Given the distance from London to New York is 5500 km
```

Here you need to configure a test database to provide the correct distance between London and New York. You could do this in many ways: inject data directly into a test database, call a web service, or manipulate a user interface. The text describes what you intend to do, but how you do this will depend on the nature of the application and on your technical choices.

The other steps are similar. For example, the first `When` step describes the action you're testing:

```
When she completes a flight between London and New York
```

Again, this step describes what you want to do. You want to record a flight from London to New York so that you can check how many points Tara earns. But how you do this requires more knowledge about your application and its architecture.

Tools like Cucumber can't turn a text scenario into an automated test by themselves; they need your help. You need a way to tell your testing framework what each of these steps means in terms of your application and how it must manipulate or query your application to perform its task. This is where step definitions come into play.

8.1.1   Step definitions interpret the steps

Step definitions are essentially bits of code that interpret the text in feature files and know what to do for each step (see figure 8.2).

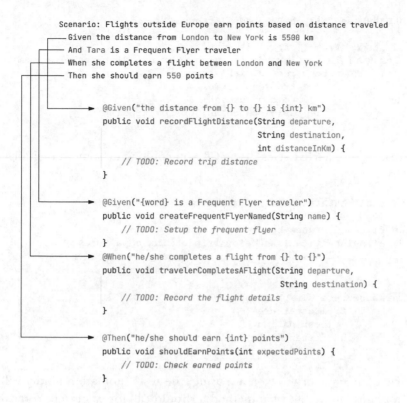

Figure 8.2   Each line (or step) of a scenario maps to a step definition test.

Step definitions can be implemented in a variety of programming languages depending on the test automation library being used. In some cases, the language used to implement the step definitions may even be different than that used to write the application.

For example, a Cucumber step definition written in Java might look like this:

```java
FlightDatabase flightDatabase = FlightDatabase.instance();

@Given("the distance from {} to {} is {int} km").
public void recordFlightDistance(String departure,
                                 String destination,
                                 int distanceInKm) {
    flightDatabase.recordTripDistance()
            .from(departure)
            .to(destination)
            .as(distanceInKm).kilometres();
}
```

What text should trigger this step definition

The step definition method

The code that implements this step

The form varies from one language to another, but the essential information is the same. In TypeScript, for example, the same example could be written like this:

```
const flightDatabase = FlightDatabase.instance();

Given('the distance from {} to {} is {int} km',
      function (origin: string, destination: string, distanceInKm: number) {
            flightDatabase.recordTripDistance()
                          .from(departure)
                          .to(destination)
                          .as(distanceInKm).kilometres()
})
```

If you are working with a .NET stack, using C#, you could write some very similar code using SpecFlow:

```
FlightDatabase flightDatabase = FlightDatabase.instance();

[Given(@"the flying distance between (.*) and (.*) is (.*) km")]
public void DefineTheFlyingDistanceForATrip(string departure,
                                            string destination,
                                            int distance)
{
    flightDatabase.recordTripDistance()
                  .from(departure)
                  .to(destination)
                  .as(distanceInKm).kilometres();
}
```

No matter what language or tool you are using, the test automation library will read the feature files and figure out what method it should call for each step. You can also tell the library how to extract important data out of the text and pass that data to the step definition method. But it's the step definition's job to do whatever needs to be done to perform this step.

Because the feature files and annotations consist of free text, there's always a risk that when the text in a feature file is modified, you may forget to update the text in the annotation, or vice versa. In this case, the affected scenario or scenarios will be flagged as pending once again. To help developers manage this sort of issue, many modern IDEs have plug-ins for BDD tools such as Cucumber and SpecFlow, which allow you to navigate from scenarios to step definition code, and that highlight steps in scenarios that don't have matching methods.

In the remainder of the chapter, we will look at how to write your step definition methods in more detail, focusing particularly on Java and TypeScript. But before we start, let's see how to set up a professional test automation project in both these languages.

8.2   *Setting up your project*

There are many BDD tools you can use to automate scenarios like the ones we've been looking at, using different languages and often targeting different environments. The choice of which tool is right for your team will depend on how comfortable the team is with a particular language and environment (and how willing they are to learn a new one!), what technology stack your project is using, and the goals and target audience of your BDD activities.

Throughout the rest of this chapter, we will learn how to write high-quality step definition code using examples in Java and JavaScript,[3] the most popular options at the time of writing. At the end of the chapter, we will give a brief overview of BDD tools for .NET and Python. The list of tools we'll study is far from exhaustive, but the techniques we'll discuss should be generally applicable no matter which tool you choose.

Automation tests are code, just like production code. It's when we think of them as simple scripts, things that can be easily and quickly written with little skill or care involved, that we get into trouble. When automated acceptance test suites are poorly designed, they can add to the maintenance overhead, costing more to update and fix when new features are added than they contribute in value to the project. For this reason, it's important to design your acceptance tests well. In this chapter, we'll also look at a number of techniques and patterns that can help you write automated acceptance tests that are meaningful, reliable, and maintainable.

To explore the features of each tool, we'll look at how you might automate scenarios involving the Flying High airline's Frequent Flyer application, introduced in the previous chapters. The Frequent Flyer program is designed to encourage flyers to fly with Flying High by allowing them to accumulate points that they can spend on flights or on other purchases. In this chapter's examples, we'll study some of the requirements around accumulating and managing Frequent Flyer points. But before we get into the code, let's see how you can set up a test automation project from scratch and start writing your own test code.

8.2.1 Setting up a Cucumber project in Java or TypeScript

In chapter 3, we saw how you can create a basic project structure using the Serenity Cucumber Starter project on GitHub (http://mng.bz/gRKV); you can clone this project yourself or use it as a template to create your own project on GitHub (see figure 8.3). The Serenity Cucumber Starter project also contains some sample configuration files and a simple web test to get you started. The Serenity/JS project also has a number of template projects you can use if you prefer TypeScript (http://mng.bz/aPp7 and http://mng.bz/yapB).

8.2.2 Organizing a Cucumber project in Java

In figure 8.4, you can see a fairly typical project organization for a Cucumber test suite written in Java and using Maven or Gradle as a build tool.

---

[3] Java is by far the most commonly used language in test automation at the time of writing, whereas JavaScript is the fastest growing. In this book we're using TypeScript, which offers all of the JavaScript features, as well as the TypeScript type system. This type of system will make it easier for you to avoid common programming mistakes and easier for your editor or IDE to understand the structure of your programs and therefore better support your work.

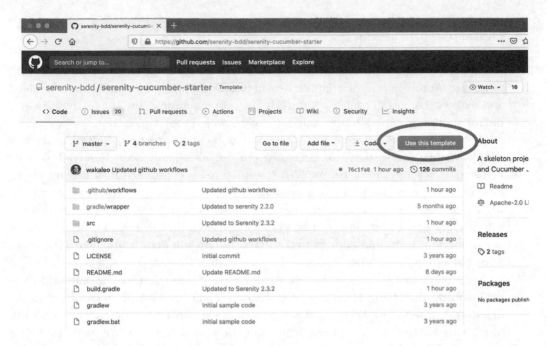

Figure 8.3   You can also create a starter project using the Serenity Cucumber Starter template on GitHub.

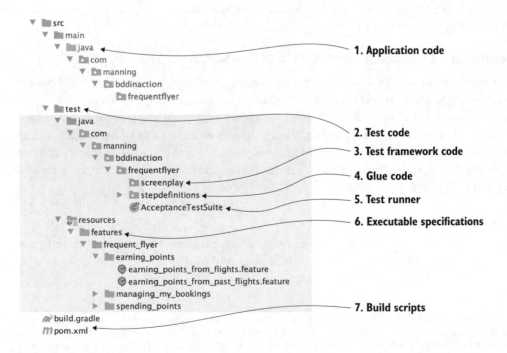

Figure 8.4   An example of a Cucumber project using Java

This project follows the Maven conventions, which are widely used in the Java world and help to make a project easier to read for developers new to the project.

Application code and resources go in the src/main folder (1). This is how we will organize our sample project, but not all projects are like this. Many larger Maven and Gradle projects often have multiple modules, with the acceptance test suite being one module among many others. In projects like this, there may be no need for any application code in the src/main/java folder.

Anything related to automated tests, including executable specifications, goes in the src/test folder (2). In this folder you will find a java subfolder, where your Java test code goes, and another folder called resources.

The java folder contains several important classes and subfolders, and they can be organized in many different ways. The one shown here is just one example. In the project shown here, the Cucumber feature files are executed by a test runner class called `AcceptanceTestSuite` (5). The code that actually executes the steps in the Cucumber scenarios is called glue code and can be found in the `stepdefinitions` package (4). Other test automation framework code goes in packages, such as the domain package shown here (3).

The resources folder contains non-Java files needed to run your tests, in particular the features directory (6), which will contain your Cucumber feature files. A common convention is to place your feature files in the src/test/resources/features folder, and this is the convention we will follow throughout this book. If there are too many feature files in the same directory, however, they become hard to read, so feature files are generally grouped by capability or in some other structure.

8.2.3   *Organizing a Cucumber project in TypeScript*

In figure 8.5, you can see a fairly typical layout of a Node.js project implemented in TypeScript and using popular Cucumber JS conventions around the structure of the features directory. In our example project, application code and resources go in the src folder (1). However, the structure and layout of Node.js projects is not as homogenous as in the Java world. You will find that different projects follow different conventions depending on their authors' preferences, as well as tools and frameworks used.

When it comes to test automation, projects using Cucumber JS tend to follow Cucumber conventions and store feature files under the features folder (2). This folder typically contains subfolders such as step_definitions that host files containing step definition libraries, or support, which contains any supporting code such as configuration, parameter types definitions, and so on. It's worth noting that Cucumber JS is typically configured to look for step definitions in all the TypeScript or JavaScript files under the features folder. However, even though using those subfolders is just a convention and your code will work even if you named them differently, many IDEs expect those conventions to be followed to provide you with code navigation support.

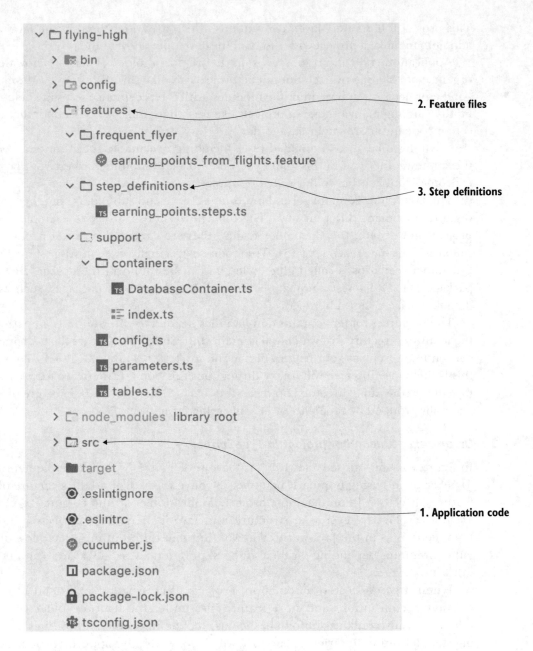

Figure 8.5   An example of a Cucumber project using TypeScript

8.3   *Running Cucumber scenarios*

A test automation project isn't much use if we can't actually run any tests. In this section, you will learn how to set up and configure test runners in Java or JavaScript that will execute your Cucumber scenarios.

8.3.1 Cucumber test runner classes in Java

In a Java project, you need to write a special class to run your scenarios. This class contains no such test code, just configuration logic. A very simple Cucumber runner class is illustrated in the following listing.

Listing 8.1 A simple Cucumber runner class

```
package com.manning.bddinaction.frequentflyer;

import net.serenitybdd.cucumber.CucumberWithSerenity;
import org.junit.runner.RunWith;
                                          The @RunWith
                                          annotation
@RunWith(Cucumber.class)
public class RunCucumberTest {}          The class itself
                                         should be empty.
```

This class will look for feature files inside the `com.manning.bddinaction.frequent-flyer` package and its subdirectories. However, in practice this can be a little confusing and make the feature files harder to find.

A better approach is to use the `@CucumberOptions` annotation to configure the finer details, as in the following listing.

Listing 8.2 The `@CucumberOptions` section to configure your test runner class

```
package com.manning.bddinaction.frequentflyer;

import io.cucumber.junit.CucumberOptions;
import net.serenitybdd.cucumber.CucumberWithSerenity;      Specifies the root
import org.junit.runner.RunWith;                           directory of your
                                                           feature files
@RunWith(CucumberWithSerenity.class)
@CucumberOptions(                                          Only runs
    features = "classpath:features",                       scenarios
    tags = "@important",                                   with this tag
    glue = "com.manning.bddinaction.frequentflyer.stepdefinitions",
    plugin = {"pretty","json:target/cucumber.json"}
)                               Extra functionality    Glue code
public class AcceptanceTestSuite {}  can be defined using   goes under
                                     Cucumber plug-ins.     this package.
```

As you can see from the example in listing 8.2, the `@CucumberOptions` annotation gives you a wide range of options. The most important of these is the features attribute, which tells Cucumber where to find your feature files, and the glue attribute, which tells Cucumber where to look for your glue code (which we will talk more about shortly). Some of the other attributes include the tags attribute, which lets you define a tag or Cucumber tag expression (more on these later) to limit test execution to a subset of your tests, and the plug-in attribute, which lets you add extra capabilities such as writing the scenarios to the console as the tests are executed, and generating the Cucumber test results as a JSON file (which is what the two plug-ins shown here do).

8.3.2   *Running Cucumber scenarios in JavaScript and TypeScript*

Projects using Cucumber JS invoke the tool using its command-line interface and don't require a runner class, as all the configuration parameters are provided as arguments on the command line:

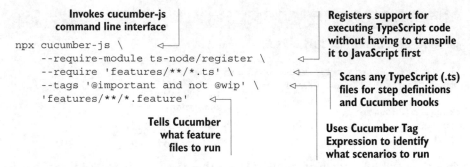

Of course, having to specify all these arguments every time we want to run our test suite would be rather inconvenient. A better way to do that is to capture them in a Cucumber profile defined in the cucumber.js file in the project root directory:

```
// cucumber.js
module.exports = {
    default: `--require-module ts-node/register --require
      'features/**/*.ts'`,
}
```

Cucumber JS detects this file automatically, which allows us to simplify the command we used previously:

```
npx cucumber-js 'features/**/*.feature'
```

We can take this a step further, though, and wire execution of Cucumber test suite to an NPM test script defined in our package.json:

```
"scripts": {
  "test": "cucumber-js 'features/**/*.feature'"
},
```

With this script definition in place, the test suite can be invoked by running

```
npm test
```

This configuration allows us to also execute scenarios matching a given name,

```
npm test -- --name='Flights outside Europe'
```

or matching a given Cucumber tag expression:

```
npm test -- --tags='@important and not @wip'
```

Note that these two commands use a double dash (`--`) to delimit the npm test command from Cucumber arguments such as `--name` or `--tags`. The double dash is a special NPM argument that instructs it to pass any arguments that follow to the script executed by the NPM test. To find out more about the available options, run

```
npx cucumber-js --help
```

8.4 Writing glue code

Tools such as Cucumber work by reading Gherkin scenarios and running a corresponding piece of code for each line in the scenario. Cucumber's job is to figure out what method it needs to call for any given line in a scenario and what test data it needs to pass to the test automation code. Let's start with the following scenario:

```
Scenario: Flights within Europe earn 100 points
  Given Tara is a Standard Frequent Flyer member
  When she flies from Paris and Berlin in Economy class
  Then she should earn 100 points
```

We can turn this scenario into an automated test by writing some *glue code*, which binds the natural language of the scenarios to the actual automation code; it is how we tell Cucumber what code it needs to execute at each step of a scenario. We call this a *step definition method*. The step definition method for the first line in the scenario shown might go something like the following.

Listing 8.3 A simple step definition method in Java

> We record the frequent flyer member in a variable to be used in the following steps.

> We create a new Frequent Flyer member using a simple builder method.

```java
FrequentFlyerMember member;

@Given("Tara is a Standard Frequent Flyer member")
public void aStandardFrequentFlyerMember() {
 member = FrequentFlyerMember.named("Tara")
                         .withStatus(FrequentFlyerStatus.Standard);
}
```

Or in TypeScript, the same step definition could look like the following.

Listing 8.4 A simple step definition method in TypeScript

> We record the frequent flyer member in a variable to use in the following steps.

> We create a new Frequent Flyer member by injecting an object literal into a domain object constructor.

```typescript
let member: FrequentFlyerMember;

Given('Tara is a Standard Frequent Flyer member', function() {
    member = new FrequentFlyerMember({
        name: 'Tara',
        status: FrequentFlyerStatus.Standard,
    });
});
```

8.4.1 *Injecting data with step definition parameters*

The step definition code we saw will run, but it isn't very flexible. There is a lot of hard-coded data embedded in the text, and this could lead to unnecessary duplication when we want to add new scenarios that are related to this one. For example, if the scenarios mentioned a Silver Frequent Flyer instead of a standard one, we would need to write another step definition method:

```java
@Given("Tara is a Silver Frequent Flyer member")
public void aSilverFrequentFlyerMember() {
  member = FrequentFlyerMember.named("Tara")
                            .withStatus(FrequentFlyerStatus.Silver);
}
```

Of course, this is wasteful. A better approach would be to have just one step definition method and to pass the Frequent Flyer category to our automation code, as follows.

Listing 8.5   A step definition method with a parameter (in Java)

```java
FrequentFlyerMember member;

@Given("{word} is a {word} Frequent Flyer member")
public void aFrequentFlyerMember(String name, String status) {
    FrequentFlyerStatus statusLevel = FrequentFlyerCategory.valueOf(status);
    member = FrequentFlyerMember.named(name).withStatus(statusLevel);
}
```

The status is defined as a variable part of the scenario text, using "{word}".

We convert the status to an enum value that can be passed to our builder method.

We pass the FrequentFlyer status as a string to our step definition method.

In the step definition annotation in listing 8.5 we replaced the word "Standard" or "Silver" with a special placeholder that represents a single word: "{word}". This notation is known as a *Cucumber Expression*.

There are many Cucumber Expressions available, depending on the type and format of data you want to pass to your step definition method. For example, we could simplify the step definition code by using the special anonymous Cucumber Expression type ("{}"), which does its best to convert the text in the scenario to the parameter type you define in your step definition method. The anonymous type works fine for enums, so we could replace the "{word}" expression we used in listing 8.4 with an anonymous expression and use an enum parameter instead of a string. You can see the result of this refactoring in the following listing.

Listing 8.6   Using the anonymous Cucumber Expression type (in Java)

```java
FrequentFlyerMember member;

@Given("{word} is a {} Frequent Flyer member")
public void aStandardFrequentFlyerMember(String name,
                                FrequentFlyerStatus status) {
    member = FrequentFlyerMember.named(name).withStatus(status);
}
```

The status is now defined using the "{}" anonymous type.

Cucumber converts the status text into the enum value automatically.

The built-in Cucumber expressions are listed in table 8.1 (also see http://mng.bz/epzQ). You can even define your own (we will learn more about this later in the chapter).

Table 8.1 Built-in Cucumber Expression types

Parameter Type	Description	Example	Matches
{int}	A whole number	There are {int} remaining tasks	There are 5 remaining tasks
{float}	A floating-point number	The box weighs {float} kg	The box weighs 7.5 kg
{word}	A single word (without whitespace)	She buys a {word} jersey	She buys a blue jersey
{string}	A string enclosed in double-quotes	She flies to {string}	She flies to "New York"
{}	Matches any expression (works with enums and most basic types)	She flies to {}	She flies to New York
{biginteger} (only applies to step definitions written in a JVM language)	A BigInteger parameter	A population of {biginteger}	A population of 5,000,000,000
{bigdecimal}	A BigDecimal parameter	A total value of {bigdecimal}	A total value of 99.9876543
{byte}	A Byte parameter	There are {byte} apples	There are 500 apples
{short}	A Short parameter	There are {short} apples	There are 5,000 apples
{long}	A Long parameter	There are {long} apples	There are 50,000,000 apples
{double}	A Double parameter	The box weighs {double} kg	The box weighs 7.4987 kg

Generating your step definitions

Cucumber gives you a couple of ways to wire your Gherkin scenarios and bind them to your test automation code. First, when you run a test runner class for a scenario with no step definitions, Cucumber will write some sample step glue code to the console output:

```
$ mvn verify
…
There were undefined steps. You can implement missing steps with the
 snippets below:
@Given("Tara is a Frequent Flyer traveler")
```

(continued)

```
public void tara_is_a_Frequent_Flyer_traveler() {
    // Write code here that turns the phrase above into concrete actions
    throw new cucumber.api.PendingException();
}
@Then("she should earn {int} points")
public void she_should_earn_points(Integer int1) {
    // Write code here that turns the phrase above into concrete actions
    throw new cucumber.api.PendingException();
}
…
```

A more convenient option, available in both IntelliJ IDEA and Eclipse (via the Cucumber Eclipse plug-in), is to run the feature or scenario (at the time of writing IntelliJ IDEA is the only IDE that supports the execution of individual scenarios from the IDE) itself directly from your IDE. This will cause the step definition snippets for any undefined steps to be written to the console.

You can then copy these snippets into your step definition classes. These snippets are a good start, but you will usually need to tweak them a bit; they may miss parameters, and at the very least, you will need to make parameter names more readable.

IDEs such as IntelliJ IDEA and Eclipse (via the Cucumber Eclipse plug-in) allow you to generate step definition code directly from your IDE, using the contextual menu.

8.4.2   *Making your Cucumber Expressions more flexible*

Executable specifications are above all a form of documentation, written in business-readable language. This is why the best Gherkin scenarios and feature files read very much like a normal specifications document, in fluent, readable business language.

Little grammatical details can go a long way to make your scenarios easier to read. When there are inconsistencies in grammar, it can distract the reader from focusing on the business intent behind the scenario and make the scenario a little bit less effective at communicating its message. For example, consider the following step definition:

```
@Then("she has been a member for {int} years")
```

This will match both "she has been a member for 5 years" and "she has been a member for 1 years," but not "she has been a member for 1 year." However, we could tell Cucumber to accept both forms by making the final "s" optional. When using Cucumber Expressions, you can make any text optional by surrounding it in parentheses, like in the following example:

```
@Then("she has been a member for {int} year(s)")
```

Another common use of optional text (in English) is to make scenario genders a bit more flexible:

```
@Then("(s)he has been a member for {int} year(s)")
```

This would match both of the following variations:

- "she has been a member for 5 years"
- "he has been a member for 1 year"

Sometimes it can be helpful to allow small variations in the scenario text. For example, suppose that business users use the words "member" and "customer" synonymously. Cucumber Expressions allow us to use the slash character to indicate alternative words in a scenario text. You can see an example here:

```
@Then("(s)he has been a member/customer for {int} year(s)")
```

This Cucumber Expression would work in all of the following cases:

- "she has been a member for 1 year"
- "he has been a customer for 5 years"

Note that this will only work for words without whitespaces; for more sophisticated options, you need to use regular expressions, which we will look at later in this chapter.

8.4.3 *Cucumber Expressions and custom parameter types*

Cucumber expressions are meant to make your step definitions more readable. One great way to do this, and to simplify your code in the process, is to use custom parameter types.

Custom parameter types allow you to make your step definition expressions more meaningful by using your own domain-related parameter types. For example, in one of the previous step definitions, we used an anonymous parameter type to pass in the frequent flyer status and then create a Frequent Flyer member:

```
@Given("{} is a {} Frequent Flyer member")
public void aFrequentFlyerMember(String name, FrequentFlyerStatus status) {
    member = FrequentFlyerMember.newMember()
                        .named(name)
                        .withStatus(status);
}
```

We could make this code a little more readable and a little more reusable by defining a parameterized type to represent Frequent Flyer members. This would allow us to pass a FrequentFlyerMember parameter directly into our step definition method, like this:

```
@Given("{} is a {frequentFlyer}")
public void aFrequentFlyerMember(String name, FrequentFlyerMember member) {
    this.member = member.named(name);
}
```

To make this work, we need a method that recognizes the text corresponding to the description of the Frequent Flyer member (e.g., "Standard Frequent Flyer Member" or "Silver Frequent Flyer member") and that converts this text into the correct parameter type. We use the `ParameterType` annotation to identify methods like in the following listing. (`ParameterType` methods can go in your step definition classes or in any other class in your glue code packages.)

Listing 8.7   A parameter type definition

This is a regular expression (more about these later) that identifies the parameter value.

We pass the status into the parameter as a String.

```
@ParameterType("(Standard|Silver|Bronze|Gold) Frequent Flyer member")
public FrequentFlyerMember frequentFlyer(String statusName) {
    FrequentFlyerStatus status = FrequentFlyerStatus.valueOf(statusName);
    return FrequentFlyerMember.withStatus(status);
}
```

We return a Frequent Flyer member with this status.

`ParameterType` methods define a regular expression to identify the piece of text in the scenario that should be converted to an object, and that defines the permitted values. The name of the parameter type is derived from the name of the method (you can also use the name attribute if you prefer).

When we define domain-specific parameter types like this, it is easy to reuse them in other step definition methods. For example, suppose we need to implement the following scenario:

```
Scenario: 50% bonus points for members who already have 10000 points
  Given Tara is a Silver Frequent Flyer member with 20000 points
  When she completes a flight from Paris to Berlin
  Then she should earn 150 points
```

Using the `frequentFlyer` custom parameter type we defined earlier, the corresponding step definition becomes much simpler.

Listing 8.8   Another step definition method using a custom parameter type

A Frequent Flyer member along with their points

```
@Given("{} is a {frequentFlyer} with {int} points")
public void aFrequentFlyerMemberWithPoints(String name,
                                           FrequentFlyerMember member,
                                           int points) {
    this.member = member.named(name).withPoints(points);
}
```

The Frequent Flyer member is converted to a FrequentFlyerMember parameter.

We can also use more precise regular expressions to define more sophisticated custom types. For example, Cucumber has no built-in date format, but it is easy to define one. Suppose we wanted to automate the following step:

`Given` Todd joined the Frequent Flyer program on 2020-01-01

We could define a custom date type called, for example, "ISO-Date," using a regular expression that matches the date format we want to use. A regular expression that matches this date format could be `"\d{4}-\d{2}-\d{2}"` (four digits followed by a dash, then two digits followed by a dash, then two more digits). We can also use the name attribute to define parameter types that don't follow a Java method name convention. Our parameter type method would like the following.

> **Listing 8.9   A custom parameter type for a date**

```
@ParameterType(name="ISO-date",                    ◁——  The name of the
               value="(\\d{4}-\\d{2}-\\d{2})")  ◁—      parameter type
public LocalDate isoDate(String formattedDate) {        The regular expression
    return LocalDate.parse(formattedDate);              that matches this type
}                                                        of parameter
```

The step definition code would then look something like this:

```
@Given("{} joined the Frequent Flyer programme on {ISO-date}")
public void justJoined(String name, LocalDate date) {…}
```

So far, we have alluded to regular expressions a few times, but not looked at them in much detail. In the next section we will take a closer look at what regular expressions are and how we use them in Cucumber.

8.4.4   Using regular expressions

Cucumber Expressions are not the only way to write your step definition methods. You can also use regular expressions, which provide a concise syntax for pattern matching in strings. Just like Cucumber Expressions, you can use regular expressions to identify parameters inside your scenario. In older versions of Cucumber, regular expressions were the only way to implement step definitions, so you may see a lot of them in older code bases. And as we saw in the previous section, we also use regular expressions when we define custom parameter types. You can see an example of the previous step definition we saw, using regular expressions, in the following listing.

> **Listing 8.10   A step definition written using regular expressions**

```
@Given("^Tara is a (.*) Frequent Flyer member with (\\d+) points")   ◁——┐
public void aFrequentFlyerMemberWithPoints(FrequentFlyerStatus status, int
    points) {
    member = FrequentFlyerMember.withStatus(status);        Regular expressions are
    member.setPoints(points);                               used to identify the status
}                                                           and points parameters.
```

Well-written regular expressions can go a long way to making your step definitions more flexible and more reusable. Regular expressions are extremely powerful but are also notorious for being hard to understand. Back in the late 1990s Netscape engineer Jamie Zawinski humorously remarked, "Some people, when confronted with a problem, think, 'I know, I'll use regular expressions.' Now they have two problems." Although you need them less often with the introduction of Cucumber Expressions, they still come in handy from time to time. Fortunately, the range and complexity of the regular expressions you need to know to write effective step definition methods are relatively limited.

SIMPLE MATCHERS

The simplest and most commonly used regular expression for Cucumber step definitions is the wildcard (.*). This reads as "any character (except for a new line), any number of times," so the following annotation would match the text we saw earlier: "she has been a member for 5 years":

```
@Then("^she has been a member for (.*) years")
```

Let's break this down.

In regular expressions, we use the caret (^) symbol to indicate the start of the string. This makes the expression less ambiguous, and some versions of Cucumber use this to know when you want to use regular expressions as opposed to Cucumber Expressions.

The regular expression (.*) is surrounded by parentheses. This is known as a group and is how Cucumber knows which parts of the text to convert into parameter variables.

MATCHING SPECIFIC TYPES OF CHARACTERS

You can also match specific ranges or types of characters. For example, in regular expressions, "d" represents a digit, and the plus symbol reads as "one or more," so the regular expression "d+" would match a sequence of one or more digits. We need to escape alphabetical symbols with backslashes, so we could rewrite our scenario definition like this:

```
@Given("^she has been a member for (\\d+) years")
```

MATCHING SETS OF POSSIBLE VALUES

Regular expressions also let you define a set of possible values, using a pipe-separated list like the one shown here.

```
@Given ("^Tara is a (Standard|Bronze|Silver|Gold) Frequent Flyer member")
public void aFrequentFlyerMember(FrequentFlyerStatus status) {…}
```

OPTIONAL CHARACTERS

We saw earlier how with Cucumber Expressions you can make a character optional by surrounding it in parentheses; for example, "(s)he" is a Cucumber Expression that will match both "she" and "he." We can do the same thing using regular expressions by using a question mark, as shown here:

```
@Given("^s?he has been a member for (\\d+) years")
```

NON-CAPTURING GROUPS

Sometimes we need to support several variations of wording in a text, which are unrelated to the parameters that we pass to the step definition methods. For example, suppose we wanted to match both "when Tara registers on the site" and "given Tara has registered on the site." Using regular expressions, we can do this using a noncapturing group. Non-capturing groups are regular expressions that will be matched but that will not be passed through to the step definition method. They are prefixed by ?:, as shown in this example:

```
@Then("^(.*) (?:registers|has registered) on the site")
public void userHasRegistered(String name){…}
```

COMMON REGULAR EXPRESSIONS

You can see a more complete list of the more useful regular expressions (and a recap of the ones we have already seen) in table 8.2.

Table 8.2   Common regular expressions used in Cucumber scenarios

Regular Expression	Description	Example	Matches
.*	Any sequence of characters (including nothing)	`^ (.*) is a frequent flyer`	Tara is a frequent flyer
.+	A sequence of one or more characters	`^ (.+) is a frequent flyer`	Tara is a frequent flyer
/d+	A sequence of one or more digits	`Tara is (/d+) years old`	Tara is 30 years old
/d{n}	A sequence of precisely n digits	`In the year /d{4}`	In the year 2020
(a|b|c)	Any one of the listed values	`The status is (red|amber|green)`	The status is red The status is amber The status is green
?	An optional character	`s?he purchases a ticket`	she purchases a ticket he purchases a ticket
?:	A non-capturing group	`Tara (?:buys|has bought) a ticket`	Tara buys a ticket Tara has bought a ticket

8.4.5   *Working with lists and data tables*

So far, we have been looking at simple data types. But very often we need to pass in more complex data structures.

WORKING WITH SIMPLE LISTS

Simple lists (tables with a single column) can generally be mapped automatically. For example, the following scenario contains a simple list of strings:

```
And the available destinations should be:
   | Berlin   |
   | Paris    |
   | New York |
```

The corresponding step definition method would simply accept a list of strings as a parameter:

```
@Then("the available destinations should be")
public void availableDestinations(List<String> destinations) {…}
```

WORKING WITH EMBEDDED LISTS

Sometimes it can be more readable to embed a short list of values inside the step text, rather than in a separate list, as you can see in this example:

```
Then the available destinations should be Berlin, Paris, New York
```

The simplest way to achieve this is to define a parameter type method that converts the list of strings in the text to an actual list of strings. (In real-world code you might even convert the values to a list of enums or domain objects using the same technique shown in the following listing.)

Listing 8.11   A parameter type that handles a list of strings

```
@ParameterType(name = "string-values", value = "(.*)")      Splits the list into
public List<String> stringValues(String destinationList) {   its individual
    return Stream.of(destinationList.split(","))              elements
               .map(String::trim)                             Trims off any
               .collect(Collectors.toList());                 white spaces
}
                                            Returns the result
                                            as a list of strings
```

The step definition code would now look like this:

```
@Then("the available destinations should be {string-values}")
public void availableDestinations(List<String> destinations) {…}
```

Lists are convenient, but we often need to express more involved data structures, and a great way to do this is using tables.

WORKING WITH TABLES

Suppose we have the following scenario:

```
Scenario: Completed flights in the past 90 days can be claimed
  Given Todd joined the Frequent Flyer program on 2020-01-01
  When Todd asks for the following flight to be credited to his account:
    | Flight Number | Date       | Status    |
    | FH-101        | 2019-12-01 | COMPLETED |
    | FH-102        | 2019-12-01 | CANCELED  |
    | FH-103        | 2019-08-01 | COMPLETED |
  Then only the following flights should be credited:
    | Flight Number | Date       | Status    |
    | FH-101        | 2019-12-01 | COMPLETED |
```

In the second step, we pass a data table containing the flight details for a number of flights. In the third step, we pass a list of the flights we expect to be credited to Todd's Frequent Flyer account.

Each row in the table represents one of the flights that Todd has completed. We could represent the concept of completed flights using a simple domain class, as follows.

Listing 8.12   A domain class representing a past flight

```java
import java.time.LocalDate;

public record PastFlight(String flightNumber,
                         LocalDate scheduledDate,
                         FlightStatus status) {}
```

By default, Cucumber will pass tables into step definition methods using its own `DataTable` class. You can use this class to extract the rows and columns of the table, as in the following listing.

Listing 8.13   Using the `DataTable` class

Cucumber provides the table's rows and cell values as a DataTable object.

```java
@When("{} asks for the following flight to be credited to his account:")
public void creditFlights(String name, DataTable flights) {
    List<PastFlight> requestedFlights = flights.asMaps()        ← Extracts the rows and cells
            .stream()                                              as a list of maps
            .map(row -> new PastFlight(                          ← Converts each map into a PastFlight domain object
                    row.get("Flight Number"),
                    LocalDate.parse(row.get("Date")),
                    FlightStatus.valueOf(row.get("Status"))))
            .collect(Collectors.toList());                      ← Returns the collection of PastFlight objects as a list
    ...
}
```

However, this code is not very readable and is more complex than we would typically expect in a step definition method. It would be much cleaner and easier to maintain if we could pass in a list of meaningful domain objects directly to the step definition method.

We can do this by refactoring the conversion logic into a separate method, which we annotate with the DataTableType annotation. This annotation tells Cucumber how to convert data tables into domain objects or lists of domain objects. You can see an example of how to use this annotation in the following listing.

Listing 8.14   Using the `DataTableType` annotation

```
@DataTableType
public PastFlight mapRowToPastFlight(Map<String, String> entry) {     ⟵── Cucumber provides a single row as a map of Strings.
    return new PastFlight(entry.get("Flight Number"),     ⟵
                    LocalDate.parse(entry.get("Date")),
                    FlightStatus.valueOf(entry.get("Status")));
}
```

Cucumber provides a single row as a map of Strings.

We convert the row to whatever domain object we need.

This method can go anywhere in your glue code—for example, in the step definition class alongside the methods that use the PastFlight domain objects, or (if the domain object is used in many places) it might go in a class of its own.

We can now pass a list of PastFlight domain objects directly to our step definition method, like this:

```
@When("{word} asks for the following flight to be credited to his account:")
public void creditFlights(String name, List<PastFlight> requestedFlights) {
    …
}
```

WORKING WITH MORE COMPLEX TABLES

Converting Gherkin tables to domain types this way does take a little extra effort initially but pays off handsomely in terms of readability and maintainability down the line. Sometimes, however, the data you need to describe is a bit more complex. In real-world scenarios, you may need to deal with complex domain objects with many fields, but where the relevant fields vary from one scenario to another. A past flight record could include many more fields than the three we saw, including fields that are not useful for these scenarios.

For example, suppose you now need to implement the following scenario:

```
Scenario Outline: Frequent flyer members are awarded extra points for late
⇒ flights
10 extra points are earned for each hour delayed after 1 hour.
  Given Tracy has traveled on the following flights:
     | Flight Number   | Delayed   | Delayed By   | Extra Points   |
     | <Flight Number> | <Delayed> | <Delayed By> | <Extra Points> |
  When the flight is credited to her account
  Then she should be credited with <Extra Points> additional points
  Examples:
     | Flight Number | Delayed | Delayed By | Extra Points |
```

```
| FH-101     | No        |           | 0         |           |
| FH-102     | Yes       | 10m       | 0         |           |
| FH-102     | Yes       | 60m       | 10        |           |
| FH-103     | Yes       | 2h30m     | 20        |           |
| FH-104     | Yes       | 5h        | 50        |           |
```

In this requirement, we use a different subset of fields. The date and status of the flights are not relevant for this scenario, but we do need to know how long each flight was delayed.

The `PastFlight` class needs some additional fields to support this requirement. You can see one possible implementation in the following listing.

Listing 8.15   A domain class representing a past flight with additional fields

```java
public record PastFlight(String flightNumber,
                         LocalDate scheduledDate,
                         FlightStatus status,
                         Boolean wasDelayed,
                         Period delayedBy,
                         String boardingPassNumber) {}
```

The tricky thing now is to give your step definition methods the flexibility they need to be able to cope with different table structures. One approach might be to check each field and use a sensible default value if none is provided. In the following listing, you can see a sample implementation of this approach.

Listing 8.16   A domain class representing a past flight with additional fields

```java
@DataTableType
public PastFlight mapRowToPastFlight(Map<String, String> entry) {
    return new PastFlight(
            optional(entry.get("Flight Number"),"FT-101"),
            LocalDate.parse(optional(entry.get("Date"), "2020-10-01")),
            FlightStatus.valueOf(optional(entry.get("Status"), "COMPLETED")),
            isDelayed(entry),
            delayDurationOf(entry));
}

private <T> T optional(T cellValue, T defaultValue) {
    return Optional.ofNullable(cellValue).orElse(defaultValue);
}

private Boolean isDelayed(Map<String, String> entry) {
    if (entry.get("Delayed") == null) { return false; }
    return (entry.get("Delayed").equalsIgnoreCase("Yes"));
}

private Duration delayDurationOf(Map<String, String> entry) {
    if (entry.get("Delayed By") == null) { return Duration.ZERO; }
    return Duration.parse("PT" + entry.get("Delayed By"));
}
```

In real-world projects there are many other ways to do this. For example, some teams use a JSON or Excel template file to contain the default values, and only update the fields specified in the table.

8.5 Setting up and tearing down with backgrounds and hooks

Test scenarios often need the system to be in a particular state. For example, certain records must be present in the database, the user must be a particular type of user or have specific permissions, or perhaps certain operations must have already been performed before the scenario can start.

Before you can automate any acceptance criteria, you need to make sure the system is in a correct and well-known initial state. Also, many automated acceptance criteria—particularly the end-to-end variety—will need to refer to or update data in a database, or maybe prepare input data in some other format. Some tests may need other services or resources, such as filesystems or remote web services, to be initialized and configured. In order to have effective automated acceptance criteria, you need to be able to set up all of these things quickly, precisely, and automatically (see figure 8.6).

Figure 8.6   Automated data setup is a key part of automated acceptance criteria.

8.5.1 Using background steps

One simple way to prepare your test environment before each scenario that we saw in the previous chapter is to use a background step, which is executed before the start of each scenario and thus is a good place to add contextual or preparatory information that is true for each scenario. For example, suppose you were working on a feature that describes rules about how Frequent Flyer members earn points when they fly:

```
Feature: Earning Frequent Flyer points from flights
  In order to improve customer loyalty
  As an airline sales manager
  I want travelers to earn frequent flyer points when they fly with us
```

The number of points a frequent flyer earns depends on factors such as the distance they travel, the cabin class they fly in, and their current status. Different routes are worth different numbers of points; the number of points for a given route is determined by the marketing department based on their own criteria. In all cases, Silver Frequent Flyers earn an extra 50% points and Gold Frequent Flyers earn double points.

You could use the following background step to capture a flight schedule and other data that might hold for several scenarios:

```
Background:
  Given the following flight points schedule:
    | From     | To          | Class    | Points |
    | London   | New York    | Economy  | 550    |
    | London   | New York    | Business | 800    |
    | London   | New York    | First    | 1650   |
    | New York | Los Angeles | Economy  | 100    |
    | New York | Los Angeles | Business | 140    |
    | New York | Los Angeles | First    | 200    |
  And the following flyer types multipliers:
    | Status   | Multiplier |
    | Standard | 1.0        |
    | Silver   | 1.5        |
    | Gold     | 2.0        |
```

You can then proceed to write more concise and focused scenarios that build on these background steps. For example, you could start with a simple scenario that illustrates how points are earned based on the route and the cabin class:

```
Scenario: Travelers earn points depending on the points schedule
  Given Stacy is a Standard Frequent Flyer member
  When she flies from London to New York in Economy class
  Then she should earn 550 points
```

Each subsequent scenario in the feature would develop and explore business rules and constraints. For instance, another scenario might build on the first one and illustrate the effect of the cabin class on the number of points earned:

```
Scenario Outline: Travelers earn more points in higher cabin classes
  Given Silvia is a Silver Frequent Flyer member
  When she flies from <From> to <To> in <Cabin> class
  Then she should earn <Points Earned> points
  Examples:
    | From     | To          | Cabin    | Points Earned | Notes             |
    | London   | New York    | Economy  | 550           | International leg |
    | New York | Los Angeles | Business | 800           | Domestic leg     |
    | New York | London      | First    | 1650          | Return trip      |
```

And a third example could explore the effect of frequent flyer status on the number of points earned:

```
Scenario Outline: Higher frequent flyer status levels earn more points
  Given Tracy is a <Status> Frequent Flyer member
```

```
When she flies from <From> to <To> in Business class
Then she should earn <Points Earned> points
Examples:
    | From     | To          | Status   | Points Earned |
    | London   | New York    | Standard | 800           |
    | New York | Los Angeles | Silver   | 210           |
    | New York | London      | Gold     | 1600          |
```

The step definition code for background steps is written in the same way as any other steps; in fact, for Cucumber, it makes no difference whether a step appears in a background step or in an ordinary scenario. For example, the following listing shows an implementation of a step definition for one of the steps shown above.

Listing 8.17   The DataTableType annotation used to convert rows from Gherkin tables

```
@DataTableType
public PointsSchedule pointsSchedule(Map<String, String> row) {
    return PointsSchedule.from(row.get("From"))
                         .to(row.get("To"))
                         .flyingIn(CabinClass.valueOf(row.get("Class")))
                         .earns(Integer.parseInt(row.get("Points")));
}


@Given("the following flight points schedule:")
public void theFollowingFlightPointsSchedule(List<PointsSchedule>
➥   pointSchedules) {
    flightDatabase.addPointSchedules(pointSchedules);
}
```

But sometimes we need to perform tasks that we don't want to expose to the business reader. Maybe they are too technical to be of interest, or maybe they are implementation dependent, and we don't want to expose them in our scenarios. That's where we need to use another technique, which we will learn about in the next section: hooks.

8.5.2   Using hooks

Not all setup steps should go in a background step. Background steps are designed to be business facing and business readable: they should only contain information that business readers care about.

But there are times when we need to set up other aspects of the system that the business isn't so interested in. For example, we may need to perform some low-level housekeeping activity such as opening a browser, setting up a database, or deleting test data once the test has completed execution. We can do this using hooks. A hook is a method that will get called at different points in your life cycle, where you can inject your own custom code to do whatever you need to do to keep your test data and environment just the way you want it.

All BDD tools support some sort of hook mechanism, though the details will vary from tool to tool. In the rest of this section, we will look at a few practical examples of using hooks to prepare and manage test environments in Cucumber.

INTERVENING BEFORE AND AFTER A SCENARIO

The most common use of hooks is likely intervening before each scenario starts. For example, if your application uses a database, you could automatically reinitialize the database schema before each test, possibly populating it with a sensible predefined set of reference data. This way, no test can inadvertently break another test by adding unexpected data into the database. It also ensures that each scenario is independent of the others and doesn't rely on another scenario to have been executed beforehand.

One of the most common situations for hooks is to use them to set up a test environment before a scenario is executed. It's a good habit to make sure each scenario takes care of its own test environment and data so that it can be run in isolation if necessary. And hook methods, safely out of view of the business reader, but still executed at the start of each scenario, are a great place to do this. In Cucumber, you use the io.cucumber.java.Before annotation, as seen in the following listing.

Listing 8.18   Hook methods running at different points in the test life cycle

```
@Before
public void prepareStaticData() {           ◁──  The Before tag tells Cucumber
    FlightDatabase.instance().setupAirports();       to run this method before each
    FlightDatabase.instance().initialiseDefaultFlightPlans();   scenario is executed.
}
```

When working with Cucumber in TypeScript, the code will look very similar, as follows.

Listing 8.19   Hook methods in TypeScript

Just like in Java, the Before tag tells Cucumber to run this function before each scenario is executed.

```
Before(async function () {           ◁──
    await FlightDatabase.instance().setupAirports();
    await FlightDatabase.instance().initialiseDefaultFlightPlans();    ◁──
});
```

All Cucumber step definition functions support asynchronous functions that return Promises.

All Cucumber step definition functions (Given, When, Then as well the hooks Before, After, BeforeAll, and AfterAll) support asynchronous functions that return Promises. Here we use the async/await syntax to simplify the implementation of asynchronous calls setting up the FlightDatabase.

GETTING MORE INFORMATION ABOUT THE SCENARIO

Sometimes you need more information about the scenario that you are running. For example, you might want to know the name of the scenario, or whether it passed or failed, for logging or troubleshooting purposes.

Listing 8.20 Passing scenario details to the hook method

> Details about the scenario will be included in the Scenario parameter.

```
@After
public void logScenarioResult(Scenario scenario) {
    System.out.println(scenario.getName() + ":" + scenario.getStatus());
}
```

INTERVENING BEFORE AND AFTER SPECIFIC SCENARIOS

The hook methods shown in listing 8.20 run for each and every scenario in a test suite. But sometimes you need to perform housekeeping for certain scenarios only. For example, suppose some of your tests are web tests that open a browser. You might want to open the browser instance in a @Before hook, and then close the browser in an @After hook. However, you don't want to open and close the browser unnecessarily if the scenario does not interact with the web UI. You can do this easily in Cucumber using tags and hooks.

The first step is to add a tag to the scenarios we want to run. For example, you could add a @web tag to the scenarios that require a browser to run:

```
@web
Scenario: Travelers earn points depending on the points schedule
  Given Stacy is a Standard Frequent Flyer member
  When she flies from London to New York in Economy class
  Then she should earn 550 points
```

Next, you add @Before and @After hook methods to open and close the browser for each scenario (see listings 8.21 and 8.22).

Listing 8.21 Hook methods that only run for specific scenarios

```
WebDriver driver;

@Before("@web")
public void prepareDriver() {
    driver = new ChromeDriver();
}

@After("@web")
public void closeBrowser() {
    driver.quit();
}
```

> Opens the Chrome browser for @web-annotated scenarios

> Closes the Chrome browser after @web-annotated scenarios

The parameter you pass to each annotation describes the tag. This parameter is known as a tag expression and can be a single tag (such as @web) or a logical combination of tags (@web and @smoketest or @web and not @backend) that describe the circumstances when these hook methods need to run.

Listing 8.22   Tag-specific hook methods in TypeScript

```
let driver: WebDriver;

Before({ tags: '@web' }, function () {          ◁────  In CucumberJS, tagged hooks
    driver = new ChromeDriver();                       are defined using an object literal
});                                                    passed as the first parameter.

After({ tags: '@web' }, async function () {     ◁────  Note that hooks can be
    await driver.close();                              asynchronous and use the
});                                                    async/await syntax, return a
                                                       Promise, or invoke a callback.
```

INTERVENING AT THE START AND END OF A FEATURE

Most scenarios need a fresh environment before they start. And this is a good practice; otherwise, the results of previous scenarios can interfere with scenarios executed later in the test suite and lead to unpredictable test failures.

But sometimes you want to prepare a test environment, or some parts of a test environment, only once, at the start of the test run. For example, if your tests need to start a Docker instance (we will see how to do this later in the chapter), you may want to start the instance only once and then reuse it for each scenario. In TypeScript, it's very easy: you can use the `BeforeAll` and `AfterAll` hooks, which are executed, respectively, before any scenario is executed, and at the end once they have all finished, as follows.

Listing 8.23   Running hooks before any scenario is executed in TypeScript

Apart from tags, another option Cucumber JS hooks support is timeout, expressed in milliseconds. Here, we overwrite the default timeout of 5 seconds and give our DatabaseContainer up to 10 seconds to start up. Increasing the default timeout can be useful if our test needs to run in environments not as powerful as the development machine we write them on.

Instantiate a DatabaseContainer, start it asynchronously, and store the reference to the started container.

```
let dbContainer: StartedTestContainer;

BeforeAll({ timeout: 10 * 1000 }, async () => {
    dbContainer = await new DatabaseContainer(dbConfig).start();   ◁────
});

AfterAll(async () => {              Stop the
    await dbContainer.stop();       container.
});
```

In Cucumber with Java, the `@BeforeAll` and `@AfterAll` hook annotations (introduced in Java in Cucumber 7) play the same role. For example, in the following listing we use a simple static variable to ensure that our database is only initialized once.

Listing 8.24   Preparing data before any scenario is executed in Java

```
@BeforeAll
public void prepareStaticData() {
    TestDatabase.instance().setupAirports();
    TestDatabase.instance().initialiseDefaultFlightPlans();
}
```

This approach is fine in many cases, but depending on how your code is implemented, it may not be thread safe. This means that if you are running your tests in parallel, you may run into trouble, as the code could be executed simultaneously in more than one thread.

USING CUCUMBER EVENTLISTENERS

Another way to intervene at different points in the test life cycle is to leverage the Cucumber EventListeners. This involves writing a bit of extra code but can result in a cleaner and more modular approach than using static variables.

Writing a Cucumber EventListener is straightforward. First, you need to write a class that implements the io.cucumber.plugin.EventListener interface. This interface has a single method, setEventPublisher(). Inside this method, you register handlers for the events you are interested in, in this case, when a test run starts and finishes. An example of a Cucumber EventListener follows.

Listing 8.25   Preparing data before any scenario is executed in Java using a static flag

```
public class DatabaseServerHandler implements EventListener {
    @Override
    public void setEventPublisher(EventPublisher eventPublisher) {
        eventPublisher.registerHandlerFor(TestRunStarted.class,
                event -> {
                    TestDatabase.instance().startServer();
                    TestDatabase.instance().initialiseDefaultFlightPlans();
                });

        eventPublisher.registerHandlerFor(TestRunFinished.class,
                event -> {
                    TestDatabase.instance().stopServer();
                });
    }
}
```

Runs this code before the test suite starts

Runs this code after the test suite finishes

The next step is to configure your test suite to use your listener class. You do this by simply including the path to your listener class in the plug-in attribute of the @Cucumber-Options annotation in your test runner class, for example, in the following listing.

Listing 8.26   Configuring a runner class to use a Cucumber EventListener

```
@CucumberOptions(
        plugin = {"com.manning.bddinaction.plugins.DatabaseServerHandler"},
        features = "classpath:features"
)
public class AcceptanceTestSuite {}
```

Include the full path to your EventListener and add it to the plug-in attribute.

8.6   *Preparing your test environments using hooks*

In this section, we look at how we can use hook methods with open source tools to set up and prepare test data and test environments.

8.6.1   Using in-memory databases

A popular use of hooks is to prepare a test database before a scenario or a set of scenarios is executed. Many teams use in-memory databases such as H2 or HSQLDB for their test data. In-memory databases are fast to create and to destroy afterward, so each scenario can use a fresh set of test data.

8.7   Using virtual test environments

In-memory databases are fast and convenient but do have some drawbacks. Some applications may use features that are only available in the production database, such as proprietary data types or stored procedures. Many applications also rely on other components, such as messaging queues, NoSQL databases, or distributed caches. For this reason, many teams prefer to run integration and end-to-end tests in a more production-like environment.

Traditionally, teams often use a dedicated test environment to run integration and end-to-end tests. However, there are some issues with this approach. Running tests this way locally is difficult, and having to deploy into a specific environment to test slows down feedback cycles and creates bottlenecks. In addition, these environments can be unstable; they might also be used for manual or exploratory testing, and testing can be unexpectedly interrupted by deployments or updates.

An alternative approach is to use virtualization to run your own production-like environment on your local machine. And the most common tool used for this purpose is Docker.

Docker is a powerful tool that lets you bundle up an application or service, along with all the dependencies it needs, and spin it up on another machine. In practical terms, this means you can package an application or service that you need to test and use whenever and wherever you need to run your tests. We call these bundled applications or services *containers.*

For example, you might want to start up a container running a Postgres or MongoDB database to test your database persistence (see figure 8.7). Or you might need to integrate with other services such as Apache Kafka for stream processing or an Elasticsearch search engine. You can even start a bespoke set of services using a tool called Docker Compose.

There are many approaches to using Docker as part of your build and testing process. If you are using Java, one of the easiest is to use an open source library called `TestContainers` (https://www.testcontainers.org).

Figure 8.7   A simple test architecture using a Docker container to run a database instance

8.7.1   *Using TestContainers to manage Docker containers for your tests*

TestContainers is an open source library that makes it easy to use databases or other services that your tests need to run. It uses Docker under the hood (see https://www .docker.com/get-started), so it can start any application or service that can be bundled into a Docker container, but it has out-of-the-box support for many common services, including relational and nonrelational databases, ElasticSearch, Kafka, and RabbitMQ. For more tailored services you can integrate with Docker Compose or create a custom image by providing your own Docker configuration file.

There are many ways to configure and use TestContainer. It integrates well with unit testing frameworks such as JUnit and Spock and is a great way to speed up conventional integration tests. In the rest of this section, we will look at a few of the more useful approaches that you can use for a Cucumber test suite.

THE TESTCONTAINERS DEPENDENCIES

Before you use TestContainers you need to add the corresponding dependencies to your Maven POM file or Gradle build script. This includes the main testcontainers library, and any dependencies for the specific containers you want to use. For example, the following code shows the Gradle dependencies for a project using Test-Containers and PostgreSQL:

```
testCompile "org.testcontainers:testcontainers:1.15.0-rc2"
testCompile "org.testcontainers:postgresql:1.15.0-rc2"
```

STARTING A TESTCONTAINERS INSTANCE

With these dependencies added, you can start using Docker in your tests. Using a Docker instance with TestContainers is as simple as instantiating a new TestContainer object. Each supported database or application has its own class, such as PostgreSQL-Container, MongoDBContainer, or KafkaContainer. You can also use the Generic-Container class if you need to use an arbitrary Docker instance. For instance, to create and start up a new PostgreSQL database instance, you could run the code in the following listing.

Listing 8.27   Starting a Docker instance with `TestContainers`

```
PostgreSQLContainer container = new PostgreSQLContainer("postgres:13.0")
        .withDatabaseName("integration-tests-database")
        .withUsername("sa")
        .withPassword("sa");

container.start();

String jdbcUrl = container.getJdbcUrl();
```

Configuration options for the Docker instance

The start() method starts the container, downloading the image if necessary.

The name and version of the Docker instance

You can use the getJdbcUrl() method to find the JDBC URL for the database.

Generally, you will want to use a container in more than one test, so it makes sense to encapsulate it in its own class, as shown in the following listing.

Listing 8.28   Encapsulating a `TestContainer` in a class

```
public class TestDatabase {
    private static PostgreSQLContainer container
            = new PostgreSQLContainer("postgres:11.1")
                    .withDatabaseName("integration-tests-db")
                    .withUsername("sa")
                    .withPassword("sa");

    public static PostgreSQLContainer getInstance() {
        container.start();
        return container;
    }
}
```

This code will create a single database instance that will be shared across every test. This is sometimes done for performance reasons, but spinning up a TestContainers instance is generally so quick that it is perfectly feasible to use a new instance for each test.

In Cucumber you could do this by creating a new instance in a `@Before` hook. Alternatively, if you want to keep the container logic separate from your glue code, you could modify the class in listing 8.28 to make it thread safe. A simple way to do this is to use the `ThreadLocal` class to maintain a separate instance of the container for each thread, as follows.

Listing 8.29   Using thread-safe `TestContainers` instances

```
public class TestDatabase {
    private static ThreadLocal<PostgreSQLContainer> container
            = ThreadLocal.withInitial(
            () -> new PostgreSQLContainer("postgres:11.1")
                    .withDatabaseName("integration-tests-db")
                    .withUsername("sa")
                    .withPassword("sa")
    );

    public static PostgreSQLContainer getInstance() {
        container.get().start();
        return container.get();
    }
}
```

INTEGRATING TESTCONTAINERS WITH CUCUMBER AND SPRINGBOOT

There are many ways to integrate these Docker instances with your test code, but one of the most challenging aspects is generally to inject the dynamically generated address of the test server into your application code so that it points to the correct database and services.

One useful trick if you are using SpringBoot is to use the `@DynamicPropertySource` annotation, which lets you override Spring configuration properties programmatically.

In listing 8.30 you can see an example of how this annotation can be used to dynamically inject the connection details for the database instantiated by `TestContainers`. (To see how to do it in TypeScript, check out the GitHub repo.)

Listing 8.30   Using `TestContainers` with Cucumber and SpringBoot

```
@SpringBootTest
@ContextConfiguration
public class EarningPointsStepDefinitions {

    @DynamicPropertySource
    static void properties(DynamicPropertyRegistry registry) {
        registry.add("spring.datasource.url",
                    TestDatabase.getInstance()::getJdbcUrl);
        registry.add("spring.datasource.username",
                    TestDatabase.getInstance()::getUsername);
        registry.add("spring.datasource.password",
                    TestDatabase.getInstance()::getPassword);
    }

    @Autowired
    PointsScheduleRepository pointsScheduleRepository;

    @Given("the following flight points schedule:")
    public void setupFlightPointsSchedule(List<PointsSchedule>
     pointsSchedules) {
        pointsScheduleRepository.deleteAll();
        pointsSchedules.forEach(
                schedule -> pointsScheduleRepository.save(schedule)
        );
    }
}
```

Summary

- To run our executable specifications, we write automated test code in the language of our choice that will be executed for each step of your Cucumber scenarios (in this chapter, we focused on Java and JavaScript/TypeScript).
- Hooks and background steps can be used to prepare your test environment or tidy up afterward.
- Many teams use Docker to create and manage virtual test environments. The `TestContainers` library is a convenient way to manage Docker instances from within your test code.

In the next chapter, you'll learn how to write automated acceptance tests that exercise a web interface.

Writing solid automated acceptance tests

9

This chapter covers

- The importance of writing high-quality automated tests
- Patterns for implementing reliable and sustainable tests

In the next few chapters, we'll look at turning the automated scenarios we discussed in the previous chapters into fully automated acceptance tests for different types of applications and technologies. Before we dive into the technical details, we need to look at the bigger picture. We need to consider how to ensure that, no matter what technology or combination of technologies we use, the quality of our tests remains high.

A good acceptance test communicates its intent clearly and provides meaningful feedback about the current state of the application. It is reliable and easy to maintain so that the value provided by the test outweighs the cost of maintaining it.

But when automated acceptance tests are poorly designed, they add to the maintenance overhead, costing more to update and fix when new features are added than they contribute in value to the project. A large number of test automation initiatives fail or become ineffective for this very reason, so it's important to design your acceptance tests well. In this chapter, we'll look at a number of techniques and patterns that can help you write automated acceptance tests that are meaningful, reliable, and maintainable. Let's start by discussing what makes an industrial-strength acceptance test.

9.1   *Writing industrial-strength acceptance tests*

It's not hard to write a simple automated test. There are plenty of books and resources on the internet that can show you how to write automated tests for all sorts of technologies, and we'll look at a few of these later on in this book. But what's harder is ensuring that your tests will stand the test of time. Will your tests continue to provide useful feedback several months down the road? Will they become harder to maintain as the code base grows? Will they become brittle and fragile, discouraging the team from fixing them when they break? Many teams spend a great deal of effort in building large and complex test suites, only to abandon them because they find that the cost of maintaining and updating them outweighs the value of the feedback they provide.

The tests in a well-written automated acceptance test suite should be either passing or pending. A failing automated acceptance test should be a red flag for the development team that demands immediate attention. But when tests fail too often due to sporadic technical problems, the team will lose confidence in them as a feedback mechanism and be less motivated to fix them when they break (see figure 9.1). This leads to a vicious circle, where there are always a few broken tests in the build. When this happens, the automated acceptance criteria no longer perform their primary role of providing feedback about the project's current health. This is what you want to avoid.

Figure 9.1   Acceptance tests that fail too often can lead to complacency.

It's an important problem, and it's worth putting in some effort up front to ensure that the time you invest automating your acceptance criteria yields its full fruits over the duration of the project and beyond. Automated tests are like any other kind of code—if you want them to be robust and easy to maintain, you need to put a little effort into their design and write them in a way that's clear and easy to understand.

Writing good, automated acceptance tests requires the same software engineering skills and disciplines, and the same level of craftsmanship, as well-written production code. The best automated acceptance tests tend to be the result of a collaborative effort between testers and developers.

Unfortunately, automated tests often don't receive the attention they need. Part of this problem is historical—for many years, test automation has been synonymous with test scripts. Teams have been reluctant to put too much effort into writing scripts when they could be writing production code. Many of the more traditional testing tools do indeed use scripting languages that have poor support for, or simply don't encourage, standard software engineering practices, such as refactoring to avoid code duplication, writing reusable components, and writing code in a clean and readable manner.

Many of these issues can be avoided if teams apply a few simple principles. A good, automated acceptance test needs to respect a few key rules:

- *It should communicate clearly.* Automated acceptance tests are first and foremost communication tools. Wording and semantics are important; the tests need to clearly explain the business behavior they're demonstrating. They need to explain to stakeholders, business analysts, testers, and other team members what business tasks the application is intended to support and illustrate how it does. Ideally, these tests will outlive the development phase of the project and go on to help the maintenance or business as usual team (BAU, the team that takes care of applications once they're deployed into production; in many organizations, this is a different team than the one developing the project) understand the project requirements and how they've been implemented.

- *It should provide meaningful feedback.* If a test fails, a developer should be able to understand what the underlying requirement is trying to achieve and how it's interacting with the application to do so.

- *It should be reliable.* To get value out of the tests, the team needs to be able to trust the test results. A test should pass if (and only if) the application satisfies the underlying business requirement and should fail if it doesn't. If a test does break for technical reasons, the problem should be easy to isolate and simple to fix. Although this sounds obvious, it can require care and discipline to ensure that the more complex tests respect this rule.

- *It should be easy to maintain.* A test that breaks too often when the application is updated or modified, or that requires constant maintenance to keep up to date, rapidly becomes a liability for the development team. If this happens too frequently, the developers will often simply cease updating the tests and leave them in a broken state. When this happens, any useful feedback from the test results is lost, and the time invested in building up the test suite is wasted.

In the rest of this chapter, we'll look at how you can write high-quality tests that respect these rules and that provide valuable feedback and are robust and easy to maintain.

9.2   Using personas and known entities

In chapter 7 we saw how fluent builders can be used to describe the initial state of an application or of objects in the system in a clean and readable manner. Another very useful technique when describing the state of a system for a scenario is to use *personas* or *known entities*. In the domain of user experience (UX), personas are fictional characters that are meant to represent the different types of people who will be using the system. A persona usually comes with a very detailed description, including everything from the fictional person's name and email address to their interests, hobbies, and work habits. Figure 9.2 shows a persona for a Flying High customer.

Casual Flying High Customer: Jane

First name:	Jane
Last name:	Smith
Email:	jane@acme.com
DOB:	29/08/1981
Phone:	0123456789
Address:	10 Partridge Street, Dandenong

Background: Jane is an account manager for a pharmaceutical company in Melbourne.
Family: Married with two children, a five-year-old boy and a two-year-old girl
Preferred communication: Email and phone
Seating preference: Aisle

Flying profile: Jane flies two to three times per month for her job. She takes whatever airline proposes the most attractive deal.

Figure 9.2   A persona is a fictional character meant to represent a category of user of the system.

9.2.1   Working with persona in your scenarios

When it comes to setting up test data for your scenarios, a persona assembles a set of precise data under a well-known name. So, when you refer to Jane in the following scenario, everyone on the team will know who you're talking about. Here's an example of one of Jane's scenarios:

```
Scenario: Registering online for a new Frequent Flyer account
  Given Jane is not a Frequent Flyer member
  When Jane registers for a new account
  Then she should be sent a confirmation email
  And she should receive 500 bonus points
```

Whenever Jane is referred to in the scenario, the test code will look up the corresponding persona details. For example, in the second step ("When Jane registers for a new account"), the test code can refer to all of Jane's details to complete the registration form, without them needing to appear in the scenario itself.

There are many ways to implement persona-based test data in your code, and the best way will depend on your specific application. Sometimes the data related to each persona is stored in external files, such as a JSON file or properties file. In other applications default persona data is stored in a test database and initialized at the start of each test. In the next section we'll look at one simple and effective strategy for storing test data in JSON-like configuration files.

9.2.2 Storing persona data in HOCON

One very convenient way to store persona data in external files is to use the Typesafe `config` library (https://github.com/lightbend/config). This open source library allows you to store data in the HOCON format (https://github.com/lightbend/config/blob/master/HOCON.md). HOCON is a superset of JSON used by many open source tools for configuration files. More flexible and readable than plain JSON, HOCON is a great way to store test data and represent the persona that figure in your scenarios. An example of a HOCON file is shown in the following listing, where we describe two persona, Jane and Terry, who have different personal details.

> **Listing 9.1 Test data stored in the HOCON format used by Typesafe `config`**

```
Jane: {
  firstName: Jane
  lastName: Smith
  email: "jane@acme.com"
  street: 10 Partridge Street
  city: Dandenong
  state: Victoria
  postCode: 3175
  country: Australia
  telephone: "0123456789"
  dateOfBirth: 1981-08-29
}
Terry: {
  firstName: Terry
  lastName: Traveler
  email: "terry@dummy-email.com"
  street: 100 Main Street
  city: Dublin
  country: Ireland
}
```

The step definition code for the first step of the scenario we saw earlier refers to the persona name to retrieve the corresponding details:

```
Traveler travelerDetails;

@Given("{} is not a Frequent Flyer member")
public void notAFrequentFlyer(String name) {
    travelerDetails = TravelerPersonas.findByName(name);
}
```

And behind the scenes, the `TravelerPersonas` class uses the Typesafe Config API to read the persona data from a test file called travelers.conf stored in the src/test/resources/testdata folder, as seen in the following listing.

Listing 9.2   Reading test data from an HOCON file

```
import com.typesafe.config.Config;
import com.typesafe.config.ConfigFactory;

public class TravelerPersonas {

    private static Config travelers
        = ConfigFactory.load("testdata/travelers");

    public static Traveler findByName(String name) {
        Config travelerDetails = travelers.getConfig(name);
        return new Traveler(
                travelerDetails.getString("firstName"),
                travelerDetails.getString("lastName"),
                travelerDetails.getString("email"),
                travelerDetails.getString("street"),
                travelerDetails.getString("city"),
                travelerDetails.getString("state"),
                travelerDetails.getString("postCode"),
                travelerDetails.getString("country"),
                travelerDetails.getString("telephone"),
                travelerDetails.getString("dateOfBirth")
        );
    }
}
```

A similar approach can be used with other types of test data. The team defines known entities—domain objects in a well-known state. For example, a banking application working on transferring bank statement files might define a few standard file types and then only specify the fields that have different values for a given scenario.

9.3   *Layers of abstraction*

Automated acceptance tests need to be stable and reliable. When small changes happen in the application, you shouldn't need to update hundreds of acceptance tests just to keep the test suite running. Maintaining your automated acceptance tests should never be a hindrance to your ability to embrace change.

Yet when many teams start automating their acceptance criteria, this is exactly what happens. Often a small change in a single, commonly used web page will break a large swath of tests, and developers will need to fix each test individually before the test suite can work again. This is thankless, unproductive work that does little to encourage the team to automate more acceptance tests.

It doesn't have to be this way. One very effective way to improve the quality of your automation code is to apply a basic principle of software engineering, known as layers of abstraction. Layers of abstraction hide implementation details inside a function or object. This makes the high-level layers cleaner and easier to understand and isolates them from changes in the implementation details hidden inside the lower layers.

When you write automated acceptance criteria, using layers can help you isolate the more volatile, low-level implementation details of your tests from the higher level, more stable business rules. High-level business rules tend to be relatively stable, and changes to them will be driven by the business rather than by technical constraints. Lower-level implementation details, such as screen layouts and field names, as well as how a low-level library is called, tend to change more frequently. When changes do happen at the lower implementation levels, the affect on the automated acceptance criteria should be minimal. Experienced BDD practitioners[1] typically use at least three layers of abstraction in their tests, like the ones illustrated in figure 9.3.

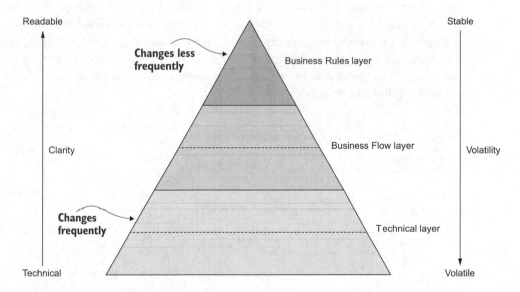

Figure 9.3   Well-written automated acceptance criteria are organized in three main layers.

Let's look at each of these three main layers.

9.3.1   *The Business Rules layer describes the expected outcomes*

The Business Rules layer describes the requirement under test in high-level business terms. If you're using a BDD tool such as Cucumber, or SpecFlow, the business rule will typically take the form of a scenario in a feature file using either a table or a narrative structure, like the one we saw earlier in the chapter. In other cases, the business

---

[1] See, for example, Gojko Adzik, "How to implement UI testing without shooting yourself in the foot," http://gojko.net/2010/04/13/how-to-implement-ui-testing-without-shooting-yourself-in-the-foot-2/.

rules layer can be automated using other test automation libraries such as JUnit or
TestNG (for Java), NUnit (for .NET), or any of the many NodeJS-based testing libraries
for JavaScript.

To get a better feel for how these layers fit together, let's work through the example we saw earlier:

```
Scenario: Registering online for a new Frequent Flyer account
    Given Jane is not a Frequent Flyer member
    When Jane registers for a new account
    Then she should be sent a confirmation email
    And she should receive 500 bonus points
```

This rule only applies to new members.

The expected outcomes

The high-level action under test

As you saw in the previous chapter, this sort of scenario focuses on the business outcomes of a requirement and isn't too worried about how the system delivers these outcomes. Requirements expressed in this way should only need to change if the business changes its mind (or its understanding evolves) about the expected outcomes.

Figure 9.4 illustrates one example of the way the Business Rules layer works together with the other layers to implement this scenario. Don't worry about the details of the code just yet; we'll discuss the technologies used in this example later in the chapter and in the following chapters.

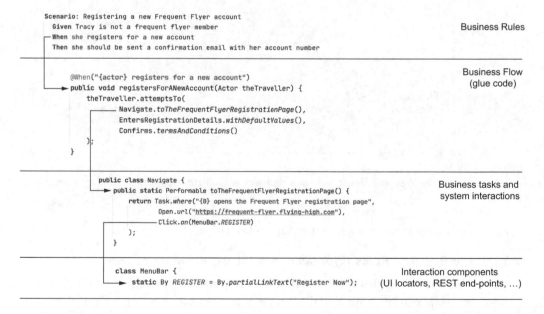

Figure 9.4   Each automation layer uses services from the layer beneath to implement a scenario.

We can relate the code in figure 9.4 back to the layers we described earlier (see figure 9.5). Business rules are described in feature files and scenarios. The step definition methods (or "glue code") describe how each step translates into business tasks and actions. These tasks and actions are represented in the next layer down, as reusable objects or methods. Finally, in the System Interactions layer, we define how we actually interact with the application. More precisely, this is where we specify how to locate elements on a web page, what REST end points to call, and so forth.

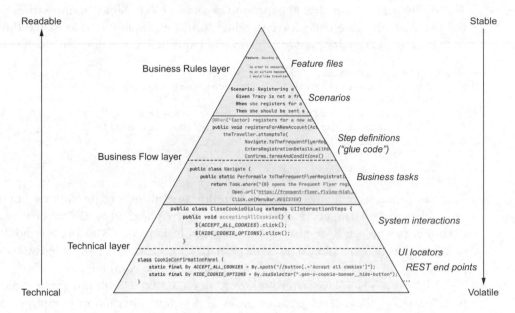

Figure 9.5   Each automation layer uses services from the layer beneath to implement a scenario.

In the following sections we will walk through each of these layers in more detail.

9.3.2   *The Business Flow layer describes the user's journey*

If the Business Rules describe business goals and constraints that the business is interested in, the Business Flow layer is where you demonstrate how the system helps users achieve these goals or respect these constraints. The aim here is not to describe the implementation of the system in detail, but to give a high-level overview, in business terms, of the tasks or steps. What high-level actions does Jane need to perform to register for a new account? How will you know that she has received the confirmation email? How would you step through the application to demonstrate this scenario?

BUSINESS GOALS AND USER JOURNEYS

This layer is where we define and describe each of the business tasks a user performs to achieve a particular goal. These tasks often come together to describe a user journey through the system. Each step in a scenario maps to a sequence of one or more of these tasks.

For example, the second step of the scenario we introduced earlier is "When Jane registers for a new account." We could break this step into the following activities:

- Jane chooses to register for a new account on the Frequent Flyer website.
- Jane enters her name and address.
- Jane confirms the terms and conditions and submits her application.

The Business Flow layer should express these steps in a readable, business-friendly way. For example, the glue code corresponding to this example might look like this (this code uses the Screenplay pattern, which we will look at in more detail in chapter 10):

```
@When("{actor} registers for a new account")
public void registersForANewAccount(Actor theTraveler) {
    theTraveler.attemptsTo(
            Navigate.toTheFrequentFlyerRegistrationPage(),
            EnterRegistrationDetails.using(travelerDetails),
            Confirms.termsAndConditions()
    );
}
```

These steps are more likely to change than the core business requirements, but they'll only need to be changed if some aspect of the application workflow changes. For example, maybe you'll need to add a step where Jane needs to provide additional details when she enters her details, or perhaps a new law means she needs to confirm her email address before the registration process can be completed.

The Business Flow layer typically never interacts directly with the application itself; it delegates to lower-level business tasks and system interaction components. For example, in the code shown, we don't talk about clicking on any buttons or links; we simply state that the traveler navigates to the registration section of the application. We don't list the fields that Jane needs to fill in when she enters her details, as they are not relevant at this level of the story. We focus purely on what she does, and the how comes later.

BIG-PICTURE SCENARIOS

For larger applications, business-flow steps can be even higher level. Suppose we are working on an online car insurance application. We could represent the overall flow with a scenario like this one:

```
Scenario: Jane applies for comprehensive insurance online
  Given Jane owns a new Toyota Prius
  When Jane applies for comprehensive car insurance
  Then she should be shown a New Hybrid Car quote
  And she should receive a copy of the quote via email
```

This is a big-picture scenario. We aren't worried about the details, such as where Jane lives, or whether she has had any accidents in the past. We are focusing on the overall flow and high-level goals—in this case getting a quote in front of our customers so they can make a purchase.

Of course, applying for a car insurance quote is a rather complex, multistep process and involves entering a lot of details. You need to know personal details such as the driver's age and address, as well as details about the type of car they drive. All these details will be required in lower-level steps. However, the focus in this big-picture scenario is the overall flow, and we don't want them muddying the picture at this high level.

To keep track of all these details, without overwhelming the reader of the scenario with unnecessary noise, we could define persona objects to contain sensible default values about the driver's car and personal details, only changing the ones that are relevant for a specific scenario. Using the techniques we saw in the previous chapter, the code for the first step might look like this:

```
@Given("{actor} owns a {newOrUsed} {word} {}")
public void ownsACar(Actor theCustomer,
                     NewOrUsed newOrUsed,
                     String make,
                     String model) {
    driverDetails = DriverPersonas.withName(theCustomer.getName())
                               .withVehicle(Vehicle.thatIs(newOrUsed)
                                   .ofMake(make)
                                   .ofModel(model));
}
```

In the next step we walk through the application process, but at a high level, showing the big steps. When Dave asks for a quote for his car, he needs to first provide details about his car (e.g., the make and model of the car, the year it was purchased, and where it is parked) and then provide details about himself (where he lives, his driving record, etc.). Finally, he needs to confirm that all the details he entered are accurate.

```
@When("{actor} applies for comprehensive car insurance")
public void appliesForComprehensiveCarInsurance(Actor theDriver) {
    theDriver.attemptsTo(
            ApplyForAutomobileInsurance.forASingleCar(),
            ProvideDetails.from(driverDetails).aboutTheirCar(),
            ProvideDetails.from(driverDetails).aboutThemselves(),
            Conforms.theApplicationDetails()
    );
}
```

Notice how high level all these tasks are. High-level tasks tend to be more stable than low-level implementation details. A customer will always need to apply for automobile insurance, choose a particular product, and provide the appropriate details. What details they need to enter about themselves may change as the application evolves, but the fact that they need to provide some personal information will not.

High-level tasks written this way are also easy to reuse and reassemble for other tests. For example, another scenario might involve purchasing motorbike insurance. This could use different tasks for choosing the product but reuse the tasks related to entering personal details and confirming the application:

```
theDriver.attemptsTo(
        ApplyForAutomobileInsurance.forAMotorcycle(),
        ProvideDetails.from(driverDetails).aboutTheirMotercycle(),
        ProvideDetails.from(driverDetails).aboutThemselves(),
        Conforms.theApplicationDetails()
    );
```

It's only inside each of these tasks that we actually interact with the application, so we only need to maintain how these interactions happen in one place for each task.

This actor-centric style of coding is known as *Screenplay* (see chapter 12), and it is just one of many approaches that teams use to layer their code. We will look at other patterns that can help achieve this kind of layering in the coming chapters. Let's look at how these individual tasks do their jobs now.

9.3.3   *Business tasks interact with the application or with other tasks*

As we have seen, well-designed test code is implemented in layers. Any given layer contains the implementation of steps in the layer above. And this implementation is done by specifying (or orchestrating) what the layer below should do (see figure 9.5).

What this generally means is that tasks in the Business Flow layer are broken down into more granular business tasks or direct interactions with the application. For example, some tasks may interact with a web page, whereas others may call a REST API or query a database.

In the previous section, we saw how, to register for a Frequent Flyer account, a traveler needs to navigate to the registration page and provide their registration details. Each of these steps hides lower-level interactions with the application. For example, to navigate to the registration page, the traveler needs to open a browser and click on a Register button (see figure 10.3). And similarly, entering registration details will involve many interactions with the application, most likely by interacting with other web pages.

Not all interactions happen via the web pages. For many scenarios, some or all steps can be performed more effectively via REST API calls, database queries, message queues, or other non-UI-based approaches. For example, one of the last steps in the scenario is "And she should receive a confirmation email." This step could be implemented using a mock web server or an email testing service. (You can find many email testing tools on the market, such as TestMail, MailSlurp, and MailHog.) Similarly, the last step, "And she should receive 500 bonus points," could be a simple call to a REST end point to query the traveler's current Frequent Flyer account balance.

9.3.4   *The Technical layer interacts with the system*

The Technical layer is made up of components that interact directly with the application in some way. Technical components typically combine two elements: some domain or application-specific details about what part of the application to interact with and a tool or library that performs the actual interaction.

For example, the following code describes how a user navigates to the registration page:

```
public static Performable toTheFrequentFlyerRegistrationPage() {
    return Task.where("{0} opens the Frequent Flyer registration page",
            Open.url("https://frequent-flyer.flying-high.com"),
            Click.on(MenuBar.REGISTER)
    );
}
```

Click on the Register link in the main menu.

Open the browser to a specific URL.

This method uses technical components: the `Open` class, to open a browser on a specific URL, and the `Click` class, which clicks on a specified element on the page. Each of these components, which are part of the Serenity Screenplay library that we will be looking at in more detail later in the book, uses Selenium WebDriver under the hood to perform the actual interactions.

The test code passes application-specific details to these components in the form of parameters. The first action uses the application URL. The second specifies where exactly the user should click using a WebDriver locator object (we'll learn much more about these in chapter 10), which we store in a separate class:

```
public class MenuBar {
    public static final By REGISTER = By.partialLinkText("Register Now");
}
```

Keeping the locators in a separate class like this is a technique we use to minimize the impact of change. Well-written technical components isolate the other layers from the impact of low-level change. For example, suppose the design of the registration page changes, involving changes to the HTML structure and field names. Such a change would modify neither the business rule nor the workflow for this requirement, and those levels wouldn't be affected. The only code you'd need to update is within the page object that encapsulates the registration page. This update would work for any scenario that uses this page.

In addition, you can implement the Business Rules and the Business Flow layers before the user interface has been implemented. The first layers are written in collaboration with the testers and business analysts and act as guidelines for development work. Only when the user interface is reasonably stable do you implement the technical components. In the following chapters we will look more closely at the tools you can use to perform these interactions for different types of applications.

Summary

- Good, automated acceptance tests should communicate clearly and provide meaningful feedback when they fail. They should also be reliable and designed with maintenance in mind.
- Using persona in your test scenarios is a good way to describe the state of the system in a more descriptive way.
- Layers of abstraction help make the automated acceptance criteria more robust by separating the what from the how at multiple levels.

In the next chapter, you'll learn how to write automated acceptance tests that exercise a web interface.

Automating acceptance criteria for the UI layer

This chapter covers

- Why and when you should write automated UI tests
- Using tools like Selenium WebDriver in Java to automate web tests
- Finding and interacting with page elements in your tests
- Design patterns to write more maintainable web tests

In the previous chapter, you learned how using a layered approach to automated acceptance testing helps make your tests clearer, more robust, and more maintainable. We discussed the three broad layers used in well-designed automated acceptance tests: the Business Rules layer, the Business Flow layer, and the Technical layer. In the following few chapters, we'll focus on approaches and tools that can be used to implement the Technical layer, starting with the user interface.

In this chapter we'll discuss techniques to automate UI tests for web-based applications. Users interact with an application through its user interface, and in modern web applications the UI implementation plays a major role in the overall user experience. The screenshots from automated web tests can be a valuable aid for testers, and they're also a great way to provide illustrated documentation describing how the application behaves.

We'll look at automated web testing from several perspectives, as well as a few popular automation libraries used for web testing:

- *Automated web tests* are very effective at testing user interactions with the UI, and for illustrating end-to-end user interactions with the application. But if they're badly designed or used to test things that would be better tested by non-UI tests, web tests can become a maintenance liability.
- *Selenium WebDriver* is a popular open source library that can be used to write automated web tests in a number of languages, such as Java, JavaScript, Ruby, C#, and Python, and is the basis for a large number of open source tools.
- WebDriver is not the only tool you can use for web automation. We will also learn about *Cypress*, an interesting and more recent alternative to Selenium WebDriver from the JavaScript space.

Possibly more so than other types of test automation, web testing efforts can suffer enormously from poor design. We will look at a number of design patterns and practices that can help make sure your tests are robust, reliable, and easy to maintain.

Although we'll focus on web testing in this chapter, many of the tools and approaches discussed here also apply to other types of user interfaces. For example, mobile apps can be tested effectively using the tool set we'll discuss here by using Appium (http://appium.io/), a WebDriver-based automation library for mobile apps, and the design patterns and best practices we discuss are applicable for any type of GUI.

To write effective automated web tests, you need to know not only how to automate web tests well, but also when you should and shouldn't automate scenarios with web tests.

10.1   When and how should you test the UI?

Web tests have some significant advantages over other types of testing:

- They reproduce end-user behavior well. While non-UI tests can be very effective at describing and documenting business rules, UI tests imitate actual user behavior more closely. Many stakeholders have a natural tendency to trust them more for this reason.
- They're a great way to demo features to stakeholders and to document how the application works.
- Some application behavior and logic happen only at the UI level and cannot be tested in any other way.
- UI tests tend to be closer to what a tester would test by hand, and so they can reduce the need for manual UI testing, which represents a significant overhead for testers.

A web test, by definition, is designed to verify UI behavior. But web tests, as end-to-end tests, can also be an effective way to illustrate and check how all the components in the system work together. Used as living documentation, a web test also often does a great job of documenting how a user will use the system to achieve a particular goal. Web tests can also help give business analysts, testers, and stakeholders more confidence in the automated acceptance tests.

10.2   Where does UI testing fit in your test automation strategy?

UI tests clearly have their uses. But you rarely need to test every aspect of a system using UI tests, and doing so is generally not a good idea. In fact, in a typical BDD project, a significant proportion of automated acceptance tests will be implemented as non-UI tests (see figure 10.1).

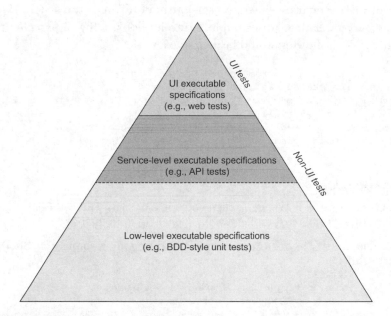

Figure 10.1   A typical BDD project will have many more non-UI automated acceptance tests than UI ones.

These non-UI tests can take many forms, as you'll see in chapter 11, including what would traditionally be classed as integration or unit tests. Many automated acceptance criteria, particularly those related to business rules or calculations, are more effectively done directly using the application code or via a REST API rather than through the user interface. Non-web tests can test specific business rules more quickly and more precisely than an end-to-end web test. Non-UI tests are also much easier to automate before development starts.

10.2.1 *Which scenarios should be implemented as UI tests?*

It can often be tricky to know whether to implement an acceptance test as a web test or a non-web test, or where to use a combination of techniques. One simple approach is to remember that you only really need a web test for four things:

- Illustrating key user journeys through the system
- Illustrating or checking what information is presented in the user interface in different circumstances
- Showing how information is rendered in the user interface
- Documenting and verifying screen-specific business logic

Let's look at each of these.

10.2.2 *Illustrating user journeys*

Many high-level BDD scenarios illustrate user journeys through the system. We call these scenarios *journey scenarios*. For example, a traveler books a flight, or a client completes a purchase. The following would be a good example:

```
Scenario: Tara books a flight from London to New York
  Given Tara is a registered Frequent Flyer member
  And she has searched for one-way flights from London to New York in Economy
  When she books the first available flight
  Then she should be informed that her booking was successful
  And the booking should appear in her My Booking section
```

Bullet point Gherkin

Some folks find the Given . . . When . . . Then notation a bit clunky and artificial for journey scenarios. They'd rather just rattle off what happened, from the user perspective.

One way to make this a bit more readable is the bullet-point notation in Gherkin, which looks like this:

```
Scenario: Tara books a flight from London to New York
  * Tara is a registered Frequent Flyer member
  * She searches for one-way flights from London to New York in Economy
  * She books the first available flight
  * She should be informed that her booking was successful
  * The booking appears in her My Booking section
```

Behind the scenes, Cucumber treats these steps identically to the ones in the Given . . . When . . . Then version, so the style you use is very much a question of personal preference or team conventions.

Scenarios like these are often good candidates for UI tests, because they do a great job illustrating how a user interacts with the system to achieve a particular business goal. But you don't need too many of them. You don't need to show every possible path through the system, just the more significant ones. More exhaustive testing can be left to faster-running tests.

You can also streamline high-level scenarios by mixing UI interactions with back-end interactions. For example, in the previous scenario, suppose that the registration feature has already been tested in another scenario. In that case we could implement the first step, "Given Tara is a registered Frequent Flyer member," with an API call rather than by registering via the web interface.

10.2.3   Illustrating business logic in the user interface

Web tests can also illustrate how business rules are reflected in the user interface. For example, suppose that when they book a flight, Frequent Flyer members should be given the option to choose their seat, a privilege not offered to other customers. This would be a good candidate for an automated web test.

A good rule of thumb is to ask yourself whether you're illustrating how the user interacts with the application or underlying business logic that's independent of the user interface. Now suppose that, when a new Frequent Flyer member registers, we need to check that the email doesn't already exist. To do this we could write a scenario like the following:

```
Rule: Duplicate usernames are not allowed

  Example: Someone tries to register with an email that is already used
  Mike Smith is an existing Frequent Flyer member.
  His wife Jenny Smith does not have a Frequent Flyer account

    Given Mike Smith is a Frequent Flyer member with the following details:
       | username | smiths@example.org |
       | password | correct-password |
    When Jenny tries to register with a username of "smiths@example.org"
    Then she should be presented with an error message containing "Email
  exists, please try another name"
    And she should also be presented with a "Forgot your password?" link
```

This is not really a full user journey; it checks a specific business rule on a specific screen. The logical way to implement this scenario would be via the user interface.

But not all cases are so cut-and-dry. For example, suppose you were testing the registration feature and that one of the acceptance criteria included the following constraints:

- The user should receive feedback indicating the strength of the password entered.
- Only strong passwords should be accepted.

The first acceptance criterion relates to the user's interaction with the web page and would need to illustrate how this feedback is provided on the login page. This would be a good candidate for an automated web test.

The second criterion, on the other hand, is about determining what makes a strong password and what passwords users should be allowed to enter. While this can be done through the user interface by repeatedly submitting different passwords, that would be wasteful. What you're really checking here is the password-strength algorithm, so an application code–level test would be more appropriate.

10.2.4 *Documenting and verifying screen-specific business logic*

Sometimes we need more fine-grained UI testing for specific screens, including scenarios that might be too detailed for a typical BDD scenario. For example, we might want to check that all the fields on a particular page are rendered correctly.

For example, when a new Frequent Flyer member registers, they need to provide a valid email, so we need to do some checks to make sure that the address they provide is well formed. We could write a scenario along the following lines to express this constraint:

```
Rule: The unique username should be a valid email address
  Scenario Outline: Only correctly structured emails should be accepted
    Given Candy does not have a Frequent Flyer account
    When she tries to register with a username of "<username>"
    Then she should be told "Not a valid email format"
    Examples:
      | username      |
      | not-an-email  |
      | notemail.com  |
      | candy@#.com   |
```

This scenario gives a few examples of invalid email formats that would need to be checked. It shows how the user is informed when they enter a bad email address.

But there are clearly many, many other examples of invalid email addresses. And we wouldn't want to test them all via the user interface—that would lead to a large number of web tests that would slow down the test suite, without adding that much additional confidence.

A more efficient approach would be to check these other cases at a lower level. In a well-designed application, we would only need to check a few examples through the user interface. Once we have established that entering an invalid email address will get you an error message, we could test the other cases with non-UI-based tests.

Many teams use separate Cucumber scenarios for more detailed scenarios like this:

```
Scenario: Email addresses need to be well formed
  Given Candy does not have a Frequent Flyer account
  When she wants to register a new Frequent Flyer account
  Then the following emails should not be considered valid:
    | Email        | Reason Rejected     |
    | not-an-email | Missing @ section   |
    | wrong.com    | Missing @           |
    | wrong@       | Mission domain      |
    | wrong@#.com  | Invalid characters  |
    |              | Cannot be empty     |
```

Scenarios like this open or navigate to a given page, and then check a number of related cases on this page. For example, here we check that each invalid email is rejected, without running a separate web test for each case. This is more efficient than the approach described in the previous scenario (where we used a scenario outline) but requires a little more logic in the step definition code to loop over the test cases. (You can see an example of how this can be implemented in the sample code for this chapter.)

But we could also use a lower-level unit testing library as well. We would typically only use Cucumber if we felt this is the best way to document these rules, and if they are something that the business care enough about to have it appear in the living documentation.

10.2.5 *Showing how information is rendered in the user interface*

Sometimes we want to check more detailed UI behavior; for example, we might want to check that all the fields on a particular page are rendered correctly, or which fields on a form are mandatory.

Gherkin isn't always the most convenient format to specify mandatory fields, but it can be done. For example, the following scenarios succinctly describe rules about mandatory fields when registering:

```
Rule: Registering members need to complete all the mandatory fields
  Scenario: Mandatory fields for registration
    Given Candy does not have a Frequent Flyer account
    When she wants to register a new Frequent Flyer account
    Then the following information should be mandatory to register:
      | Field     | Error Message If Missing   |
      | email     | Please enter your email    |
      | password  | Please enter your password |
      | firstName | Please enter your first name |
      | lastName  | Please enter your last name |
      | address   | Please enter your address  |
      | country   | Please enter a valid country |

  Scenario: Customers must agree to the registration terms and conditions
    Given Candy does not have a Frequent Flyer account
    When she tries to register without approving the terms and conditions
    Then she should be told "Please confirm the terms and conditions"
```

Now that we've had a look at the kind of scenarios where we might want to use user interface automation, let's look at how we can do this. We'll start with the most commonly used open source web testing library: Selenium WebDriver.

10.2.6 *Automating web-based acceptance criteria using Selenium WebDriver*

In this section, we'll look at automating web tests using Selenium WebDriver. Selenium WebDriver is a popular open source web browser automation library that can be used to write effective, automated web tests. It also forms the basis for many higher-level web-testing tools. In this chapter we will focus on working with WebDriver in Java, and in the next chapter we will look at how these techniques work in JavaScript. But the principles and techniques we'll discuss in these chapters will be generally applicable to any WebDriver-based testing.

WebDriver is a browser-automation tool. It lets you write tests that launch and interact with a real browser. This interaction can include simple clicks on buttons or links, or more sophisticated mouse operations such as hovering or dragging and dropping.

WebDriver lets you check the test outcomes by inspecting the state of the page in the browser. WebDriver also gives you the ability to take screenshots along the way—screenshots that can be used later as part of the test reports or living documentation.

Figure 10.2 shows a high-level view of WebDriver, which supports a large number of web browsers, including Firefox, Chrome, and Microsoft Edge. This allows you to test your application in different environments and with different browsers.

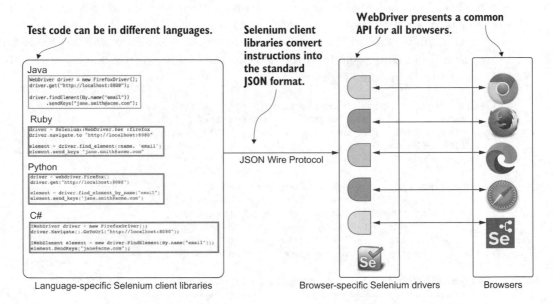

Figure 10.2   Overview of the WebDriver architecture

You write a WebDriver test using a language-specific client library. Many languages are supported, including Java, JavaScript, Ruby, C#, and Python. The WebDriver API varies little from one language to another, so you can generally use the language you're most comfortable with, or the one that provides the most value for you in terms of ease of writing, maintainability, and living documentation.

The WebDriver client libraries use a standard format, defined in the W3C Webdriver Specification (`https://w3c.github.io/webdriver/`), to manage communication between the client and a browser-specific driver. Drivers exist for most of the main browsers, such as Chrome, Firefox, Internet Explorer, and Microsoft Edge.

This same protocol also works for remote browsers. You can set up a network of servers using Selenium Grid, which allows you to control browsers on real or virtual remote machines. This makes scaling your test suite by running your tests in parallel much easier. Many commercial services, such as SauceLabs and BrowserStack also propose to manage and maintain a Selenium Grid for you.

The WebDriver API is powerful and flexible, but there are several open source libraries for different platforms that can help you build on WebDriver to write web tests more efficiently and more expressively, including Serenity BDD and Selenide (Java), Serenity/JS, Protractor, Webdriver.io (JavaScript), Watir (Ruby), and Geb (for Groovy), just to name a few. For most of this chapter, you'll see how to use the WebDriver API with Java and JavaScript, which are, at the time of writing, the most commonly seen options.

10.2.7 Getting started with WebDriver in Java

Let's start with a very simple example of web browser automation with WebDriver. You'll illustrate WebDriver's features using a simple version of the Flying High Frequent Flyer website that we've discussed in previous chapters.

If you want to follow along, you can download both the website and the sample code from either the GitHub repository or from the Manning website. The sample code repository contains two directories:

- The flying-high-app directory contains the sample website (see sidebar).
- The subdirectories in the chapter-09 directory (java) contain the sample WebDriver code we'll discuss during the chapter.

> ### Running the sample website
> The Frequent Flyer website you'll use is a simple standalone website that will run on any web server. It's a simple JavaScript-based web application. You can either deploy it to your own web server or run it as a standalone website. One way to do this is to use Node.js, a lightweight JavaScript platform used to build and run JavaScript-based server-side applications. You don't need to know anything about Node.js to run the sample site; just follow the instructions.
>
> First, you need to install Node.js, which you can download from the Node.js website (http://nodejs.org/). Once you've done this, go into the flying-high-app directory and into the server subdirectory and install the project dependencies:
>
> ```
> $ npm install
> ```
>
> Next, start the website with the following command:
>
> ```
> $ nest start
> ```
>
> To view the running application, open a web browser and go to http://localhost:3000. You should see a page similar to the one in figure 10.3.

Suppose you're testing the sign-in feature of your Frequent Flyer website. Registered members need to enter their email address and password to access their account details. The login screen looks something like the one in figure 10.3.

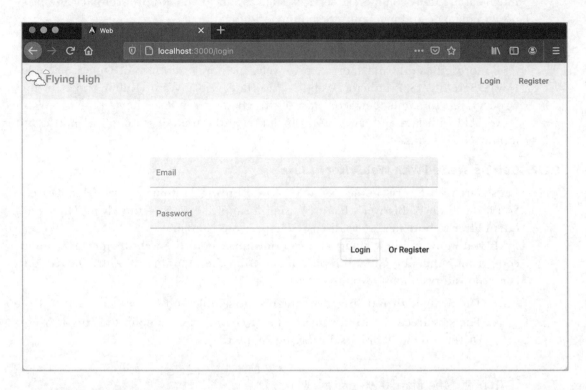

Figure 10.3   Flying High Frequent Flyer members identify themselves using their email address and a password.

Once a member has entered a matching email and password, they'll be welcomed to the member's area with a friendly message (see figure 10.4). We could represent this requirement using a simple scenario like this:

```
Business Need: Authentication

  Registered Frequent Flyer members can access their account using their
  email
  and password

  @webtest
  Example: Tracy successfully logs on to the Frequent Flyer app
    Given Tracy is a registered Frequency Flyer member
    When Tracy logs on with a valid username and password
    Then she should be given access to her account
```

Now let's dive straight into the step definitions and see how this scenario could be implemented using WebDriver in Java.

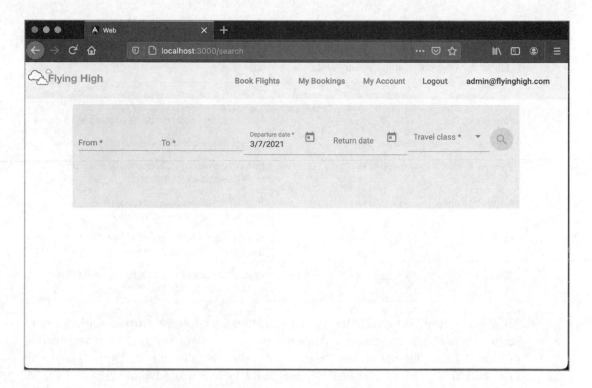

Figure 10.4   Authenticated members can book flights and see their bookings and earned points.

10.2.8   Setting up a WebDriver driver

One of the first things we need to do in any Selenium web test is to spin up a browser to run our tests in. As we saw earlier, Selenium WebDriver gives us a standard API that we can use to interact with different types of browsers.

The first thing you do is declare a new `WebDriver` instance. This object, which implements the WebDriver interface, is the starting point for all your interactions with the application. There is a separate implementation class for each different type of browser.

For example, the following code creates a new `WebDriver` instance for Chrome (it also opens an instance of the Chrome browser to interact with):

```
WebDriver driver = new ChromeDriver();
```

If we wanted to use Firefox, the code would look like this:

```
WebDriver driver = new FirefoxDriver();
```

This code needs a WebDriver driver binary to work. Each browser needs a specific driver, a binary executable that knows how to control and interact with the browser. One option is to download the binaries for the browsers of your choice (see table 10.1) and place them on your system path. This is not always the most robust approach, as it can make your tests dependent on your local environment installation.

Table 10.1   Where to find the various WebDriver drivers

Browser	WebDriver implementation	Download site
Firefox	`Geckodriver`	https://github.com/mozilla/geckodriver/releases
Chrome	`ChromeDriver`	https://chromedriver.chromium.org/downloads
Internet Explorer	`InternetExplorerDriver`	https://github.com/SeleniumHQ/selenium/wiki/InternetExplorerDriver
Microsoft Edge	`edgedriver`	https://developer.microsoft.com/en-us/microsoft-edge/tools/webdriver/
Opera	`OperaDriver`	https://github.com/operasoftware/operachromiumdriver/releases
Safari	`SafariDriver`	https://developer.apple.com/documentation/webkit/testing_with_webdriver_in_safari

Another option is to use the WebDriverManager[1] library (https://github.com/bonigarcia/webdrivermanager), which downloads the right binary driver for you automatically. That's the option we'll use in our code examples in this chapter. To download and set up the WebDriver binaries for Chrome using `WebDriverManager`, we would include the following code:

```
WebDriverManager.chromedriver().setup();
```

Now that we've seen how to create a new `WebDriver` instance, let's see how all this fits into our Cucumber code.

Configuring your browser

When you create a new `WebDriver` instance, you can also pass configuration options to the browser.

Each browser has its own configuration classes. For example, for Chrome, you can use the `ChromeOptions` (http://chromedriver.chromium.org/capabilities) class, which you pass as a parameter to the `ChromeDriver` class constructor

```
ChromeOptions options = new ChromeOptions();
options.addArguments("start-maximized",
                "headless",
                "disable-extensions",
                "disable-popup-blocking",
                "disable-infobars");
WebDriver driver = new ChromeDriver(options);
```

---

[1] In the more recent versions of Selenium, this feature has been integrated into the Selenium library itself, so it is no longer necessary to configure drivers manually.

10.2.9 Integrating WebDriver with Cucumber

For our Cucumber scenario, we can use a `@Before` hook to define a method that will be run before each scenario that involves a user interface test (which we can identify using a tag):

```
public class AuthenticationStepDefinitions {           The WebDriver interface allows
                                                       us to interact with the browser
    WebDriver driver;                          ◁───    using a WebDriver client.

    @Before("@webtest")                        ◁───    Run this code before each
    public void setupWebdriver() {                     scenario with the @webtest tag.
        WebDriverManager.chromedriver().setup();   ◁───    Uses WebDriverManager
        driver = new ChromeDriver();           ◁───        to download and set up
    }                                                      the chromedriver binary
                                                           (optional)
    @After("@webtest")
    public void closeWebdriver() {
        driver.quit();          ◁──    Closes the          Creates a new WebDriver
    }                                  browser at the      instance to open and
}                                      end of each test    connect to a Chrome
                                                           browser
```

10.2.10 Sharing WebDriver instances between step definition classes

The code sample shown is a little too simple to be realistic. In general, we need to share the `WebDriver` instance across multiple step definition classes.

We could do this by storing the `WebDriver` instance in a static field. However, this will not work if you ever want to run your features or scenarios in parallel (more on this later).

A better approach is to use a `ThreadLocal` object, a *static* field that is shared between all the objects created in a given thread. Since each scenario will run in its own thread, this approach will create a separate `WebDriver` instance for each scenario but still let us share the `WebDriver` instance among all of the step definitions in a given scenario.

An example of this approach is shown here:

```
public class WebTestSupport {

    private static ThreadLocal<WebDriver> DRIVER = new ThreadLocal<>();

    @Before("@webtest")
    public void setupDriver() {
        WebDriverManager.chromedriver().setup();
        WebDriver driver = new ChromeDriver(options);
        DRIVER.set(driver);
    }

    public static WebDriver currentDriver() {
        return DRIVER.get();
    }
```

```
    @After("@webtest")
    public void closeDriver() {
        DRIVER.get().quit();
    }
}
```

10.2.11 Interacting with the web page

So far, we have just set up `WebDriver` instance and opened a browser. The next step
("Tracy logs on with a valid username and password") is where we actually interact
with the browser, and where things get a bit more interesting. In this step, we need to
do three things:

- Open the browser on the right page.
- Enter Tracy's login details.
- Click on the Login button and proceed to the home page.

Let's see how we would implement these steps in our Cucumber glue code.

In this scenario we log in to the application as Tracy ("Given Tracy is a registered
Frequent Flyer member"). Tracy is the name of our test user, who is created automatically when we start the server. In the previous chapter, we saw how to use configuration files to keep track of test user data like this. In this case, we will opt for a simpler
approach and create an enum to contain test user emails and passwords:

```
public enum FrequentFlyer {
    Tracy("tracy@flyinghigh.com","trac3");

    public final String email;
    public final String password;

    FrequentFlyer(String email, String password) {
        this.email = email;
        this.password = password;
    }
}
```

We can then use this enum as a parameter to the corresponding step definition method:

```
FrequentFlyer frequentFlyer;

@Given("{} is a registered Frequency Flyer member")
public void frequentFlyerMember(FrequentFlyer frequentFlyer) {
    this.frequentFlyer = frequentFlyer;
}
```

Next, we need Tracy to interact with the Chrome browser. We do this by using the
`driver` object once again; the `WebDriver` class has a wide range of methods you can
call to manipulate the web browser. For example, to open the browser on a given URL,
we use the `get()` method:

```
driver.get("http://localhost:3000");
```

To interact with a field or element on the page, we first need to find it on the page using the `findElement()` method. This method allows us to locate the element using a range of different strategies, which we will look at in detail in the next section. It returns a `WebElement` object, which gives us access to a number of other methods we can use to manipulate and query the individual element on the page.

For example, the following code locates the login link on the application home page, based on the text in the link:

```
WebElement loginLink = driver.findElement(By.linkText("Login"));
```

Once we obtain the element, we can use methods such as `click()` and `sendKeys()` (to click on or type some text into an element, respectively). For example, the following method will click on the link we just located:

```
loginLink.click();
```

You can see all of these techniques in action in the method:

```
@When("{} logs on with a valid username and password")
public void logsOnWithAValidUsernameAndPassword()
    WebDriver driver = WebTestSupport.currentDriver();

    driver.get("http://localhost:3000");
    driver.findElement(By.linkText("Login")).click();
    driver.findElement(By.id("email")).sendKeys(frequentFlyer.email);
    driver.findElement(By.id("password")).sendKeys(frequentFlyer.password);
    driver.findElement(By.id("login-button")).click();
}
```

Annotations:
- **Opens the application in Chrome**
- **Clicks on the login link and navigate to the login page**
- **Enters Tracy's username and password**
- **Clicks on the login button**

The last thing we need to do in this scenario is to check that Tracy gets taken to the right page once she has logged in. We can do this by checking the email address in the menu bar (see figure 10.3). The `findElement()` method returns a `WebElement` class and also gives us methods to fetch information about an element, such as its text content. The glue code for this step could be written as follows:

```
@Then("he/she should be given access to his/her account")
public void shouldBeGivenAccessToTheAccount() {
    WebDriver driver = WebTestSupport.currentDriver();
    String currentUser = driver.findElement(By.id("current-
user")).getText();
    assertThat(currentUser).isEqualTo(frequentFlyer.email);
}
```

Now that we've had a quick overview of WebDriver in action, let's look at the various WebDriver API features in more detail.

10.2.12 *How to locate elements on a page*

When it comes to writing automated web tests, locating elements on a page is one of the most fundamental skills you need to learn. In WebDriver, any object you'd like to inspect or manipulate in some way is represented by the `WebElement` class. You can find a web element on a page using the `findElement()` method. This method uses a fluent API to identify objects in a very readable manner. For example, in the code in figure 10.5, you find the email field by looking for an HTML element with the name `attribute` set to `email`.

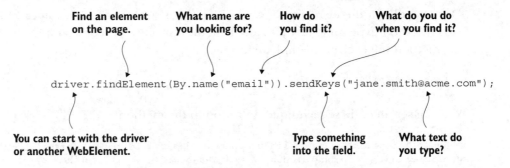

Figure 10.5   Locating elements on a page using the WebDriver API

Once you have the element, you can query or manipulate it as required. In the preceding code line, you use the `sendKeys()` method to simulate a user typing something into the field. Later in the test, you click on the login button (identified by its id attribute) using the `click()` method:

```
driver.findElement(By.id("login-button")).click();
```

Finally, at the end of the test, you check the text contents of the logged-in user, conveniently identified by an `id` attribute:

```
    String currentUser = driver.findElement(By.id("current-
➥ user")).getText();
    assertThat(currentUser).isEqualTo(frequentFlyer.email);
```

One of the nice things about this API is that it's not only very readable, but it's very easy to use. In modern IDEs, the auto-complete feature can be used to list the available methods for the various objects and classes used in the WebDriver API (see figure 10.6). This makes the API both easy for new developers to learn and very productive for more experienced developers.

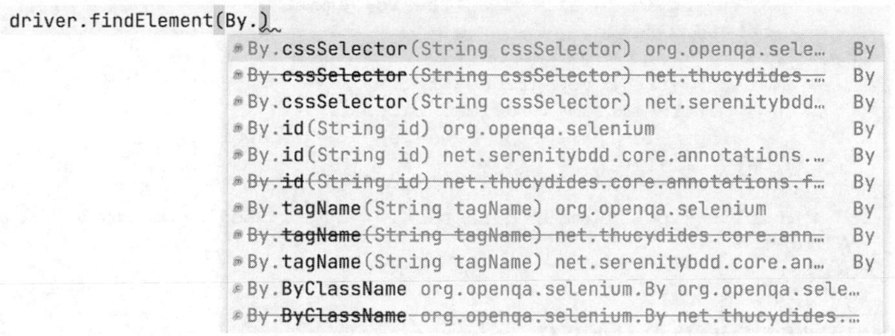

```
driver.findElement(By.)
```

```
 By.cssSelector(String cssSelector) org.openqa.sele…   By
 By.cssSelector(String cssSelector) net.thucydides.…   By
 By.cssSelector(String cssSelector) net.serenitybdd…   By
 By.id(String id) org.openqa.selenium                  By
 By.id(String id) net.serenitybdd.core.annotations.…   By
 By.id(String id) net.thucydides.core.annotations.f…   By
 By.tagName(String tagName) org.openqa.selenium        By
 By.tagName(String tagName) net.thucydides.core.ann…   By
 By.tagName(String tagName) net.serenitybdd.core.an…   By
 By.ByClassName org.openqa.selenium.By org.openqa.sele…   By
 By.ByClassName org.openqa.selenium.By net.thucydides.…
```

Figure 10.6   Modern IDE features, such as auto-completion, make the WebDriver API easy to work with.

IDENTIFYING ELEMENTS BY ID OR NAME

In the previous example we used the HTML `id` and `name` attributes to identify elements on this page. This strategy is a common one; it is easy and convenient, and these attributes are less likely to change when the structure or style of the page changes. In fact, it's a good idea to make sure that all semantically significant elements in a page have a unique ID or name.

This example is relatively straightforward, as the fields and buttons are easy to find. In real-world applications, this isn't always the case, and there are some situations where other strategies are more convenient. Fortunately, WebDriver provides a number of other ways to identify web elements.

IDENTIFYING ELEMENTS USING DATA ATTRIBUTES

While the `id` and name `attribute` are unlikely to change when the page layout changes, they are still fairly tightly coupled to the implementation of the page, particularly when JavaScript frameworks are used. The `id` field is often associated with JavaScript event handling, and the name attribute is often used in HTML forms, for example.

If you have control over the HTML source code, a much more independent strategy is to use an HTML data attribute. HTML data attributes are specifically designed to let you store additional information in standard HTML elements, without overriding the usage of more conventional HTML attributes.

For example, the `data-testid` attribute is a popular convention for identifying elements on a page in your tests. You can see some examples of this convention in the HTML code in the following listing.

Listing 10.1   Using a data attribute to identify a field

```html
<div class="login-container">
    <form [formGroup]="form" (submit)="login(form)">
        <mat-form-field appearance="fill">
            <mat-label>Email</mat-label>
```

```
              <input id="email" data-testid="email">
        </mat-form-field>
        <br>
        <mat-form-field appearance="fill">
            <mat-label>Password</mat-label>
            <input id="password" data-testid="password">
        </mat-form-field>
        <br>
        <button type="submit" data-testid="login">Login</button>
    </form>
</div>
```

IDENTIFYING ELEMENTS BY LINK TEXT

When you write automated web tests, you often need to click on links, either to navigate to another page or to trigger some action. For example, on the welcome page of our Frequent Flyer site, a user can choose to search flights, to view the current bookings, or to view the account details (see figure 10.7).

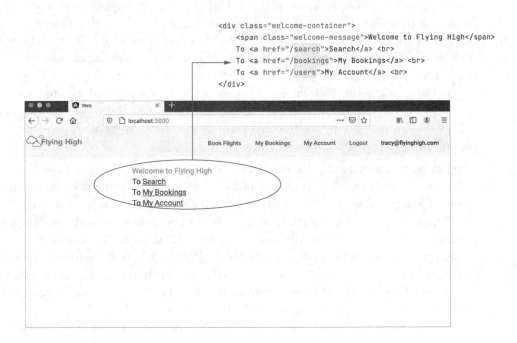

Figure 10.7   Hyperlinks can often be identified by the text they contain.

Links like this may not have a `name`, `id`, or `data` attribute that you can use to identify them. But you can use the next best thing—the text of the link itself. To click on the Search link, you could write the following:

```
driver.findElement(By.linkText("Search")).click();
```

You can also search the link texts for a partial match. To click on the My Bookings link, the following call would work:

```
driver.findElement(By.partialLinkText("Bookings")).click();
```

Identifying links by their text content is simple, intuitive, and relatively robust, though the test will obviously break if the displayed text is modified.

IDENTIFYING ELEMENTS USING CSS

A more flexible way of identifying elements is to use *CSS selectors*, patterns designed to identify different parts of a web page for formatting and styling, but they're also a great general-purpose way to identify elements on the page.

For example, in figure 10.7, the welcome message text is only identified by its CSS class. You can find web elements with CSS selectors by using the `By.cssSelector()` method. In CSS, you identify an element with a given class by using the "`.`" notation, like this:

```
driver.findElement(By.cssSelector(".welcome-message"));
```

We could also do this using the `By.className()` method. But CSS selectors become more valuable when you need to find web elements without clean `id` or `name` attributes, or where elements are nested inside other elements. For example, if there were several welcome messages on the page and we wanted to identify the welcome message inside the welcome-container component (see figure 10.7), we could write something like this:

```
driver.findElement(By.cssSelector(".welcome-container .welcome-message"));
```

Some of the more useful CSS selectors are listed in table 10.2.

Table 10.2   Useful CSS selectors

Selector	Example	Notes
`.class`	`.navbar`	Matches all elements with the class `navbar`
`#id`	`#welcome-message`	Matches the element with an `id` of `welcome-message`
`tag`	`img`	Matches all the `<img>` elements
`element element`	`.navbar a`	Matches all the `<a>` elements inside an element with the class `navbar`
`element > element`	`.navbar-header > a`	Matches `<a>` elements directly under an element with the class `navbar-header`
`[attribute=value]`	`a[href="#/book"]`	Matches `<a>` elements with an `href` value of `#/book`

Table 10.2   Useful CSS selectors *(continued)*

Selector	Example	Notes
`[attribute^=value]`	`a[href^="#"]`	Matches `<a>` elements with an `href` value that starts with #
`[attribute$=value]`	`a[href$="book"]`	Matches `<a>` elements with an `href` value that ends in `book`
`[attribute*=value]`	`a[href*="book"]`	Matches `<a>` elements with an `href` value that contains `book`
`:nth-child(n)`	`.navbar li:nth-child(3)`	Matches the third `<li>` inside an element of class `navbar`

Let's look at a more practical example. One of the requirements you've defined with the marketing folk goes along the following lines:

```
Scenario: Displaying featured destinations
Given Jane has logged on
When Jane views the home page
Then she should see 3 featured destinations
And the featured destinations should include Singapore
```

On the Frequent Flyer home page, each featured destination appears inside a `<div>` element with the featured class. The destination title is nested inside a `<span>` element with the featured-destination class. The rendered HTML code looks something like this:

```
<div id="featured">                          ⟵ All the featured
    <div class="featured-destination"...>       destinations appear
                                                within this <div>.
        <img src="img/singapore.png"></img>   ⟵ Each featured
        <span class="destination-title">Singapore</span>   destination has
        <span class="destination-price">$900</span>        its own <div>.
    </div>
    <div class="featured-destination">...</div>
    <div class="featured-destination">...</div>
</div>
```

Sets the featured destination's image → (points to `<img src="img/singapore.png">`)

Sets the featured destination's title ← (points to `<span class="destination-title">Singapore</span>`)

Other featured destinations like this follow.

In CSS, you can match elements with a given class by using the period (.) prefix. Using a CSS selector, you could find all the `<div>` elements that represent the featured destinations like this:

```
List<WebElement> destinations
    = driver.findElements(By.cssSelector(".featured-destination"));
assertThat(destinations).hasSize(3);
```

Checks the number of matching featured destination elements

Finds all the featured destination elements

Note that you're using the `findElements()` method rather than the `findElement()` method you saw previously. As the name suggests, the `findElements()` method returns a list of matching web elements, rather than just a single one. You then check the size of the returned list, using the `AssertJ` library (https://assertj.github.io/doc/) to make the test more readable.

This would be enough if you just wanted to count the number of featured destinations, but if you need to check the destination titles, you'll need to drill further. Fortunately, CSS selectors are flexible. You could retrieve the titles directly by finding all the web elements with the destination-title class:

```
driver.findElements(By.cssSelector(".destination-title"));
```

This would work, but it may not be robust. If destination titles were used elsewhere on the page, you'd retrieve too many titles. A safer approach would be to limit your search to the elements nested within the `<div>` that contains all the featured destinations:

```
driver.findElements(By.cssSelector("#featured .destination-title"));
```

Once you have a list of matching web elements, you need to convert it to a list of strings that you can verify. You could write something like this:

```
List<WebElement> destinations
  = driver.findElements(By.cssSelector("#featured .destination-title"));
List<String> destinationTitles = new ArrayList<String>();
for(WebElement destinationElement : destinations) {
    destinationTitles.add(destinationElement.getText());
}
assertThat(destinationTitles).contains("Singapore");
```

Converts these web elements into a list of strings

Finds all featured destination title elements

Uses getText() to extract the string contents of each element

Checks the contents of the list

First, retrieve the list of matching web elements. To get the text content of a `WebElement`, you use the `getText()` method, so loop through the web elements and extract the text contents of each one. Finally, check that the destination titles do indeed contain "Singapore."

We've just scratched the surface of CSS selectors here, but they're very useful for working with modern jQuery-based UI frameworks. You can find more details on the W3 website (http://www.w3.org/TR/CSS21/selector.html). Most modern browsers have excellent native support for CSS selectors, which means that tests using CSS selectors will generally be very fast.

IDENTIFYING ELEMENTS USING XPATH

CSS selectors are flexible and elegant, but they do run into limits from time to time. A more powerful alternative is to use XPath, a query language designed to select elements in an XML document. *XPath expressions* are path-like structures that describe elements within a page based on their relative position, attribute values, and content. In the context of WebDriver, you can use XPath expressions to select arbitrary elements within the HTML page structure. A list of useful XPath expressions can be found in table 8.3.

Table 10.3   Useful XPath expressions

XPath expression	Example	Notes
`node`	`a`	Matches all of the `<a>` elements
`//node`	`//button`	Matches all of the `<button>` elements somewhere under the document root
`//node/node`	`//button/span`	Matches `<span>` elements that are situated directly under a `<button>` element
`[@attribute=value]`	`//a[@class='navbar-brand']`	Matches `<a>` elements whose `class` attribute is exactly equal to `navbar-brand`
`[contains(@attribute, value)]`	`//div[contains(@class, 'navbar-header')]`	Matches `<div>` elements whose `class` attribute contains the expression `navbar-header`
`node[n]`	`//div[@id='main-navbar']//li[3]`	Matches the third `<li>` inside the `<div>` with an id of `main-navbar`
`[.=value]`	`//h2[.='Flying High Frequent Flyers']`	Matches the `<h2>` element with text contents equal to `Flying High Frequent Flyers`

You can find an element via an XPath expression by using the `By.xpath()` method. You could find the welcome message heading by using the following expression:

```
driver.findElement(By.xpath("//h3[@id='welcome-message']"));
```

XPath requires more knowledge of the document structure than CSS, and it doesn't benefit from the intimate understanding of HTML that's built into CSS selectors. This makes simple selectors more verbose than their equivalents in CSS. For example, in the previous section you saw how you could find the list of featured destination titles using the following CSS selector:

```
driver.findElements(By.cssSelector(".destination-title"));
```

The equivalent in XPath might be something like this:

```
driver.findElements(By.xpath("//span[@class='destination-title']"));
```

This will find all the `<span>` elements anywhere on the web page that have an attribute named `class` that's equal to destination-title.

You could make this more generic by using a wildcard (`*`) instead of `span`:

```
driver.findElements(By.xpath("//*[@class='destination-title']"));
```

This would find elements whose class was exactly equal to `destination-title`.

Unfortunately, modern web applications will sometimes add extra classes to the `class` attribute, so you can't rely on an exact match. A more reliable solution is to use the XPath `contains()` function, matching elements that have a `class` attribute with a value that contains `destination-title`:

```
driver.findElements(By.xpath("//*[contains(@class,'destination-title')]"));
```

The full power of XPath becomes more apparent when you need to find elements based on their content—something that's not currently supported in CSS. For example, the featured destinations you saw earlier are rendered in HTML like this:

```
<div class="featured-destination"...>
    <img src="img/singapore.png"></img>
    <span class="destination-title">Singapore</span>
    <span class="destination-price">$900</span>
</div>
<div class="featured-destination">...</div>
```

You could find the `<span>` element containing the text `Singapore` using the following XPath expression:

```
//span[.='Singapore']
```

You could take this further. Suppose you need to find the price displayed for the `Singapore` featured destination. XPath supports relative paths using the "`..`" notation, so you could find the neighboring `<span>` notation with a class of destination-price like this:

```
//span[.='Singapore']/../span[contains(@class,'destination-price')]
```

XPath isn't without its disadvantages. XPath expressions are generally more verbose and less readable than CSS selectors. XPath expressions can also be fragile if they aren't well crafted. XPath has no native support in Internet Explorer, so tests that use XPath on Internet Explorer may run very slowly. But XPath is more powerful than CSS, and there are cases where XPath will be the only way to reliably identify the elements you're looking for.

USING NESTED LOOKUPS

When you write automated tests with WebDriver, it's important to keep expressions as simple and readable as possible. Simpler expressions tend to be easier to understand

and to maintain, and in many cases they're more reliable. One useful strategy when it comes to writing simpler WebDriver code is to use nested lookups.

So far, you've found web elements using the WebDriver instance. But you can also call the findElement() and findElements() methods directly on WebElement instances. For example, suppose there are several Book links at different places on the page, and you need to click on the Book link in the main menu. You could do this by first finding the main menu using its ID and then finding the menu entry within the main menu's web element using the linkText selector:

```
driver.findElement(By.id("main-navbar"))        ◁──        Narrows down the
       .findElement(By.linkText("Book"))        ◁────      search for elements
   ┌──▷ .click();                                           to the main navbar
   │                            Looks for a link
 Clicks on                      within the navbar
 the link
```

This approach is clear and intuitive and tends to be less error-prone than using complex XPath expressions or CSS selectors.

10.2.13 *Interacting with web elements*

Interacting with web elements in WebDriver is usually fairly intuitive, and it involves a relatively small number of methods. You can use the click() method on any web element (not just buttons and links) to simulate a mouse click. The sendKeys() method can be used to simulate user input. And the getAttributeValue() and getText() methods let you retrieve attribute values and the text contents of a web element.

The Frequent Flyer registration page illustrated in figure 10.8 has many fields that can illustrate these ideas. Let's walk through one of the scenarios we saw in the previous chapter to see how this works. The scenario we will automate is the following:

```
Rule: Customers must register to be able to use the Frequent Flyer members
➥ area
Example: Trevor registers as a Frequent Flyer member
  Given Trevor does not have a Frequent Flyer account
  When he registers as a Frequent Flyer member
  Then Trevor should be able to log on to the Frequent Flyer application
  And he should have a Frequent Flyer account with:
    | Status Level | STANDARD |
    | Points       | 0        |
```

Let's see how we automated each of these steps.

PREPARING THE TEST DATA
The first step simply defines the persona we will be using for this scenario. We saw this approach in chapter 9.

```
Given Trevor does not have a Frequent Flyer account
```

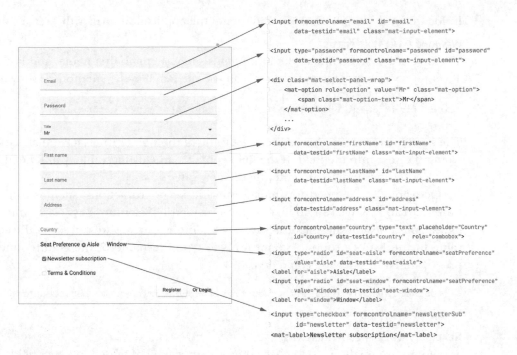

Figure 10.8   The Frequent Flyer registration page

The step definition method uses a persona class called `Traveler`, which defines all the fields we need to use in the registration process:

```
Traveler newMember;

@Given("{} does not have a Frequent Flyer account")
public void notAFrequentFlyerMember(String name) {
    newMember = TravelerPersonas.findByName(name);
}
```

The actual values are defined in a HOCON configuration file, and look like this:

```
Trevor: {
  firstName: "Trevor"
  lastName: "Traveler"
  email: "trevor@traveler.com"
  password: "tr3vor"
  title:"Mr"
  address: "10 Partridge Street, Dandenong"
  country: "Australia"
  seatPreference: "Aisle"
}
```

Now let's see how we use this persona object to interact with the registration page:

```
When he registers as a Frequent Flyer member
```

Inside this step, we will complete and submit the application form with Trevor's details.

WORKING WITH TEXT FIELDS

The first task is to complete the input fields such as email, first name, and last name. To enter a value into a text field, you can use the `sendKeys()` method, as shown here:

```
driver.findElement(By.id("email")).sendKeys(newMember.getEmail());
```

The `sendKeys()` method doesn't set the value of the field; rather, it simulates the user typing the text into the field. If the field contains an existing value, you'll need to use the `clear()` method before entering the new value.

Occasionally, we need to simulate specific keyboard actions, such as hitting the Enter or Tab key. We can do that by simply using the Selenium Keys class, which gives us a set of values for these special keys. For example, one way we can select the country value in the list of proposed countries is to type the name of the country and then press Tab. Here's how we could do this:

```
driver.findElement(By.id("country")).sendKeys(newMember.getCountry(),
                                              Keys.TAB);
```

READING VALUES FROM TEXT FIELDS

Sometimes we might need to check the current value contained in a text field. This is stored in the value attribute of the corresponding input element. To retrieve an attribute value, you can use the `getAttribute()` method, as shown here:

```
String email = driver.findElement(By.id("email")).getAttribute("value");
```

This approach will also work for any other form field that uses the value attribute, such as check boxes or the newer HTML5 input field types like email and date. The exception is `<textarea>` fields, which don't have a value attribute. You can retrieve the contents of a `<textarea>` field by using the `getText()` method.

RADIO BUTTONS AND CHECK BOXES

The simplest way to select a radio button value is to find the radio button you want and to click on it. This can be a little tricky because the `name` attribute isn't unique, and the `id` attribute isn't always defined or directly related to the value. For example, the HTML code for the radio buttons in our registration form looks like this:

```
<input type="radio" id="aisle" formcontrolname="seatPreference"
       name="seatPreference" value="aisle" data-testid="seat-aisle">
<label for="aisle">Aisle</label>
<input type="radio" id=" window" formcontrolname="seatPreference"
       name="seatPreference" value="window" data-testid="seat-window">
<label for="window">Window</label>
```

One approach in this case might be to use the value attribute in conjunction with the name attribute (which identifies the group of radio buttons):

```
driver.findElement(
    By.cssSelector("input[name='seatPreference'][value='aisle']")
).click()
```

We might also opt to click on the corresponding label element, as shown in this example where we use an XPath expression to identify the Window label element:

```
driver.findElement(By.xpath("//label[.='Window']")).click()
```

And in the case of our application, we could create an XPath selector dynamically from the persona attributes we pass to the step definition method:

```
String seatPreference = String.format("//label[.='%s']",
                                       newMember.getSeatPreference());
driver.findElement(By.xpath(seatPreference)).click();
```

This approach will also work for check boxes, which behave in exactly the same way.

DROP-DOWN LISTS

Drop-down lists are a common element of web interfaces. These can come in the form of traditional HTML SELECT elements or as framework-specific JavaScript components.

For SELECT elements, WebDriver provides a convenient helper class for dealing with drop-down lists. The `Select` class is used to wrap a web element representing a drop-down list to add drop-down-specific methods, such as `selectByVisibleText()`, `selectByValue()`, and `selectByIndex()`. On the booking page, you could set the travel class to "Business" using the following code:

```
WebElement travelClassElt = getDriver().findElement(By.id("travel-class"));
new Select(travelClassElt).selectByVisibleText("Business");
```

The `Select` class also provides a number of methods that you can use to learn about the current state of the drop-down list, including `getFirstSelectedOption()` and `getAllSelectedOptions()`.

10.2.14 Working with modern UI library components

More modern applications often use nonstandard HTML tags to implement UI components. For example, our Frequent Flyer application uses the `Angular Material` library (https://material.angular.io/), a UI component library for Angular JS applications. You can see an example of one of these components in figure 10.9, which shows the Title dropdown list on the registration page. Let's see how we would automate this sort of component using Selenium WebDriver.

Although the `Title` field looks like an HTML SELECT field, the corresponding HTML code is quite different. The dropdown field uses the `mat-select` tag, and looks something like this:

```
<mat-select role="listbox" id="title" data-testid="title">
    ...
</mat-select>
```

When you click on the dropdown field, a block of HTML elements similar to the following are dynamically added to the DOM, showing the dropdown values you see in figure 10.9:

```
<div class="mat-select-panel-wrap">
    <div class="mat-select-panel mat-primary" id="title-panel">
        <mat-option role="option" value="Mr" class="mat-option">
            <span class="mat-option-text">Mr</span>
        </mat-option>
        <mat-option role="option" value="Ms" class="mat-option">
            <span class="mat-option-text">Ms</span>
        </mat-option>
        <mat-option role="option" value="Mrs" class="mat-option">
            <span class="mat-option-text">Mrs</span>
        </mat-option>
    </div>
</div>
```

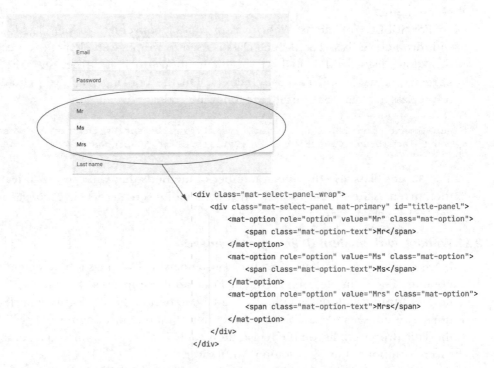

Figure 10.9   An example of a nonstandard HTML UI component found in many modern web applications

To select a value in the dropdown, we first need to click on the `mat-select` element, and only then click on the corresponding `mat-option` entry.

The first step is easy. We simply click on the `mat-select` element, which we could do like this:

```
driver.findElement(By.id("title")).click();
```

For the second step, we have a couple of options. One might be to click on the `mat-option` element, which has a convenient value field. For example, we could use the following code to identify the `'Mr'` entry:

```
driver.findElement(By.cssSelector("mat-option[value='Mr']")).click();
```

Alternatively, we might want to avoid using the value label (which might not be a human-readable value in all cases) and use the displayed text value instead. We could do this using an XPath expression instead of the CSS one we showed:

```
driver.findElement(By.xpath("//*[@class='mat-option-
➥ text'][.='Mr']")).click();
```

The last step would be to make this expression depend on our test data, which we could do using an approach similar to the one we used for seat preference.

```
String titleOption = String.format("mat-option[value='%s']",
                                   newMember.getTitle());
driver.findElement(By.cssSelector(titleOption)).click();
```

This process is fairly typical of working with nonstandard UI frameworks like this. However, there is one aspect we haven't considered: the dropdown list may not appear immediately. It may retrieve the list from a backend service and take a short instance before the list appears. In this case, the code we just wrote may fail because the dropdown list entry it is looking for hasn't been populated yet. In the next section we will learn how to deal with this situation as well as other cases where we need to wait for things to happen.

10.2.15 Working with asynchronous pages and testing AJAX applications

Most modern web applications use AJAX in one way or another. AJAX-based Java-Script libraries allow developers to write applications with vastly improved usability and user experience. But the asynchronous nature of AJAX can present challenges when it comes to automated web testing.

In a conventional web application, when you click on a link or submit a form, an HTTP request is sent to the server and a new page is returned. In these cases, Web-Driver will automatically wait for the new page to load before proceeding. But with an AJAX application, the web page will send queries to a server and update the page directly, without reloading. When this happens, WebDriver will not know if or when it needs to wait for updates, which may cause the test to fail unexpectedly.

Timing problems can also come into play even when data loading is not involved. For example, many UI component libraries use animation; the popular `Toastr` (https://codeseven.github.io/toastr/) library for example uses fading animation for nonblocking notification messages. This kind of animation is used in the registration scenario we saw earlier:

```
Then Trevor should be able to log on to the Frequent Flyer application
```

When Trevor logs on to his new account, a notification message appears briefly (see figure 10.10). The message fades in and then fades away after a few seconds.

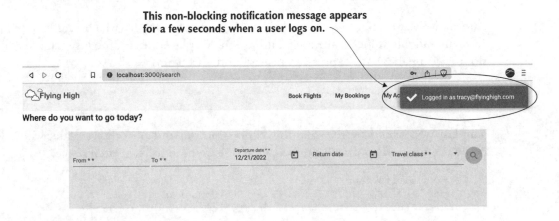

Figure 10.10   The green dialog message appears briefly when a user logs on to the application.

The previous step checks that when Trevor logs on, this message appears and contains the correct email address. But if we look for the notification message as soon as we complete the login process, the test will fail; the message hasn't yet appeared. We need to tell Selenium to wait for the message to appear. WebDriver gives us a few options as to how to do this.

EXPLICIT AND FLUENT WAITS

One approach is to use *explicit waits*, which let us wait for specific events. We can do this using the `WebDriverWait` and `ExpectedConditions` classes. The `WebDriverWait` class creates the initial framework, waiting until some condition is met or a given time-out expires.

```
WebDriverWait wait = new WebDriverWait(driver, Duration.ofSeconds(5));
```

This object won't do anything by itself, though; we need to tell it to wait for something. And that's where the `ExpectedConditions` class comes into play. This class provides a large number of useful predefined conditions, including waiting for elements to be present (or not present), visible (or invisible), clickable, and so forth.

If we want to wait for the Toastr success message to be visible, we would simply use the `visibilityOfElementLocated()` method, as illustrated here:

```
wait.until(
    ExpectedConditions.visibilityOfElementLocated(
        By.cssSelector(".toast-success")
    )
);
```

This code will wait up to five seconds or until the Toastr success message appears, whichever comes first.

A neat trick with the `WebDriverWait` methods is that they return the element you are waiting for as a result, so you can interact directly with the web element once you find it. In the following code sample, we wait for the Toastr message to appear, and then retrieve the text content of the message, so that we can make an assertion about the value of the message. Note how we are using a static import from the `Excepted-Conditions` class to make the code read more fluently.

```
WebDriverWait wait = new WebDriverWait(driver, Duration.ofSeconds(5));
String successMessage = wait.until(visibilityOfElementLocated(
                                    By.cssSelector(".toast-success")))
                        .getText();

assertThat(successMessage).isEqualTo("Logged in as "
                                    + newMember.getEmail());
```

There are many, many other pre-bundled `Wait` conditions; some of the more commonly used ones are outlined in table 10.4.

Table 10.4   Useful WebDriver wait conditions

Method (with example)	Purpose
`visibilityOfElementLocated(By.id("#elt"))`	Wait for an element to be both on the page and visible.

`visibilityOfNestedElementsLocatedBy(`
`    By.id("#parent"),By.id("#elt")`
`)`
	Wait for a child element to be both on the page and visible.

`textToBePresentInElementLocated(`
`    By.id("elt"),"expected text"`
`)`
	Wait for a specified text to be present in a specified element.

`invisibilityOfElementLocated(By.id("#elt"))`	Wait for an element to disappear.

`invisibilityOfElementWithText(`
`    By.id("#elt"),`
`    "Disappearing text"`
`)`
	Wait for an element containing some specified text to disappear.

`numberOfElementsToBeMoreThan(By.id("#list"), 3)`	Wait for the number of elements matching a specified locator to appear.

Table 10.4   Useful WebDriver wait conditions *(continued)*

Method (with example)	Purpose
`titleContains("some title")`	Wait until the page title contains some specified value.
`urlContains("/search")`	Wait until the URL contains some value.
`alertIsPresent()`	Wait until a JavaScript Alert dialog appears.

`and(`
`    visibilityOfElementLocated(By.id("#elt-1")),`
`    visibilityOfElementLocated(By.id("#elt-2"))`
`)`
	Wait until several conditions are met.

These predefined conditions cover many common situations. But occasionally you'll need to do something more specific. Again, WebDriver offers several options. The `FluentWait` class allows you to create arbitrary wait parameters on the fly using a readable, fluent API:

```
Wait<WebDriver> wait = new FluentWait<>(driver)    Wait for up to
    .withTimeout(Duration.ofSeconds(30))           30 seconds.
    .pollingEvery(Duration.ofSeconds(1))           Check the page
    .ignoring(NoSuchElementException.class);       every second.
                                    Don't fail if an element
                                    isn't found yet.
```

You can use this `wait` object with one of the predefined conditions from the `Expected-Conditions` class, or you can write your own condition. A condition takes the form of a Java 8 Function object, and it typically returns either a `WebElement` (if you're waiting for a web element to become available) or a Boolean (if you're waiting for some more general condition).

For example, we could wait until the Toastr notification message contained an email address of a particular format like this:

```
wait.until(driver
        -> driver.findElement(By.cssSelector(".toast-success"))
            .getText()
            .contains("@traveler.com")
    );
```

Fluent waits are a little more complicated to write, but they open infinite possibilities when it comes to waiting for arbitrary events.

10.3   *Test-friendly web applications*

The style and quality of your web application code has a significant influence on how easy or hard it will be to test. Applications with clean HTML code, identifiers, names, and CSS classes for all the significant elements on a page make testing easier and more reliable. When applications have messy or inconsistent HTML code, the elements can be hard to identify, which results in more complicated and more brittle selector logic. And the opposite is true, too: as we have seen, simply using test-specific attributes can go a long way in making your tests more robust.

The technology stack you choose can have a major effect on testability. Frameworks that limit the control you have over the rendered HTML are a major source of difficulty.

In Java web application development, for example, some frameworks automatically generate element identifiers for their own use, making it difficult to use the simplest and fastest of the WebDriver selectors. (Many JSF-based frameworks fall into this category.) Applications that use plug-in technologies such as Flash and Silverlight, which are opaque to testing tools like WebDriver, also make testing very difficult.

10.4 Next steps

So far you have seen the fundamentals of how to interact with a web application using Selenium WebDriver, and how to automate Cucumber acceptance criteria that manipulate the user interface. To keep things simple, we have focused almost entirely on the WebDriver API.

However, the style of coding we have been using is not really suitable for anything beyond simple tutorial projects. To understand why this is the case, let's revisit one of the step definition methods we implemented earlier in the chapter:

```
@Then("{} should be able to log on to the Frequent Flyer application")
public void shouldBeAbleToLoginAs(String name) {
    WebDriver driver = WebTestSupport.currentDriver();       ← Obtains the WebDriver instance
    driver.get("http://localhost:3000/login");

    driver.findElement(By.id("email")).sendKeys(newMember.getEmail());
    driver.findElement(By.id("password")).sendKeys(newMember.getPassword());
    driver.findElement(By.id("login-button")).click();

    WebDriverWait wait = new WebDriverWait(driver, Duration.ofSeconds(5));
    String successMessage
        = wait.until(visibilityOfElementLocated(
                    By.cssSelector(".toast-success"))
                ).getText();

    assertThat(successMessage)
            .isEqualTo("Logged in as " + newMember.getFirstName());
}
```

Opens the login page / *Interacts with the login form* / *Waits for the login notification message to appear* / *Checks that the correct message is displayed*

Even for a simple example like this, the code shown here is relatively long and would be quite hard to maintain:

- We are exposing the WebDriver API in our test logic, which means the test is tightly coupled to the WebDriver implementation. If we wanted to refactor the test (e.g., to use API calls or a different testing technology), we would need major changes to the code.

- The URL we are navigating to for the login screen is hard-coded, which would make it difficult to run the test on a remote server.
- The locators are embedded in our test code, which means that if these elements are used in other step definition methods, they will need to be maintained in several places.
- The code contains implementation details, such as the need to wait for the Toastr notification message to appear, which are not relevant.

The following sample, which uses the Screenplay Pattern we will discover in chapter 12, arguably does a much better job of expressing the intent of this step while hiding the implementation details in other classes where they will be easier to find and maintain:

```
@Then("{} should be able to log on to the Frequent Flyer application")
public void shouldBeAbleToLoginAs(Actor frequentFlyer) {
    frequentFlyer.attemptsTo(Login.usingTheirCredentials());
    frequentFlyer.should(
            seeThat(the(LOGIN_NOTIFICATION_MESSAGE),
                    containsText("Logged in as " + frequentFlyer.getName())))
    );
}
```

In the following chapters, we will learn a number of techniques that can help make your test automation code more maintainable and more robust.

Summary

- You can automate UI acceptance tests for web-based applications in Java using Selenium WebDriver.
- Automated web tests are a powerful testing tool, but should be used sparingly in order to avoid slowing down your test suite too much.
- Selenium Webdriver is one of the most common and well-established open source browser automation libraries.
- Building testability into our applications (e.g., by including meaningful ids or css classes for key elements) makes it much easier to write reliable, sustainable test automation code.
- When testing asynchronous applications, we can use different types of wait conditions (e.g., explicit and fluent waits) to wait until the application is in an expected state before proceeding with our test.

In the next chapters we will look at a number of techniques you can use to make your web test automation code more robust, easier to extend, and easier to maintain.

Test automation design patterns for the UI layer

This chapter covers

- The limitations of unstructured test scripts
- Page Objects and Page Component Objects
- Modeling user interfaces and user behavior
- Action classes and DSLs

In the previous chapter, you learned how to automate a web page using basic Selenium WebDriver code. In this chapter, you will learn how to organize and structure your UI test code to make it easier to extend and easier to maintain.

11.1 The limitations of unstructured test scripts

Thus far we've explored the WebDriver API using very simple code samples. These examples work well to illustrate the various WebDriver methods, but you wouldn't want to write code like this for real-world automated tests. For example, to log on to the Frequent Flyer website, you used the following code:

```
@When("he/she logs on with a valid username and password")
public void logsOnWithAValidUsernameAndPassword() {
    WebDriver driver = WebTestSupport.currentDriver();
```

```
driver.get("http://localhost:3000");
driver.findElement(By.linkText("Login")).click();
driver.findElement(By.id("email")).sendKeys(frequentFlyer.email);
driver.findElement(By.id("password")).sendKeys(frequentFlyer.password);
driver.findElement(By.id("login-button")).click();
}
```

This code wouldn't scale well. You'd need to duplicate the same or similar lines for every scenario involving a user logging on, and any change to this logic would need to be updated at every place that it's used.

Another problem is that you're mixing selector logic (like `By.id("email")`) with the test data we pass to it (`frequentFlyer.email`). When we keep two things together in our code, it is hard to change one without risking changing the other.

This also means that if we want to interact with this field somewhere else in our tests (e.g., if we wanted to enter different or invalid email values in a different scenario), we would need to duplicate the locator logic. And that, in turn, means more maintenance and more places that need changing if, for example, the ID of the email field were to change.

11.2 *Separating location logic from test logic*

A better approach would be to refactor the selector logic into one place so that it can be reused across multiple tests. For example, you could rewrite the script we saw in the previous section more cleanly by placing the selector logic in a single class:

```
public class LoginPage {
    private static final By EMAIL_FIELD = By.id("email");          Locator strategies
    private static final By PASSWORD_FIELD = By.id("password");     for the elements
    private static final By LOGIN_BUTTON = By.id("login-button");   in this form

    private final WebDriver driver;          ◁──── Declares a WebDriver
                                                    instance that can be used to
    public LoginPage(WebDriver driver) {    ◁──    interact with the browser
        this.driver = driver;
    }                                               Passes in the
                                                    WebDriver instance
    public void open() {
        driver.get("http://localhost:3000/login");
    }

    public void signinWithCredentials(String email, String password) {
        driver.findElement(EMAIL_FIELD).sendKeys(email);
        driver.findElement(PASSWORD_FIELD).sendKeys(password);
        driver.findElement(LOGIN_BUTTON).click();
    }
}                          Rather than hard-coding selectors, we
                           represent them as reusable constant values.
```

Opens the login page → (annotation for `public void open()`)

Enters user credentials and signs in to the application → (annotation for `public void signinWithCredentials(...)`)

This class wraps the lines of code you saw earlier into a single method called `signin-WithCredentials()`. It also provides an `open()` method to get to the right page. The code needs a `WebDriver` instance, which is provided in the constructor.

Notice how we are no longer hard-coding the locators in the `findElement()` methods. The locator strategies for the elements used in the login process are defined as constant values at the top of the class. This does two things. First, the locators are centralized in one place, which makes them easier to find if they need updating. And second, by using readable constant names, when we read the code in the method we can focus on what element the code is looking for rather than how the element is located.

This principle also applies when we use the `LoginPage` class, which allows your test code to focus on the test data and the intent of the actions rather than on how the individual web elements are found or manipulated:

```
@When("he/she logs on with a valid username and password")
public void logsOnWithAValidUsernameAndPassword() {
    LoginPage loginPage = new LoginPage(driver);
    loginPage.open();
    loginPage.signinWithCredentials("jane.smith@acme.com", "s3cr3t");
}
```

Opens the login page ⟶ (points to `loginPage.open();`)

Signs in with the specified credentials ⟵ (points to `loginPage.signinWithCredentials(...)`)

11.3 *Introducing the Page Objects pattern*

The class we just looked at is an example of the *Page Objects* pattern. A Page Object is a class that models a specific part of the user interface and that presents a set of more business-focused methods for tests to use, sparing them from the implementation details of the actual HTML page. A Page Object has two main roles:

- It isolates the technical implementation of the page from the tests, making the test code simpler and easier to maintain.
- It centralizes the code that interacts with a page (or a Page Component) so that when the web page is modified, the test code only needs to be updated in one place.

A well-structured automated acceptance test suite is typically made up of at least three layers:

- The Business Rules layer describes the expected business outcomes.
- The Business Flow layer relates the user's journey through the application.
- The Interaction layer interacts directly with the system.

Page Objects belong in the interaction layer (see figure 11.1). They provide business-friendly services to the Business Flow layer and implement the interactions with the web pages using the WebDriver API.

What exactly does a Page Object do? Let's find out.

11.3.1 *Page Objects are responsible for locating elements on a page*

The primary role of a Page Object is to know where things are on a web page and how to interact with them. In other words, a Page Object is responsible for locating the

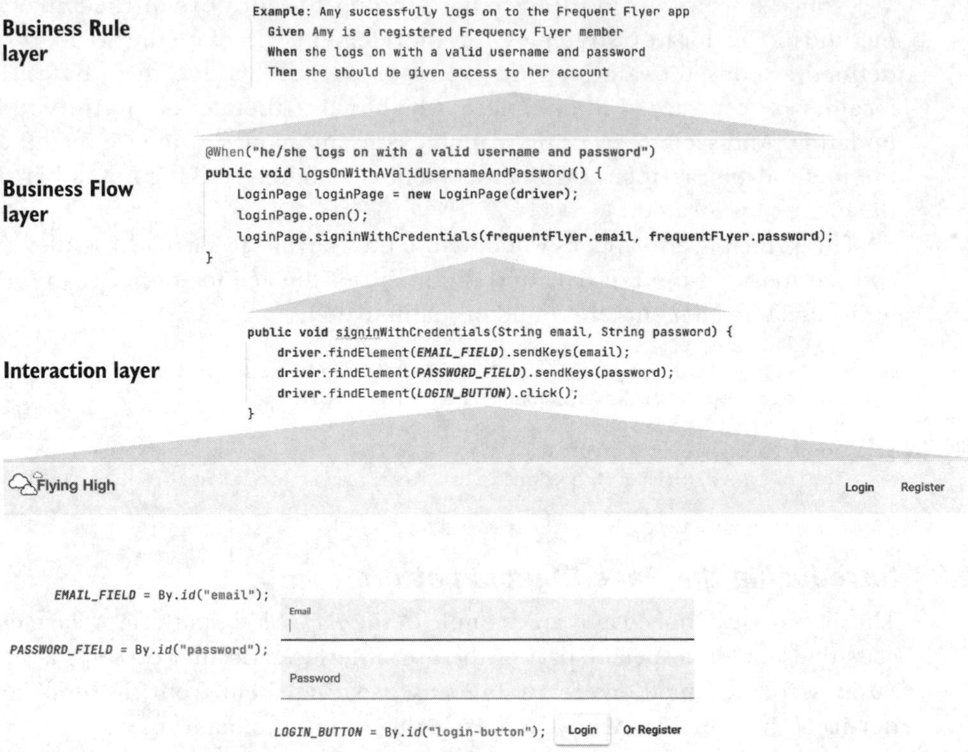

Business Rule layer

```
Example: Amy successfully logs on to the Frequent Flyer app
   Given Amy is a registered Frequency Flyer member
   When she logs on with a valid username and password
   Then she should be given access to her account
```

Business Flow layer

```
@When("he/she logs on with a valid username and password")
public void logsOnWithAValidUsernameAndPassword() {
    LoginPage loginPage = new LoginPage(driver);
    loginPage.open();
    loginPage.signinWithCredentials(frequentFlyer.email, frequentFlyer.password);
}
```

Interaction layer

```
public void signinWithCredentials(String email, String password) {
    driver.findElement(EMAIL_FIELD).sendKeys(email);
    driver.findElement(PASSWORD_FIELD).sendKeys(password);
    driver.findElement(LOGIN_BUTTON).click();
}
```

Flying High   Login   Register

```
EMAIL_FIELD = By.id("email");
```
Email

```
PASSWORD_FIELD = By.id("password");
```
Password

```
LOGIN_BUTTON = By.id("login-button");   Login   Or Register
```

Figure 11.1　Page Objects play a role in the interaction layer.

elements your test code needs to interact with.[1] The Page Object knows what locator strategy to use and stores them in a place that is easy to find and update when needed. This avoids duplication; if the web element changes, there is only one place that the locator strategy will need to be modified.

For example, in the LoginPage class we saw earlier in this chapter, the locator strategies are represented by constant values at the top of the class:

```
public class LoginPage {
    private static final By EMAIL_FIELD = By.id("email");
    private static final By PASSWORD_FIELD = By.id("password");
    private static final By LOGIN_BUTTON = By.id("login-button");
    ...
```

Sometimes, locator logic can be a little more sophisticated. For example, the Frequent Flyer application has a menu bar that appears at the top of almost every screen (see figure 11.2).

---

[1] In some approaches (such as the Action classes and Screenplay Patterns, which we will look at later in this book), we take this concept even further, and this becomes the only responsibility of the Page Object classes.

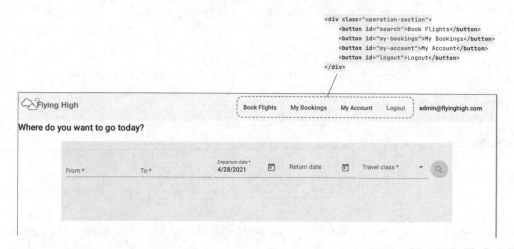

Figure 11.2 The Frequent Flyer menu bar

We could choose to group the locators for these in a single class, with a locator for each button, like this:

```
public class MenuBar {

    private static final By BOOK_FLIGHTS_BUTTON
        = By.xpath("//button[contains(.,'Book Flights')]");
    private static final By MY_BOOKINGS_BUTTON
        = By.xpath("//button[contains(.,'My Bookings')]");
    private static final By MY_ACCOUNT_BUTTON
        = By.xpath("//button[contains(.,'My Account')]");
    private static final By LOGOUT_BUTTON
        = By.xpath("//button[contains(.,'Logout')]");
    …
```

> We define a different XPath locator for each of the buttons in the menu bar.

But the HTML structures and the corresponding XPath locators for each link are very similar, so this feels like duplicated work. A more flexible approach might be to have a single locator strategy across all the buttons, and just make the name of the button parameterizable. Using this strategy, the complete Page Object class might look something like this:

```
public class MenuBar {

    private WebDriver driver;

    public MenuBar(WebDriver driver) {
        this.driver = driver;
    }

    private static By buttonWithLabel(String label) {
        return By.xpath("//button[contains(.,'" + label + "')]");
    }
}
```

> We define a generic XPath locator that can work for any of the buttons and a method to find the specific locator based on the text label of a button.

```
public void navigateToBookFlights() {
    driver.findElement(buttonWithLabel("Book Flights")).click();
}

public void navigateToMyBookings() {
    driver.findElement(buttonWithLabel("My Bookings")).click();
}

public void navigateToMyAccount() {
    driver.findElement(buttonWithLabel("My Account")).click();
}

public void logout() {
    driver.findElement(buttonWithLabel("Logout")).click();
}
}
```

We use this method to locate and interact with each of the buttons in the menu bar.

Once again, the location logic is hidden inside the class itself, and any modifications only need to be done in one place.

11.3.2 Page Objects represent objects on a page, not an entire page

Despite their name, Page Objects do not typically represent an entire page. Modern web applications are usually too rich and complex to be represented as a single object. Just think about all the things that you typically see on a page: menu bars, navigation elements, search boxes, search results, and so forth. If you put all these things in the same class, the code would quickly become large and unwieldy, hard to read, and hard to understand.

A more accurate term is *Page Component Objects* because they represent some reusable component on the page. Martin Fowler, in his seminal article on Page Objects from 2013, puts it like this: "Despite the term 'page' object, these objects shouldn't usually be built for each page, but rather for the significant elements on a page" (https://martinfowler.com/bliki/PageObject.html). For example, you might use a Page Object to represent the main menu bar that appears on every screen, or for the list of featured destinations if this appears in several places (see figure 11.3).

11.3.3 Page Objects tell you about the state of a page

Page Objects can also report what they see on a page in business terms, hiding the details of how this information is located. This both keeps WebDriver logic hidden from your test code and makes it easier to express the intent of your tests.

For example, in the previous chapter we implemented the "Then she should be given access to her account" step by checking the email address displayed in the top right corner of the screen. The code looked like this:

Locates the current user description on the page

```
@Then("he/she should be given access to his/her account")
public void shouldBeGivenAccessToTheAccount() {
    String currentUser = driver.findElement(By.id("current-user"))
                                .getText();
    assertThat(currentUser).isEqualTo(frequentFlyer.email);
}
```

Fetches the text content of this field

Compares it with the expected current user's email address

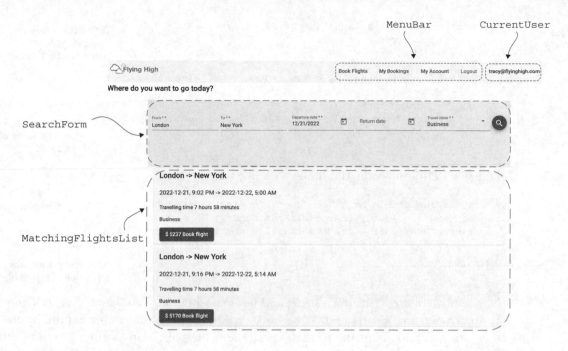

Figure 11.3   Web pages often contain many distinct components.

Here we are interacting directly with the WebDriver API and doing many things at once: locating the element, fetching the text, and comparing it to an email value. Lumping all this together makes it harder to read.

It also makes the code harder to maintain; even in this simple example, there are many reasons this code might need to change. For example, the locator for the current user field might change, or we might switch to displaying the user's first name with a friendly welcome message like "Welcome, Amy!" instead of a boring email address. The second case is a change in business logic, which should be reflected in the step definition code, but the first is an implementation detail about how we get the user description from the screen; if it changes, our step definition code should not be affected.

When you use the Page Object model (or the other patterns recommended in this book), you never interact directly with web elements inside your step definition methods. Instead, you interact with other classes, such as Page Objects, using more readable and business-centric method names that make the intent of your test code more obvious.

For example, using the Page Object model strategy, we could refactor the previous code sample like this:

```
public class CurrentUserPanel {

    private WebDriver driver;
```

```
    public CurrentUserPanel (WebDriver driver) {
        this.driver = driver;
    }

    private static final By CURRENT_USER = By.id("current-user");

    public String label() {
        return driver.findElement(CURRENT_USER).getText();
    }
}
```

Define the location
strategy for the
current user field.

Fetch and return
the test value of
this field.

Our step definition code would now look like this:

Creates a
new object

```
@Then("he/she should be given access to his/her account")
public void shouldBeGivenAccessToHisAccount() {
    CurrentUserPanel currentUserPanel = new CurrentUserPanel(driver);
    assertThat(currentUserPanel.label()).isEqualTo(frequentFlyer.email);
}
```

Fetches and returns the
test value of this field

Notice how we are returning a string and not exposing the WebElement itself? There is no getCurrentUserElement() method. Page Objects should never expose implementation details about the page or component they're encapsulating. Page Object methods should accept and return simple types such as strings, dates, Booleans, or domain-specific objects. They should never expose WebDriver or WebElement classes.

11.3.4 *Page Objects perform business tasks or simulate user behavior*

Page Objects hide away the WebDriver implementation and present a more business-friendly façade to the world. For example, the LoginPage class we saw earlier does not expose each web element for users to interact with. We would not typically write code like this, where we return the WebElements themselves for our code to interact with:

```
loginPage.getEmailField().sendKeys(frequentFlyer.email);
loginPage.getPasswordField().sendKeys(frequentFlyer.password);
loginPage.getLoginButton().click();
```

In some situations, we might write individual methods that interact with these elements, like this:

```
loginPage.enterEmail(frequentFlyer.email);
loginPage.enterPassword(frequentFlyer.password);
loginPage.clickLoginButton();
```

But not always. For example, in this case, logging in is a single business action; we would never enter an email alone, without clicking on the login button, so instead of having three separate steps, it would be much more convenient to group them all into a single more business-friendly method, like this:

```
loginPage.signinWithCredentials(frequentFlyer.email,
                                frequentFlyer.password);
```

The `signinWithCredentials()` method focuses on the business intent of this action and hides the details of how we actually interact with the fields themselves inside the method.

Another example could be the flight search form (see figure 11.4). On this form, the `From`, `To`, and `Travel class` fields are mandatory, and the search button is disabled until they are filled in.

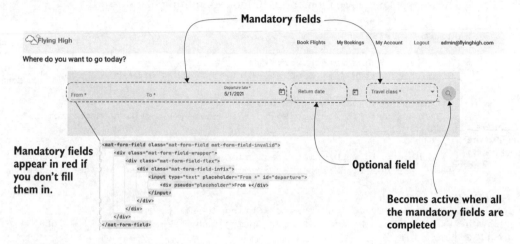

Figure 11.4   The Flying High search form

We could write a scenario for this business rule like this (http://mng.bz/aMjz):

```
Background:
  Given Amy is a registered Frequency Flyer member
  And she has logged on with a valid username and password

Rule: Travellers must provide at least departure, destination and travel
 class
  Scenario Template: Missing mandatory fields should be highlighted
    When she tries to search for flights with the following criteria
      | From   | To     | Travel Class    |
      | <From> | <To>   | <Travel Class>  |
    Then the search should not be allowed
    And the <Missing Field> field should be highlighted as missing
    Examples:
      | From   | To        | Travel Class  | Missing Field |
      |        | Hong Kong | Economy       | From          |
      | Sydney |           | Economy       | To            |
      | Sydney | Hong Kong |               | Travel class  |
```

Now suppose we want to implement this scenario using Page Objects. We might define a `SearchForm` class to encapsulate the search form and its fields. One approach is to have a method for each of these input fields (e.g., `enterFrom()`, `enterTo()`, and `selectTravelClass()`), like in the following example:

```
@When("she/he tries to search for flights with the following criteria")
public void searchBy(FlightSearch search) {
    menuBar.navigateToBookFlights();
    searchForm.setDeparture(search.from());
    searchForm.setArrival(search.to());
    searchForm.setTravelClass(search.travelClass());
}
```

The `SearchForm` Page Object might look something like this:

```
public class SearchForm {

    private WebDriver driver;
    public SearchForm (WebDriver driver) { this.driver = driver; }

    public void setDeparture(String departure) {
        driver.findElement(By.id("departure")).sendKeys(departure);
    }

    public void setDestination(String destination) {
        driver.findElement(By.id("destination")).sendKeys(destination);
    }

    private By optionWithLabel(String label) {
        return By.xpath("//mat-option[normalize-space(.)='" + label + "']");
    }

    public void setTravelClass(TravelClass travelClass) {
        driver.findElement(By.id("travel-class")).click();
        driver.findElement(optionWithLabel(travelClass.getLabel())).click();
    }
}
```

Annotations:
- **Enters a value into the departure field** → `driver.findElement(By.id("departure")).sendKeys(departure);`
- **Enters a value into the destination field** → `driver.findElement(By.id("destination")).sendKeys(destination);`
- **Finds the dropdown entry with a given text** → `return By.xpath(...);`
- **Clicks on the option we want** → `driver.findElement(optionWithLabel(travelClass.getLabel())).click();`
- **Clicks on the dropdown field to make the dropdown options appear**

This approach presents a business-readable representation of the information while still hiding the implementation details of how the values are actually entered on the page: the departure and arrival fields are text fields, for example, whereas the travel class is a JavaScript dropdown component, which involves some more complex Web-Driver code to complete. All these details are hidden away behind readable and friendly methods.

Alternatively, if we prefer to always enter all these criteria in a search (even if some might be empty for our negative tests), we could also opt for a more concise approach using a single method, such as the `enterSearchCriteria()` method shown here:

```
searchForm.enterSearchCriteria("Sydney", "London", TravelClass.ECONOMY);
```

The full step definition would then look something like this:

```
@When("she/he tries to search for flights with the following criteria")
public void searchBy(FlightSearch search) {
    menuBar.navigateToBookFlights();
```

```
                searchForm.enterSearchCriteria(search.from(),
                                                search.to(),
                                                search.travelClass());
        }
```

11.3.5 Page Objects present state in business terms

Page Objects should also convert information about the state of the page into business terms. For example, in the screen shown in figure 11.4, when a field is not completed in the search form it is highlighted in red and the search button is disabled.

To check that the search button is disabled, we can simply check the state of the web element like this:

```
public boolean searchIsEnabled() {
    return driver.findElement(By.id("search-button")).isEnabled();
}
```

And the step definition method could simply be:

```
@Then("the search should not be allowed")
public void searchShouldNotBeAllowed() {
    assertThat(searchForm.searchIsEnabled()).isFalse();
}
```

Notice how, if the logic needed to check the state of the search button changes, our step definition method will remain unchanged.

Checking for the highlighted field labels is a bit trickier. We could check the CSS color attribute, but this will tie your code to the whims of the graphic designer. A better approach is to look for a CSS selector that identifies the text labels as incomplete. As it turns out, incomplete fields are tagged with the `mat-form-field-invalid` class (see the HTML snippet in figure 11.4).

We could add a method to the `SearchForm` class to fetch all the web elements matching this selector and extract the text value of each element:

```
                                                  Finds all the matching input
                                                  fields that are displayed in red
public List<String> missingFields() {
    return driver.findElements(By.cssSelector(".mat-form-field-invalid")).  ◄─┘
            .stream()
            .map(label -> label.getText().trim().replace(" *",""))  ◄───
            .collect(Collectors.toList());  ◄──┐            Extracts the field
}                                              Returns these labels   label and strip off the
                                               as a list of strings   trailing "*" character
```

The Page Object hides these details from the test code and exposes the results as an easy-to-consume list of field names. Using this method, we could check that the From field is marked as a missing field with the following assertion:

```
    assertThat(searchForm.missingFields()).containsExactly("From");
```

Notice once again how the Page Object method hides the implementation details of how this information is obtained and simply returns the results in an easy-to-consume format.

11.3.6   *Page Objects hide wait conditions and other incidental implementation details*

Oftentimes in our tests we need to wait for certain conditions to be met before continuing. We saw some ways you can do this earlier. But details such as wait conditions should never appear directly in our tests; they are rarely relevant to the business logic that a test demonstrates and just add noise to the test code.

Page Object methods are a great place to hide away these implementation details. For example, when we perform a search in our Flying High app, a spinner appears while the flights are retrieved (see figure 11.5).

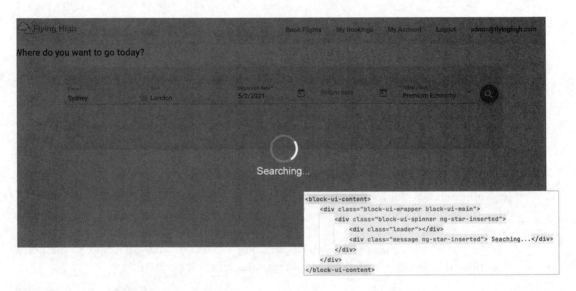

Figure 11.5   A spinner appearing on the Flying High app when you search for flights

Now imagine we need to automate the following scenario:

```
Rule: Travelers can search by departure, destination and travel class
  Scenario Outline: Searching for flights by travel class
    When she searches for flights with the following criteria
      | From   | To   | Travel Class   |
      | <From> | <To> | <Travel Class> |
    Then the returned flights should match the travel class <Travel Class>
    Examples:
      | From    | To        | Travel Class    |
      | Sydney  | Hong Kong | Economy         |
      | London  | New York  | Premium Economy |
      | Seoul   | Hong Kong | Business        |
```

During the first step, we need to wait for the spinner to disappear before we can check the actual search results. But this is an implementation detail; perhaps tomorrow the search results might be returned differently, without the spinner, but this should not affect our scenario or our step definition code.

So, we hide the interaction details about how we deal with the spinner inside a Page Object method. For example, to perform the actual search, we could extend the `SearchForm` class with a `submitSearch()` method, which clicks on the Search button and waits for the spinner to disappear:

```
                                                                    How to locate
    How to locate the search button                                 the spinner

    private static final By SEARCH_BUTTON = By.id("search-button");
    private static final By SPINNER = By.cssSelector(".block-ui-spinner");

    public void submitSearch() {
        driver.findElement(SEARCH_BUTTON).click();              Clicks on the
        Wait<WebDriver> wait = new FluentWait<>(driver)         search button
                .withTimeout(Duration.ofSeconds(10))
                .pollingEvery(Duration.ofMillis(100));
        wait.until(invisibilityOfElementLocated(SPINNER));      Waits for the spinner
    }                                                           to disappear
```

We can then call this method in the step definition code without needing to know anything about the spinner:

```
@When("she/he searches for flights with the following criteria")
public void performSearch(FlightSearch search) {
    this.searchCriteria = search;
    menuBar.navigateToBookFlights();
    searchForm.enterSearchCriteria(search.from(),
                                    search.to(),
                                    search.travelClass());
    searchForm.submitSearch();
}
```

This way, our step definition code can focus exclusively on the user interactions involved with this step.

11.3.7 *Page Objects do not contain assertions*

In the previous example, we saw how our Page Object returns a list of invalid fields so that the test code can assert whether these values were the expected ones. This is the typical way you use Page Objects: they report the state of a page but don't make judgment calls about whether this state is as expected.

In other words, your Page Objects should not contain assertions. Burying assertion logic inside Page Object code makes the Page Objects larger and more complex and also makes it harder to read what a test is actually testing.

For example, in the code we saw earlier, we used the `label()` method in the `CurrentUserPanel` Page Object to return the email of the currently connected user:

```
@Then("he/she should be given access to his/her account")
public void shouldBeGivenAccessToHisAccount() {
    CurrentUserPanel currentUserPanel = new CurrentUserPanel(driver);
    assertThat(currentUserPanel.label()).isEqualTo(frequentFlyer.email);
}
```

Here, the Page Object is responsible for returning the currently displayed user ID. The separation of concerns is clear: the step definition code describes what we expect (in the form of an assertion), and the Page Object tells us what it sees on the screen.

We would never include this assertion logic inside the Page Object itself. For example, the following code would break the separation of concerns rules we are trying to enforce by separating the UI interaction code from our test logic:

```
public void checkThatUserEmailDisplayedIs(String expectedEmail) {
    assertThat(driver.findElement(CURRENT_USER).getText())
            .isEqualTo(expectedEmail);
}
```

Anti-pattern—we violate the separation of concerns between Page Objects and test code.

This would add unnecessary complexity to our Page Object classes (imagine if we needed to add assertion methods for every check we needed to do!) and makes it harder to know what is being tested in each test.

Now that we have a better idea of what a Page Object should (and shouldn't) do, let's look at some of the features Selenium gives us to support writing Page Objects more easily.

11.3.8 *WebDriver Page Factories and the @FindBy annotation*

Although you can write your own Page Objects from the ground up, invoking the WebDriver methods for each interaction quickly becomes repetitive. Fortunately, WebDriver does give us another option.

This support comes in the form of the `PageFactory` class and the `@FindBy` annotation. Together, these can be used to locate web elements much more efficiently.

The `@FindBy` annotation lets you specify how you want to locate the different web elements your Page Object needs to use. And the `PageFactory` class knows how to scan your class for annotated web elements and configure them so that they are retrieved on the fly using the right locator strategy, whenever you interact with them.

Using this approach, you could rewrite the `LoginPage` Page Object we saw earlier like this (the `open()` method has been excluded for simplicity):

```
public class LoginPage {
    @FindBy(id="email")              Looks up the
    WebElement emailField;           email field

    @FindBy(id="password")           Looks up the
    WebElement passwordField;        password field
```

```
@FindBy(id="login-button")                    Looks up the
WebElement loginButton;                        login field

public LoginForm(WebDriver driver) {                        Initializes
    PageFactory.initElements(driver, this);                 the email and
}                                                           password fields

public void signinWithCredentials(String email, String password) {
    emailField.sendKeys(email);
    passwordField.sendKeys(password);          Looks up the web elements on
    loginButton.click();                       the web page before using them
}
}
```

The @FindBy annotation tells WebDriver how to look up a WebElement field. When you mark fields this way, you can use the PageFactory.initElements() method in the constructor to instantiate these fields for you. Each time you use these fields, WebDriver performs the equivalent of a driver.findElement(By...) call to bind them to the corresponding element on the web page. The @FindBy annotation supports all of the different selector methods available when you use driver.findElement(By...) (see table 11.1).

Table 11.1 Different ways to use the @FindBy annotation

@FindBy expression	Description
@FindBy(id="welcome-message")	Find by ID
@FindBy(name="email")	Find by name
@FindBy(className="typeahead")	Find by CSS class name
@FindBy(css=".typeahead li")	Find by CSS selector
@FindBy(linkText="Book")	Find by link text
@FindBy(partialLinkText="Book")	Find by partial link text
@FindBy(tagName="h2")	Find by HTML tag
@FindBy(xpath="//span[.='Singapore']")	Find by XPath expression

If the name of the WebElement fields in your Page Object matches either the name or ID of the corresponding HTML element, you can skip the @FindBy annotation entirely:

```
public class LoginForm {
    WebElement email;                   You don't need the
    WebElement password;                @FindBy annotation here.

    @FindBy(id="login-button")
    WebElement loginButton;

    ...
```

In this case, WebDriver automatically instantiates the email and password fields. The email field, for example, is the equivalent of first trying `@FindBy(id="email")`, and if that fails, `@FindBy(name="email")`.

11.3.9 Finding collections

The `@FindBy` annotation isn't limited to individual fields; you can also use this notation to retrieve collections of web elements. For example, in one of the scenarios we saw earlier, we need to check that all the returned flights match certain criteria (see figure 11.6):

```
Rule: Travelers can search by departure, destination and travel class
  Scenario Outline: Searching for flights by travel class
    When she searches for flights with the following criteria
      | From   | To    | Travel Class    |
      | <From> | <To>  | <Travel Class>  |
    Then the returned flights should match the travel class <Travel Class>
    Examples:
      | From   | To        | Travel Class    |
      | Sydney | Hong Kong | Economy         |
      | London | New York  | Premium Economy |
      | Seoul  | Hong Kong | Business        |
```

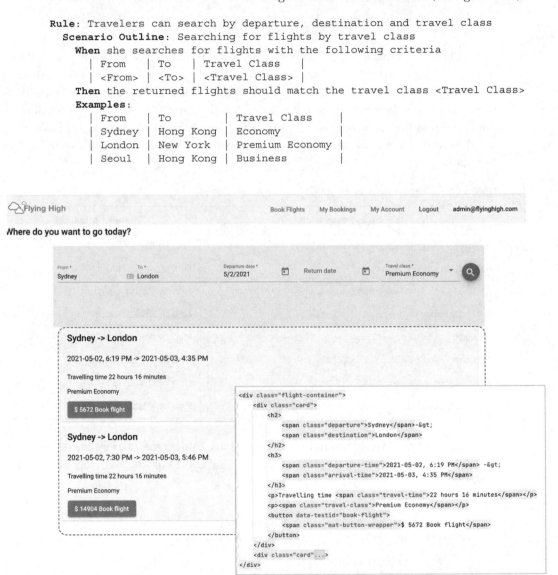

Figure 11.6   The list of matching flights

To implement this logic, we could define a `MatchingFlightsList` Page Object, responsible for returning a list of matching flights in a format that we can use in our step definitions. In this class, we could use the `@FindBy` annotation to retrieve the list of web elements that correspond to the matching flights:

```
@FindBy(css = ".flight-container .card")
private List<WebElement> matchingFlights;
```

But we need to return these results not as a list of WebElements, but in a business-friendly format we can use in our step definition code. For example, we might model the entries in the search results using a Java record (a language feature available in Java 14 or higher) structure like this:

```
public record MatchingFlight(String departure,
                             String destination,
                             TravelClass travelClass) {}
```

This way we could convert the web elements into MatchingFlight objects. Using Java 8 streams, the code might look like this:

```
matchingFlights.stream()
        .map(element -> new MatchingFlight(
                element.findElement(By.cssSelector(".departure")).getText(),

    element.findElement(By.cssSelector(".destination")).getText(),
                TravelClass.withLabel(
                        element.findElement(
                                By.cssSelector(".travel-class")
                        ).getText())
        )).collect(Collectors.toList());
```

After a little refactoring, the full class might now look like this:

```
public class MatchingFlightsList {

    private WebDriver driver;

    public MatchingFlightsList(WebDriver driver) {
        this.driver = driver;
        PageFactory.initElements(driver, this);
    }

    @FindBy(css = ".flight-container .card")          ◄─ Finds the list of web elements
    private List<WebElement> matchingFlights;            for each flight result

    private final static By DEPARTURE = By.cssSelector(".departure");
    private final static By DESTINATION = By.cssSelector(".destination");
    private final static By TRAVEL_CLASS = By.cssSelector(".travel-class");

    public List<MatchingFlight> matchingFlights() {   ◄─ Converts the list of matching
        return matchingFlights.stream()                  flights to MatchingFlight records
```

Defines locator strategies for the elements within the search form

Finds the departure, destination, and travel class for each flight using a nested query

```
            .map(element -> new MatchingFlight(
                element.findElement(DEPARTURE).getText(),
                element.findElement(DESTINATION).getText(),
                TravelClass.withLabel(
                    element.findElement(TRAVEL_CLASS).getText()
                )
        )).collect(Collectors.toList());
    }
}
```

Creates a new MatchingFlight for each section

The final piece of the puzzle is then simply to retrieve the list of `MatchingFlight` records and check that each one matches the expected travel class:

Fetches the matching flights currently displayed

```
@ParameterType("Economy|Premium Economy|Business")
public TravelClass travelClass(String value) {
    return TravelClass.withLabel(value);
}


@Then("the returned flights should match the travel class {travelClass}")
public void shouldMatchTravelClass(TravelClass expectedClass) {
    assertThat(matchingFlightsList.matchingFlights())
            .isNotEmpty()
            .allMatch(flight -> flight.travelClass() == expectedClass,
                    "should have a travel class of " + expectedClass
    );
}
```

Defines a Cucumber parameter type to convert the travel class label into the corresponding Enum value

All of the flights should be in the expected travel class.

There should be at least one matching flight.

11.3.10 Page Objects in Serenity BDD

In the code samples in the next few chapters, we will use the WebDriver support built into Serenity BDD (http://serenity-bdd.info/). There's nothing we will discuss that you can't do without using Serenity BDD, but it does allow us to write more automation code with less boilerplate and setup.

Serenity BDD provides a number of shortcuts that make Page Objects easier and more convenient to write. For example, Serenity BDD handles setting up and shutting your WebDriver instance, so you don't need to do that yourself.

Serenity BDD also enhances the WebDriver API, notably through the `PageObject` and `WebElementFacade` classes. For example, the `type()` method extends the send-Keys() method provided by the `WebElement` class by ensuring that the field is ready and clearing it before sending the key values.

The `LoginPage` Page Object we saw earlier could be implemented using Serenity BDD like this:

Defines the relative or absolute URL to be used when this Page Object is opened

All Serenity BDD Page Objects extend the PageObject class.

```
@DefaultUrl("/login")
public class LoginPage extends PageObject {
```

```
@FindBy(id="email")
WebElementFacade email;                    ◁──┐  The optional
                                               │  WebElementFacade class
                                               │  enhances WebDriver's
@FindBy(id="password")                         │  WebElement class.
WebElementFacade password;

@FindBy(id="login-button")
WebElementFacade loginButton;

public void signinWithCredentials(String emailValue,
                                  String passwordValue) {
    email.type(emailValue);
    password.type(passwordValue);       ┐  Defines a Cucumber
    loginButton.click();                │  parameter type to convert
}                                       │  the travel class label into the
}                                       ┘  corresponding Enum value
```

Serenity will also instantiate any Page Object fields in your tests for you, so you don't
need to explicitly create them. Our step definition code could be written like this:

```
                                              Serenity will automatically initialize
                                              this field with a Page Object configured
LoginPage loginPage;         ◁───┤           with the current WebDriver instance.

@When("^s?he (?:logs|has logged) on with a valid username and password$")
public void logsOnWithAValidUsernameAndPassword() {
    loginPage.open();
    loginPage.signinWithCredentials(frequentFlyer.email,
                                    frequentFlyer.password);
}
```

You can read more about Serenity BDD on the Serenity BDD website (http://serenity
-bdd.info/).

11.4   Going beyond Page Objects

So far, we have seen how to use Page Objects to make our UI automation code easier
to read and maintain by isolating WebDriver code inside Page Object classes and
methods, away from the test code itself.

Well-written Page Objects are much more maintainable than simple test scripts
and work well for small applications. However, as an application grows, we often run
into limitations. For example, a Page Object is by definition focused on the user interface; if all you have are Page Objects, there can be a temptation to test everything
through the UI and miss the opportunity to streamline tests by implementing certain
steps with faster and more reliable API calls.

Page Objects can also become large and bloated, mixing business-focused logic
(e.g., "search for flights") with UI-implementation details ("select travel class from the
dropdown menu"). Many folks fall into the trap of writing Page Objects that closely
model and duplicate the structure of the user interface, which can make the Page
Object classes more complicated and fragile.

A good way to avoid these problems is to introduce an additional layer of abstraction between your step definitions and your interaction layer. This approach has a number of advantages for larger or more complex applications:

- A much cleaner separation between the business-focused steps in the Cucumber scenarios (the what), and the nitty-gritty details of how these steps are implemented (the how)
- More options to reuse business steps between different scenarios, without having to add complexity to our Page Objects

We sometimes call this approach a domain-specific language (DSL), because it models the business domain in a very readable way. We call the classes and objects that implement this layer *actions* (to distinguish them from Page Objects). Let's see how this approach works in practice.

11.4.1 Action classes

Earlier in the chapter we looked at a simple scenario describing how a Frequent Flyer member can connect to the Flying High site using their credentials:

```
Example: Amy successfully logs on to the Frequent Flyer app
  Given Amy is a registered Frequency Flyer member
  When she logs on with a valid username and password
  Then she should be given access to her account
```

The step definition code using Page Objects looked something like this:

```
@When("he/she logs on with a valid username and password")
public void logsOnWithAValidUsernameAndPassword() {
    LoginPage loginPage = new LoginPage(driver);
    loginPage.open();

    loginPage.signinWithCredentials(frequentFlyer.email,
                                    frequentFlyer.password)

}
```

Opens the login page

Signs in with some valid credentials

Reads the email displayed on the screen and compares it with the expected one

This code is very tightly coupled to the user interface implementation. For example, in the first step, we explicitly open a page and enter the credentials. This is fine as it stands, but it means that we can only perform this step via the UI. If we wanted to streamline things (for example by providing our authentication details via a Cookie, or using some other authentication mechanism), we would need to rewrite the whole step. Now imagine if we had a class whose job it was to model the login process from a business perspective—not the login screen, but the login process as a whole, regardless of whether we were logging in via the UI or using some other mechanism.

We could have a `Login` class that knows how to authenticate as a given Frequent Flyer user:

```
@Steps
Login login;          A Serenity BDD annotation that automatically
                      instantiates this class and any nested Page Objects

@When("^s?he (?:logs|has logged) on with a valid username and password$")
public void logsOnWithAValidUsernameAndPassword() {
    login.as(frequentFlyer);
}
```

The Login Action class represents the high-level action of logging in.

The `Login` class would implement the `as()` method and know how to open the login page and enter the correct user credentials, using the Page Object class we defined earlier. Logging in involves two steps: opening the login page and then entering the correct credentials, so we could implement the `Login` class like this:

```
public class Login {            The Page Object field will be    A Serenity BDD
                                automatically initialized by      annotation that
    LoginForm loginForm;        Serenity BDD.                     makes this method
                                                                  call appears as a step
    @Step("Login as {0}")                                         in the test report.
    public void as(FrequentFlyer frequentFlyer) {                 "{0}" represents the
        loginForm.open();                                         first parameter of the
        loginForm.enterCredentials(frequentFlyer.email,           method, the frequent
                        frequentFlyer.password);                  flyer in this case.
        loginForm.submit();
    }
}
```

The `Login` class is an example of an Action class, a class that encapsulates a specific business task or action. Action classes know which pages (or APIs) they need to interact with but don't need to know implementation details such as how to locate a particular element on a page.

11.4.2   Query classes

Another type of Action class, that we sometimes call a Query class, focuses on reading the state of the system and returning it to the test code in business-friendly terms. Earlier we saw how to write Page Object methods to do this. The step definition code got the email address displayed on the screen and compared it to that of the current user:

```
@Then("he/she should be given access to his/her account")
public void shouldBeGivenAccessToHisAccount() {
    CurrentUserPanel currentUserPanel = new CurrentUserPanel(driver);
    assertThat(currentUserPanel.email()).isEqualTo(frequentFlyer.email);
}
```

But this can add unnecessary complexity to our Page Object classes, especially if different tests need to obtain different information from the same page. It also binds our test class to the implementation. For example, what happens if we decide to display the user's first name instead of their email? The intent of the step ("he/she should be given access to his/her account") wouldn't be any less valid. But the implementation would break.

Rather than adding this method to a Page Object, we could write a dedicated query class responsible for knowing if the current user matches the expected one. Using the Serenity BDD support classes we could write a Query class like this:

A Serenity BDD base class used for Action or Query classes that interact with the user interface

Compare the expected email with the currently displayed value. The textOf() method returns the text value of an element located by a given locator.

```
public class CurrentUser extends UIInteractionSteps {
    public boolean isConnectedAs(FrequentFlyer frequentFlyer) {
        return frequentFlyer.email.equals(textOf("#current-user"));
    }
}
```

Now our step definition just needs to check whether the current user is connected as the expected one, without having to know how this is done:

```
@Then("he/she should be given access to his/her account")
public void shouldBeGivenAccessToHisAccount() {
    assertTrue("the current user should be shown as " + frequentFlyer,
            currentUser.isConnectedAs(frequentFlyer));
}
```

The (optional) extra text parameter helps describe what we are asserting more clearly.

Checks that the current user matches the expected one

11.4.3 DSL layers and builders

Modeling our business flow in Action classes gives us a lot of flexibility; it makes it possible to write highly expressive and readable application code that models the behavior of our users and of the system, which makes our test code easier to write, easier to understand, and cheaper to maintain.

Let's look at another example to see what we mean. Earlier we looked at the following search scenario:

```
Scenario Outline: Searching for flights by travel class
  When she searches for flights with the following criteria
    | From   | To    | Travel Class   |
    | <From> | <To>  | <Travel Class> |
  Then the returned flights should match the travel class <Travel Class>
  Examples:
    | From   | To        | Travel Class    |
    | Sydney | Hong Kong | Economy         |
    | London | New York  | Premium Economy |
    | Seoul  | Hong Kong | Business        |
```

We've seen a few ways to implement this test code using Page Objects, which work very well for this specific scenario. But suppose we had other scenarios, such as for a return trip or a multistop journey?

One approach would be to use a Fluent Interface to make our code more flexible and more expressive. A *Fluent Interface* is an API that uses method chaining to improve readability. Our step definition code might look something like this if we use one:

```
@When("she/he searches for flights with the following criteria")
public void performSearch(FlightSearch search) {
    searchFlights.from(search.from())
            .to(search.to())
            .inTravelClass(search.travelClass())
            .andViewResults();
}
```

If we needed to test return trips, for example, we could easily extend the API to cater to the extra condition like this:

```
@When("she/he searches for return flights with the following criteria")
public void performSearch(FlightSearch search) {
    searchFlights.from(search.from())
            .to(search.to())
            .inTravelClass(search.travelClass())
            .withAReturnTrip()
            .andViewResults();
}
```

And a multistop journey might look like this:

```
        searchFlights.from("London")
                .to("New York")
                .thenTo("Los Angeles")
                .inTravelClass(TravelClass.ECONOMY)
                .withAReturnTrip()
                .andViewResults();
```

There are many ways to implement a class like this, and writing DSLs is a topic worth a book in its own right. But by using our existing Page Objects, we could simply invoke one or more Page Objects as required for each method of the class:

```
public class SearchFlights extends UIInteractionSteps {

    @Steps
    Navigate navigate;
    SearchForm searchForm;

    public SearchFlights from(String departure) {
        navigate.toTheBookFlightsPage();
        searchForm.setDeparture(departure);
        return this;
    }

    public SearchFlights to(String destination) {
        searchForm.setDestination(destination);
        return this;
    }
```

```
public SearchFlights inTravelClass(TravelClass travelClass) {
    searchForm.setTravelClass(travelClass);
    return this;
}

public void andViewResults() {
    searchForm.submitSearch();
}
}
```

This is a very simple example of a Fluent Interface, a coding style that allows us to write much more flexible and readable code in our step definitions.

Summary

- You can use Page Objects to make the step definition code for UI scenarios more maintainable.
- You can use Action classes and Fluent Interfaces to isolate your step definition code from the WebDriver API.

In the next chapter, we will look at a more advanced way of writing step definition code called the Screenplay Pattern.

Scalable test automation with the Screenplay Pattern

12

As your test automation framework grows, you quickly realize that your biggest problem isn't knowing how to automate each new scenario; it's being able to add these new scenarios while at the same time keeping your code base simple and maintainable. As your test suite interacts with different UI components, APIs, databases and more, keeping your code simple and consistent can be harder and harder to do.

The Screenplay Pattern, which we will be covering in this chapter, is an approach to keeping this complexity under control as our frameworks grow. The Screenplay Pattern is an actor-centered approach to modeling executable specifications. It uses functional composition to help you capture the domain language and represent the various workflows your system needs to support in a way that's easy to understand by both technical and nontechnical audiences.

Let's start with a quick example of how the Screenplay Pattern can help us write cleaner, more maintainable test automation code. Screenplay helps us model user behavior in terms of the tasks a user wants to achieve and the interactions with the application that the user needs to do to perform these tasks. In this chapter, we will see how modeling user behavior makes our code both more readable and more reusable, and also makes it easier to build large test suites that are easy to maintain and extend.

12.1   *What is the Screenplay Pattern, and why do we need it?*

In chapters 8, 9, and 10, we saw a few other approaches to help keep your test automation code clean. Page Objects are one example. We've seen how the Page Object model can help to separate low-level WebDriver code from your step definition code, which can reduce duplication and simplify your step definition code.

However, Page Objects can lead to two major problems as our application grows. First, when tests rely too heavily on Page Objects alone, they tend to place too much emphasis on how the user interface is built. They spend a lot of time describing which fields are on which pages, and how to navigate from one page to another, which makes it harder to step back and see what the user is really trying to achieve in business terms—not to mention that, by their very nature, Page Objects are focused on modeling interactions only with the graphical user interface. This means that incorporating API, batch processing, or database-based interactions into your tests might feel awkward and inconsistent with the UI-based interactions.

A second problem is maintenance. For larger applications, Page Object classes often try to do way too much. For example, they try to model too many unrelated fields or page elements, simply because they appear on the same page of an application. Or they use complex class hierarchies to try to imitate the way pages are organized in the actual application.

One way to avoid these problems is to add a different layer of abstraction between the business behavior our scenarios describe (the what) and what our code must do to deliver this behavior (the how). This helps to keep the Page Objects simpler and easier to understand and frees up our test code to focus more on the user journey and business tasks instead.

The Action classes pattern that we looked at in chapter 11 is one way to make this separation. With Action classes, behavior is modeled as methods or functions; each method describes a particular business task. Let's look at a concrete example of the Action classes pattern in practice. In figure 12.1 we can see the search page of our Frequent Flyer application.

Figure 12.1   The search screen of our Frequent Flyer application accepts a number of search criteria that we need to enter.

In chapter 11 we saw an example of a scenario that tests this feature:

```
Rule: Travelers can search by departure, destination, and travel class
   Scenario Outline: Searching for flights by travel class
      Given Amy is logged on as registered Frequency Flyer member
      When she searches for flights with the following criteria
         | From    | To    | Travel Class    |
         | <From>  | <To>  | <Travel Class>  |
      Then the returned flights should match the travel class <Travel Class>

      Examples:
         | From    | To        | Travel Class    |
         | Sydney  | Hong Kong | Economy         |
         | London  | New York  | Premium Economy |
         | Seoul   | Hong Kong | Business        |
```

We also saw how to implement this scenario using Action classes. The code for the *when* clause used an Action class called `SearchFlights` to perform this action. This class has methods for the various steps Amy needs to do when she performs a search. The code looked something like this:

```
@Steps
SearchFlights searchFlights;

@When("she/he searches for flights with the following criteria")
public void performSearch(FlightSearch search) {
    searchFlights.from(search.from())
                 .to(search.to())
                 .inTravelClass(search.travelClass())
                 .andViewResults();
}
```

The `SearchFlights` class in turn contained methods that interacted with the application itself. For example, to select the departure airport, the Serenity BDD code might look something like this:

```
public void to(String destination) {
    $("#destination").type(destination);
    waitingForNoLongerThan(1).second()
        .find("/span[contains(.,'{0}')]", destination)
        .click();

}
```

Enters the destination into the destination field

Finds a dropdown entry containing the destination city

Then clicks on the matching destination entry

Waits for up to one second for the dropdown to populate

This approach is clean and readable and works well for simple scenarios. It is not as reusable as we might like, though: the dropdown logic shown here would need to be duplicated whenever we encounter a similar dropdown field anywhere in the application. This code also makes an implicit assumption that there's only one external actor interacting with the system, so things can become tricky and boundaries between the different parts of a workflow blurred if more than one actor is involved.

And in real-world projects, many scenarios do need more than one actor. When we test complex business applications, we often need to demonstrate multi-user workflows, with different activities performed by different people. For example, a loan application may need a client to make the application, and then one or more bank employees to review and approve or reject the application. Chat systems and games are other common examples where various actors interact with each other.

Another limitation of the Action-class approach is reuse. While it is easy to reuse individual methods, if we want to combine a sequence of methods (say, search flights, select a flight, and book the flight) into a single task (say, make a booking), we need to create a new method for that. This can lead to large Action classes with lots of methods.

The Screenplay Pattern proposes a different approach, an approach that many testers find more flexible and more elegant. Screenplay uses an *actor-centric* approach, where we model *actors* that interact with the application, as well as the *tasks* that these actors perform to achieve their goals. Once written, tasks are particularly easy to reuse and to combine, which makes this pattern well suited to large applications.

Using the Screenplay Pattern, we could automate the second step of our scenario, "When she searches for flights with the following criteria," using the following code:

In Screenplay, actors (in this case the traveler) are the starting point of most activities.

```
@When("{actor} searches for flights with the following criteria")
public void performSearch(Actor traveler, FlightSearch searchCriteria) {
    traveler.attemptsTo(
            SearchFlights.matchingCriteria(searchCriteria).
    );
}
```

Actors perform tasks, which are represented by sequences of command objects and passed as parameters to the attemptsTo() method.

The `SearchFlights` class encapsulates the logic of this search form and hides the interaction details behind a business-readable façade:

```
public class SearchFlights {
    public static Performable matching(FlightSearch searchCriteria) {
        return Task.where("Search for matching flights",
            Navigate.toBookFlights(),
            Type.theValue(searchCriteria.from())
                .into(SearchFlightsForm.FROM),
            Type.theValue(searchCriteria.to())
                .into(SearchFlightsForm.TO),
            Select.option(searchCriteria.travelClassName())
                .from(SearchFlightsForm.TRAVEL_CLASS_DROPDOWN),
            Click.on(SearchFlightsForm.SEARCH_BUTTON),
            WaitUntil.the(SearchResultsList.SEARCH_RESULTS,isVisible())
                .forNoMoreThan(5).seconds()
        );
    }
}
```

Opens the book flights page

Enters the Departure city in an input field

Enters the Destination city in an input field

A human-readable description of the task, to be used in test report

Clicks on the search button

Waits until the results appear

Selects a travel class in a dropdown menu

Even without understanding the finer points of the pattern, this code remains very readable. Each step describes what the actor is doing and what element they are interacting with. In many ways that is the essence of the Screenplay Pattern: at each layer, we focus on describing what is happening at that layer, leaving the how for the layer underneath.

Whereas a Page Object architecture describes things in the language of the solution (pages, UI element, etc.), with Screenplay we model things using the language of the business or the problem domain. In this way, the Screenplay Pattern works very naturally with a behavior-driven approach to writing acceptance tests. We'll see how this code works in more detail as we explore the Screenplay Pattern in the rest of the chapter.

The origins of the Screenplay Pattern

The Screenplay Pattern has grown in popularity over the past few years. However, it is not a new idea—the core concepts have been around for a while.

It all started at the Agile Alliance Functional Testing Tools workshop (AAFTT) back in 2007.

"In Praise of Abstraction," a talk given by Kevin Lawrence, inspired Antony Marcano to implement a fluent DSL based on Kevin's idea to use the language of interaction designers to model the layers of abstraction in an acceptance test. With the help of Andy Palmer, this fluent DSL became JNarrate a year later (2008).

In the late 2012, Antony and Andy joined forces with Jan Molak. Their experiments with Kevin's model, combined with a desire to address problems with shortcomings of the Page Object pattern and apply SOLID design principles to acceptance testing is what became known in 2013 as `screenplay-jvm` (https://github.com/screenplay/screenplay-jvm).

And in 2015, when Antony, Andy, and Jan started working with John Ferguson Smart, what became known as the Screenplay Pattern found its way into Serenity BDD, and from there into the broader test automation community.

12.2   *Screenplay fundamentals*

Despite the word "screen" in its name, the Screenplay Pattern has nothing to do with computer screens. On the contrary, it is a general method of modeling user-centered acceptance tests interacting with any external interface of our system.

The name of the pattern takes inspiration from the world of film production. There, a screenplay describes the actors who take part in the performance, their dialogues, and the various tasks they perform. Here, in the world of test automation, we use actors to represent the users of our system. We model their behavior and micro-goals as tasks, which instruct the actors what activities to perform and what things to check. Those sequences of activities, expressed using the domain-specific test language you create and performed by the various actors you define, become screenplays.

This approach helps us to describe both user and system behavior more clearly and makes it easier to encapsulate behavior in the form of reusable code. It also steers us toward clean, well-designed layers of abstraction, which helps to make our code base easier to understand and maintain. This focus on users and user behavior makes the Screenplay Pattern a great fit for many BDD scenarios.

The Screenplay Pattern is beautiful in its simplicity. It's made up of five elements we combine to express any functional acceptance test we need, no matter how sophisticated or how simple it has to be:

- *Actors*—Who represent users and external systems interacting with ours
- *Interactions*—Which represent the most basic activities an actor can perform in our system, such as clicking on a button or sending a request to an API
- *Abilities*—Which enable the actors to interact with the system through its various interfaces
- *Questions*—Which, when answered by the actors, provide information about the state of the system
- *Tasks*—Which allow us to group, combine, and reuse sequences of interactions or other tasks

You can see an overview of how these elements fit together in figure 12.2. In the following sections we'll look at each of these components in more detail.

12.3   *What is an actor?*

The Screenplay Pattern is a user-centric model, which means that actors are its key element and a starting point of every test scenario we write. An actor represents someone or something who interacts with the system under test, such as a user, or even an external system. Actors can also correspond to the personas we introduced in chapter 7 (see section 7.6.5) and that we have been using in our Gherkin scenarios.

When actors represent user personas, we often give them easy-to-remember names, such as Tracy the Traveler or Amy the Account Manager. Here's an example of how we define a new Screenplay actor in Java using Serenity BDD:

```
Actor tracy = Actor.named("Tracy");
```

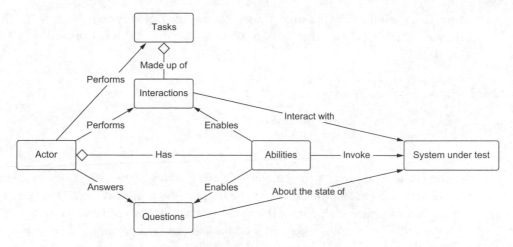

Figure 12.2   The Screenplay Pattern is an actor-centric model.

But defining an actor is just the start. After all, a star who never appears on stage isn't much of a star. An actor only becomes interesting when they play a role in the movie. Likewise, in a Screenplay scenario, we want to see our actors in action, performing business tasks and getting stuff done. Let's look at how this happens.

> **Screenplay: A design pattern, not a library**
>
> In the rest of this chapter, we'll be giving code examples in Java using the Serenity BDD implementation of the Screenplay Pattern. However, it's important to remember that Screenplay is a design pattern, not a library, and there are many Screenplay implementations out there. Some of the more notable ones include Serenity/JS (JavaScript/TypeScript), ScreenPy (Python), Boa Constrictor (.NET), and Cucumber Screenplay (JavaScript/TypeScript).

12.4   Actors perform tasks

Like real actors in a film, Screenplay actors have a role to play in a test. They have well-defined business goals they want to achieve, such as purchase a plane ticket, issue an invoice, or approve a loan. And to achieve these goals, they need to perform a sequence of business tasks, such as search for a flight, locate a customer, or perform a credit check.

These tasks are expressed in business or domain language and model what the actor needs to do in business terms, not in terms of screens, buttons, or APIs. For example, if an actor (say, Tracy) wants to book a flight, one of the things she will need to do is search for the available flights.

Those tasks might be composed of subtasks; for example to raise an invoice an actor would need to find the customer details and provide the details of the sale. To find the customer details they'd need to use the CRM system, search for the customer, and so on. In a Screenplay test, we would model this action with a task, possibly like this:

```
tracy.attemptsTo(
    BookAFlight.from("London")
              .to("New York")
              .inClass(Business)
              .departingIn(2).days()
);
```

Notice how we try to talk the language of the business—the task does not specify any particular implementation and could be implemented in many ways. But here the key is that we are representing what the actor needs to do in business terms.

We will come back to tasks and see how you can create your own, later in the chapter. But first, we need to understand how Screenplay helps us model how the actor interacts with the application in order to perform these tasks.

12.5 Interactions model how actors interact with the system

Tasks represent how the actor sees the world, independently of any particular implementation. But to perform a task, the actor must in turn interact with the system under test so that they can achieve these goals (see figure 12.3).

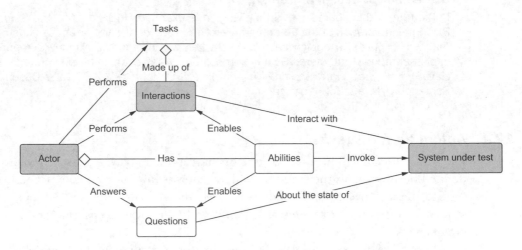

Figure 12.3   Actors interact with the system under test using Interaction classes.

These interactions can come in many forms. Our actor may need to navigate to a particular URL, to click on a button or enter a value into a field, or maybe send an HTTP request to a REST API.

But no matter what system we are interacting with, in the Screenplay Pattern we use the same pattern: the `actor.attemptsTo()` method, and then provide a list of the activities we would like our actor to perform. (We say "attempts to" rather than a more confident expression such as "performs" or "does" because, after all, this is a test, and something might go wrong.)

Imagine that we want Tracy to click on the search icon in figure 12.1, which can be identified by the CSS expression "#search-button". The Screenplay code to click on this button would look something like this:

```
tracy.attemptsTo(Click.on("#search-button"));
```

Or if we prefer a more explicit style, we could use a Selenium locator like this:

```
tracy.attemptsTo(Click.on(By.id("search-button")));
```

In both cases, we are using the `Click` interaction class to do the actual work. Under the hood this class will find the WebDriver instance for this actor and execute the appropriate Selenium commands for us. `Click` is one of hundreds of built-in interaction classes that Screenplay libraries like Serenity BDD provide for you out of the box, so you typically don't have to implement the low-level interactions yourself.

12.5.1 Actors can perform multiple interactions

Typically, an actor will want to do more than one thing to achieve their goals. For example, when Tracy logs on to the application, she needs to enter her email address and her password, and then click the Login button (see figure 12.4).

Figure 12.4   The Frequent Flyers login page

To implement these actions we could simply repeat the calls to the `attemptsTo()` method, like this (the `Enter` interaction class that we use here is the equivalent to the Selenium `sendKeys()` method; it enters a text value into a specified field):

```
tracy.attemptsTo(Open.url("http://localhost:3000/"));
tracy.attemptsTo(Click.on("//button[normalize-space()='Login']");
```

```
tracy.attemptsTo(Enter.theValue("tracy@traveler.com").into("#email"));
tracy.attemptsTo(Enter.theValue("secretPassword").into("#password"));
tracy.attemptsTo(Click.on("#login-button"));
```

But this would become repetitive and distract from the flow of the actions, making the code harder to read. A cleaner approach would be to use a single call to the attemptsTo() method and pass in a sequence of activities:

```
tracy.attemptsTo(
    Open.url("http://localhost:3000/"),                          ← Opens the application home page
    Click.on("//button[normalize-space()='Login']"),             ← Goes to the login page
    Enter.theValue("tracy@traveler.com").into("#email"),         ← Enters the email
    Enter.theValue("secretPassword").into("#password"),          ← Enters the password
    Click.on("#login-button")                                    ← Clicks on the login button
);
```

Interaction classes like these are designed to make interacting with a user interface simple and intuitive. Screenplay implementations such as Serenity BDD (http://serenity -bdd.info and https://serenity-bdd.github.io) and Serenity/JS (https://serenity-js.org) typically come bundled with a large number of interactions for different situations. You can see some of the more common UI Screenplay interaction classes in table 12.1.

Table 12.1   Some common Screenplay UI Interaction classes

Interaction	Usage	Example
Clear	Clear a text field	`Clear.field("#email")`
Click	Click on an element	`Click.on("#login-button")`
Enter	Type a value into a field	`Enter.theValue("secretPassword")` `    .into("#password")`
Open	Open a given URL (in Serenity BDD)	`Open.url("https://www.google.com")`
Navigate	Open a given URL (in Serenity/JS)	`Navigate` `    .to("https://www.google.com")`
Scroll	Scrolls the browser to the specified element	`Scroll.to("#login-button")`

SelectFromOptions	Select a dropdown list value (in Serenity BDD)	`SelectFromOptions`
		`    .byVisibleText("Economy")`
		`    .from("#travel-class")`

Select	Select a dropdown list value (in Serenity JS)	`Select.option("Economy")` `    .from(travelClass)`

12.5.2 Interactions are objects, not methods

One important detail, that is easy to overlook at first glance, is that each interaction in the code shown is not a method of a class, but an object in its own right. This is a core Screenplay principle and is what gives the pattern a lot of its flexibility.

In conventional WebDriver code, if you want to click on a button, you might write code along the following lines:

```
WebElement loginButton = driver.findElement(By.id("#login-button"));   ◁─┐
loginButton.click();   ◁─┐                                               │
```

┌───────────────────────────┐   ┌───────────────────────────┐
│ **Invokes the click()**   │   │ **Locates the element we** │
│ **method on this object** │   │ **want to interact with** │
└───────────────────────────┘   └───────────────────────────┘

But in Screenplay, we take a different approach. As we have seen, the actor uses the `attemptsTo()` method to perform a series of interactions,[1] so the equivalent code would look something like this:

```
tracy.attemptsTo(           ◁─┐  The actor performing
    Click.on("#login-button")  │  the action
);                          ◁─┐  The action being
                               │  performed
```

On the surface, the second code sample looks very similar to the first. In both cases, we are clicking on a button, but rather than invoking the `click()` method, we create and pass a new instance of the `Click` class to the `attemptsTo()` method.

This gives us a much more flexible architecture. We don't have to modify our existing classes when we want to add new behavior; we simply create a new interaction class. And by not having to change our existing code so much, we reduce the risk of inadvertently breaking something.

For example, the `WebDriver` class has no method to perform a double-click. If we want to do that, we need to introduce the WebDriver `Actions` class and use a different coding style:

```
WebElement loginButton = driver.findElement(By.id("#login-button"));
Actions action = new Actions(driver);
action.doubleClick(loginButton).perform();
```

In Screenplay, on the other hand, we simply use a different interaction class:

```
tracy.attemptsTo(
    DoubleClick.on("#login-button")
);
```

Screenplay libraries generally come with a wide range of bundled interaction classes for different situations, but they are easy to write yourself, too. We'll see how later in this chapter.

---

[1] Technically, each interaction implements a special Screenplay interface called performable, and the `attemptsTo()` method accepts a list of performable objects as parameters.

> ### Screenplay Actors and Interactions use the Command pattern
>
> In Object-Oriented Design, the Command Pattern[a] is a design pattern where an object containing all the information necessary to perform some action is passed to a function or method that can perform the action. It's a bit like when you are in a restaurant: the waiter takes your order, writes it down on a piece of paper (the object), and passes this piece of paper to the kitchen, where your meal is prepared. In the same way the Interaction Object only contains instructions of what the actor should do; it is the actor who performs them.
>
> ———————————
>
> [a.] Erich Gamma et al., *Design Patterns: Elements of Reusable Object-Oriented Software* (Addison-Wesley, 1994).

12.5.3 *Interactions can perform waits as well as actions*

When working with modern applications, we often need to wait for things to happen. Maybe we need to wait for an API call to return results to the screen, for a back-end system to update the state of a record, or for our application to receive some message or event.

The Screenplay Pattern gives us an elegant way to wait for a particular state. For example, when we search for flights, we need to wait until the results are returned from the server. This is visually represented by a spinner (see figure 12.5).

Figure 12.5   **Waiting for the search results**

In Serenity BDD, we could wait for this spinner to disappear using the `WaitUntil` interaction, like this:

```
tracy.attemptsTo(
        WaitUntil.the(".block-ui-spinner", isNotVisible())    ← Waits until the spinner disappears
                .forNoMoreThan(10).seconds()    ← Sets a maximum time to wait to 10 seconds
    )
```

Alternatively, we could wait until the search results are visible on the new page, like this:

```
tracy.attemptsTo(
      WaitUntil.the(".flight-container", isVisible())
               .forNoMoreThan(10).seconds()
   )
```

Waits until the search results appear

Sets a maximum time to wait to 10 seconds

The expressions `isNotVisible()` and `isVisible()` come from the `WebElement-StateMatchers` class, which contains many similar methods. Some of the more common ones are listed in table 12.2.

We can use the Selenium `ExpectedConditions` class to access a wide range of wait conditions:

We use the ExpectedConditions.titleIs() method to define the expected condition.

```
tracy.attemptsTo(
      WaitUntil.the(titleIs("Search Results"))
               .forNoMoreThan(Duration.of(3, SECONDS))
   );
```

As before, we can also specify how long we want to wait.

We could even wait until some arbitrary function is completed, using the `Wait` class:

We wait for a Boolean function to return a value of true.

```
tracy.attemptsTo(
      Wait.until(() -> fileIsProcessed()).
           .forNoMoreThan(Duration.of(3, SECONDS))
   );
```

Once again we can specify how long we want to wait.

As you can see, Screenplay gives us a great deal of flexibility when it comes to wait conditions, but each variation follows the same general style and patterns we have seen so far.

Table 12.2 Wait conditions and usages

Wait Conditions	Usage	Example
`isVisible()`	Wait until the element is rendered	`WaitUntil.the(".flight-container", isVisible())`
`isNotVisible()`[a]	Wait until the element is not rendered	`WaitUntil.the("#login-button", isNotVisible())`
`isEnabled`	Element is enabled	`WaitUntil.the("#search-button", isEnabled())`
`isPresent`	Element is present in the DOM	`WaitUntil.the("#search-button", isPresent())`
`containsText`	A given element contains the specified text value	`WaitUntil.the(".status-message", containsText("Done"))`

a. Most wait conditions have a *not* version (e.g. `isNotVisible()`, `isNotEnabled()`, etc.).

12.5.4   *Interactions can also interact with REST APIs*

Thus far we've focused on interacting with the application through the UI. But one of the great things about the Screenplay Pattern is its flexibility. Actors can interact with the browser via Selenium WebDriver, Webdriver.io, Playwright, or some other technology, depending on the interaction classes they choose to use. But they can also interact with the system in other ways.

Suppose we need to register a new user, and we have two options. The first option is to open the Frequent Flyer site, go to the registration page, enter the details, and submit the form. The second option is to use a REST API.

```
Traveler trevor = new Traveler("trevor@traveler.com","secret");   ◁──  Creates a
actor.attemptsTo(                                                       new traveler
        Post.to("/users")                              ◁──               to register
            .with(request -> request.body(trevor))     ◁──  Sends a POST
);                                                                 request . . .
                                  . . . with a request body.
```

We'll look at interacting with REST APIs in more detail, both with and without Screenplay, in the next chapter.

12.6   *Abilities are how actors interact with the system*

Thus far we've seen how actors can interact with the system under test to achieve their goals. To do that, they might need to use a web browser, make a call to an API, query a database, or interact with a mainframe—the possibilities are endless! But how does this work? This is where the concept of *abilities* comes into play (see figure 12.6).

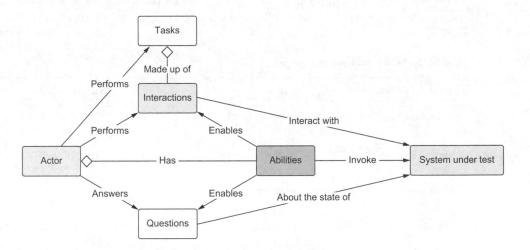

Figure 12.6   **We give actors abilities that enable them to interact with the system.**

Abilities are what enable an actor to interact with all these different systems. They give our actors their special powers, if you will.

For example, each actor can have their own browser instance, so we need to tell our actors which browser they should use. In Serenity BDD and Serenity/JS, we can give an actor the ability to interact with a web browser using WebDriver by using the `BrowseTheWeb` ability:

Create a   **Create a new WebDriver instance**
new actor.   **to open a Chrome browser.**   Sally can now use all the
                                                                          WebDriver interactions
```
WebDriver driver = new ChromeDriver();              we saw in the previous
Actor sally = Actor.named("Sally");                 section.
sally.can(BrowseTheWeb.with(driver));
```

In a similar way, we can give an actor the ability to query a REST endpoint:

```
sally.can(CallAnApi.at("http://my.api.server:8000"));
```

Once we have given an ability to our actors, they can use this ability to perform interactions or ask questions. For example, the `BrowseTheWeb` ability assigns a unique Web-Driver instance to each actor. We can access this instance using the `BrowseTheWeb.as()` static method. Suppose we wanted to get the current URL directly from the actor's Web-Driver instance. We can do just that with the following code:

```
String currentUrl = BrowseTheWeb.as(actor).getDriver().getCurrentUrl();
```

This makes Screenplay a very extensible model: you can easily add new abilities without having to change the actor implementation for each new system you need to interact with.

> **Abilities are an implementation of the Adaptor Pattern**
>
> If you are familiar with Object-Oriented Design patterns, an ability is an implementation of the Adaptor Pattern.[a] An adaptor is a thin interface that allows two systems to work together, without having to change the code in either system. An ability, then, is a thin wrapper around a lower-level, interface-specific client such as a web browser driver, a HTTP client, a database client, and so on. When you need to complete a task using an external system, you invoke this interface to interact with that system.
>
> ---
> [a.] Erich Gamma et al.

12.7   *Writing our own interaction classes*

The reason an actor has abilities is to use them in interaction and question classes to interact with and retrieve information from the system under test. Most Screenplay implementations will generally come with all the interaction classes you will need for most standard scenarios.

Interaction classes are easy to write. With Serenity BDD, the simplest way to do it is to use the `Interaction.where()` method, which allows us to create a new `Interaction` class dynamically using a Java 8 lambda expression.

Let's look at an example. Imagine we need to switch to another window. With Web-Driver we can do that using the WebDriver `switchTo()` method. If we wanted to write a Screenplay interaction class to do this, we could write something like this:

```
public class SwitchTo {
    public static Interaction parent() {
        return Interaction.where("{0} switches to the parent frame",
            theActor -> {
                WebDriver driver = BrowseTheWeb.as(theActor).getDriver();
                driver.switchTo().parentFrame();
            }
        );
    }
}
```

Passes the actor into a closure to perform low-level UI actions

Switches to the parent frame using the actor's browser

Uses the BrowseTheWeb class to retrieve this actor's browser

Now Sally can use this interaction class to switch to the parent frame like this:

```
sally.attemptsTo(SwitchTo.parent());
```

12.8 Questions allow an actor to query the state of the system

Assertions are an essential part of any test, and in Screenplay, questions are how we write our assertions. Actors can answer questions about the state of the system (see figure 12.7) so that we can decide whether this state is what we expect it to be.

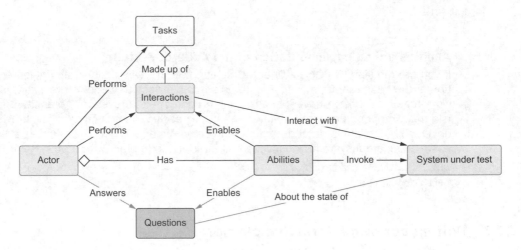

Figure 12.7   Actors can answer questions about the state of the system, using their abilities.

Question classes use the abilities of the actor to query the state of the system, from the perspective of the actor. For example, if an actor has the ability to use WebDriver to interact with a web application, `Question` classes can use this ability to report on the contents of the web pages that the actor sees. Let's see how this works more closely.

12.8.1   Questions query the state of the system

Suppose we need to read the current point balance on the account page of our Frequent Flyer application (see figure 12.8).

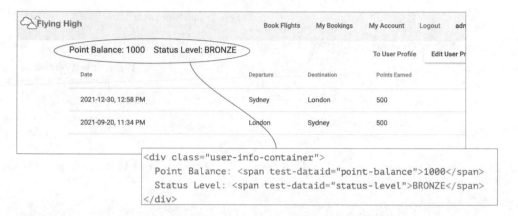

Figure 12.8   We give actors abilities that enable them to interact with the system.

Just like the interaction classes we saw earlier, Screenplay questions are represented by classes and objects. And just like interaction classes, Screenplay libraries typically come bundled with a range of predefined Question classes that you can use to query your application state.

In Serenity BDD, a question to query the text value of the status level would look like this:

```
Text.of("[test-dataid='status-level']")
```
← **Get the text content of the status-level element.**

The Question class comes with a range of transformation methods that you can use to convert a value into the type you need. For example, you could use the following code to retrieve the point balance as a numerical value:

```
Text.of("[test-dataid='point-balance']").asInteger()
```
← **Turn this text value into an integer.**

Or we could even ask whether the point balance is visible, using the Visibility question class like this:

```
Visibility.of("[test-dataid='point-balance']")
```

All of these code snippets are examples of Screenplay questions. But none will do much by themselves. A Question class in Screenplay is a bit like an online poll: if you don't ask anyone to answer the questions, you won't get much information.

To get the actual information, we need to ask an actor to answer the question. We do this with the answeredBy() method, like this:

```
String statusLevel = Text.of("[test-dataid='status-level']")     ◁          Finds the text
                         .answeredBy(sally);         ◁                      of the status-
                                                                            level field
                              As seen in Sally's browser
```

Or if we needed an integer value, we could use the asInteger() method we saw earlier:

```
                                          We want text content of the
                                             point balance element.

Integer pointBalance = Text.of("[test-dataid='point-balance']")   ◁
                          .asInteger()              ◁          We want to use it as
   Uses the value Sally    .answeredBy(sally);                 an integer value.
   sees in her browser
```

And if we wanted to ask Sally whether she sees the point balance field, and store the result, we could write something like this:

```
boolean balanceIsVisible = Visibility.of("[test-dataid='point-balance']")
                             .answeredBy(sally);
```

Questions are a convenient way to get information about the state of the application. You can see an overview of some of the more commonly used UI Question classes in Serenity BDD in table 12.3.

Table 12.3 Common Screenplay question classes in Serenity BDD

Question	Usage	Example
Attribute	Find a specific HTML attribute value for a given element	Attribute.of(".item-details-link") .named("href")
Disabled	Check whether a given field is disabled	Disabled.of("#login-button")
Enabled	Check whether a given field is enabled	Enabled.of("#login-button")
SelectedValue	The value of the selected element in a dropdown list	SelectedValue.of("#travel-class")
Text	The text value of an element	Text.of("[test-dataid='name']")
Value	The value of a form field (from the "value" CSS attribute)	Value.of("#firstName")
Visibility	Check whether an element is visible on the page	Visibility.of(".error-message")

12.8.2   *Domain-specific Question classes make our code more readable*

It is also easy to write your own `Question` classes, either to perform more sophisticated queries about the user interface or to query other parts of the system under test as well. Sometimes, you might write a custom question class simply for better readability.

For example, we saw how to read the status level displayed on the account page (see figure 12.8) using the `Text` question class earlier on. We could create a simple question that reads the current point balance and converts it to an integer value like this:

```
public class Account {
    public static Question<Integer> pointBalance() {
        return Text.of(("[test-dataid='point-balance']").asInteger();
    }
}
```

We can now retrieve the current point balance level directly in a more readable manner:

```
int pointBalance = Account.pointBalance().answeredBy(sally);
```

But there is another way we use questions using the Screenplay Pattern: to make assertions about the state of the system.

12.8.3   *Actors can use questions to make assertions*

We have seen how `Question` classes can be used to retrieve information about the state of the system under test. We can then use this information to make assertions and describe the outcomes we expect. For example, using a conventional assertion library, we could check that the Sally's current point balance is 1,000 with the following code:

```
sally.attemptsTo(Click.on("#my-account"));           Opens the My
                                                     Account page
    int pointBalance = Account.pointBalance().answeredBy(sally);
    Assert.assertEquals(1000, pointBalance);          Checks that it is
                                                     equal to 1,000
Retrieves the current
point balance for Sally
```

Alternatively, we can often use Screenplay library features to make our assertions more fluent and more readable. For example, with Serenity BDD we can use the `Ensure` class to weave our assertion into the normal flow of interactions, like this:

```
sally.attemptsTo(                                    Navigates to the
    Click.on("#my-account")                          My Accounts page
    Ensure.that(Account.pointBalance()).isEqualTo(1000)   Checks that the
);                                                        point balance is
                                                         equal to 1,000
```

The `Ensure` class in Serenity BDD provides a fluent interface to make assertions about questions or other values, so the assertion methods you get depend on the type of question you ask. For example, if you ask a question that returns a `String` value, we can make `String`-related assertions, whereas if you ask a question that returns an integer, we can make numerical assertions.

```
Ensure.that(Account.statusLevel()).isEqualTo(UserLevel.BRONZE)
```

Other Screenplay libraries have similar capabilities. For example, Serenity/JS also has the `Ensure` class, though with a slightly different syntax:

```
Ensure.that(Account.pointBalance(), equals(1000))
```

The `Ensure` class is a good example of how the Screenplay Pattern helps us make our code more readable and expressive, and to illustrate the business intent behind our actions more clearly.

We also saw how we can create new domain-specific questions to make our code relate more closely to our domain. But what if we could do the same thing with interactions? What if we could turn low-level UI interaction, like "Click on Submit" or "Enter 'Jane' into the #firstname field," into more business-meaningful ones, such as "Register new customer" or "Enter personal details"? It turns out we can, using the concept of tasks. Let's see how.

12.9 Tasks model higher-level business actions

We've seen how actors can invoke the system under test using interactions and query its state using questions. However, expressing our test scenarios using such low-level constructs alone would not be much of an improvement over doing so by directly calling WebDriver or REST client APIs. It could also lead to lengthy tests in which the higher-level business-specific concepts are difficult to discern and easy to miss in the noise of actors clicking on buttons and sending HTTP requests. And as we have seen, the Screenplay Pattern offers a construct called *tasks* to model those higher-level abstractions. In essence, tasks represent sequences of interactions that an actor needs to perform in order to achieve some micro goal (see figure 12.9).

12.9.1 Simple tasks improve readability

Some tasks can be incredibly simple and modeled using just one interaction. To do this, we can use the `Task.where()` method, providing a description of the task as well as the interactions or tasks that make up this task.

For example, we might want to introduce a task where the user opens the application home page using the `Open.url()` interaction we saw earlier in the chapter:

```
public class Navigate {
  public static Performable toTheHomePage() {
    return Task.where("{0} goes to the login page",    ◁──┐  A short description of the
            Open.url("https://www.frequent-flyers.bddinaction.com")   ◁──  task ("{0}" is a placeholder
    );                                                                      for the name of the actor)
  }
}
```

A task is made up of a description and one
or more interactions or other tasks.

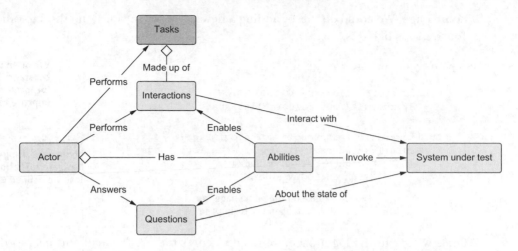

Figure 12.9   Tasks allow us to group interactions into meaningful and reusable blocks.

Now, rather than opening a specific URL, our actors will be able to "Navigate to the home page":

```
sally.attemptsTo(
  Navigate.toTheHomePage()
);
```

See how this allows us to focus more on what our actor is trying to achieve and less on how they make it happen? Introducing small tasks like the one above might not seem like much, but it allows us to reap several benefits of following the Screenplay Pattern:

- It helps us introduce higher-level abstractions and encapsulate bits of reusable behavior. Now every other actor will be able to navigate to the home page too, without having to remember what URL they need to open.
- Tasks, even as small as the one shown, help us avoid having to duplicate information such as URLs and element selectors and instead offer a single place to maintain and update these details.
- Each custom task has its own description, which helps to produce far more informative test execution reports than simply listing all the "clicks" and element selectors.

But that's not all. The main purpose of tasks is not simply to improve readability; it's to make our code more reusable and less brittle. Let's see how that works.

12.9.2   *More complex tasks enhance reusability*

The real power of tasks is when we combine a sequence of other interactions and tasks into a reusable chunk of business functionality. For example, suppose we wanted our actors to be able to open the login page without having to explicitly mention the home page. We could do this by adding a new `toTheLoginPage()` method to our `Navigate` class like this:

```
public class Navigate {
  ...
  public static final By LOGIN_BUTTON
    = By.xpath("//button[normalize-space()='Login']");

  public static Performable toTheLoginPage() {
    return Task.where("{0} goes to the login page",
            Navigate.toTheHomePage(),
            Click.on(LOGIN_BUTTON)
    );
  }
}
```

> We often use constants like this for locators to improve readability.

> Opens the home page using the Navigate.toTheHomePage() task we defined earlier

> Once on the home page, we can open the login page.

Once we get to the login page, we need to enter the user's email and password, and click on the login button, to access the application. We saw how to do this using low-level interactions, but we could also define a much more reusable task that combines all these interactions. It might look something like this:

```
public class Login {
  public static Performable usingCredentials(String username,
                                             String password) {
    return Task.where("{0} logs in as " + username,
            Navigate.toTheLoginPage(),
            SendKeys.of(username).into("#email"),
            SendKeys.of(password).into("#password"),
            Click.on("#login-button")
    );
  }
}
```

Which would lead to much more readable and reusable code for our test cases:

```
tracy.attemptsTo(
  Login.usingCredentials("tracy@traveler.com","secretpassword")
);
```

Reusability is at the heart of the Screenplay Pattern. In test automation, we often think of reusability in terms of the locators and fields we interact with on a page, or of the low-level interactions we perform.

But Screenplay takes the concept of reusability much further. Screenplay makes it easy to define reusable tasks made up of other tasks and interactions, and to use these tasks both to execute tests and to build other, even higher-level tasks.

Bringing all of these elements together, we end up with test code that is more succinct and more readable and that reflects the business flows and expected outcomes much more clearly. We can see a full example in the following code:

```
WebDriver driver;

@Before
public void openBrowser() {                    Opens a new
  driver = new ChromeDriver();          ◁───    browser before
}                                               any test starts

@Test
public void viewAccountBalance() {                          Assigns the
  Actor sally = Actor.named("Sally")                        browser to
              .whoCan(BrowseTheWeb.with(driver));   ◁───    Sally
```

Sally
logs on. └▷
```
  sally.attemptsTo(
    Login.usingCredentials("sally@flying-high.com","secretpassword"),

    Navigate.toMyAccount(),          ◁──    Sally views her
                                            account details.
```
We check
that the
expected
values are
displayed.
```
    Ensure.that(Account.pointBalance(), isEqualTo(1000)),
    Ensure.that(Account.statusLevel()).isEqualTo(UserLevel.BRONZE).
  );

  @After
  public void closeBrowser() {
    driver.quit();              ◁──    Shuts down the browser in an
  }                                    @After method to ensure that
                                       it happens even if the test fails
}
```

But how does this relate to the Cucumber scenarios we've seen in the previous chapters? Let's find out!

12.10 Screenplay and Cucumber

In the code we have seen so far, we know who our actors are. We create our actors by giving them a name directly in our test code, like this:

```
Actor tracy = Actor.named("Tracy");
```

But in a Cucumber scenario, the name of the actor is often announced in the scenario text, not in the test code. For example, imagine we want to automate a scenario about the account page we saw in figure 12.8. Suppose we are using predefined users for our scenarios, who are set up at the start of each test run. For example, Stan is a standard Frequent Flyer member with zero points.

A simple scenario to illustrate how Stan checks his account status might look like this:

```
Scenario: Stan checks his balance
  Stan is a standard frequent flyer member with 0 points

  Given Stan has logged into his account
  When he views his account details
  Then his account status should be:
    | Point Balance | Status Level |
    | 0             | STANDARD     |
```

In this scenario, Stan is our actor, but in other scenarios we might work with Silvia (who's a Silver Frequent Flyer member) or Bryony (a Bronze member). In other words, the name of the actor needs to be a variable that we pass to our scenario. Because the name of the actor can change, we need to pass the name to our step definition method before we set up our actor.

12.10.1 Actors and casts

We could simply pass in the name of the actor and create a new actor using the `Actor.named()` method we saw earlier:

```
@Given("{} has logged into his/her account")
public void memberHasLoggedIntoTheirAccount(String actorName) {
  Actor actor = Actor.named(actorName);
  actor.can(BrowseTheWeb.with(driver);
  …
}
```

But, unlike a self-contained Screenplay test case, the actor will need to be used in other step definition methods, possibly in other classes, so we need to keep track of the actor between these steps.

Fortunately, Screenplay libraries have a way to make this easier for us: the *Cast*. A Cast allows us to manage the actors who take part in our Screenplay scenario. We can define their abilities and refer to them by name so that we don't need to keep track of the `Actor` objects between steps.

We can set up a Cast before our scenarios start using the `OnStage.setTheStage()` method. We can also use the special `OnlineCast` class to give us a Cast of actors, each equipped with their own `WebDriver` instance so that they can interact with the application using the WebDriver interaction classes we saw earlier in the chapter:

```
@Before                                        ◁——┐  Performs before each Cucumber
public void setTheStage() {                        │  scenario is executed
  OnStage.setTheStage(new OnlineCast());       ◁——    Defines a Cast of
}                                                      actors equipped with
                                                       WebDriver instances
```

12.10.2 The Screenplay stage

Now that we have set the stage, we can summon an actor any time we need one using the `OnStage.theActorCalled()` method:

```
@Given("{} has logged into his/her account")
public void memberHasLoggedIntoTheirAccount(String actorName) {
  Actor actor = OnStage.theActorCalled(actorName);
  actor.attemptsTo(…);
}
```

The second step of this scenario reads "When *he* views his account details." We don't explicitly name our actor; we simply use a pronoun. Libraries like Serenity BDD and

Serenity/JS will recognize common pronouns, so the following step definition code will assume that "he" is talking about Stan, the last actor referred to in this scenario:

```
@When("{} views his/her account details")
public void viewsAccountSummary(String actorName) {
  OnStage.theActorCalled(actorName).attemptsTo(Navigate.toMyAccount());
}
```

In some cases, we need to refer to an actor indirectly, and the name of the actor is not mentioned in the step. In that case, we can use the `OnStage.theActorInTheSpotlight()` method, which will retrieve the last active actor in the current scenario.

12.10.3 Defining a custom parameter type for actors

We can also make our Screenplay step definition code more concise and expressive by defining a custom parameter type for our actors:

```
@ParameterType(".*")
public Actor actor(String actorName) {
    return OnStage.theActorCalled(actorName);
}
```

This way an actor can be referred to by name (or by pronoun) in the Cucumber scenario, and automatically converted into an `Actor` parameter in the step definition code:

The actor is now passed into the step definition as a parameter.

```
@Given("{actor} has logged into his/her account")
public void memberHasLoggedIn(Actor actor, String actorName) {
  actor.attemptsTo(…);
}
```

As a result, the actor can be used directly in the step definition code.

12.10.4 Defining persona in enum values

Sometimes we need to know more details about the actors in our scenarios. For example, in the previous scenario, we need to know Stan's name and his email address and password so that he can log on to the application. If other scenarios use other actors, we'll need to know their details too.

There are many ways to do this, but one very simple approach is to define an enum with the names of the actors along with their credentials:

```
public enum FrequentFlyer {
    Stan("stan@flyinghigh.com", "secret"),
    Bryony("bryony@flyinghigh.com", "secret"),
    Silvia("silvia@flyinghigh.com", "secret");

    public final String email;
    public final String password;
```

```
        FrequentFlyer(String email, String password) {
            this.email = email;
            this.password = password;
        }
}
```

We can now refer to this enum directly in our step definition:

```
@Given("{} has logged into his/her account")
public void memberHasLoggedIntoTheirAccount(FrequentFlyer member) {
    theActorCalled(member.name()).attemptsTo(
            Login.usingCredentials(member.email, member.password)
    );
}
```

12.10.5 Screenplay assertions in Cucumber

Performing Screenplay assertions in Cucumber is no different than performing them in a self-contained scenario, except that the expected results generally come from the scenario text. For example, the final step of our scenario reads like this:

```
Then his account status should be:
  | Point Balance | Status Level |
  | 0             | STANDARD     |
```

As with the other styles of Cucumber automation we have seen in previous chapters, we could define a @DataTypeType method to convert the table data into a more convenient domain object:

```
@DataTableType
public AccountStatus accountStatus(Map<String, String> statusValues) {
    Integer points = Integer.parseInt(statusValues.get("Point Balance"));
    UserLevel level =  UserLevel.valueOf(statusValues.get("Status Level"));
    return new AccountStatus(level, points);
}
```

Now we need to use the OnStage.theActorInTheSpotlight() method to retrieve our actor (since he is not referred to directly in the scenario). The resulting step definition code might look something like this:

```
@Then("his/her account status should contain:")
public void accountStatusShouldContain(AccountStatus expected) {
  OnStage.theActorInTheSpotlight().attemptsTo(
      Ensure.that(MyAccount.statusLevel())
            .isEqualTo(expected.userLevel()),
      Ensure.that(MyAccount.pointBalance())
            .isEqualTo(expected.pointBalance())
    );
}
```

As you can see, writing Cucumber step definitions using the Screenplay Pattern is not much different from writing self-contained Screenplay scenarios. The only real differences are the use of the `Cast` and `OnStage` classes to set up and manage the scenario actors.

Summary

- You can use the Screenplay Pattern to write more reusable and more expressive test code. Screenplay is an actor-centric approach where actors interact with the system under test using tasks and interactions and query the state of the system using questions.
- Actors model our application users.
- Actors have abilities, which allow them to interact with the system in different ways (e.g., by opening a browser or calling an API).
- Actors use these abilities to perform interactions with the application. Interactions allow us to describe and model actor behavior into the form of reusable objects.
- Actors can ask questions to query the state of the system. We use questions to make assertions to determine whether the application behaves as we expect.
- We can combine interactions and tasks into higher-level tasks, allowing us to reason about our test code at a much higher level of abstraction when we need to, but still being able to look at detailed interactions with the system when necessary.
- Screenplay also integrates well into Cucumber; actors are provided dynamically, via a `Cast` object, and managed between scenario steps using the `OnStage` class.

In the next chapter, we will explore how these principles, and the concepts of BDD in general, apply to the world of APIs and web services.

13

BDD and executable specifications for microservices and APIs

This chapter covers

- API and Microservice-based architectures and how to test them
- The difference between broader user journey requirements and more specific business rule requirements, and how user journey requirements can often be automated using API interactions
- Using RESTAssured to interact with REST APIs
- Using JSONPath to query the responses returned by REST API calls

Thus far we have focused on automating tests that exercise the user interface. But, as we discussed in chapter 10, user interface tests shouldn't be the only tool in your automated acceptance testing toolbox. It's important to know when to use them and when to look for alternative strategies. In this chapter, you'll learn about other ways to automate your acceptance tests that don't involve exercising the user interface.

In chapters 10 and 11, you learned how to automate acceptance tests using automated web testing tools such as Selenium WebDriver. Web tests are a great way to simulate the user's journey through the system, to illustrate interactions with an application, and to document the key features of your application. Stakeholders can easily relate to web tests, as they're highly visual and intuitive and map closely to the user experience. Automated web tests can also be used to demonstrate new features, which is a great way to increase confidence in the tests. Automated web tests are also the only way to effectively test business logic that's implemented directly within the user interface (UI).

But you also saw that end-to-end web tests tend to execute significantly more slowly than tests that don't involve the UI. Interacting with a browser adds significant overhead in terms of execution time and system resources. Web tests that rely on a real browser are also more subject to technical or environment-related problems that are hard to control. For example, web tests can fail because the wrong version of a browser is installed on a test machine, because the site is responding slowly, or because the browser crashes. Tests that fail for reasons unrelated to the application logic waste development time and resources and can reduce the team's confidence in the test suite.

Although they can have great value, web tests shouldn't be your only option when it comes to automating your BDD scenarios:

- Most applications need a judicious mix of both automated UI tests and automated tests for non-UI components.
- Non-UI tests can work at different levels of the application, including tests that exercise the business rules implemented in the application code directly and tests that work with remote services.
- Non-UI tests can also be used to verify nonfunctional requirements, such as performance.
- Implementing non-UI acceptance tests, and the corresponding application code, is also a great way to discover what components your application needs and to design clean, effective APIs within your application.

It is also important to understand the role BDD scenarios play in microservice architectures, which are an increasingly popular approach for large applications, and the way these architectures are built can play a major role in how we specify and test features designed to run on them.

Let's start with looking at what APIs and microservices are all about and how you should find the correct balance between UI and non-UI acceptance testing techniques for your projects and acceptance tests.

13.1   APIs and how to test them

API is short for *Application Programming Interface*; an API describes how an application can interact with another application programmatically. In other words, an API defines how you can write code to interact with some underlying application or service. It describes the actions you can perform, the queries you can ask, and the data structures you can send to and receive from the application. Common API architectures that you are likely to encounter include service-oriented architectures (SOA) and microservices.[1]

Testing applications using APIs is a bit more technical and requires a deeper understanding of the application architecture than testing via the user interface, but it opens up the possibility of faster, more robust, and more comprehensive testing than we could do with the UI alone. To give you a feel for how API testing can help, we will look at a number of common scenarios where API testing can help make writing automated acceptance tests easier.

13.2 *Defining a feature using a web UI and a microservice*

In this section, you will learn how to write an executable specification for a simple requirement involving a single microservice. When a traveler registers as a frequent flyer, they open the Flying High website and navigate to the registration page. Alternatively, they might have clicked on a link in an email sent by the marketing department. In both cases, they end up on a registration page, where they enter their details.

Once they have entered their details, they are sent an email with a link they can click to confirm their email address; this activates their account and allows them to log in and access their account details. The general architecture for this feature is illustrated in figure 13.1.

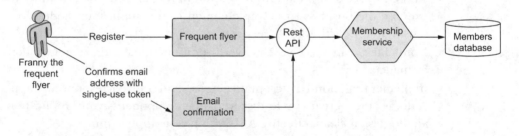

Figure 13.1   The Frequent Flyer membership service presents a REST API that allows a frequent flyer to view their points history and to confirm their email address when they first register.

13.2.1 *Understanding the requirements*

Before they start work, the development team members get together with Marcus from marketing to run through this requirement in more detail. This feature seems straightforward enough, but it's always worth making sure everyone is on the same page.

After a quick Example Mapping session, the team comes up with a set of business rules and examples (see figure 13.2) and uncovers the following details:

- The primary goal of the feature is to allow travelers to sign up as frequent fliers on the Flying High website.

---

[1] For a more in-depth treatment of microservice architectures, see *Microservice APIs* by José Peralta (Manning, 2022) and *Microservice Patterns* by Chris Richardson (Manning, 2018).

- New frequent flyers need to provide their name, address, and email.
- If an account already exists with a given email, the user should be presented with the option to reset their password.
- Having a valid email is particularly important, as Marcus wants to send members promotions and marketing material. For this reason, new frequent flyers will have to validate their email before their account can be activated.
- Compliance and legal want new frequent flyers to approve the terms and conditions before joining.
- These validation emails can get lost or overlooked, so if an email address doesn't get validated after a certain amount of time, a follow up email should be automatically sent out.
- When a member signs up, they should receive a welcome email message. The details and sequencing of the message are managed by the marketing department using specialized software.

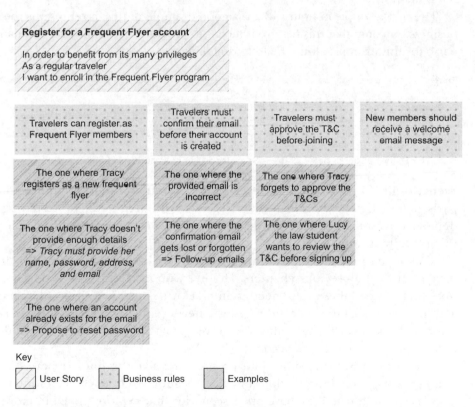

Figure 13.2   The Example Map for the registration feature

13.2.2   *From requirements to executable specifications*

From these rules and examples, we can define a set of executable specifications that capture the intent of these rules. However, the requirements we discussed earlier are a mixture of high-level user journeys (e.g., "Travelers can register as new members"), more granular requirements (e.g., "Travelers must approve the terms and conditions before joining" or "A traveler must provide a valid email address"), and requirements that involve systems potentially outside the team's scope (e.g., "New members should receive a welcome email when they join"). Let's take a closer look at the different kinds of acceptance criteria we typically come across and how we can express them using Gherkin.

EXECUTABLE SPECIFICATIONS THAT GIVE US THE BIG PICTURE

It is always a good idea to capture the key business outcomes as a few succinct, easy-to-read scenarios before drilling more into the details. This helps us document the intent of a feature more clearly and keep the focus on the business outcomes that really matter.

The first example in figure 13.2 is a good example of this: it represents the overall business outcome that this feature is meant to provide. We might write a detailed scenario for this example along the following lines:

```
Rule: Travelers can register as new members on the Flying High website

   Example: Tracy registers as a new Frequent Flyer
     Given Tracy does not have a Frequent Flyer account
     When she registers for a new Frequent Flyer account with valid details
     And she confirms her email address
     Then she should have a new Standard tier account with 0 points
```

Scenarios like this give us an overview of the overall user journey and the different parts of the UI a user will need to interact with. They can be tested against a deployed, running application (though ideally a developer should be able to run them locally as well).

This scenario could be demonstrated with a UI-based scenario, like those we have seen in the previous chapters. However, upon closer observation, we might note that none of these steps need to interact with the UI. We can interact directly with the membership service to register a new Frequent Flyer account, to confirm the email address using the link the server provides, and also to check the existence and status of the new account.

In other words, for business journey scenarios like this one, we have the option of automating the UI interactions or of performing a sequence of API interactions. This is especially true if we have other scenarios that explore the UI in more detail. Later in the chapter, we will see how we could automate a scenario like this without using UI tests.

EXECUTABLE SPECIFICATIONS THAT EXPLORE THE USER JOURNEY

Now that we have a scenario that illustrates the bigger picture, we can start to explore the user journey in more detail. For example, the second rule ("Travelers must confirm their email before their account is activated") breaks down the process of registering and validating the email address. We could document this process with a series of smaller scenarios, like the following (for this chapter's source code, see http://mng .bz/710m):

```
Rule: Travelers must confirm their email before their account is created

  Example: Tracy's account is initially pending activated
    Given Tracy does not have a Frequent Flyer account
    When Tracy registers for a new Frequent Flyer account
    Then she should be sent an email with an email validation link
    And her account should be pending activation

  Example: Tracy cannot access her account before having activated her
  email
    Given Tracy has registered for a new Frequent Flyer account
    But she has not yet confirmed her email
    When she attempts to access her Frequent Flyer account details
    Then she should be invited to first confirm her email address

  Example: Tracy confirms her email
    Given Tracy has registered for a new Frequent Flyer account
    When she confirms her email address
    Then her account should be activated
```

Note that in the third scenario we have not included a clause like "And she should be able to log in" to illustrate the effect of her confirming her email address. While we could include this step, it is not strictly necessary (we have already demonstrated that a user can log in after confirming their email in the "Tracy registers as a new Frequent Flyer" scenario we saw earlier), and adding the extra step would make the scenario slower and potentially less stable.

We could also explore more detailed scenarios, such as the negative example, "the one where the provided email is correct." On the surface of it, this sounds like a simple field format check, but Marcus from marketing places a lot of value on acquiring good-quality leads for his marketing campaigns. So, in addition to basic syntax checking, Marcus wants to make sure the emails come from valid domains and are not disposable email addresses.

These requirements could be illustrated by a few representative examples, like the ones shown here:

```
A granular business rule implemented at the API level

Rule: Travelers mush provide a valid email address
  Scenario Outline: Emails must be correctly formed and non-disposable
    Given Tracy does not have a Frequent Flyer account
```

```
When she registers with an email of <email>
Then the email address should be <Accepted/Rejected> with the message
  "<Reason>"

Examples: Correctly-formed emails should be accepted
  | email                     | Accepted/Rejected | Reason    |
  | sarah@example.org         | Accepted          |           |
  | sarah-jane@example.org    | Accepted          |           |

Examples: Invalid emails should be rejected
  | email                       | Accepted/Rejected | Reason                |
  | example.com                 | Rejected          | email must be an email |
  | #@%^%#$@#$@#.com             | Rejected          | email must be an email |
  | email@example..com          | Rejected          | email must be an email |
  | email@inexistant-domain.com | Rejected          | Invalid email address  |
```

The user will see the error message mentioned in the Reason column on the registration page, just like other field validation errors. However, the actual email validation is performed on the server, so this scenario could be implemented via API calls without needing to refer to the user interface.

EXECUTABLE SPECIFICATIONS THAT FOCUS ON UI BEHAVIOR

Other scenarios can be tested in a more isolated context. For example, most of the field validation rules in the second example could be tested in isolation using a UI component test. We might implement these with more granular scenarios like the following:

```
Rule: New members need to complete all the mandatory fields and approve the
➡ terms & conditions
  Scenario: Candy fails to enter to enter a mandatory field
    Given Candy does not have a Frequent Flyer account
    When Candy wants to register a new Frequent Flyer account
    Then the following information should be mandatory to register:
      | email     |
      | password  |
      | firstName |
      | lastName  |
      | address   |
      | country   |
```

The requirements related to approving the terms and conditions are similar:

```
Example: Tracy forgets to agree to the Terms and Conditions
    Given Tracy does not have a Frequent Flyer account
    When Tracy tries to register without approving the terms and conditions
    Then she should be told "Please confirm the terms and conditions to
➡ continue"
```

Other scenarios might focus on UI interactions but use API services to set up test data and verify the outcomes. For example, when a user tries to register with an email that already exists, they should be presented with the option to reset their password. The core business need here is to avoid multiple accounts, so we could come up with a more colorful example like this one:

```
Rule: Duplicate accounts with the same email address are not allowed

  Example: Someone tries to register with an email that is already used

  Trevor is an existing Frequent Flyer member.
  His wife Candy does not have a Frequent Flyer account

    Given Harry Smith has registered as thesmiths@example.org
    When Candy tries to register with the same email
    Then she should be informed that this email address is already in use
    And she should be presented with the option to reset her password
```

This is a good example of a scenario that involves both API and UI interactions. In the first step of this scenario, we learn that Harry has already registered for a Frequent Flyer account. This step would typically be implemented via an API call. We have already illustrated how a user interacts with the registration page to register, and there is little value in repeating those interactions here.

However, the following steps illustrate how Candy tries to enter the same email but is not allowed to register; instead, she is proposed with the option to reset her password. This is a very UI-focused flow, with Candy completing the registration form and being redirected to the appropriate password reset page.

EXECUTABLE SPECIFICATIONS THAT ILLUSTRATE HOW SYSTEMS INTERACT

Other scenarios may need to interact with external services. For example, the second business rule in figure 13.2 discusses how a new Frequent Flyer needs to validate their email address before their account can be activated. We might express this business rule in Gherkin with scenarios along the following lines:

```
Rule: Travelers must confirm their email before their account is created
  Example: Tracy's account is initially pending activated
    Given Tracy does not have a Frequent Flyer account
    When Tracy registers for a new Frequent Flyer account
    Then she should be sent an email with an email validation link
    And her account should be pending activation

  Example: Tracy cannot access her account before having activated her
email
    Given Tracy has registered for a new Frequent Flyer account
    And she has not yet confirmed her email
    Then she should be invited to confirm her email address when she
attempts to login

  Example: Tracy confirms her email
    Given Tracy has registered for a new Frequent Flyer account
    When she confirms her email address
    Then her account should be activated
```

Having Tracy register through the UI for these scenarios would be slow and wasteful (since we have already illustrated that user journey elsewhere). It would be much more efficient to register Tracy's account directly via an API call for both these scenarios.

Now suppose that emails are sent by a separate service, outside of the scope of our team. It would be inefficient to physically check whether Tracy received her confirmation email in her inbox, especially if the email service is not in our scope of work or perhaps is a completely external system developed by a separate company. Instead, we can simply ensure that the correct message is sent to the email service. We'll see how this could work in the next section.

13.3 *Automating acceptance tests for microservices*

As we have seen, even a simple feature can lead to a range of requirements and acceptance criteria. And very often, many of these acceptance criteria can be automated and validated with little or no reference to the UI.

When we automate scenarios, we want to do so in the most effective way possible, on a case-by-case basis. Some scenarios might require UI interactions, whereas others might be possible entirely via API calls, while still others might need a combination of UI and API calls. And that's fine. The focus at this stage is not to test a specific layer of the application; it is to illustrate what the application should do in business terms. Once we understand what the application should do, and what examples of behavior will give us confidence that the feature is performing as expected, we can consider how we will go about demonstrating these examples.

API testing, or testing with APIs

Traditional thinking about test automation encourages us to think in terms of application layers: end-to-end tests, UI tests, API tests, integration tests, unit tests, and so forth. There is a clear segregation between the testing libraries and techniques used for each layer.

However, when we are writing and automating executable specifications, our thinking needs to be a little different. The goal is to illustrate and automate an example of a business use case or business rule, *not* to exercise a specific layer of the application, such as the UI or an API.

In other words, while our automated tests interact with the interfaces of our system, including UI and API components, their purpose is not to test those interfaces themselves. Their goal is to ensure that our system sports a given business scenario and that business rules hold. Interacting with the interfaces is just a means to an end rather than a goal on its own.

13.4   *The microservice architecture under test*

In this section, we walk through an example of how we can automate the scenarios we have seen so far, using only API interactions. Let's start by taking a closer look at the Frequent Flyer membership APIs, which are illustrated in figure 13.3.

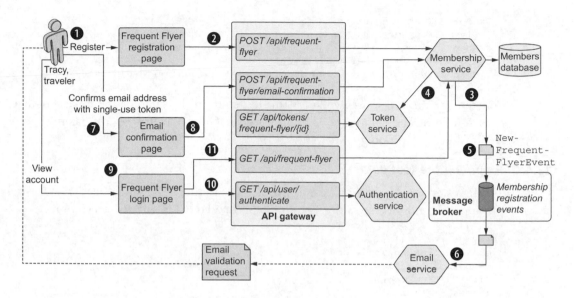

Figure 13.3   The Frequent Flyer membership architecture

When a new frequent flyer registers on the registration page (1), a POST request is sent to the Frequent Flyer endpoint with details about the new member (2). The Frequent Flyer service adds a new pending Frequent Flyer account in the membership database (3) and requests a new single-use token from the token service (4).

The token will be used to create an email confirmation message sent to the new Frequent Flyer member. This happens in a separate service, the email service, which is maintained by a different team.

Our application uses an event-based architecture to coordinate and send these emails. The Frequent Flyer service publishes a `NewFrequentFlyerEvent` event to a dedicated channel on a message broker (5); other services interested in this event, such as the email service, can subscribe to these events. This way, whenever a new Frequent Flyer registers, the email service will prepare and send an email confirmation message to the appropriate address, with a link containing the single-use token (6).

When the new member receives the email confirmation message, they click on the link in the message to confirm their email address (7). This in turn sends a POST request to the email confirmation endpoint (8), which updates the status of the member's account to active.

Tracy can now log on to her account via the login page, which uses the authentication service endpoint to validate her email and password (10), and then the membership service to provide her with an overview of her account (11).

Let's walk through the process of automating the first scenario we saw, using this architecture:

```
Example: Tracy registers as a new Frequent Flyer
  Given Tracy does not have a Frequent Flyer account
  When she registers for a new Frequent Flyer account
  And she confirms her email address
  Then she should have a new Standard tier account with 0 points
```

You can see the full source code for this test suite in the chapter-13/api-acceptance-tests folder in the sample code repository on Github (https://github.com/bdd-in-action/second-edition.git).

13.4.1 Preparing the test data

The first step involves setting up our prospective Frequent Flyer member, Tracy. A simple approach might be to store Tracy's details in a HOCON file, as shown here:

```
Tracy: {
  email: "tracy@example.org"
  password: "trac1"
  firstName: "Tracy"
  lastName: "Traveler"
  address: "10 Pinnack Street, Reading"
  country: "United Kingdom"
  title:"Mrs"
}
```

In our Java code, we represent this information in the form of a simple Java Record, like this one:

```
public record TravelerRegistration(String firstName,
                                   String lastName,
                                   String title,
                                   String email,
                                   String password,
                                   String address,
                                   String country) {}
```

Suppose we are storing our traveler registration details in a file called travelers.conf. We can load these details from this file using the TypeSafe Config library (https://github.com/lightbend/config), like this:

```
public class TravelerRegistrationConfig {

    public static TravelerRegistration forTravelerNamed(String name) {
        Config travelerDetails
            = ConfigFactory.load("travelers").getConfig(name);
```

```
        return new TravelerRegistration(
                travelerDetails.getString("firstName"),
                travelerDetails.getString("lastName"),
                travelerDetails.getString("title"),
                travelerDetails.getString("email"),
                travelerDetails.getString("password"),
                travelerDetails.getString("address"),
                travelerDetails.getString("country")
        );
    }
}
```

This makes our first step definition code a simple matter of capturing the name of the traveler (in this case, Tracy) and loading the corresponding registration details from the traveler.conf configuration file:

```
TravelerRegistration newMember;

@Given("{} does not have a Frequent Flyer account")
public void has_no_frequent_flyer_account(String name) {
    newMember = travelerRegistrationConfig.forTravelerNamed(name);
}
```

13.4.2 Performing a POST query: Registering a Frequent Flyer member

The next step is where we first interact with one of the Membership API endpoints. We need to send a POST query to the api/frequent-flyer URL and retrieve the Frequent Flyer number that the service returns to us (we will need this for the steps to follow). Behind the scenes, this will record a new Frequent Flyer account in the membership database and publish a NewFrequentFlyerEvent to the message broker. This flow is illustrated in figure 13.4.

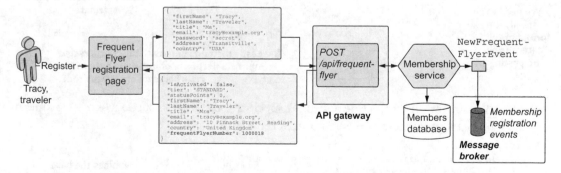

Figure 13.4 Registering a frequent flyer member

It is good practice to avoid interacting directly with our application layers (UI or APIs) in our step definition methods. This is why, in previous chapters, we saw how to use action classes and Screenplay tasks to create a more readable and more reusable layer of abstraction that we use for our step definition code. We can do something similar with the API layers.

Let's imagine a dedicated class, called `MembershipAPI`, which will contain methods to interact with the Frequent Flyer membership API endpoints. Our step definition class could look something like this:

```
MembershipAPI membershipAPI = new MembershipAPI();          ◁──  Create a new instance
                                                                 of the MembershipAPI
@When("he/she registers for a new Frequent Flyer account")       class.
public void registers_for_a_new_frequent_flyer_account() {
    newFrequentFlyerNumber = membershipAPI.register(newMember);  ◁──
}
                                          We interact with the API by calling
                                          methods of the MembershipAPI class.
```

The `register()` method will perform the actual API interaction; more precisely, it will perform the POST request and extract the frequent flyer number from the response.

To perform the POST request, we could really use any REST client library we like. However, when writing test automation code, Rest Assured (https://rest-assured.io/) is a great choice. As we will see, Rest Assured gives us a readable DSL to both interact with REST APIs, but also to extract data from, and make assertions about, the responses.

By default, our test application runs on port 3000, so when we run the application on our local machine, we can access the API endpoints on http://localhost:3000/api.[2] The Rest Assured code to submit a POST request to http://localhost:3000/api/frequent-flyer looks something like this:

```
                          All Rest Assured queries start with a
                          static call on the RestAssured class.
                                                                           RestAssured will
                                                                           automatically convert
Response response = RestAssured.given()     ◁──                            our Java record into a
                    .contentType(ContentType.JSON)                         JSON format.
We need to          .body(newMember)                    ◁──
specify the         .post("http://localhost:3000/api/frequent-flyer");     ◁──
format of the
data we will                    The post() method submits the POST query and
be posting.                     returns a Response object that contains the
                                returned data and status code.
```

We can simplify this code a little by specifying the `RestAssured.baseURI` property at the start of our test cases, as shown here:

```
RestAssured.baseURI = "http://localhost:3000/api";    ◁──  Defines the base
Response response = RestAssured.given()                    URL to be used for
                    .contentType(ContentType.JSON)         all RestAssured
                    .body(newMember)                       queries in a test
                    .post("/frequent-flyer");
```

---

[2] In a real application, and in the sample project on Github, this address is configurable to be able to interact with different environments. However, for simplicity, this will not be shown in the code samples in this chapter.

If we wanted to reuse this configuration logic across several similar API clients, we might create a base class like this one, that reads the base URL from the serenity.conf configuration file,[3] like this one:

```
public class ConfigurableAPIClient {
    public ConfigurableAPIClient() {
        RestAssured.baseURI = Serenity.environmentVariables()
                                .getProperty("base.url",
                                    "http://localhost:3000/api");
    }
}
```

Loads the serenity.conf configuration properties

Reads the base.url configuration property if defined

Otherwise uses a sensible default value

The serenity.conf file uses a simple HOCON format and typically contains project configuration details such as the driver to use for web tests and other reporting options. For this project, it simply contains the base.url property:

```
base.url = "http://localhost:3000/api"
```

The `Response` object allows us to extract information from the response returned to us from the API call. When a new Frequent Flyer account is created, the endpoint will return a complete JSON structure containing details about the new frequent flyer, like this one:

```
{
    "isActivated": false,
    "tier": "STANDARD",
    "statusPoints": 0,
    "firstName": "Tracy",
    "lastName": "Traveler",
    "title": "Mrs",
    "email": "tracy@example.org",
    "address": "10 Pinnack Street, Reading",
    "country": "United Kingdom",
    "frequentFlyerNumber": 1000036
}
```

However, in this case we only need the frequent flyer number. Remember, we are testing functionality via the API, not testing the API itself (there will be other tests for that), so it makes more sense to simply extract the `frequentFlyerNumber` field from this response. Limiting ourselves to a single field reduces our dependency on the structure of the JSON response; if another field is added to the structure, for example, our test will not fail.

In `RestAssured`, we use a notation called JSONPath to extract data from a JSON response. JSONPath is similar to XPath, but for JSON documents. It allows sophisticated queries to retrieve individual values or collections of values from complex JSON structures.

---

[3] In a Serenity BDD project, test configuration data is stored in a file called serenity.conf, which you will find in the src/test/resources directory.

In this case, the `frequentFlyerNumber` attribute is at the top level of the JSON structure, so we can retrieve it by name, using the `jsonPath()` method like this:

```
response.jsonPath().getString("frequentFlyerNumber")
```

Adding in this code, the complete `MembershipAPI` class, including the method to create a new Frequent Flyer member and retrieve the new frequent flyer number, might look like this:

```
public class MembershipAPI extends ConfigurableAPIClient {

  public String register(TravelerRegistration newMember) {
      RestAssured.baseURI = "http://localhost:3000/api";        Sends a POST
      Response response = RestAssured.given()              ◁──  query to the
          .contentType(ContentType.JSON)                       API endpoint
          .body(newMember)
          .post("/frequent-flyer");
      return response.jsonPath().getString("frequentFlyerNumber");   ◁─
  }                                    Returns the value of the 'frequentFlyerNumber'
}                                                   field in the response object
```

This is a very simple example of how we can use JSONPath to retrieve key data from a JSON response. In the next section, we will learn how to use JSONPath to query more complex JSON structures.

13.4.3 *Querying JSON responses with JSONPath*

Suppose we are working with an API call that returns some of the Frequent Flyer account details, along with a list of their past flights. The exact JSON structure is shown in the following listing.

Listing 13.1   A sample JSON response

```
{
  "frequentFlyerNumber": 1000036,
  "firstName": "Tracy",
  "lastName": "Traveler",
  "email": "tracy@example.org",
  "flightHistory": [
    {
      "from": "London",
      "to": " Paris",
      "date": "2021-12-15"
    },
    {
      "from": "Paris",
      "to": " London",
      "date": "2021-12-21"
    }
  ],
  "passport": {
    "number": "12345678",
```

```
    "country": "United Kingdom"
  }
}
```

Let's see how we can use JSONPath to query this JSON document using Rest Assured.

READING TOP-LEVEL FIELD VALUES

Field values at the top level of a JSON structure can simply be referred to by name. For example, to read Tracy's last name, we could use the following:

```
String lastName = response.jsonPath().getString("lastName");
```

We can also convert values to other types. For example, if we need the frequent flyer number as an integer, we could use the getInt() method instead:

```
int number = response.jsonPath().getInt("frequentFlyerNumber");
```

READING NESTED FIELD VALUES

We can access nested field values by using the "dot" notation. For example, the following code will read Tracy's passport number:

```
int passport = response.jsonPath().getInt("passport.number");
```

READING PARTS OF A STRUCTURE AS AN OBJECT

Sometimes we might want to retrieve a collection of fields as a Java domain object. For example, suppose we wanted to represent Tracy's passport details using the following Java record:

```
public record Passport(int number, String country) {}
```

We could read this object directly from the JSON response by calling the getObject() method and specifying the class we want to store the values in:

```
Passport passport = response.jsonPath().getObject("passport",
                                                 Passport.class);
```

READING COLLECTIONS OF OBJECTS

JSONPath is not limited to extracting individual values or objects. Sometimes we might want to read all of the items matching a given path. For example, the flightHistory.to JSONPath expression will match the destination fields of each flight in the flight history list. We could get them all by using the getList() method, like this:

```
List<String> cities = response.jsonPath().getList("flightHistory.to");
```

We can also retrieve a list of entries as a list of objects. For example, suppose we had a simple Java record to represent the flight history records, like this one:

```
public record Flight(String from, String to, String date) {}
```

We could load a list of `Flight` records from the JSON response simply by specifying the record class:

```
List<Flight> flights
            = response.jsonPath().getList("flightHistory",Flight.class);
```

JSONPath is a powerful tool, which allows us to extract just the information we need for a particular scenario. By only getting the information we really need, and ignoring incidental fields, we can help make our test automation code more flexible and robust. We will see more of its use later in this chapter.

13.4.4 *Performing a GET query: Confirming the frequent flyer address*

The next step in our scenario is where Tracy confirms her email address. Figure 13.5 describes this process in more detail.

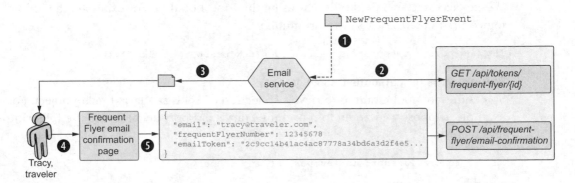

Figure 13.5   Confirming the email address

The process starts when the email service receives a `NewFrequentFlyerEvent` from the message broker (1). The email service fetches a single use token from the token service (2) and sends an email to Tracy containing a link where she can confirm her email address (3). When Tracy clicks on the link (4) the email confirmation page sends a POST request to the Membership API with a message containing Tracy's email and frequent flyer number along with the single-use token (5).

For our test scenario we only need to focus on this last step. Generating and sending the email is done by the email service, which is being developed by a separate team. One of the advantages of decoupled architectures like this one is that it makes it much easier for work to be done independently and in parallel. We do not need to have a working email service to be able to implement the email confirmation logic; all we need is to agree on how the single use token service will work.

In concrete terms, the third step ("when she confirms her email address") needs to do two things:

1 Fetch the single-use token from the Token API.
2 Confirm the email address using the Membership API.

Both of these steps interacts with a different endpoint. We could include all of this logic in the same class, but it would be cleaner and more maintainable to keep the Token API logic separate from the membership API code. To interact with the Token API, we will create a new `TokenAPI` class.

Using this class, the step definition code would look like this:

```
TokenAPI tokenAPI = new TokenAPI();

@When("he/she confirms her email address")
public void confirms_email_address() {
    emailToken = tokenAPI.getEmailToken(newFrequentFlyerNumber);
    membershipAPI.confirmEmail(newFrequentFlyerNumber,
                               newMember.email(),
                               emailToken);
}
```

FETCHING THE SINGLE-USE TOKEN

The first method we need to implement is `getEmailToken()`, which retrieves the single-use token using a GET request:

```
public class TokenAPI extends ConfigurableAPIClient {

    public String getEmailToken(String frequentFlyerNumber) {
        return RestAssured.given()
                    .pathParam("id", frequentFlyerNumber)
                    .get("/tokens/frequent-flyer/{id}")
                    .getBody().asString();
    }
}
```

> **Defines an "id" variable that we can use in the path expression** → `.pathParam("id", frequentFlyerNumber)`

> **Performs a GET operation, injecting the frequent flyer number into the {id} placeholder** → `.get("/tokens/frequent-flyer/{id}")`

> **Retrieves the returned value as a string** → `.getBody().asString();`

Many GET operations return more complex JSON structures, which we need to process or convert to a Java class or record. But since this API returns a simple string expression, we can simply return and use this value directly in our code.

CONFIRMING THE EMAIL ADDRESS

The final step is to confirm the email address. To do this, we need to send a simple JSON structure containing three fields: name, frequent flyer number, and email address. One of the simplest way to do this would be to use a Java record:

```
public record EmailValidation(String frequentFlyerNumber,
                              String email,
                              String token){}
```

The confirmEmail() method will be similar to the register() method, where
➡ we pass a Java object into the body of the request:

```
public void confirmEmail(String frequentFlyerNumber,
                         String email,
                         String token) {
    RestAssured.given()
        .contentType(ContentType.JSON)
        .body(new EmailValidation(frequentFlyerNumber, email, token))
        .post("/frequent-flyer/email-confirmation")
        .then().statusCode(201);
}
```

This object will be converted to a JSON document and submitted in the request body.

Submits a POST request

Checks the status code of the response and throws an exception if it is not the expected value

Checking outcomes with the then() method

The then() method in the last line is a convenient way to check the response and to make sure that the operation was successful. This method lets us check the status and content of the response using both simple values and more sophisticated Hamcrest matchers. For example, the following code checks that the status code has a value of 201, the frequentFlyerNumber field is equal to the one we passed in, and that the token field is not empty:

```
RestAssured.given()
        .contentType(ContentType.JSON)
        .body(new EmailValidation(frequentFlyerNumber, email, token))
        .post("/frequent-flyer/email-confirmation")
        .then()
        .statusCode(201)
        .body("frequentFlyerNumber", equalTo(frequentFlyerNumber))
        .body("token", not(emptyOrNullString()));
```

We can also make assertions about collections of objects, using JSONPath expressions. For example, the following code will check the list of destinations in the flight history:

```
RestAssured.when()
        .get("/frequent-flyer/{id}/history", id)
        .then()
        .body("flightHistory.to", hasItems("Paris", "London"));
```

13.4.5   *Partial JSON Responses: Checking the new Frequent Flyer account details*

The last step of the scenario involves checking that the new Frequent Flyer account has been successfully created and activated:

```
Then she should have a new Standard tier account with 0 points
```

We can read the current membership details by sending a GET query to the `/api/frequent-flyer/{id}` endpoint, and specifying the member's frequent flyer number (see figure 13.6).

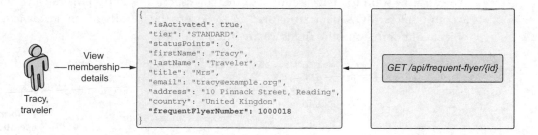

Figure 13.6 Retrieving membership details

This query will return a JSON document like the following, containing various details about the Frequent Flyer:

```
{
  "isActivated": true,
  "tier": "STANDARD",
  "statusPoints": 0,
  "firstName": "Tracy",
  "lastName": "Traveler",
  "title": "Mrs",
  "email": "tracy@example.org",
  "address": "10 Pinnack Street, Reading",
  "country": "United Kingdon",
  "frequentFlyerNumber": 1000018
}
```

As the application grows, this data structure might grow, with additional fields needed for other requirements. However, for the purposes of our test, we really need only three fields: the `isActivated` field (to know the activation status), the number of points, and the membership tier.

We can extract this data from the response object by using a Java record:

```
public record TravelerAccountStatus(int statusPoints,
                                    MembershipTier tier,
                                    boolean isActivated) {}
```

However, there is a catch. By default, Rest Assured will try to find a property for every field in the JSON document and throw an error when it doesn't find them. To work around this constraint, we can use the `@JsonIgnoreProperties` attribute, like this:

```
@JsonIgnoreProperties(ignoreUnknown = true)
public record AccountStatus(int statusPoints,
                           MembershipTier tier,
                           boolean isActivated) {}
```

We can now submit a GET request to the corresponding endpoint, retrieve the full account status JSON data structure, and convert the results to an `AccountStatus` object containing only the fields we are interested in:

```
public AccountStatus getMemberStatus(String frequentFlyerNumber) {
    return RestAssured.given()
                 .get("/frequent-flyer/{number}", frequentFlyerNumber)   ◁┄┐
                 .jsonPath()
                 .getObject(".", AccountStatus.class);   ◁┄┐
}
```

Performs a GET operation using the frequent flyer number in the path

Converts the JSON document to an AccountStatus object

In the step definition method, we can now use the `getMemberStatus()` method to retrieve this data and compare their values with the expected ones:

```
@Then("he/she should have a new {tier} tier account with {int} points")
public void should_have_a_new_account_with_points(MembershipTier tier,
                                                  Integer points) {
    TravelerAccountStatus accountStatus
        = membershipAPI.getMemberStatus(newFrequentFlyerNumber);

    assertThat(accountStatus.statusPoints()).isEqualTo(points);
    assertThat(accountStatus.tier()).isEqualTo(tier);
}
```

This completes the step definitions for the scenario, so this scenario should now run. However, there is one more thing we need to do: once the scenario has finished, we will need to delete the Frequent Flyer member we have created and restore the system to its initial state.

13.4.6   *Performing a DELETE query: Cleaning up afterward*

In a typical REST API, we can use the HTTP DELETE command to delete a record from the system. Our membership API service is no exception: we can delete a Frequent Flyer account by sending a DELETE request to the `/api/frequent-flyer/{id}` endpoint.

We don't want to have to do this in the last step of every scenario, though; that would be hard to maintain. A simpler approach is to use the Cucumber `@After` annotation. Methods annotated with `@After`, like the one shown here, will be executed at the end of each scenario. Let's implement a method called `deleteFrequentFlyer()`:

```
@After
public void deleteFrequentFlyerAccount() {
    membershipAPI.deleteFrequentFlyer(newFrequentFlyerNumber);
}
```

The implementation is simple:

```
public void deleteFrequentFlyer(String frequentFlyerNumber) {
    RestAssured.when()
            .delete("/frequent-flyer/{id}", frequentFlyerNumber)
            .then().statusCode(200);
}
```

Performs a DELETE operation using the frequent flyer number in the path

Makes sure the operation succeeded

Using the @After annotation along with REST endpoints is often a fast and effective way to clean up test data after a scenario has terminated.

13.5   *Automating more granular scenarios and interacting with external services*

The scenario we have seen so far is a high-level user-journey scenario that maps out the full registration process, but these journey scenarios should only make a very small proportion of our acceptance criteria. The bulk of our acceptance criteria will take the form of smaller, more granular, and more nimble scenarios that explore specific business rules within a user journey.

The second scenario we wrote is a good example of one of these more granular examples:

```
Example: Tracy's account is initially pending activated
    Given Tracy does not have a Frequent Flyer account
    When she registers for a new Frequent Flyer account
    Then she should be sent an email with an email validation link
    And her account should be pending activation
```

When we automate scenarios like this one, we can generally use very similar techniques to those we saw in the previous section, and very often, we can reuse the API client code we wrote for previous steps. In this case, the first two steps are identical to our previous scenario, and we only need to focus on the third and fourth ones.

The third step is interesting, because we cannot simply call one of our service endpoints. In this step, we need to check that the email validation message was sent to the new frequent flyer.

There are a few ways we could perform this check. We could set up an email server and monitor the inbox of our frequent flyer.[4] And there are some scenarios where the importance or risks involved may make this a useful strategy. However, in other cases these services may be implemented and managed by other teams or departments. If we are using an event-driven architecture, as is the case for the Frequent Flyer application, it may be enough to simply listen for the appropriate event, without needing to check the actual email delivery.

---

[4] There are even companies, such as Mailinator (https://www.mailinator.com/) that can provide you with a test infrastructure where you can test email and SMS messages in a realistic way.

In both cases, the automation code in the step definition method should try to express the intent of the step rather than the implementation. For example, we could create an `EmailMonitor` class to encapsulate this logic and hide the details in an appropriately named method:

```
@Steps
EmailMonitor emails;

@Then("he/she should be sent an email with an email validation link")
public void shouldBeSentAnEmailWithAnEmailValidationLink() {
    assertThat(
        emails.newAccountConfirmationMessageSentTo(newMember.email()))
    .isTrue();
}
```

The `EmailMonitor` class is then free to choose whether to query the event bus logs, subscribe to a particular message type, or use an external service to monitor the email messages that go out.

13.6   *Testing the APIs or testing with the APIs*

The scenarios we have seen so far are designed to define and explore the business rules and behavior, through the APIs. They are *not* designed to test the APIs themselves. Testing the details of your API design, such as what fields are included and what error codes are returned, are often easier to do using unit or integration testing tools and with the same technology stack as the development itself.

Summary

- We can describe and test business requirements that involve interacting with microservices and other API layers.
- We can test many business requirements more quickly and more reliably using API calls than by interacting with the user interface. Even user-journey scenarios can often be automated uniquely via API interactions.
- Rest Assured is an open source library that we can use to perform various REST API calls as part of our automated acceptance tests.
- JSONPath is a query language we can use to query the responses we receive from API calls and check that they contain the expected results.
- Teams practicing BDD can also use BDD techniques such as cross-team API discovery sessions to explore exactly what services each API should provide.

In the next chapter, we move away from Java and see how we can implement BDD practices and test automation techniques for projects using JavaScript.

Executable specifications for existing systems with Serenity/JS

This chapter covers
- Using Journey Mapping to identify and visualize high-value workflows and test scenarios
- Using layered architecture and Serenity/JS to design scalable test automation systems

So far, you've learned how to use automated acceptance tests as a design tool that helps your team evolve a software system gradually, together with your growing understanding of the rules the system needs to implement and the business scenarios it needs to support. However, you might not always have the luxury of starting fresh on a greenfield project, and you could find yourself in a situation where you need to retrofit acceptance tests to an existing or partially existing system before you can use them to guide development of any new features.

To help you prepare for that, in this chapter we'll pretend that most of the Flying High Airlines' system has already been built without any acceptance test coverage. As is typically the case, our first task is to create a safety net of automated tests around the critical parts of the system to enable the development team to introduce improvements and reduce the risk of such improvements causing regressions, which would negatively affect the existing functionality.

While it might be tempting to try to fulfill our task by writing or generating as many test scripts as possible, there is a far more effective way to go about this. In this chapter, you'll learn Journey Mapping—a powerful facilitation technique to identify high-value workflows and visualize high-priority test scenarios. Then, we'll investigate using layered architecture to design scalable test automation systems and begin to explore the Serenity/JS test automation framework to give you an overview of both Java and JavaScript-based tools to support BDD adoption on your team. (You can learn more about Serenity/JS at https://serenity-js.org and about examples and reference implementations at https://github.com/serenity-js.)

14.1 Navigating an uncharted territory with Journey Mapping

Automating tests of an existing software system often feels like wandering into an uncharted territory; you might take a route that's much longer than necessary, miss a shortcut, trip over an unexpected obstacle, or walk in circles as you're trying to get your bearings. In practical terms, this typically means limiting automation to end-to-end tests running against a fully assembled and deployed system, missing opportunities to integrate tests with programmatic APIs, not paying enough attention to the context in which the system operates, or not taking the business priorities and risks into consideration.

Even though the BDD techniques you've learned about so far are typically used to guide development of new features and new functionality, you can use them to guide the development of automated tests for existing systems as well. In this section, we'll show you how to use a technique called Journey Mapping to identify the critical scenarios that our system needs to support and to help us prioritize our test automation work accordingly. In chapter 15, you'll learn how to model those scenarios in code to create automated tests.

Since we're working with a system that's already been built, the overall approach, as shown in figure 14.1, is to shift our focus from discovering what features should be delivered to discovering how the existing features are used and which ones are on the critical path to actors achieving their goals.

14.1.1 Determine actors and goals to understand the business context

Before writing any automated tests of an existing system, it's crucial to understand the system not just from the technical perspective but, more importantly, from the business perspective. This means you need to gain an understanding of the business context in which the system operates—not only *how* the system is built, but also *what* the system is and *who* it's built for.

Having a good understanding of the reasons that motivated the creation of the system, the most important workflows the system is expected to support and the audiences it is expected to serve, is critical to helping you prioritize your automation work more effectively and focus on the workflows that matter the most.

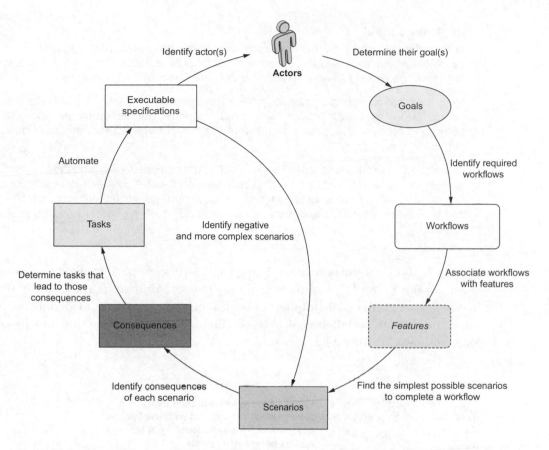

Figure 14.1   The overall approach to creating Journey Maps for existing systems requires us to shift focus from discovering what features need to be built to discovering how the existing features are used.

To do that, the first thing you need to do is to explore the business need that motivated the creation of the system, the business problem the system strives to address. To help you focus on implementing test scenarios that have the highest business value, you'll also need a good understanding of the critical workflows the system enables and the audiences who rely on them to work as expected. For example, the business purpose of an online store could be to sell products to your customers so that they don't have to visit the physical locations. The most important workflows here could be for the customers to find and purchase the products they're interested in and request a refund or replacement of products that did not meet their expectations. While a typical online store will most likely have a lot of additional functionality, such as star ratings, reviews, recommendations, and so on, if the core functionality of finding the right product and making the purchase doesn't work, the whole system might as well cease to exist.

Beginner's mind

At first glance, asking the business sponsors about the purpose of a system might seem like an exercise in futility. After all, shouldn't it be obvious why a system exists? Aren't we the experts they've hired to do the job? Shouldn't we just know?

Even if we have worked on similar types of systems in the past, it's important to approach our task with a beginner's mind, dropping our assumptions, expectations, and preconceived ideas about what the system should and shouldn't do in our opinion.

Asking each stakeholder about their perspective will help us understand the business context of the system better and highlight any inconsistencies and contradictions sooner. It will also give us an opportunity to capture and visualize them in an objective and blameless way and build a shared understanding of the system and its goals sooner.

What is the business purpose of the Flying High Airlines app? A business sponsor representing the Flying High Airlines might say that the primary purpose of the flight booking system is to enable travelers to book a flight. This helps us to identify the first actor, the traveler, and their goal, to book a flight, which we can capture on a Journey Map, as shown in figure 14.2.

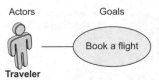

Figure 14.2   Actors and their goals on a Journey Map. You can add additional actors and goals as your understanding of the system under test expands.

Of course, most software systems will support multiple categories of actors, each with multiple goals, and you might find it useful to add other actors to your Journey Map as your understanding of the system expands. To keep things simple for now, we'll limit our Journey Map to just one category of actors, the travelers, and a single goal to book a flight.

14.1.2 Determine what workflows support the goals of interest

Now that you understand why the system exists and who its primary audience is, you need to understand more about how a representative of such audience would go about accomplishing their goal of booking a flight. To do that, you need a high-level view of any workflows such actor would need to complete to accomplish their goal. For example, you might learn that to book a flight a traveler needs to find a flight of interest and then make a booking, as shown in figure 14.3.

It's important to note that even though we've only just started working on our Journey Map, we're already using it to identify the boundaries between the different

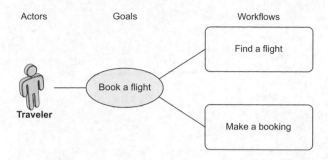

Figure 14.3 Visualizing the workflows required to accomplish a given goal helps to identify the critical capabilities of our system, as seen from the perspective of a person using the system.

parts of high-level workflows. In this case, we can think of the workflow required to accomplish a goal of booking a flight as consisting of two separate and reasonably independent sequences of activities: to find a flight and to make a booking. The reason we'd want to think of them as separate is that because an actor is looking for a flight doesn't necessarily mean that they want to make a booking. It could be that they want to check the departure and arrival times or compare its price. The same goes for the flight-booking workflow. While the actor could book a flight they found using the flight-finder feature, they might have entered the booking workflow right after clicking on an ad or a link in the newsletter, therefore bypassing the flight finder altogether.

> **NOTE** Understanding where the boundaries lie between the different workflows is critical in designing reusable test code.

Once you understand the workflows required to accomplish a given goal, it's always worth asking about any other activities an actor would need to perform before they could start with their first workflow (i.e., any prerequisites they need to meet). Such knowledge becomes invaluable when designing automated tests as it helps you get a better understanding of any test data and runtime dependencies you'll need to consider.

Here, again, a good way to learn about any dependencies on other workflows is to ask the business stakeholder, or the person providing the overview of the system, to show you step by step how they'd initiate the first workflow if they were to do it themselves. If you hear, for example, that a given workflow can't be done "without coordinating with a third party," "locking down the test environment to avoid interference from other testers," or "running an overnight batch process to set up the test data," you'll know right away that you need to incorporate solving those problems into your test automation approach.

For example, in the case of the Flying High Airlines, the system supports only authenticated travelers. This means that to use the system a traveler who's not authenticated would need to sign in, and a traveler who doesn't have an account would need to sign up first. We expand our Journey Map to capture this new information as shown in figure 14.4.

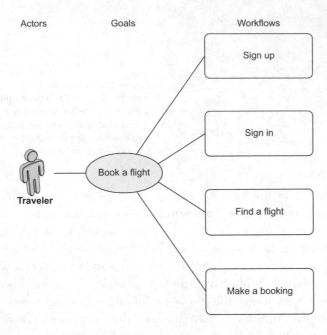

Figure 14.4   Adding prerequisite workflows to the Journey Map helps to identify any additional steps an automated test will need to take.

Thinking about the system from the perspective of an actor completing various workflows will help you to quickly build an understanding of the problems the system is trying to solve, the ways it does it, and any dependencies it requires. It will also help you to identify business-critical workflows and focus on automating test scenarios that cover those parts of the system that matter the most to its stakeholders.

Furthermore, this approach will also help you design reusable test code and spot opportunities for optimizations sooner. For example, while the test actor is required to complete the workflows to sign up and sign in before they can find their flight and make a booking, perhaps they could do so using a more efficient method like an API call or seeding the test database instead of the slower method of using a web browser. We'll talk more about this when we investigate blended testing in section 15.1.5 in the next chapter.

14.1.3 *Associate workflows with features*

Once you've identified the high-level workflows necessary to accomplish the actor's goal, the next step is to group such workflows logically and associate them with the high-level system features that enable those workflows. You can see this association depicted in figure 14.5.

Visualizing this high-level association between actor-centric workflows and system-centric features like registration, authentication, flight finder, or bookings will help you to better understand the scope of the automated tests needed to provide sufficient coverage of a given workflow. It also demarcates a convenient boundary for other types and levels of testing you might want to incorporate in your testing strategy, both automated and exploratory.

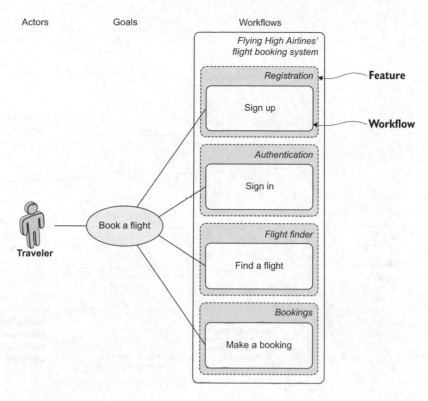

**Figure 14.5   System features associated with the workflows they enable. Note that
to accomplish a goal an actor typically needs to interact with multiple system
features.**

You'll find that typically any given high-level feature enables multiple workflows, as
shown in figure 14.6. For example, the authentication feature enables a sign-in workflow, but also a reset password workflow. The flight finder might offer its users an
option to remember their favorite destinations; the bookings feature might allow the
actors to add extra services to their booking, reschedule a flight, or request a refund.
Just like with any new actors and goals you discover, here it also could be useful to add
those additional workflows to your Journey Map. However, try to maintain the right
balance between breadth and depth of this discovery exercise and be mindful not to
attempt to map out every single workflow the system supports upfront.

   As shown in figure 14.1 earlier, a good approach is to start with one or a handful of
actors and their goals, identify only the critical workflows required to accomplish
those goals, and complete the automation test automation cycle before iterating on
the Journey Map again. Another technique that's particularly useful in helping you to
stay on track is to establish a steel thread, which we'll investigate next.

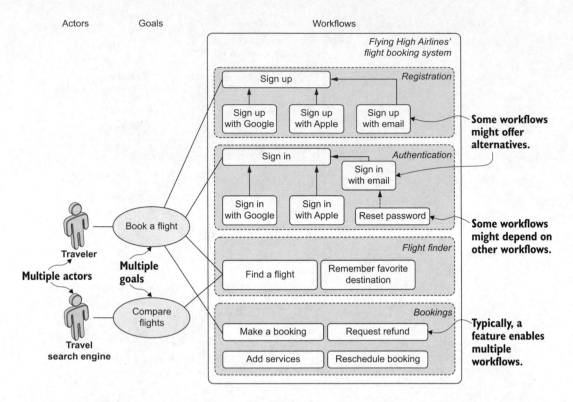

Figure 14.6   A typical software system supports multiple actors, with multiple goals, and offers features enabling dozens of workflows. Instead of trying to map out the entire system upfront, focus first on those workflows that support the high-priority actor goals you've identified.

14.1.4 Establish a steel thread of scenarios that demonstrate the features

Typically, any given high-level feature supports multiple actor workflows, each workflow utilizing a given feature has multiple usage scenarios, and those scenarios tend to support numerous business rules.

Because of this inherent complexity of the software systems we create, it is easy to get bogged down in details and spend a significant amount of time developing automated tests for features that are not necessarily on the critical path of the actor accomplishing their goal. To make sure you stay on track, it's useful to start the implementation of our automated test suite from a steel thread.

Just like what the bridge builders used to do when constructing a bridge across a valley, you don't start with a 5-foot piece of the whole bridge, as the bridge would fall down, unsupported. You begin with a simple cable right across, a steel thread, which you then use to pull over the first narrow beam. Then you attach other parts to that beam until you have a bridge.

This is similar to what we do when implementing acceptance tests for an existing system, but here, rather than building a bridge, we focus on exercising the absolute minimum of scenarios within each feature required for the actor to achieve their goal.

It is also important for those scenarios to exercise the system end to end. However, bear in mind that here, and contrary to popular opinion, "end to end" doesn't mean running the tests against a fully assembled and deployed system through its web interface. Far from it. When talking about end to end we mean the ends of the workflow, focusing on its breadth rather than its depth. While you'll want to exercise the workflow from its beginning to its end, in our case from user sign up through sign in, finding a flight, and making a booking, you could choose to perform parts or even the whole workflow against its APIs not the Web UI, or against in-memory databases rather than a production-like DB server.

This technique of establishing a steel thread is well known in software architecture and has many benefits in test automation too. It allows you to see whether your overall understanding of how the system is supposed to work is correct and helps to surface any assumptions you and your team might be making, often without realizing it. It will also help you see any dependencies that the team or the business sponsors might not have been aware of, and since you detect them early it will give you more time to do something about them.

All that improves your chances of being successful with your test automation effort, as it creates opportunities for you to react sooner and address risks before they become problems. It also helps you buy time to make changes to the architecture of your automated test suite, or the system under test itself. This early feedback mechanism can also help you to avoid an unfortunate yet common scenario where dependencies go undetected for weeks or months, only to appear at the last minute when you realize that, for example, even though you've built a state-of-the-art test automation system, setting up the test data it needs to run is a manual process that takes weeks and needs to be performed by a different team that you don't control.

How do you establish the minimum set of scenarios you need to exercise to ensure that the system allows the actor to accomplish their goal? You use a variation of Feature Mapping, a technique you first encountered in section 6.5, and start from finding the simplest possible successful scenario within each feature that allows the actor to progress toward their goal of making a booking.

For example, the easiest way to get through the sign-up workflow is to sign up with valid traveler details and use an email-based registration workflow rather than one that requires interacting with a third party. To pass the sign-in workflow without any fuss from any form validation rules, the actor needs to provide valid authentication credentials. To find a flight that will let the actor book it, the actor needs to search for the simplest possible journey configuration, such as a one-way direct flight in an economy class. This minimal set of simplest possible successful scenarios is shown on our updated Journey Map in figure 14.7.

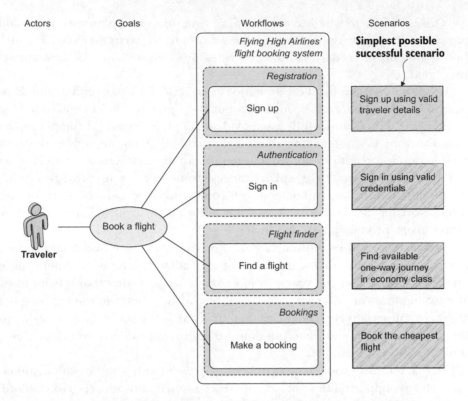

Figure 14.7   Establishing a steel thread of simplest possible scenarios required to accomplish a given goal

You might have noticed in figure 14.7 that, so far, our steel thread covers only the simplest possible "happy path scenarios," those positive cases confirming the system works as expected when provided with valid inputs. Of course, this gives us only rudimentary coverage of the functionality offered by the system. It is, nevertheless, a great place to start and makes it easier for us to evolve our automated test suite while ensuring that there's always a reliable safety net around the most critical workflows.

Another advantage of this approach is that it offers a mental model that helps us to avoid getting overwhelmed by the combinatorial explosion of all the possible paths an actor could take through the system. Instead, we will consider this variability within a much more manageable scope of each individual feature. We won't ignore the "unhappy path scenarios" in our acceptance tests, and we'll talk about how to incorporate them shortly.

14.1.5   *Determine verifiable consequences of each scenario*

Once you've gone through the exercise of establishing the purpose of the system under test, identifying some of the actors who interact with it, the goals they want to accomplish, the workflows that enable achieving those goals, and a steel thread of scenarios to exercise the critical features along the way, it's time to think about the specific activities the actors would perform. Thankfully, our Journey Map already contains a list of important workflows, as well as scenarios within those workflows that we'll need to investigate in more detail. Let's start with the sign-up workflow since other workflows depend on it.

The easiest way to capture a workflow so that it can be then turned into an automated test is perhaps slightly counterintuitive: we'll start from the outcome and then work our way back. How would we know if a given workflow was successful? What consequences would we need to verify to determine that? And on the other hand, how would we know if a given workflow was *not* successful? Answering those questions helps us build a mental model of the observable responses the system will produce to the stimuli the actors provide. It will also help us think about the assertions our automated tests need to perform.

In the case of the sign-up workflow it's easy to identify the expected consequences: the workflow is completed successfully when the traveler's account is created, and the actor can move on to the sign-in workflow, as depicted in figure 14.8. Since we're not yet sure what exact tasks an actor needs to perform this outcome, we add a placeholder card to our Journey Map and mark it as TBC, or to be confirmed.

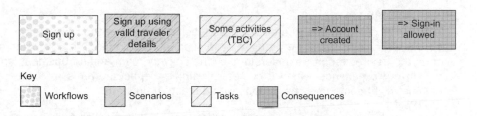

Figure 14.8   Visualizing a workflow using conventions from Feature Mapping

When visualizing each scenario, we use color convention, similar to what you saw in chapter 6 (section 6.5) when you learned about Feature Mapping: white cards on the left of the board signify the workflows, green cards describe the scenarios, and purple cards are the consequences. The yellow cards in the middle, even though they contain only rudimentary notes for now, will soon expand to describe the exact activities an actor needs to perform in order to achieve a given outcome.

It's important to observe that while so far we have focused on a handful of happy path scenarios, our Journey Map should not neglect the so-called unhappy path scenarios either. Those negative cases where things go wrong, errors occur, and the actor is prevented from achieving their goal. For example, a negative variation of a positive sign-up scenario is one where the actor is not allowed to proceed to sign-in, perhaps because they've provided invalid registration details. In this case, the sign-up form validation rules should kick in, the account should not get registered, and the actor should be advised on how to fix any problems with their registration (see figure 14.9).

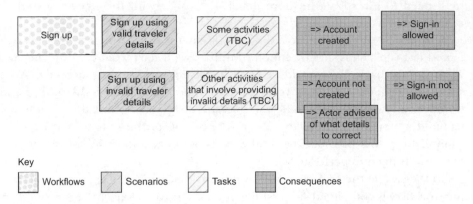

Key

Workflows   Scenarios   Tasks   Consequences

Figure 14.9   Visualize both happy and unhappy path scenarios to highlight their different consequences.

Expectations vs. reality

Note that when describing the outcomes of each scenario we tend to use the word "should." This is because we visualize each scenario starting from its expected outcome, the desired result as understood by the delivery team and its business sponsors. In our experience, when it comes to complex legacy systems, the expected outcome might sometimes be at odds with the actual outcome.

Establishing what a system is expected to do, and what each workflow is expected to yield, tends to be a better starting point than simply mirroring the current behavior of the system in your automated tests as it steers us toward building a shared understanding of the desired outcome. This strategy will also help you to highlight, discuss, and reconcile any potential inconsistencies between the expected and actual state instead of risking to replicate any defects and misunderstood requirements from the system into your test suite.

Just like in Feature Mapping, here too we use blue index cards to record any business rules we discover along the way and pink cards to capture any unanswered questions or topics to consider in exploratory testing.

Capturing business rules on our Journey Map helps us get an indication of the complexity of a given workflow, and the ratio of scenario to rule cards is an indication of its variability. Capturing business rules also has another advantage as it offers us an opportunity to "split by rule" when implementing the automated tests. This means that instead of trying to automate all the scenarios of a given workflow in one go, we could instead divide them by business rules they support and implement in much smaller batches, one business rule at a time (see figure 14.10).

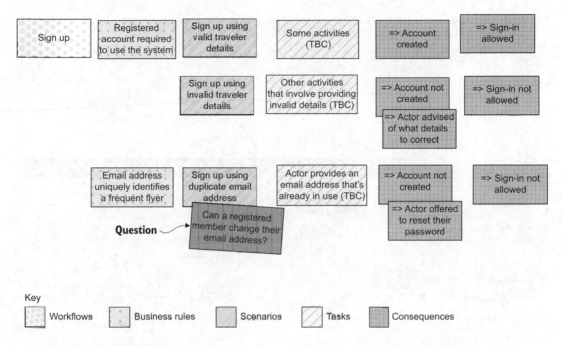

Figure 14.10   Visualizing business rules helps us gauge the complexity of a workflow and spot opportunities to split automation work by business rule.

As you've noticed, we haven't dived too deep into the details of the activities an actor would need to perform to reach a given consequence, and instead we've settled for some rudimentary notes, as seen on the yellow task cards. However, that's exactly what we need since at this stage we are interested in enumerating scenarios and their outcomes within a given workflow and spotting any business rules they need to obey. We'll investigate how exactly the actors would go about reaching the outcomes of each scenario next.

14.1.6   *Using task analysis to understand the steps of each scenario*

Now that we understand what outcomes a given workflow should lead to, the next step is to analyze the high-level activities the actor needs to perform to reach those outcomes. To do that with an existing system, we will need to experiment with it a bit and learn about how it responds to the stimuli we provide.

When working with web-based user interfaces, it's also a good idea to keep the developer tools console of your favorite web browser open to see any requests exchanged between the frontend and the backend components (see figure 14.11). This will help you spot opportunities to make your tests interact directly with the APIs, which we'll talk more about when we investigate blended testing in chapter 15.

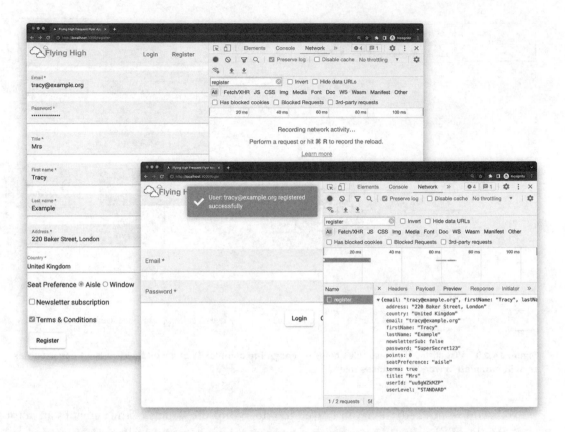

Figure 14.11   Submitting the registration form results in a POST request from the web UI to the backend. This suggests that instead of filling out the form, an automated test could also send an HTTP request directly to the server to arrive at the same outcome.

In the case of the Flying High app, the sign-up workflow we investigate is rather simple and requires the actor to perform a single high-level task to sign up via web UI, as shown in figure 14.12. This task consists of several subtasks for the actor to locate the registration form, fill it out, and submit it while also ensuring that the submission was successful. If the notification confirming a successful result of the operation is shown, the actor can assume that they can proceed with the sign in workflow.

Of course, each of the activities that constitute the task to sign up could be broken down further using the same pattern. Each higher-level activity becomes a mini-goal (the what) of a sequence of lower-level activities (the how). Locating the registration form, filling it out, submitting it, and confirming that the submission was successful

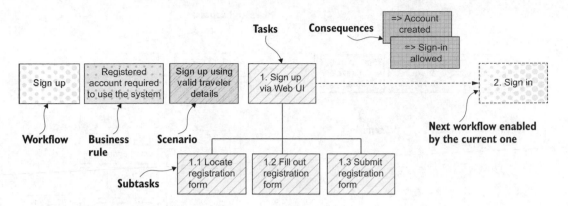

Figure 14.12   The "Sign up using valid traveler details" scenario consists of a high-level task to sign up via Web UI and allows the traveler to proceed to the sign-in workflow when all three subtasks are completed successfully.

allows the actor to accomplish the goal of registering an account. Navigating to the Flying High homepage and clicking on the link to register allows the actor to accomplish the goal of locating the registration form and so on and so forth. If we followed the same pattern all the way from the high-level domain-specific concept of signing up to low-level implementation-specific interactions of clicking on buttons and entering text into form fields we might end up with a part of a Journey Map that looks like figure 14.13.

This approach of presenting activities involved in a workflow as a hierarchy of tasks and subtasks is based on a technique known in the field of user experience research as *Hierarchical Task Analysis* (HTA). As you can see, even a relatively simple scenario within a short workflow like the one to sign up can involve quite a few lower-level activities. If we were to expand all the specific tasks just like we did with the one to specify salutation in figure 14.13, we'd end up with over a dozen low-level interactions! Of course, it makes perfect sense for our automated tests to exercise this workflow at least once through the web-based interface. After all, this is the interface that the actual end users interacting with our system will use. However, exercising it in full every single time a scenario requires the test actor to be signed up is rather wasteful.

Thankfully, we had the developer tools console open when we performed the workflow manually, and we know that the same outcome of registering an account could be achieved by much simpler means. Namely, we've observed that the frontend component of our system submits the filled-out form to the registration API using an HTTP POST request. This is exactly what our automated tests could do in those scenarios where we want to focus on the outcome of the actor getting registered rather than the web-based interactions that get them there, as shown in figure 14.14.

This observation that the same outcome can be achieved by interacting with different interfaces of the system under test will be useful when we talk about blended testing in chapter 15.

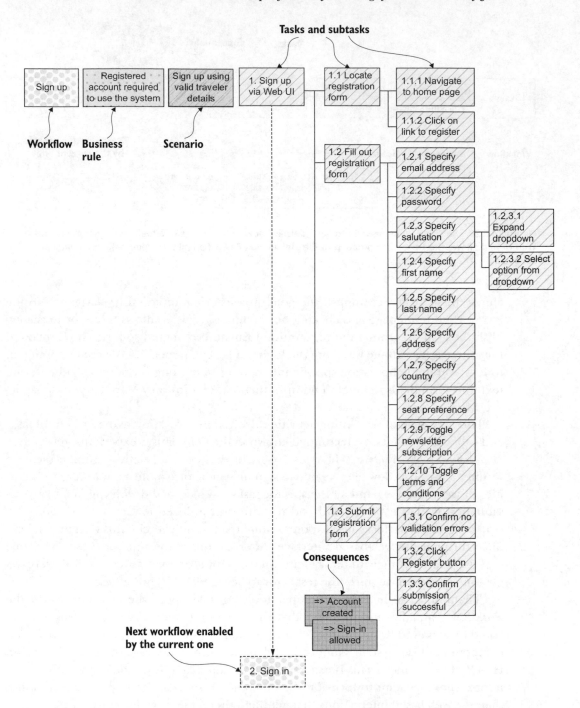

Figure 14.13   One of the branches of the Journey Map expanded to highlight the tasks involved in the workflow to sign up. Note that to fit on a page the tasks of the workflow are laid out vertically rather than horizontally. Both layouts are valid, and you can use them interchangeably to work with the medium you have available, like a physical or virtual whiteboard, a computer screen, or sticky notes on a wall.

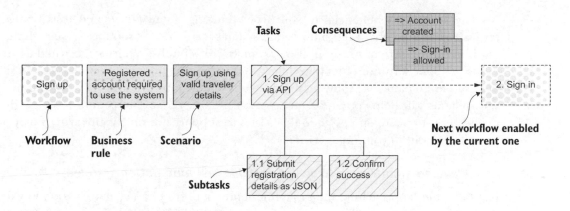

Figure 14.14   The task to sign up could be accomplished by submitting a single POST request to the traveler registration API.

14.2 *Designing scalable test automation systems*

Now that we have a good understanding of the first workflows we need to automate and the different interfaces of our system that we can interact with, let's talk about how to approach the process of test automation itself. Of course, the end goal we're after is a test suite that helps us verify if the system meets and continues to meet its acceptance criteria as expressed in our test scenarios. Furthermore, we'd like such a test suite to provide a foundation to help us test-drive any new functionality added to the system in the future.

However, just like with many other things in life, the way we think about our automated tests is the way we treat them, and the way we treat them is what they become. Since our goal is to have fast, reliable, high-quality tests that support rather than obstruct our work we need to depart from the way they're often viewed by developers and testers alike.

The view still often held in our industry is that automated acceptance tests are nothing more than a bunch of unsophisticated scripts—that it's fine for them to look like spaghetti code of low-level interactions, devoid of business domain meaning. Unfortunately, even teams using executable specification tools like Cucumber will often try to implement such sequences of low-level interactions directly in their step definition libraries and end up with slow, flaky tests, not to mention difficult-to-understand and reused test code that fails to yield the benefits of reliable test automation.

What's the alternative? A better way to look at the task of designing reliable test automation is not from the perspective of writing tests but from the perspective of creating a test automation system, so a specialized supporting system we develop to verify and document the behavior of the system under test. To do that, we need to think about test scenarios as just one piece of a larger whole and consider them in the context in which they operate, including the frameworks and libraries they use, and any custom glue code that integrates it all together.

The reason it's beneficial to shift from thinking about automated tests or test scripts to thinking about test automation systems is because as soon as we start thinking in terms of systems we should see parallels with what we've already learned as an industry about software systems architecture, domain modeling, functional composition, or design patterns. Applying those lessons to how you structure your test automation systems will help you and your team create fast, reliable tests and design high-quality, easy-to-maintain test code that scales to support not only your team, but also other teams within your organization.

14.2.1 *Using layered architecture to design scalable test automation systems*

Just like when approaching the task of designing a production system, a good way to approach designing a test automation system is to follow a well-defined set of principles, a set of guidelines that help us decide how to structure our code and where to draw boundaries between the responsibilities of the different components.

A software architecture style that lends itself well to designing test automation systems is called layered, or *n-tier architecture* (see figure 14.15). While in a typical production system those layers might represent user interface, application logic, and data layers, test automation systems based on Serenity/JS test automation framework typically have three main layers:

- *Specification layer.* The Specification layer is responsible for capturing the workflows, business rules, and usage examples that the stakeholders of the system find important. This layer is the interface between the test automation system and the people accepting the functionality of the system under test. While Serenity/JS enables us to implement the Specification layer using popular test runners, such as Mocha, Jasmine, or Playwright, using Cucumber makes it easier for us to capture additional information about the business context of a given feature. It also improves the accessibility of our automated tests by offering a convenient way for specifications to be expressed in languages other than English—for example French, Spanish, or German.
- *Domain layer.* The domain layer uses code and Serenity/JS Screenplay pattern APIs from the Integration layer and introduces additional abstractions to model the exact activities required to complete the workflows expressed in the Specification layer. It is also responsible for associating business meaning with sequences of lower-level activities, as you'll see in chapter 15.
- *Integration layer.* The Integration layer bridges the gap between the business domain and the technology domain. It translates actors' activities expressed in the Domain layer to exact low-level interactions with the specific external interfaces of the system under test. This includes integration with test tools, identifying interactable elements, setting up test data, test reporting, and so on.

The essential principle of any layered architecture is that an element of a given layer depends only on other elements in the same layer, or elements that belong to the

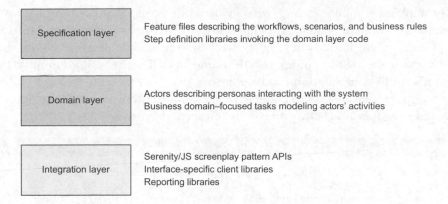

Figure 14.15   **Layers of a typical test automation system based on Serenity/JS, with their contents**

layer directly below it. The value of layers is that each one specializes in a particular aspect of the test automation system. This specialization allows for more cohesive design of each aspect and makes these designs much easier to understand.

A common design error often seen in many test suites is to skip the Domain layer and invoke low-level integration APIs, such as Selenium WebDriver APIs, directly in the Specification layer. This ties the Specification layer with interface-specific interactions and tools and acts as an obstacle to introducing more advanced techniques such as blended testing or reusable test code.

To help you get a better understanding of how this layering works in practice, we'll now continue with our outside-in approach and turn the first workflow from our Journey Map into a suite of executable specifications. Next, we'll talk about how we'd evolve them into a test automation system.

14.2.2 *Using actors to link the layers of a test automation system*

The Screenplay Pattern, modeling the expected behavior of the system under test in terms of tasks an actor needs to perform to achieve their goals, is deeply embedded in the design philosophy of Serenity/JS and the executable specifications and test automation systems based on this framework.

Actors represent external users, systems, and processes interacting with the system under test. What's interesting from the perspective of designing layered test automation systems, though, is that actors are also the link connecting all those layers—performing activities and providing abilities abstracting away the low-level integration tools like Selenium WebDriver or an HTTP client.

Similar to Serenity BDD, with Serenity/JS we also use the concept of a Cast to inform the framework what actors to engage (or, in more technical terms, we tell Serenity/JS what factory class implementing the cast interface to use to configure the actors).

In implementations in which we only have one actor, or those in which we don't need to differentiate between the different actor personas, we can configure Serenity/JS with a generic cast where every actor has the same abilities enabling them to interact with the system under test the same way. If we're using Serenity/JS with Cucumber, this configuration can be done in Cucumber with the `BeforeAll` hook, as shown in the following listing. Using `BeforeAll` ensures that we configure Serenity/JS actors exactly once and before any of the test scenarios run.

Listing 14.1   Configuring a generic cast of actors to use Playwright

```
import { BeforeAll, AfterAll } from '@cucumber/cucumber'
import { configure, Cast } from '@serenity-js/core'
import { BrowseTheWebWithPlaywright } from '@serenity-js/playwright'
import * as playwright from 'playwright'

let browser: playwright.Browser          Uses BeforeAll
                                          to setup the
BeforeAll(async () => {                   framework       Instantiates
                                                          browsers or other
  browser = await playwright.chromium.launch({   ◁──     dependencies
    headless: true,
  })
                                 Configures
  configure({                    Serenity/JS
    actors: Cast.whereEveryoneCan(

      BrowseTheWebWithPlaywright.using(browser),   ◁──  Uses appropriate abilities
    )                                                   to link actors with
  })                                                    integration libraries
})

AfterAll(async () => {        Uses AfterAll
  await browser.close()       to release any
})                            dependencies
```

In listing 14.1, we use a web integration library called Playwright. We also rely on the Serenity/JS Playwright integration module to provide a Screenplay Pattern "ability" to `BrowseTheWebWithPlaywright`. This ability acts as a wrapper around Playwright and offers an abstraction layer around its APIs.

Serenity/JS provides several web integration modules that offer abilities that wrap popular integration tools such as Playwright, WebdriverIO, or Selenium WebDriver. More importantly, they also offer a consistent Screenplay Pattern–style programming interface to allow your test scenarios to be portable across current and future web integration tools.

14.2.3 Using actors to describe personas

In the case of the Flying High Airlines app, we want our actors to represent different personas, with different user details, and different authentication credentials. This means that the generic implementation of the `Cast` interface you saw in listing 14.1, which assumed that all the actors are the same, will not be sufficient. In such slightly more sophisticated cases like ours we can provide Serenity/JS with a custom implementation of the `Cast` interface, as shown in the following listing.

Listing 14.2   Configuring actors using a custom `Cast`

```
import { BeforeAll, AfterAll } from '@cucumber/cucumber'
import {
  Actor, configure, Cast, TakeNotes, Notepad
} from '@serenity-js/core'
import {
  BrowseTheWebWithPlaywright, PlaywrightOptions
} from '@serenity-js/playwright'
import { CallAnApi } from '@serenity-js/rest'
import * as playwright from 'playwright'

class Actors implements Cast {

  constructor(
    private readonly browser: playwright.Browser,     ◁──┐ Dependencies and
    private readonly options: PlaywrightOptions,           configuration injected
  ) {                                                       via constructor
  }
                                              ┌── Actors can
  prepare(actor: Actor): Actor {              │   have multiple
    return actor.whoCan(              ◁───────┘   abilities.

      BrowseTheWebWithPlaywright.using(this.browser, this.options),

      CallAnApi.at(this.options.baseURL),

      TakeNotes.using(
        Notepad.with<TravelerNotes>({
          travelerDetails: TravelerDetails.of(actor.name),
        }),
      ),
    );
  }
}

BeforeAll(() => {
  // ... initializing the browser omitted for brevity
  configure({
    actors: new Actors(browser, {            ◁──┐ Uses custom Actors
      baseURL: 'http://localhost:3000/')           class instead of the
    })                                             generic Cast
  })
})
```

In listing 14.2, each actor receives an ability to `BrowseTheWebWithPlaywright`, just like they did in the earlier implementation from listing 14.1. Apart from that, they also receive an ability to `CallAnApi`, provided by the Serenity/JS REST module, which acts as a wrapper around an HTTP client and which will help us interact with REST APIs in chapter 15.

The last ability they get is one to `TakeNotes`, which receives a notepad that holds some initial data the actors will use for activities such as registering an account or logging in. Apart from reading this initial state, actors can use their notepads during a test scenario to record information of interest to be used later. For now, the data structure describing `TravelerNotes` held in the notepad from listing 14.2 contains a single entry to describe the `TravelerDetails`, as seen in the following listing.

> **Listing 14.3   `TravelerNotes` describes the state object held by the actors**

```
export interface TravelerNotes {
    travelerDetails: TravelerDetails
}
```

Personal details of an actor, as described by `TravelerDetails`, is what associates the actor with the persona they are meant to represent. While this information could be read from a JSON or CSV file, or even a database, to demonstrate the pattern of generating it dynamically we've decided to use a simple factory class, which you can see in the following listing.

> **Listing 14.4   `TravelerDetails` generates personal details describing each actor**

```
export abstract class TravelerDetails {
  title: string;
  firstName: string;
  lastName: string;
  email: string;
  password: string;
  address: string;
  country: string;
  seatPreference: 'window' | 'aisle';

  static of(actorName: string): TravelerDetails {
    return {
      title: 'Mx',
      firstName: actorName,
      lastName: 'Traveler',
      email: `${ actorName }.Traveler@example.org`,
      password: 'P@ssw0rd',
      address: '35 Victoria Street, Alexandria', country: 'Australia',
      seatPreference: 'window'
    }
  }
}
```

TypeScript structural type system

Invoking the static method `TravelerDetails.of(actorName)` returns a plain JavaScript object with fields such as `firstName`, `lastName`, `email`, `password` and so on.

It's worth pointing out that this returned object is compatible with the interface of the `TravelerDetails` abstract class, even though it does *not* inherit from it.

This works because TypeScript uses a structural type system (http://mng.bz/m2wM), where objects with the same types of fields are considered compatible even though they might not extend the same base class.

Note that this is different than in Java, where its nominal type system[a] makes using structures like enums more appropriate (see chapter 11).

---

[a] Benjamin J. Evans and David Flanagan, *Java in a Nutshell*, 6th edition (O'Reilly Media, Inc., 2014), chapter 4.

14.3 *Capturing business context in the Specification layer*

The Specification layer acts as a human-friendly interface between the test automation system and its audience responsible for specifying the intended behavior of the system under test. Using a tool like Cucumber.js makes it easy for us to express the scenarios using business vocabulary and enrich them with additional context. This typically includes the motivation behind a feature, or even hyperlinks to external documentation, diagrams, and so forth.

Additionally, Gherkin, the language of Cucumber, supports expressing test scenarios not just in English, but also in over 70 other languages (https://cucumber.io/docs/gherkin/languages/), including Spanish, French, German, Japanese, or Arabic. This is an important feature to remember, as it can greatly improve the accessibility of our scenarios to non-native English speakers and help to keep them engaged.

Apart from accessibility, another important factor that greatly improves the likelihood of business audiences engaging in the process of creating and reviewing the scenarios is their comprehensibility. Since our target audience typically has a very limited amount of time to dedicate to reviewing and providing feedback on our test scenarios, it's important to ensure those scenarios are succinct and highlight only the important steps directly affecting the outcome.

A great way to help us create such scenarios is to ensure that their steps correspond to the high-level tasks from the Journey Map. For example, the happy path sign-up workflow we discussed could be expressed using a scenario with only two steps, as seen in listing 14.5, and corresponding to the two high-level tasks to sign up and sign in, as depicted in figure 14.12.

Listing 14.5   Positive scenario of signing up using valid traveler details

```
Feature: Sign up

  Customers must sign up to the Frequent Flyer program to book flights
  that earn them Frequent Flyer points.

  Rule: Registered Frequent Flyer account is required to use the system

    Scenario: Sign up using valid traveler details

      When Tracy signs up using valid traveler details
      Then she should be able to sign in
```

The negative test scenario, mentioned in figure 14.10, where the traveler tries to sign up using an email address that's already been registered could be expressed using at most four steps, as seen in the following listing.

Listing 14.6   Negative scenario of signing up using duplicate email address

```
Feature: Sign up

  # ...

  Rule: Duplicate usernames are not allowed

    Scenario: Sign up using duplicate email address

      Mike Smith is an existing Frequent Flyer member.
      His wife Jenny Smith does not have a Frequent Flyer account.

      Given Mike has signed up using the following details:
        | email | smiths@example.org |
       When Jenny tries to sign up using:
        | email | smiths@example.org |
       Then she should be advised of an error: "Email exists"
        And she should be presented with an option to reset password
```

Note that both the scenarios from listings 14.5 and 14.6 highlight only the important steps that affect the final outcome and use metadata in the form of scenario descriptions and rule names to provide additional context.

Under the hood, each of the high-level steps captured in a Cucumber feature file corresponds to one or at most a handful of high-level tasks from our Journey Map, each represented by a Screenplay Pattern task. Let's look into how this mapping between Cucumber steps and Screenplay tasks is done.

Similar to Cucumber JVM, Cucumber.js also uses the concept of step definitions to map a scenario step such as "When Tracy signs up using valid traveler details" to executable code that performs the necessary interactions with the system under test.

Listing 14.7   Example step definition implementation with Cucumber.js

```
// "When Tracy signs up using valid traveler details"
When('{actor} signs up using valid traveler details', (actor: Actor) =>
  actor.attemptsTo(
    SignUp.using(
      notes<TravelerNotes>().get('travelerDetails')
    ),
    VerifySubmission.succeededWith('registered successfully')
));
```

Even though the step definition presented in listing 14.7 is short and concise, there's quite a lot going on there, so let's go through it line by line:

1 We use a Cucumber expression (https://github.com/cucumber/cucumber -expressions) to define a pattern Cucumber should use to match a scenario step with our step definition. Cucumber will also substitute the {actor} token, called a Cucumber expression parameter, with a Serenity/JS actor thanks to a custom Cucumber expression parameter type definition.

2 Next, we use the `actor.attemptsTo(…activities: Activity[])` API to create a mapping between a Cucumber step and a sequence of Screenplay Pattern tasks. This informs the actor what activities it should perform to accomplish the step.

3 We instantiate a custom task to `SignUp` via its static factory method `SignUp.using`, which we'll investigate in detail in chapter 15.

4 We parameterize the task to `SignUp` with a note on `travelerDetails`. This note retrieves the data required to perform the task to sign up from the actor's notepad; a construct you first encountered in listing 14.2.

5 Finally, we provide another custom task to verify if our form submission was successful.

Transformations that take place in listing 14.7 are depicted in figure 14.16.

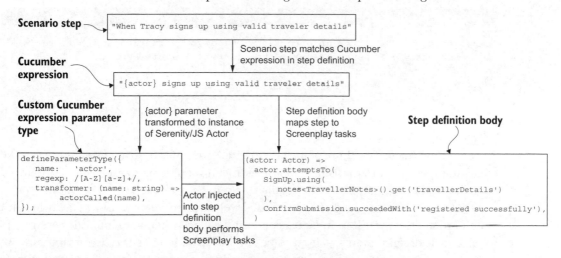

Figure 14.16   A scenario step is transformed and mapped to Screenplay Pattern tasks.

Cucumber parameter types and Serenity/JS actors

By default, Cucumber.js will not be able to interpret the {actor} and {pronoun} tokens in our step definition since they're not part of its standard vocabulary. To expand it, we need to define custom parameter types (http://mng.bz/5meD):

```
import { defineParameterType } from '@cucumber/cucumber'
import { actorCalled, actorInTheSpotlight } from '@serenity-js/core'

defineParameterType({
    name: 'actor',
    regexp: /[A-Z][a-z]+/,
    transformer: (name: string) => actorCalled(name)
})
defineParameterType({
    name: 'pronoun',
    regexp: /he|she|they|his|her|their/,
    transformer: () => actorInTheSpotlight()
})
```

The custom parameter type {actor} makes Cucumber.js invoke the Serenity/JS API actorCalled(name). This method retrieves the actor that's already been instantiated or instantiates one and passes it to our implementation of the Cast interface, where the actor is configured with abilities and the initial state of the Notepad. The other custom parameter type ,{pronoun}, simply retrieves the most recently accessed actor.

Note that the regular expressions work for scenarios expressed in English and will need to be adjusted to support other languages you might want to use with your audience.

We define the step "she should be able to sign in" in a similar manner, this time relying on Cucumber to replace the token {pronoun} with the most recently accessed actor, as follows.

Listing 14.8   Using pronouns to reference most recently used actor

```
Then('{pronoun} should be able to sign in', async (actor: Actor) => {
    const details = notes<TravelerNotes>().get('travelerDetails')

    await actor.attemptsTo(
        SignIn.using(details.email, details.password),
    )
})
```

Since it's more natural to think of the task to SignIn as only requiring two arguments, the email and the password, in listing 14.8 we extract a variable, travelerDetails, to avoid code duplication and then pass the required parameters individually to the task.

You might have noticed that the high-level tasks to SignUp and SignIn haven't been implemented yet. It is, in fact, a common practice when working with Serenity/JS to approach designing any such custom, domain-specific tasks the exact same way we approach designing the rest of our test automation system. We start from the outside and optimize the interfaces in each layer for the experience of its intended audience. And just like we optimize the Cucumber scenarios for the reading experience of the business audience, we optimize our custom Serenity/JS tasks for the reading experience and to reduce the cognitive load of the technical audience.

This consistent outside-in approach repeated throughout all the layers of our test automation system makes our code not only easier to read, comprehend, and maintain; it also helps to improve its cohesion and reduce coupling and make our code much easier to reuse. We'll talk about it more when we discuss implementing the Domain layer in chapter 15.

Implementation patterns for asynchronous step definitions

Serenity/JS fully embraces the asynchronous nature of JavaScript, and thus all the APIs provided by the framework are asynchronous by default.

What this means in practice is that the `actor.attemptsTo(...)` API returns a `Promise` (http://mng.bz/69p6). This `Promise` needs to be returned to any test runner that invokes Serenity/JS code, in this case Cucumber.js, so that it can correctly synchronize its execution.

There are two main step definition implementation patterns you can apply here, depending on the complexity of a given step definition.

The first pattern involves using an arrow function expression (http://mng.bz/o5wv) and is applicable with simple step definitions that require invoking just the `actor.attemptsTo(...)` method, for example:

```
Given('{actor} has signed up', (actor: Actor) =>
  actor.attemptsTo(/* activities */)
)
```

This minimal bracket-less arrow function expression helps us avoid the syntax noise of the equivalent but much more verbose traditional anonymous function:

```
Given('{actor} has signed up', function (actor: Actor): Promise<void> {
  return actor.attemptsTo(/* activities */)
})
```

The second pattern involves using the `async/await` (http://mng.bz/new4) syntax and works better for the more complex step definitions with multiple actors or introducing additional variables:

```
// When Alice sends a message "hello!" to Bob

When('{actor} sends a message {string} to {actor}',
  async (sender: Actor, messageText: string, receiver: Actor) => {
    await sender.attemptsTo(
      SendMessage.with(messageText).to(receiver.name)
    )
```

(continued)

```
    await receiver.attemptsTo(
      Ensure.that(Messages.received(), contain(messageText)),
    )
  }
)
```

This second pattern requires the function to use the `async` keyword, the curly brackets to be present, and any asynchronous calls in the function body to use the `await` keyword.

Summary

- Journey Mapping is a visual technique that helps to create a mental model of workflows supported by the system and associate them with external actors and their goals.
- Journey Mapping can be used to identify candidate workflows to be exercised using automated tests and influence which ones to work on first.
- Specification layer is the top layer of a test automation system. It is responsible for capturing the workflows, business rules, and usage examples that the stakeholders of the system find important and should be expressed in a language the stakeholders can understand and are comfortable with reading.
- The Domain layer is the middle layer of a test automation system. It models the exact activities required to complete the workflows expressed in the Specification layer. Test automation systems based on Serenity/JS use Screenplay Pattern APIs to model the tasks performed by the actors.
- The Integration layer is the bottom layer of a test automation system. It bridges the gap between the business domain and the technology domain. It translates actors' activities expressed in the Domain layer to exact low-level interactions with the specific external interfaces of the system under test and manages the low-level clients of those interfaces, like an HTTP client or a web browser driver.
- An end-to-end test scenario performs a full workflow but doesn't have to run against a fully assembled and deployed system.
- Splitting by rule helps us to avoid big batches of test automation work and allows us to automate scenarios one business rule at a time.
- Serenity/JS Screenplay Pattern tasks can be parameterized to enable variations in workflows.
- Actors use `Notepad` and the ability to `TakeNotes` to manage scenario-related data.
- All Serenity/JS APIs are compatible with native JavaScript Promises and offer a first-class support for the asynchronous nature of the language.
- Experiment with the test automation system in this chapter's repository to learn more.

Portable test automation with Serenity/JS

In chapter 14, you learned how following the layered architecture pattern can support you in designing scalable test automation systems. You've also seen how introducing a Specification layer can help you capture information about the business context and its rules, workflows, and scenarios, as well as the actors interacting with the system and the goals they're trying to accomplish.

In this chapter, we'll continue to explore the idea of layering the architecture of our test automation system. We'll investigate ways to reflect the concepts and vocabulary from the business domain in our test automation code. We'll also study patterns that help to focus our implementation on modeling the business process and abstracting the lower-level test integration tools.

In our exploration, we'll identify Serenity/JS APIs to help to make our test code portable. You'll also see how designing with portability in mind helps to create reusable test code that can be used in different contexts and scale to support not only multiple test suites within your project, but also multiple teams across your organization.

If you'd like to experiment with the example test automation system we'll be exploring in this chapter, you can find it in this book's GitHub repository or download it from the Manning website.

15.1 Designing the Domain layer of a test automation system

A typical enterprise system is responsible for representing concepts of the business domain: information about the business situation. More importantly, however, it is responsible for ensuring that any external actors interacting with it through its external interfaces do so in accordance with its business rules and follow the supported use cases. For example, a flight booking system would model business domain concepts such as a flight, flight schedule, or booking. It would store information about the business situation, such as what flights are currently available, and their details. It would also ensure that any external actors, such as the travelers, don't book tickets for dates in the past or flights that don't exist, which is something that would be against its business rules.

The purpose of a test automation system, on the other hand, is to help guide the evolution of the system under test to this stage. It is also to verify the correctness of its actual behavior and ensure that the business rules it needs to obey are adhered to.

To do that effectively, a test automation system must interact with the system under test, simulating the activities of the external actors and verifying how the system under test responds. Such interactions are typically achieved through the external interfaces exposed by the system under test, such as a Web UI, a mobile app, or programmatic APIs, such as REST. However, it is a mistake to focus on the external interfaces themselves as the subjects of our acceptance tests (there will be other tests for that). Rather, external interfaces are the means for a test automation system to interact with the business logic implemented by the system under test—doors through which the tests can interact with concepts from the business domain. Note that this is similar to how the actual external actors perceive the interfaces of our enterprise systems: the reason for a traveler to use a Web UI is to book a plane ticket, not to interact with the UI for the sake of it.

Since a test automation system is developed to simulate the activities of external actors, its Domain layer focuses on modeling those activities and associating them with business domain meaning. Just like in the real world, we don't reason about the activities performed by an actual traveler in terms of sequences of meaningless clicks; neither should our acceptance tests. A real traveler would search for a flight, adjust a departure date, fill out the registration form, pick the cheapest flight, and so on.

Of course, those higher-level activities are composed of lower-level activities, which are composed of even lower-level activities, all the way to the lowest-level, interface-specific interactions like clicking on a button, entering a value into a form field, or sending an HTTP request. Nevertheless, those low-level activities are an implementation detail, the *how* of the much more important *what*, and the even more important *why*.

15.1.1   *Modeling business domain tasks*

To implement a smooth transition between the why, the what, and the how, we need to gradually decompose the higher-level tasks into lower-level ones, one layer of abstraction at a time. Consider the task to sign up that we already visualized on our journey map in chapter 14 (figure 14.12) and repeated here with additional details in figure 15.1. The goal, or the why, of this high-level task is for the actor to sign up. What the actor needs to do to accomplish that goal is represented by the three subtasks: locate the registration form, fill it out, and submit it. Successful completion of these three subtasks implies a successful completion of the main task and results in the user account created and the actor allowed to sign in. Conversely, a failure to complete the three subtasks successfully results in the user account not getting created, the actor not being allowed to sign in, and advice given on how to correct the information they provided in their registration form. The former outcome is marked in figure 15.1 as positive scenario consequences, and the latter as negative scenario consequences.

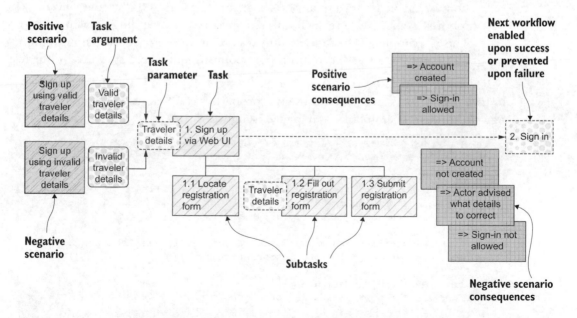

Figure 15.1   The task to sign up via Web UI allows the traveler to proceed to the sign-in workflow whenall three subtasks are completed successfully. Depending on the traveler details provided, performing the task leads to positive or negative scenario consequences.

Note that as presented in figure 15.1, the only factor that affects the outcome of the task to sign up is what traveler details the actor provides. If the actor provides valid traveler details the task is successful, and if they provide invalid details the task results in a failure.

If we were to use a functional programming analogy and think of the task to sign up as a *function*, traveler details are a *parameter* of such function, while a concrete example of valid or invalid traveler details is a *function argument*. This distinction will become useful when we discuss ways to implement Serenity/JS Screenplay Pattern tasks in the next section.

15.1.2 *Implementing business domain tasks*

Like with Serenity BDD, the easiest way to define a custom Serenity/JS Screenplay Pattern task is to use the `Task.where` API. It has the following signature:

```
Task.where(description: string, ...activities: Activity[]): Task
```

Serenity/JS Screenplay Pattern tasks are essentially aggregates of subtasks or interactions, and this method has two interesting properties that help us create such aggregates:

- It uses the rest parameter syntax (see MDN "Rest Parameters": http://mng.bz/neK2) to accept one or more "activities." This makes it easy to quickly compose tasks from subtasks or interactions.
- If activities are omitted, the method produces a `Task` object which upon execution by an actor throws an `ImplementationPendingError`, and Serenity/JS reports scenarios where such an error occurred as pending implementation. This is a simple way to define empty tasks that we're not yet sure how to implement and get a test execution report pointing out where they are in our test scenarios.

In listing 15.1, you can see how those two properties can help us implement a task to sign up and its three subtasks, as depicted in figure 15.1.

Listing 15.1   Implementing a pending task to SignUp

```
import { Task } from '@serenity-js/core'

const LocateRegistrationForm = () =>
    Task.where('#actor locates registration form')

const FillOutRegistrationForm = (travelerDetails: TravelerDetails) =>
    Task.where('#actor fills out registration form')

const SubmitRegistrationForm = () =>
    Task.where('#actor submits registration form')

const SignUp = (travelerDetails: TravelerDetails) =>
    Task.where('#actor signs up',
        LocateRegistrationForm(),
```

```
FillOutRegistrationForm(travelerDetails),
SubmitRegistrationForm(),
)
```

In listing 15.1, we use arrow function expressions, a construct you first encountered in section 14.3, to define functions producing tasks to locate registration form, fill it out, and submit it. All of which omit the list of their sub-tasks in their definition, which means they'll get reported as pending implementation. We've also defined a function producing a task to sign up, which accepts a task parameter of traveler details (presented in detail in listing 14.4).

Even though our tasks don't yet do anything meaningful, they already help us to capture business domain concepts and vocabulary, such as traveler details or signing up. This pattern of using business domain vocabulary to name tasks helps to establish consistent terminology and ubiquitous language shared by both the business and technology folk.[1]

Also, having even this rudimentary implementation in place allows us to continue with the outside-in approach to implementing our test automation system. In particular, we can already plug our task from listing 15.1 into our Cucumber step definition:

```
When('{actor} signs up using following details:',
    (actor: Actor, data: DataTable) =>
        actor.attemptsTo(
            SignUp(data.rowsHash()),
        )
);
```

At this level of abstraction, we try to avoid using any vocabulary specific to the integration interface in task names, and even the implementation of the task to sign up from listing 15.1 is still perfectly understandable to both the technology and nontechnology audience. The next step is for us to dive one level of abstraction deeper and investigate the how—a way to make the tasks perform the actual interactions with the system under test.

15.1.3   *Composing interactions into tasks*

Similar to Serenity BDD, for a Serenity/JS task to provide stimuli to the system under test it needs to delegate to an interaction. Serenity/JS interactions are low-level activities that directly invoke methods on actors' abilities. Those methods then invoke the low-level, external interface-specific integration tools, such as a Web browser driver or an HTTP client.

Serenity/JS integration modules, like `@serenity-js/web` (https://www.npmjs.com/package/@serenity-js/web) and `@serenity-js/rest` (https://www.npmjs.com/package/@serenity-js/rest) provide dozens of such low-level interactions, and in this

---

[1] Eric Evans, *Domain-Driven Design: Tackling Complexity in the Heart of Software* (Addison-Wesley Professional, 2003), pp. 32–35.

section, you'll see how to compose them into meaningful tasks. The following code shows an example implementation of the task to locate the registration form, as expressed by a composition of interactions to navigate to the home page and click on a button that says Register.

```
import { Task } from '@serenity-js/core'
import { Click, Navigate } from '@serenity-js/web'

const LocateRegistrationForm = () =>
    Task.where(`#actor locates the registration form`,
        Navigate.to('/'),
        Click.on(Form.buttonCalled('Register')),
    )
```

Note that in listing 15.2, interactions to click and to navigate come from the Serenity/JS Web module. This module is agnostic of the low-level integration tool used. More specifically, it provides a consistent abstraction that works as well with Playwright, as it does with WebdriverIO or Selenium WebDriver, even though, when used directly, those web browser integration tools offer different interfaces and programming models.

Another thing to note in listing 15.2 is the custom helper class called `Form`, which makes it easier to identify form fields of the Flying High Airlines app user interface. We'll investigate both in detail in section 15.2, when we discuss implementing the Integration layer of our test automation system.

15.1.4 *Using an outside-in approach to enable task substitution*

Before we discuss implementing the Integration layer, let's point out one more benefit of our outside-in approach: defining acceptance test tasks from the perspective of an external actor and naming the tasks to describe the business domain goal they help to accomplish, as opposed to how they do it.

When used consistently, this outside-in approach enables substituting one task for another without affecting the tests that rely on it. That is, of course, if the tasks in question accomplish the same goal. For example, it's correct to define the task to locate the registration form using two interactions, one to navigate to the home page and one to click on the registration button, as per listing 15.2. However, it would also be acceptable to define an alternative implementation using a single interaction that navigates directly to the registration page instead, which would accomplish the same goal but be a bit faster, as per the following listing.

```
import { Task } from '@serenity-js/core'
import { Navigate } from '@serenity-js/web'
```

```
const LocateRegistrationForm = () =>
  Task.where(`#actor locates the registration form`,
      Navigate.to('/register'),
  )
```

Some scenarios, however, might require us to not only replace one implementation with another altogether for performance or similar reasons, but to have several alternative implementations of a given task available simultaneously. Typically, this happens when we need to represent different means of achieving the same goal.

In those cases, it can be useful to group the alternative implementations of a given task under a single class named after the goal the task helps to accomplish. In our example, such a class could be called `LocateRegistrationForm` and have its method names indicate what makes the alternative implementations different (e.g., `LocateRegistrationForm.viaHomePage` or `LocateRegistrationForm.viaDirect-Navigation`). An example of implementing this pattern is shown in the following listing.

Listing 15.4   Grouping alternative implementations of the same task

```
import { Task } from '@serenity-js/core';
import { Click, Navigate } from '@serenity-js/web';

export class LocateRegistrationForm {
    static viaHomePage = () =>
        Task.where(`#actor locates registration form via home page`,
            Navigate.to('/'),
            Click.on(Form.buttonCalled('Register')),
        );

    static viaDirectNavigation = () =>
        Task.where(`#actor registration form via direct navigation`,
            Navigate.to('/register'),
        );
}
```

This idea of substituting one task for another that accomplishes the same goal works at all the levels of abstraction and is the foundation of blended testing, which we'll discuss next.

15.1.5   Leveraging non-UI interactions with blended testing

While Serenity/JS provides numerous mechanisms to make interacting with web interfaces easier, it's always useful to remember that, in general, interacting with web UIs tends to be considerably slower and more tricky than interacting directly with any backend services those UIs use. In this section we'll look at blended testing: interacting with different external interfaces of the system under test in a single scenario to play to their strengths.

A web-based system typically offers at least two main types of external interfaces: web UI and HTTP-based programmatic APIs, such as REST or GraphQL. Since web

UIs are optimized for the experience of a human interacting with them, they often apply user experience patterns that can make them difficult to interact with for an automated test. For example, a lengthy insurance claim form could be split across numerous pages to help the user make sense of where they are in the process. An online payment system might introduce artificial delays to help make its users feel that a transaction is more secure since it "takes longer." It is also common for UIs to use animations to make interacting with them more engaging, and so on. Each one of those patterns increases the amount of time an automated test needs to spend interacting with the UI.

In the case of the Flying High Airlines app, every traveler needs to register an account in order to use the system. It is perfectly sensible, of course, to have an automated test fill out the web-based registration form at least once to ensure that the registration process works as expected for users. However, doing so for every single scenario in our test suite to perform test data setup would be wasteful.

A better way to approach it is to leverage the registration API you might remember from figure 14.11. Using a backend API to register test user accounts will considerably speed up UI test scenarios that require a registered account but that don't particularly mind how that account gets created.

A simple convention that works quite well here is to use the When keyword and *active voice* for steps that need to demonstrate how a given step is done and use the Given keyword and *passive voice* for steps that only care about that something is done.

For example, let's take the step where the user registers an account. According to this convention, the following step describes a precondition and doesn't necessarily care about how Tracy has signed up, as long as she has signed up:

```
Given Tracy has signed up
```

On the other hand, a step describing an action and expressed using active voice demonstrates the part of the scenario we want to demonstrate:

```
When Tracy signs up
```

Since the steps are expressed using two grammatical voices, it's easy to differentiate between them when implementing their associated step definitions since they use a different Cucumber expression to match the step. The precondition step can delegate to a task registering the actor using a programmatic API, while the action step delegates to a task registering the actor via the web interface:

```
Given('{actor} has signed up', (actor: Actor) =>
    actor.attemptsTo(
        SignUp.viaApiUsing(
            notes<TravelerNotes>().get('travelerDetails'),
        ),
    ))
```

```
When('{actor} signs up', (actor: Actor) =>
    actor.attemptsTo(
        SignUp.using(
            notes<TravelerNotes>().get('travelerDetails'),
        ),
    ))
```

The implementation of the two variations of the task `SignUp` are shown in listing 15.5, where the task to `SignUp.viaApiUsing(travelerDetails)` uses HTTP interactions provided by the @serenity-js/rest module. Note that the two variations of the task `SignUp` accept a task parameter of `QuestionAdapter<T>`, which we'll talk about in section 15.1.6.

Listing 15.5   Implementing variations of a task interacting with different interfaces

```
import { Answerable, QuestionAdapter, Task } from '@serenity-js/core'
import { Send, PostRequest } from '@serenity-js/rest'
import { Ensure, equals } from '@serenity-js/assertions'

class SignUp {
  using =(travelerDetails: QuestionAdapter<TravelerDetails>) =>
    Task.where(`#actor signs up`,
      LocateRegistrationForm(),
      FillOutRegistrationForm.using(travelerDetails),
      SubmitRegistrationForm(),
    )

  viaApiUsing = (travelerDetails: QuestionAdapter<TravelerDetails>) =>
    Task.where(`#actor signs up (via API)`,
      Send.a(PostRequest.to('/api/auth/register')
         .with(travelerDetails)),
      Ensure.that(LastResponse.status(), equals(201)),
    )
}
```

It's worth noting that not all the systems provide HTTP or similar APIs that could be readily available for test automation purposes. In those cases, it's worth considering creating test-specific programmatic APIs that help with test-specific tasks, such as registering test accounts, setting up test data, or accessing information about the state of the system under test that might not be available through the user interface.

System-level tests versus component tests

When considering patterns such as blended testing when deciding on your test automation approach, it is also important to consider the extent to which the system needs to be assembled for the test to provide meaningful results and give us sufficient confidence that a given feature works as expected.

A common mistake is to execute all the acceptance tests only against a fully assembled system deployed to a production-like environment.

> **(continued)**
>
> A good alternative is to limit the level of assembly for those scenarios that don't require the entire system to be present, and can therefore be executed, for example, against a web UI connected to mock web services, or against individual web UI components rendered using a tool like Storybook, or Playwright Component Tests.

15.1.6   *Using tasks as a mechanism for code reuse*

Because the activities required to locate the registration form are encapsulated within a single task, any other tasks that rely on it, like the task to sign up, don't need to worry about its implementation details, only that it helps the actor to accomplish a mini goal of locating the registration form. Of course, if it were important to differentiate between the two ways of locating the form, we could easily capture them as two separate tasks, as per listing 15.4.

This design approach of focusing on modeling our acceptance tests using tasks at different levels of abstraction helps us make our code much easier to understand. When the names of those tasks use the same domain-specific vocabulary our audience uses, our code becomes comprehensible even for audiences not used to programming or test automation in general. Additionally, tasks make our code much easier to reuse. That's because a task to "sign up" could be plugged into any workflows that require a signed-up user, and any test reusing such a task doesn't need to worry about how that user has found the registration form, or even if they used the web browser at all. The same goes for other parts of our test automation system that need to reuse only parts of the workflow, perhaps to simulate error conditions, which we're going to discuss now.

To see how we'd go about reusing the tasks we've already written, consider the duplicate email scenario, originally described in listing 14.6, and repeated in the following listing for your convenience.

Listing 15.6   Negative scenario: Signing up using duplicate email address

```
Feature: Sign up

  Rule: Duplicate usernames are not allowed

    Scenario: Sign up using duplicate email address

      Mike Smith is an existing Frequent Flyer member.
      His wife Jenny Smith does not have a Frequent Flyer account.

      Given Mike has signed up using the following details:
        | email | smiths@example.org |
      When Jenny tries to sign up using:
        | email | smiths@example.org |
      Then she should be advised of an error: "Email exists"
```

In the first step, we want the actor called `Mike` to have a registered Frequent Flyer account so that in the next step we can verify that the business rule of not allowing duplicate email addresses is adhered to when `Jenny` tries to sign up using the same email address.

> **NOTE**   While technically speaking we could have two actors with the same email address defined in their traveler notes and not mentioned in the feature file at all, highlighting the address in the scenario itself can help to get the point across better and draw readers' attention to this key detail.

The task to sign up we defined in listing 15.1 already accepts a task parameter of `TravelerDetails`, and thus looks like a good candidate to reuse in the duplicate email scenario:

```
const SignUp = (travelerDetails: TravelerDetails) =>
    Task.where('#actor signs up',
        LocateRegistrationForm(),
        FillOutRegistrationForm(travelerDetails),
        SubmitRegistrationForm(),
    )
```

The Cucumber step definition we already have in place also allows us to pass a data table with traveler details defined in the scenario to the task to `SignUp`:

```
When('{actor} signs up using following details:',
    (actor: Actor, data: DataTable) =>
        actor.attemptsTo(
            SignUp(data.rowsHash()),
        )
)
```

However, our current step definition requires all the traveler details to be provided in one go. This is not ideal as it would seriously clutter the feature file and distract the reader from noticing the important details, not to mention the duplication of data this would cause across scenarios that require the same configuration:

```
Scenario: Sign up using valid traveler details

    When Tracy signs up using following traveler details:
        | firstName      | Tracy                              |
        | lastName       | Traveler                           |
        | email          | Tracy.Traveler@example.org         |
        | password       | P@ssw0rd                           |
        | title          | Mx                                 |
        | address        | 35 Victoria Street, Alexandria     |
        | country        | Australia                          |
        | seatPreference | window                             |
    Then she should be able to sign in
```

A better approach from both code reuse and readability perspectives is to

- Provide each actor with a data set describing the persona they're meant to represent.
- Implement our Cucumber step definitions so that they inject this default data set as task argument when invoking the task.
- Partially override the default data set in scenarios that need to simulate error conditions.

The first point can be accomplished by providing each actor with an ability to Take-Notes, which you first encountered in section 14.2.3, with necessary cast configuration repeated here:

```
class Actors implements Cast {

  constructor(
    private readonly browser: playwright.Browser,
    private readonly baseURL: string,
  ) {
  }

  prepare(actor: Actor): Actor {
    return actor.whoCan(
      BrowseTheWebWithPlaywright.using(this.browser, {
        baseURL: this.baseURL
      }),

      CallAnApi.at(this.baseURL),

      TakeNotes.using(
        Notepad.with<TravelerNotes>({
          travelerDetails: TravelerDetails.of(actor.name),
        }),
      ),
    );
  }
}
```

The TravelerDetails class, as presented originally in listing 14.4, dynamically generates valid traveler details based on the actor's name. This helps us to avoid having to specify them explicitly in our feature files:

```
export abstract class TravelerDetails {
  title: string;
  firstName: string;
  lastName: string;
  email: string;
  password: string;
  address: string;
  country: string;
  seatPreference: string;
```

```
static of(actorName: string): TravelerDetails {
  return {
    title: 'Mx',
    firstName: actorName,
    lastName: 'Traveler',
    email: `${ actorName }.Traveler@example.org`,
    password: 'P@ssw0rd',
    address: '35 Victoria Street, Alexandria', country: 'Australia',
    seatPreference: 'window'
    }
  }
}
```

However, to use the traveler details coming from an actor's notepad as task argument in our Cucumber step definition, we need to make one change to our current implementation. Right now, our task accepts a *static* and *synchronous* data structure of TravelerDetails:

```
const SignUp = (travelerDetails: TravelerDetails) => Task
```

While this is sufficient in cases where all the data is known and provided upfront, this signature is not compatible with the data returned from the Notepad. That's because the notepad uses *dynamic* and *asynchronous* data structures to allow you to work with both static and dynamic/lazy-loaded data structures simultaneously using a consistent API. To make this work, the notepad creates a proxy object called a QuestionAdapter, which wraps the returned data structure. This requires us to change the signature of our task as follows:

```
import { QuestionAdapter, Task } from '@serenity-js/core'

const SignUp = (travelerDetails: QuestionAdapter<TravelerDetails>) => Task
```

Conveniently, all built-in Serenity/JS Screenplay APIs accept static and dynamic arguments. With the task signature updated to accept a QuestionAdapter<TravelerDetails> we can now define a Cucumber step that registers the traveler using information found in their notepad:

```
When('{actor} signs up using valid traveler details', (actor: Actor) =>
  actor.attemptsTo(
    SignUp.using(
      notes<TravelerNotes>().get('travelerDetails')
    ),
  ));
```

We can also define a step that partially overrides the default details to support simulating error conditions. Here, we use Question.fromObject API, which allows us to merge static, dynamic, or partially dynamic data structures and produce a Question-Adapter:

```
import { Actor, Question } from '@serenity-js/core'
import { When, DataTable } from '@cucumber/cucumber'

When('{actor} tries to sign up using:', (actor: Actor, data: DataTable) =>
    actor.attemptsTo(
        SignUp.using(
            Question.fromObject<TravelerDetails>(
                notes<TravelerNotes>().get('travelerDetails'),
                data.rowsHash() as Partial<TravelerDetails>,
            )
        )
    ));
```

As you can see, parameterized tasks offer an excellent mechanism for code reuse, and task arguments provide an easy way to introduce variations in the workflow exercised by the tests.

Furthermore, the QuestionAdapter API allows us to reference fields and methods of the proxied object and work with it just like we would with a regular, static data structure. Any fields we reference will also get wrapped in such proxy objects recursively, providing a consistent programming model.

What this means is that we can define the task to fill out the registration form simply, as follows, referencing the relevant bits of traveler details to pass them to subtasks:

```
export const FillOutRegistrationForm =
    (travelerDetails: QuestionAdapter<TravelerDetails> | TravelerDetails) =>
      Task.where(`#actor fills out the registration form`,
        SpecifyEmailAddress(travelerDetails.email),
        SpecifyPassword(travelerDetails.password),
        SpecifySalutation(travelerDetails.title),
        SpecifyFirstName(travelerDetails.firstName),
        SpecifyLastName(travelerDetails.lastName),
        SpecifyHomeAddress(travelerDetails.address),
SpecifyCountryOfResidence(travelerDetails.country),
SpecifySeatPreference(travelerDetails.seatPreference),
ToggleNewsletterSubscription.off(),
ToggleTermsAndConditions.on(),
)
```

Implementing similar Cucumber steps

When looking for opportunities for code reuse it's important to look for both similarities and differences between the code and step definitions we've already written and those we're about to write. For example, the step to sign up using a nondefault email address is defined using a data table:

```
Given Mike has signed up using the following details:
      | email | smiths@example.org |
```

And looks very similar to the step we already have:

```
When Tracy signs up using valid traveler details
```

While the new step requires the actor to use a nondefault email address, all the other details, such as first name, last name, or seat preference, should remain at their default values.

You might have also noticed that our new step uses a Cucumber data table (http://mng.bz/vXV4) rather than the more traditional way to specify step parameters inline, such as

```
Given Mike has signed up using email address of "smiths@example.org"
```

The reason for using a data table is that it allows us to easily alter other default parameters as well, if needed, and to specify multiple overrides at the same time without having to define a separate Cucumber step for each override.

If we wanted to override other default properties as defined in `TravelerDetails`, we could expand our data table to include their names and values as well:

```
Given Mike has signed up using the following details:
  | firstName      | Michael            |
  | seatPreference | aisle              |
  | email          | smiths@example.org |
```

Using a data table rather than inline step parameters makes the step more flexible, as we can override different details depending on the scenario, without having to create more Cucumber step definitions than necessary.

15.1.7 Implementing verification tasks

One aspect of automated tests that we haven't discussed yet is how to make them verify if the actual state of the system is what we expect it to be at a given stage in the scenario. Similar to Serenity BDD, Serenity/JS also provides a Screenplay Pattern-compatible assertions library that can help with this and that is available as part of the @serenity-js/assertions module (https://www.npmjs.com/package/@serenity-js/assertions). To see how it works in practice, let's consider the duplicate email address scenario again.

In our scenario, when the actor provides registration details containing an email address that's already present in the system, the user interface shows an error message, as depicted in figure 15.2. The error message is a *toast*: a brief, temporary notification that's shown when the actor submits the form, and that disappears shortly afterward. This user experience design means that to verify the advice shown to the actor, the text of the error message, we have to do three things:

1 Trigger the error state by submitting a registration form with an email address that's already present in the system. We can do this using our task to `SignUp`, parameterized with a `TravelerDetails` argument containing a duplicate email address.

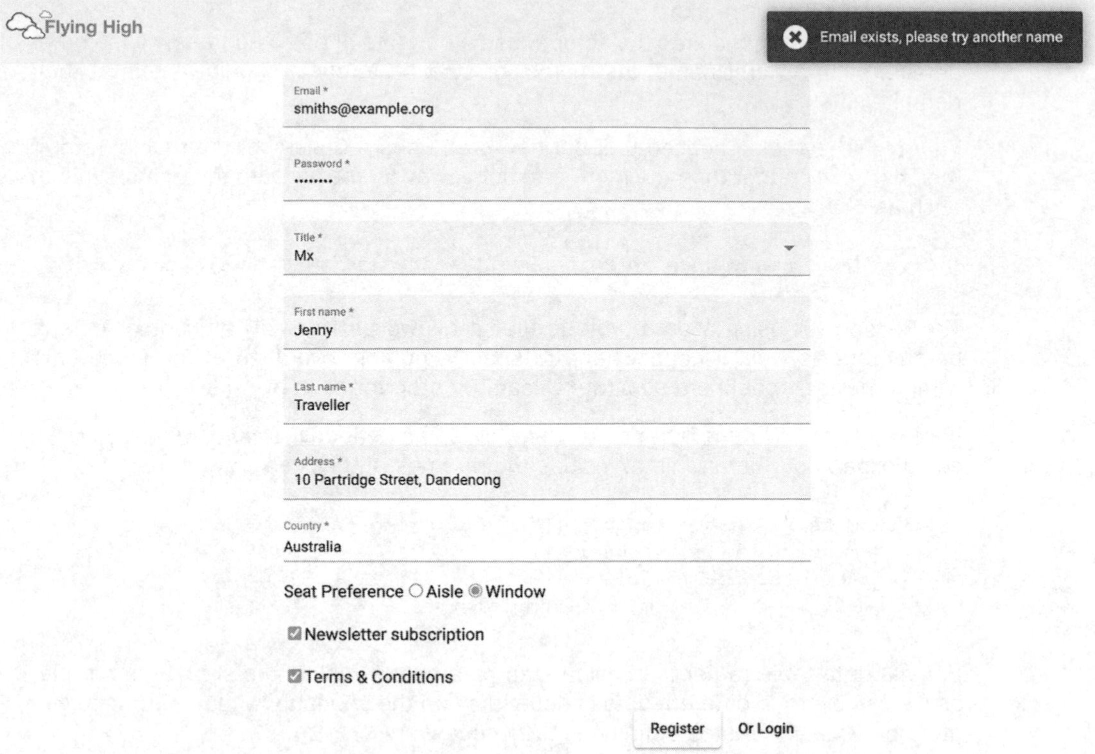

Figure 15.2   Error message displayed in the duplicate email address scenario is a brief, temporary notification displayed when the form is submitted.

2 Next, we need to wait for the error message to appear on the screen, which happens after a short animation.

3 Then, verify that the text of the message meets what we expected to see.

4 And finally, avoid having to wait for the transition animation by dismissing the message.

While we'll discuss interacting with web interfaces in detail in section 15.2, let's cover some of the basics already and look at how we can make our test scenario interact with the HTML structure generated by the toaster widget to verify its state. The HTML structure of the widget looks as follows:

```
<div class="ngx-toastr toast-error">
    <div class="toast-message">
        Email exists, please try another name
    </div>
</div>
```

Serenity/JS uses the concept of page elements to represent web elements the test scenario interacts with. A page element is identified using an element selector, such as

By.css, By.xpath, and so on, and optionally given a custom description to be used when reporting interactions with the element. We could define a page element representing the toaster message like this:

```
import { By, PageElement } from '@serenity-js/web'

const ToasterMessage = () =>
    PageElement.located(By.css(`.ngx-toastr > .toast-message`))
        .describedAs('toaster message')
```

> **NOTE** While Serenity/JS By selectors are designed to provide a similar "look and feel" to what you might be familiar with from other frameworks like Selenium WebDriver, they are integration tool agnostic. This means you can use the same page element definitions no matter the underlying integration tool you decide to use. We'll investigate this design in detail in section 15.2.2.

Now that we've defined the page element to identify the toaster message, we can use the Serenity/JS Assertions library to implement the last scenario step from listing 15.6:

```
Then she should be advised of an error: "Email exists"
```

Specifically, we'll need the following APIs:

- Wait.until to inform the actor to wait until the given expectation is met
- Ensure.that to verify that the text of the toaster message is what we expected
- Click.on to dismiss the message

If we were to use those APIs directly in our Cucumber step definition, its implementation could look as follows:

```
import { Actor, Wait } from '@serenity-js/core'
import { Click } from '@serenity-js/web'
import { Ensure, includes, isPresent, not } from '@serenity-js/assertions'

Then('{pronoun} should be advised of an error: {string}',
  (actor: Actor, expectedMessage: string) =>
    actor.attemptsTo(
      // wait for the message to appear
      Wait.until(ToasterMessage(), isPresent()),

      // verify the message
      Ensure.that(Text.of(ToasterMessage()), includes(expectedMessage)),

      // dismiss the message
      Click.on(ToasterMessage()),

      // wait for the message to disappear
      Wait.until(ToasterMessage(), not(isPresent())),
  )
)
```

However, while this implementation works, it's far from ideal as it violates the design principle we discussed in section 14.2.1, the one for the component of the specification layer (the Cucumber step definition) not to directly invoke components of the interface-specific Integration layer (the low-level web interactions). To avoid violating this design principle, we can follow the same pattern we discussed in section 15.1.3, which was to compose the low-level interactions into higher-level, business domain-specific verification tasks. Such improved implementation could look like this:

```
Then('{pronoun} should be advised of an error: {string}',
  (actor: Actor, expectedMessage: string) =>
    actor.attemptsTo(
      VerifySubmission.failedWith(expectedMessage),
  )
)
```

Such higher-level, business domain-specific verification tasks provide a great way to reflect business-specific concepts in our code; compare the clarity of "verify submission failed with an expected message" versus the low-level sequence of interactions to "wait, check, click, wait."

Another advantage of composing assertions (`Ensure.that`) and any associated synchronization statements (`Wait.until`) into higher-level tasks is that it offers a convenient mechanism for code reuse across both Cucumber steps and other tasks. Furthermore, we can apply the pattern you first encountered in listing 15.4 to gather variations of a given verification task under one class. This way we could arrive at the higher-level class representing tasks to verify submission, with two possible variations of verifying either success or failure:

```
class VerifySubmission {
  static succeededWith(expectedMessage: string): Task {
    /* … */
  }

  static failedWith(expectedMessage: string): Task {
    /* … */
  }
}
```

We can then incorporate the task to verify successful submission into the step for the actor to sign up using valid traveler details:

```
When('{actor} signs up using valid traveler details',
  (actor: Actor) =>
    actor.attemptsTo(
      SignUp.using(
        notes<TravelerNotes>().get('travelerDetails')
      ),
      VerifySubmission.succeededWith('registered successfully'),
    )
)
```

We can also use the failure case variation of our verification task in the step from listing 15.6 that checks the error message shown to the user. After all, error messages shown to the user form an important part of business communication with the customers, so it's useful to surface the acceptance criteria around them to the Specification layer:

```
Then she should be advised of an error: "Email exists"
```

To verify the error message, we can update the step definition as follows:

```
Then('{pronoun} should be advised of an error: {string}',
  (actor: Actor, expectedMessage: string) =>
    actor.attemptsTo(
      VerifySubmission.failedWith(expectedMessage),
    )
)
```

The finished implementation of the tasks to verify success or failure of the registration form submission is shown in the following listing. Here, both the tasks to verify successful and failed variation are composed of three subtasks to verify the message, its notification status (manifesting itself as a CSS class added to the widget and affecting its color), and to dismiss it.

Listing 15.7   Implementing verification tasks

```
import {
  Ensure, equals, includes, isPresent, not
} from '@serenity-js/assertions';
import { Task, Wait } from '@serenity-js/core';
import { Click, Text } from '@serenity-js/web';
import { Toaster } from './Toaster;

export class VerifySubmission {
  static succeededWith(expectedMessage: string) {
    return Task.where(`#actor confirms successful form submission`,
      VerifySubmission.hasMessage(expectedMessage),
      VerifySubmission.hasStatus('success'),
      VerifySubmission.dismissMessage(),
    );
  }

  static failedWith(expectedMessage: string) {
    return Task.where(`#actor confirms failed form submission`,
      VerifySubmission.hasMessage(expectedMessage),
      VerifySubmission.hasStatus('error'),
      VerifySubmission.dismissMessage(),
    );
  }

  private static hasMessage(message: string) {
    return Task.where(`#actor confirms notification includes ${ message }`,
      Wait.until(Toaster.message(), isPresent()),
      Ensure.that(Text.of(Toaster.message()), includes(expectedMessage)),
```

```
    );
  }

  private static hasStatus(status: 'success' | 'error') {
    return Task.where(`#actor confirms form submission ${ status }`,
      Wait.until(Toaster.message(), isPresent()),
      Ensure.that(Toaster.status(), equals(status)),
    );
  }

  private static dismissMessage() {
    return Task.where(`#actor dismisses the message`,
      Wait.until(Toaster.message(), isPresent()),
      Click.on(Toaster.message()),
      Wait.until(Toaster.message(), not(isPresent())),
    );
  }
}
```

As you might have noticed in listing 15.7, expectations from the Serenity/JS Assertions module, such as isPresent(), equals(), or includes(), are compatible and can be used together with both synchronization statements (Wait.until) and verification statements (Ensure.that). Serenity/JS uses this pattern throughout the various parts of the framework to offer a consistent programming experience whenever you need to make a decision, depending on whether an expectation is met. As you'll soon see in section 15.2, expectations are also the foundation of the Serenity/JS Page Element Query Language, which gives you a portable way to identify page elements of interest.

The second thing to note about listing 15.7 is that Serenity/JS synchronization statements, such as Wait.until(value, expectation) or Wait.for(duration), are part of the Serenity/JS Core module and are not tied to web testing. This means you can use them, for example, to keep polling a REST API until it returns a response that meets your expectation. This pattern can be useful when testing batch processing systems that process data asynchronously.

The third thing to note is that listing 15.7 references a class called Toaster, representing the toaster widget, and its two public methods, Toaster.message and Toaster.status, represent the interesting interactable elements of the widget, or the information about it, respectively. This class is called a *Lean Page Object*, and this pattern will be important for you when implementing portable web-based acceptance tests as it helps to bridge the gap between the business Domain layer and the Integration layer. Let's discuss it next.

15.2 *Designing a portable Integration layer*

The Integration layer of a test automation system is responsible for integrating it with the external interfaces of the system under test. Those typically involve web interfaces, mobile apps, or programmatic APIs, such as REST or GraphQL. However, apart from the system under test, a test automation system also needs to integrate with its test execution environment, test infrastructure, and perhaps counterintuitively, with people and processes executing the tests and analysing their results. In this section we'll discuss some of the common challenges related to those integrations and propose solutions to help you overcome them on your projects.

15.2.1 Writing portable tests for the web interfaces

Web-based testing is arguably one of the most challenging types of integration testing there is. This is partially because the scope being tested tends to be broad, particularly with the workflow-based acceptance testing. It also tends to be deep, as not every system allows for its user interface layer to be tested in isolation from the backend components, which can result in such backend components causing interference or management overhead.

Apart from that, the popular web test integration tools, like Selenium WebDriver, WebdriverIO, Puppeteer, Playwright, or Cypress, as great as they are on their own, each use different programming models and different APIs. This cross-tool incompatibility prevents test code written for one test integration tool from being used with another.

This incompatibility also becomes problematic when we want our test code to be portable across the various test suites we have for a typical system. For example, we might want to use Playwright to implement UI component tests, interacting with UI widgets running in isolation. We might also want to use Playwright as an integration tool for our smoke tests—basic workflow tests executed against a deployed system—making sure that the critical features work as intended. This tool choice tends to work well since Playwright (https://playwright.dev/) offers fast execution, good developer experience, and supports modern rendering engines.

However, a typical web-based system, especially at larger organizations, needs to support not just the modern rendering engines, but also some of the previous versions. Since this is not a use case Playwright supports, it means that for those high-level, cross-browser compatibility-focused tests we need to use a different integration tool.

Many organizations have also invested in in-house or third-party Selenium grids to centralize the management of web browsers used in the tests. In those cases, an integration tool like Selenium WebDriver or WebdriverIO is more appropriate, since thanks to their native support of the WebDriver protocol (https://www.w3.org/TR/webdriver/) they offer excellent support for running cross-browser tests on remote web browser grids.

As you might have already guessed, instead of writing numerous test suites, each tied to a specific test integration tool, a far more portable design is to introduce an abstraction layer between the integration tools and the rest of our test automation system. Such an abstraction layer can enable us to make our code portable across the lower-level integration tools, which then allows for the most appropriate integration tool to be chosen for the given context. In our example, we could use Playwright for component tests and WebdriverIO for cross-browser tests without having to change the test code. (Using both Playwright and WebdriverIO simultaneously is demonstrated in the repository with code samples for this chapter: http://mng.bz/49Yj.)

Introducing an abstraction layer between the lower-level integration tools and the rest of our test automation system also helps us to avoid integration tool lock-in. This is particularly important for the larger software projects with hundreds or thousands of tests, as it mitigates the risk of the scenario where the maintainers of a given integration tool stop to support it.[2] That's again because an Integration layer designed with portability in mind allows us to switch to an alternative integration tool without having to rewrite all the tests we already have.

For the web Integration layer to be portable, though, it needs to abstract the underlying test integration tool and provide both a programming model and APIs that can be used consistently and reliably across the various implementations. Let's now look at the portability mechanisms proposed by Serenity/JS and how you can use them to make your test automation system agnostic of the integration tool.

15.2.2   *Identifying page elements*

The Serenity/JS web module (https://serenity-js.org) provides Screenplay Pattern APIs for interacting with web interfaces. Its main abstractions relevant in the context of locating web elements are

- `Page`, modeling a Web browser tab
- `PageElement`, modeling a single web element (http://mng.bz/Qnzv)
- `PageElements`, modeling a collection of web elements and offering Page Element Query Language APIs (see section 15.2.6)
- `By` selector, providing a common abstraction around locating elements of interest using CSS or XPath queries

While Serenity/JS By selector implementations, such as `By.css`, `By.deepCss`, `By.xpath`, or `By.id`, are designed to provide a look and feel familiar to developers who used Selenium WebDriver–based frameworks, each one of them is integration tool agnostic. This means they work the same no matter the integration tool you use, since Serenity/JS translates the selectors internally to an equivalent tool-specific version.

To see how to use those abstractions in practice, let's consider the toaster widget you're already familiar with. Upon a successful registration, the toaster displays a message, as depicted in figure 15.3.

Figure 15.3   The toaster widget displaying a message confirming successful registration

---

[2] This was the case with the hugely popular Angular Protractor, which received its last commit back in 2020 and reached an official end-of-life with Angular v16, expected in the summer of 2023: https://blog.angular.io/the-state-of-end-to-end-testing-with-angular-d175f751cb9c.

The HTML structure produced by the widget and shown in listing 15.8 is almost the same as the one you're already familiar with from section 15.1.6. Here, however, the widget presents a success message, which manifests itself with a toast-success CSS class on the container element.

Listing 15.8   The toaster widget

```html
<div class="ngx-toastr toast-success">
    <div class="toast-message">
        User: alice@example.org registered successfully
    </div>
</div>
```

Serenity/JS offers two main ways to identify a specific web element, such as toast-message.

The first method is to use a By selector relative to the current browsing context, such as a browser tab or a frame within it, for example:

```js
import { By, PageElement } from '@serenity-js/web'

const ToasterMessage = () =>
    PageElement.located(By.css(`.ngx-toastr > .toast-message`))
        .describedAs('toaster message')
```

CSS selector identifies the element.

The second is to describe the page element in relation to another containing element:

```js
import { By, PageElement } from '@serenity-js/web'

const Toaster = () =>
    PageElement.located(By.css(`.ngx-toastr`))
        .describedAs(`toaster`)

const ToasterMessage = () =>
    PageElement.located(By.css(`.toast-message`))
        .of(Toaster())
        .describedAs('message')
```

Parent page element

Child page element

Establishes a relationship between the child element and the parent element

You can use both those methods together to define a chain of PageElement objects dynamically or to combine different types of selectors. This can be particularly useful when a given web element can occur multiple times on a given page and we need to differentiate between the various instances based on their containing element. Another use case for chaining PageElement objects is when the host element only becomes known at runtime and we need to inject it dynamically:

```js
import { By, PageElement } from '@serenity-js/web'

const Toaster = () =>
    PageElement.located(By.css(`.ngx-toastr`))
        .describedAs(`toaster`)
```

```
const ToasterMessage = () =>
    PageElement.located(By.css(`.toast-message`))
        .of(Toaster())
        .describedAs('message')


const NotificationsSection = () =>
    PageElement.located(By.id(`notifications`))
      .describedAs(`notifications section`)



const SpecificMessage = ToasterMessage()
    .of(NotificationsSection())
```

A hypothetical notification section hosting the toaster

A toaster message element resolved in relation to a dynamically injected host element

Of course, defining each page element individually becomes rather unwieldy fairly quickly, so let's look into structural design patterns to help us organize page elements into classes representing widgets or collections of widgets.

15.2.3   *Implementing Lean Page Objects*

As you already know from chapter 11 (section 11.3) where you learned about the Page Objects pattern, classic Page Objects have two responsibilities:

- They provide a way to locate web elements of interest.
- They also model interactions available with a given web page or widget.

Since Serenity/JS follows the Screenplay Pattern you learned about in chapter 12, the framework encourages you to place focus on the actors interacting with the system under test and uses concepts like tasks and interactions to describe how such actors go about accomplishing their goals. This means that objects representing web widgets in this world have a simplified role, and instead of modeling both the structure and behavior, Serenity/JS Lean Page Objects have a single responsibility of providing information about the widget.

An example of a Lean Page Object representing the toaster widget is shown in the following listing, where you can also see how the `QuestionAdapter` produced by the `CssClasses.of(pageElement)` API allows us to transform the low-level concept of a CSS class into a much more meaningful concept of the "success" or "error" state of the widget.

Listing 15.9   Lean Page Object representing the toaster widget

```
import { By, CssClasses, PageElement } from '@serenity-js/web'
import { QuestionAdapter } from '@serenity-js/core'

export class Toaster {
    private static component = () =>
        PageElement.located(By.css(`.ngx-toastr`))
            .describedAs('toaster')
```

```
        static message = () =>
            PageElement.located(By.css(`.toast-message`))
                .of(Toaster.component())          ◁──┐  PageElement is located
                .describedAs('message')              │  relative to another
                                                     │  page element.
        static status = () =>
  ┌─────▷  CssClasses.of(Toaster.component())
  │             .filter(cssClass => cssClass.startsWith('toast-'))        ◁──────────┐
  │             .map(cssClass => cssClass.replace('toast-', ''))                     │
  │             .slice(0, 1)[0]                                                      │
  │             .describedAs('toaster status') as QuestionAdapter<string>   ◁──┐     │
  │     }                                                                      │     │
  │                                                              Custom description to be
  │                                                                used for reporting
  QuestionAdapter wraps
  an array of CSS classes.                                       Proxied operations on an
                                                              asynchronously returned value
```

15.2.4   Implementing Companion Page Objects

Even though the Screenplay Pattern was originally proposed as an alternative to the Page Objects Pattern,[3] it can be beneficial to apply learnings from both patterns at the same time; particularly when designing test code to be shared with user interface widget libraries.

To make it easier for developers to discover test code related to a given widget, we could create test-specific companion Page Objects shipped in the same module as the widget. Such companion Page Objects provide test methods that interact with the widget and return information about its state. Additionally, we could restructure the original code from listing 15.9 to allow for the host element to be injected by the caller to make our design more flexible.

This implementation, as shown in the following listing, looks similar to regular Page Objects. The important difference, however, is that all the methods of the companion Page Object return tasks and question adapters to make it easy to compose their results into higher-level types.

Listing 15.10   Companion Page Objects

```
import { By, Click, CssClasses, PageElement } from '@serenity-js/web'
import { QuestionAdapter, Task, Wait } from '@serenity-js/core'
import { isPresent, not } from '@serenity-js/assertions'

export class Toaster {
  constructor(private readonly hostElement: QuestionAdapter<PageElement>) {}

  message = () =>
    PageElement.located(By.css(`.toast-message`))
      .of(this.hostElement).describedAs('message');
```

---

[3] Antony Marcano, Andy Palmer, John Ferguson Smart, and Jan Molak. "Page Objects Refactored: SOLID Steps to the Screenplay Pattern" 2016, https://dzone.com/articles/page-objects-refactored-solid-steps-to-the-screenp.

```
    status = () =>
      CssClasses.of(this.hostElement)
        .filter(cssClass => cssClass.startsWith('toast-'))
        .map(cssClass => cssClass.replace('toast-', ''))
        .slice(0, 1)[0]
        .describedAs('toaster status') as QuestionAdapter<string>

  dismissMessage = () =>
    Task.where(`#actor dismisses the message`,
      Wait.until(this.message(), isPresent()),
      Click.on(this.message()),
      Wait.until(this.message(), not(isPresent())),
    )
}
```

15.2.5 *Implementing portable interactions with Page Elements*

As Simon Stewart, creator of Selenium WebDriver, once said: "If you have WebDriver APIs in your test methods, you're doing it wrong." What he was pointing out is that directly invoking the low-level APIs of your web interface integration tool in your tests makes those tests brittle and difficult to maintain.

Simon's proposed solution was to apply design patterns that help to encapsulate such low-level API calls and hide them behind domain-friendly abstractions; we've looked at several such patterns in chapter 11. Serenity/JS takes this idea of abstracting the low-level API calls one step further, which enables you to abstract the entire web interface integration tool by providing a set of standardized web interaction interfaces (while still allowing access to the low-level APIs, if needed). What this means in practice is that with Serenity/JS acting as an abstraction layer around the lower-level integration tools, such as Selenium WebDriver, WebdriverIO, Playwright, and others, your tests can become agnostic of both the subtle and the not-so-subtle differences between those tools while remaining compatible with all of them.

To enable this, the Serenity/JS Web interaction module, @serenity-js/web, provides a set of Screenplay Pattern–compatible abstractions, such as the interactions that enable your actors to interact with the system under test. Those interactions include `Navigate.to(url)`, `Click.on(element)`, `Scroll.to(element)`, or `Enter.the(value)` `.into(input)`, among others.

The web module also provides Screenplay questions about `Text.of(element)`, `Value.of(input)`, or `CssClasses.of(element)`. Just like the interactions, those APIs provide an integration tool-agnostic way to get information about the state of the system through its web interface.

Serenity/JS web interactions and questions are designed for functional composition with `PageElement` objects you've learned about in section 15.2.2. For example, to click on the toaster message element, we'd compose the interaction to `Click` with a page element representing the toaster message:

```
Click.on(Toaster.message())
```

To retrieve the text of the `Toaster.message()` from listings 15.9 and 15.10, we'd compose the question about text with one about the page element:

```
Text.of(Toaster.message())
```

Note that just like `PageElement` API returns a `QuestionAdapter<PageElement>`, `Text.of` API returns a `QuestionAdapter<string>`, both compatible with the verification task to `Ensure`:

```
Ensure.that(Toaster.message(), isPresent())
Ensure.that(Text.of(Toaster.message()), includes('registered
➥ successfully'))
```

15.2.6 *Using Page Element Query Language to describe complex UI widgets*

One of the challenges particularly related to automating tests interacting with complex web interfaces is finding the right selector to allow us to uniquely identify the interactable element of interest, ideally one that we don't have to change with every slightest change of the web UI. As you already saw in chapter 10, tools like Selenium provide a number of basic locator strategies such as `By.id`, `By.css`, or `By.xpath`. Since Serenity/JS Web module is an abstraction layer around Selenium WebDriver, WebdriverIO, Playwright, and other web integration tools, it supports those basic locator strategies as well. Apart from that, it also provides an integration tool-agnostic Page Element Query Language that is useful when automating interactions with the more sophisticated web interfaces.

To put this in context, consider the registration form of the Flying High Airlines app, built using the popular Angular Material framework (https://material.angular.io/) and shown in figure 15.4.

Let's pretend for a moment that our web UI doesn't offer any test-friendly HTML identifiers (such as the `data-test-id` attributes), and instead we need to find an input element based on the text of its label. While ideally you should be able to alter the interface of the system under test to add those friendly test identifiers, this might not always be possible or desirable.

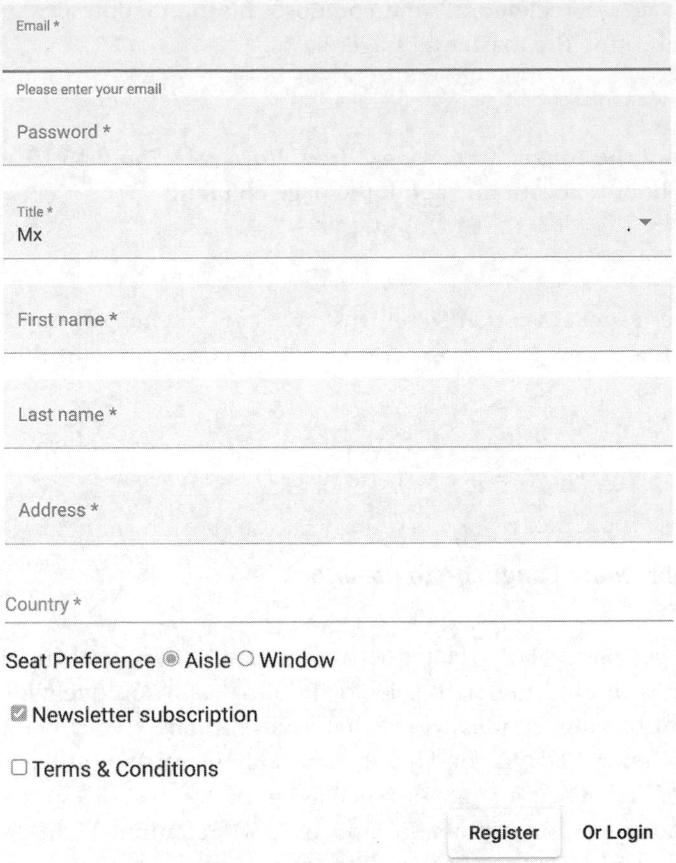

Email *

Please enter your email

Password *

Title *
Mx

First name *

Last name *

Address *

Country *

Seat Preference ⦿ Aisle ○ Window

☑ Newsletter subscription

☐ Terms & Conditions

Register   Or Login

Figure 15.4   Flying High account registration form

To better understand how the Page Element Query Language could help us with this task, let's first look at one of the form field widgets of the registration form from figure 15.4 (see figure 15.5).

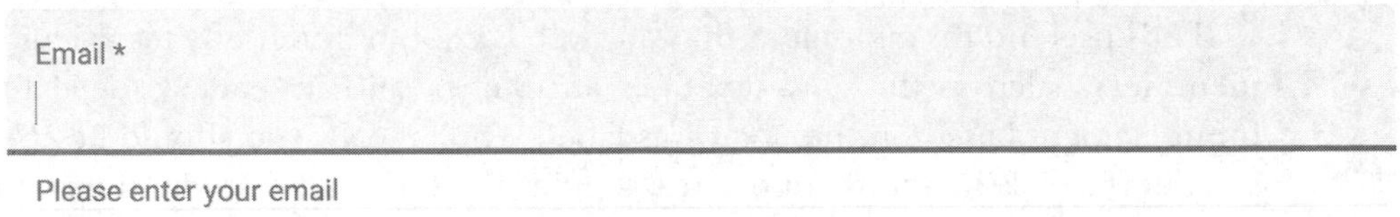

Email *

Please enter your email

Figure 15.5   Flying High account registration form field widget

The HTML structure generated for this widget, rendered in figure 15.5 and that you can inspect in your web browser developer tools (using Chrome DevTools to inspect an element: https://developer.chrome.com/docs/devtools/open/), looks as follows (some of the CSS classes not relevant in the example were removed):

```
<mat-form-field>
    <div class="mat-form-field-wrapper">
        <div class="mat-form-field-flex">
            <div class="mat-form-field-infix">
                <input name="email">
                <span>
                    <label for="email" aria-owns="email">
                        <mat-label>Email</mat-label>
                    </label>
                </span>
            </div>
        </div>
        <div>
            <mat-error>Please enter your email</mat-error>
        </div>
    </div>
</mat-form-field>
```

Since we want to find an input field by text displayed in its `<label>` element, we first define how to identify form fields in general. In our example, a form field widget generated with angular material uses a custom HTML tag called `mat-form-field`.

We define *form fields* as all the page elements with this tag name, using the `Page-Elements` API you first encountered in section 15.2.2:

```
import { PageElements, By } from '@serenity-js/web'

class Form {
    public static fields = () =>
        PageElements.located(By.css('mat-form-field'))
            .describedAs('form fields')
    // ...
}
```

Next, we describe how to identify an individual label, which the angular material UI renders using another custom HTML tag, `mat-label`:

```
import { PageElement, By } from '@serenity-js/web'

class Form {
    public static label = () =>
        PageElement.located(By.css('mat-label'))
            .describedAs('label')
    // …
}
```

Those two building blocks are enough for us to define a method, `Form.field-Called(name)`, that finds a form field with the desired label text. This method uses the Page Element Query Language, which relies on the same expectations you use to define assertion, synchronization, and flow-control clauses, and which you can extend with your own expectations and questions:

```
import { Text } from '@serenity-js/web'
import { isPresent, equals } from '@serenity-js/assertions'

class Form {
    private static fieldCalled = (name: string) =>
        Form.fields()
            .where(Form.label(), isPresent())
            .where(Text.of(Form.label()), equals(name))
            .first()
    // ...
}
```

Find fields with a label.

Find fields where the label has the desired text.

Return the first element that meets our expectations.

When the correct field is identified, referencing its `<input>` element becomes trivial, since we can use the `.of` API you know from section 15.2.2:

```
class Form {
    // ...
    static inputFor = (name: string) =>
        Form.input()
            .of(Form.fieldCalled(name))
            .describedAs(`the "${ name }" field`)
}
```

And with the `Form` class providing an easy way to identify the fields of interest, tasks such as the one to `SpecifyEmailAdress` you saw earlier become simple one-liners:

```
export const SpecifyEmailAddress = (emailAddress: Answerable<string>) =>
    Task.where(`#actor specifies their email address`,
        Enter.theValue(emailAddress).into(Form.inputFor('Email')))
```

The completed implementation of the Form class is shown in the following listing.

Listing 15.11   Completed Form class using Page Element Query Language

```
import { matches, includes, isPresent } from '@serenity-js/assertions'
import { By, PageElement, PageElements, Text } from '@serenity-js/web'

export class Form {
    static buttonCalled = (name: string) =>
        Form.buttons()
            .where(Text, includes(name))
            .first()
            .describedAs(`the "${ name }" button`)

    static inputFor = (name: string) =>
        Form.input()
            .of(Form.fieldCalled(name))
            .describedAs(`the "${ name }" field`)

    static errorMessageFor = (name: string) =>
        Text.of(
            Form.errorMessage()
                .of(Form.fieldCalled(name))
```

```
                .describedAs(`the error message for "${ name }" field`)
        )

    private static fieldCalled = (name: string) =>
        Form.fields()
            .where(Form.label(), isPresent())
            .where(Text.of(Form.label()), matches(new RegExp(name, 'i')))
            .first()

    public static buttons = () =>
        PageElements.located(By.css('button'))
            .describedAs('buttons');

    public static fields = () =>
        PageElements.located(By.css('mat-form-field'))
            .describedAs('form fields');

    public static label = () =>
        PageElement.located(By.css('label > mat-label, label > span'))
            .describedAs('label')

    private static input = () =>
        PageElement.located(By.css('input'))

    private static errorMessage = () =>
        PageElement.located(By.css('mat-error'));
}
```

Now that you know how to identify page elements, organize them into more meaningful structures using patterns like Lean and Companion Page Objects, and interact
with them using Serenity/JS APIs, let's dive a bit deeper to understand how the integration between Serenity/JS and test integration tools like Playwright or WebdriverIO
work under the hood.

15.2.7 Configuring web integration tools

As you already know, the @serenity-js/web module provides Screenplay Pattern APIs,
allowing the actors to interact with the web interface of the system under test. The
module itself, however, does not depend on, nor interact directly with, any test integration tools such as Playwright, Selenium WebDriver, WebdriverIO, and so on. Instead, it
follows the service provider framework architecture.[4] This means that it relies on
other Serenity/JS modules, such as @serenity-js/playwright or @serenity-js/webdriverio,
to provide implementations of concepts such as Page or PageElement, and to integrate with their respective test tools.

However, you wouldn't invoke classes like WebdriverIOPage or PlaywrightPage-
Element provided by those modules directly in your tests. Instead, you'd use service
access APIs like Page.current() or PageElement.located(By.css('.selector')) to

---

[4] Joshua Bloch, *Effective Java*, 2nd edition (Addison-Wesley, 2008).

obtain an instance of a given service class appropriate to your current execution context. This mechanism is what allows your tests and test automation systems based on Serenity/JS to be agnostic of the underlying test integration tool and portable across the various implementations.

But how does Serenity/JS know what test integration tool to use if all your test code is test integration tool agnostic? There's one part that isn't, and that part is the tool-specific implementation of the ability to `BrowseTheWeb`, such as `BrowseTheWeb-WithWebdriverIO` or `BrowseTheWebWithPlaywright`, that you first encountered in chapter 14 (section 14.2.2). This tool-specific implementation provided when you configure your `Cast` of Serenity/JS actors is what's responsible for instantiating an appropriate version of service classes such as `Page` or `PageElement`, interacting with the test integration tool, and providing a consistent API:

```
import { actorCalled, configure, Cast } from '@serenity-js/core'
import { BrowseTheWebWithPlaywright } from '@serenity-js/playwright'
import * as playwright from 'playwright'

const browser: playwright.Browser = await playwright.chromium.launch()    ◁─────┐
                                                                    Obtains an
configure({                                                  instance of the test
  actors: Cast.whereEveryoneCan(                               integration tool
    BrowseTheWebWithPlaywright.using(browser)
  )
})

actorCalled('William').attemptsTo(
  Click.on(PageElement.located(By.css('.selector'))),    ◁────  Tool-agnostic
)                                                               interaction and
                                                               PageElement
Uses a tool-specific version of
the ability to BrowseTheWeb
```

To see for yourself how Serenity/JS Web module and its associated tool-specific plugins enable the same test code to be executed with both WebdriverIO and Playwright, explore the code repository for this chapter.

15.2.8 *Sharing test code across projects and teams*

The consistent Screenplay Pattern APIs, with first-class support for the asynchronous nature of JavaScript, as well as a test integration tool-agnostic programming model, allow for the test automation code based on Serenity/JS to be easily reused across the various test suites a software system might have. However, those characteristics of consistency, portability, and predictability can help you solve a common organizational problem too.

More specifically, a common model for software delivery organizations working on large-scale projects is to have dedicated teams responsible for developing shared components. Those shared components, such as the web UI widgets or REST APIs, are then used by consumer teams as building blocks to be assembled into software systems. This organizational pattern is prevalent, for example, among companies that build dashboard-based apps and have central component teams producing UI widgets and supporting backend services to ensure a consistent look and feel across all such dashboards.

A common problem in this model, however, is that even though the component teams might have automated the testing of their work product to the highest possible standard, consumer teams typically don't benefit from that at all when writing their end-to-end tests interacting with such shared components. Furthermore, consumer teams typically end up with a substantial amount of additional work as they must discover for themselves how to make their tests work with the shared components or what selectors to use to locate the interesting elements of a web UI widget. What's worse, consumer teams need to keep their higher-level tests in sync with any changes introduced by the component teams to the structure or behavior of their UI widgets or supporting services.

The problem here is not just the duplication of code and effort. There's also the inherent risk of component teams unknowingly breaking other teams' tests when they introduce changes to the shared components. This typically happens when a UI component team changes the HTML structure of their component, or an API team changes the shape of some data structure supported by their API. While you could mitigate the latter to a degree with contract tests, the problem of duplicated code and effort remains.

Assuming the teams involved are comfortable with using a JavaScript-compatible language (like TypeScript) to implement both the component-level and higher-level tests, the programming model and code reuse patterns like Companion Page Objects and Screenplay tasks can offer a solution to this problem. To use it in our scenario, component teams would need to publish the Serenity/JS-based test code they've already used to test the components independently and make it easy for the consumer teams to associate such test code with the version of the component it is appropriate for. A mechanism that works well for sharing UI widget-related test code is to publish it as part of the same Node module used to ship the widgets, but under a separate entry point to avoid interference of shared test code with production code.

Summary

- In automated acceptance testing, external interfaces of the system under test are the means for a test automation system to interact with the business logic, not the focus.
- Tasks are aggregates of subtasks or interactions.
- Task parameters enable variations in the consequences of a task.
- A task argument is the concrete value of a task parameter (e.g., if traveler details are a task parameter, a concrete example of valid traveler details passed to a task is a task argument).
- Interactions are low-level activities, directly invoking methods on actor's abilities.

- The outside-in approach enables task substitution, substituting one task for another that accomplishes the same goal.
- Blended testing is an approach that helps leverage non-UI interactions in otherwise UI-focused workflow tests.
- Serenity/JS Page Element Query Language offers a reusable and portable alternative to low-level element selectors, like XPath.
- Serenity/JS Lean Page Objects define the intractable elements of a web UI widget, together with their descriptions.
- Companion Page Objects are a Screenplay Pattern–style variation of the Page Objects pattern, designed to support cross-project test code reuse for Web UI widget libraries.
- The service provider framework architecture followed by the @serenity-js/web module enables your test automation systems based on Serenity/JS to be agnostic of the underlying test integration tool, like Playwright or WebdriverIO.
- All Serenity/JS APIs are compatible with native JavaScript Promises and offer a first-class support for the asynchronous nature of the language.
- Serenity/JS offers a consistent and easy-to-learn programming model, you can use as a foundation to enable code reuse across projects and teams.
- The best way to learn Serenity/JS is to try it out! Experiment with the example test automation system in this chapter's repository to learn more.

Living documentation and release evidence

This chapter covers

- What we mean by "living documentation"
- Keeping track of project progress using feature readiness and feature coverage
- Organizing your living documentation
- Technical living documentation

In this chapter, we focus on an important part of BDD that you need to understand if you're to get the most out of whatever BDD strategy you adopt. You've seen how BDD encourages teams to express requirements in terms of executable specifications that can be run in the form of automated tests. These executable specifications become the definitive reference (often referred to as the "source of truth") for the current set of application requirements. The definitive form of these executable specifications is generally source code, so they fit neatly into the overall development process and drive the automated tests. The reports generated by the automated tests refer to the original executable specifications. These reports, which combine the original specifications, acceptance criteria, and test results, are what we call *living documentation*.

Living documentation is a key part of the BDD process. Business stakeholders can use it to review what a feature does and confirm that it corresponds to business needs and constraints. Testers can use it as a starting point for exploratory testing, saving time in routine manual testing of basic features. And developers can use it to understand what an existing feature does and how it works.

Many organizations also use the business-readable test reports produced as part of a BDD process to document what features go into a particular release, what business rules they relate to, and how they were tested. This may simply be for communication with stakeholders or might be required for audit or compliance purposes. We often call living documentation reports produced for this purpose *released evidence*. In this chapter you will learn how to generate and organize effective living documentation and see some of the tools and techniques you can use to streamline your own projects.

16.1   *Living documentation: A high-level view*

BDD reports don't simply provide a list of test outcomes, in terms of passing or failing tests. First, BDD reports document and describe what the application is expected to do, and they report whether the application performs these operations correctly. When you drill into the details, a BDD report also illustrates how a particular feature or functionality is performed, from the user's perspective.

A living document is a document that is always up to date and that always reflects the current state of the system. When we write feature files in collaboration with customers or product owners, we are creating executable specifications. When we automate these specifications using tools like Cucumber, they become living documentation. The term *living documentation* can refer to the feature files themselves (assuming they are automated and executed) or the test reports that are generated when the tests are executed.

Living documentation targets a broad audience (see figure 16.1). You've seen how BDD encourages teams to collaborate to define acceptance criteria in the form of concrete examples, scenarios, and executable specifications, and how these guide the development and delivery of the features being built. As features are delivered, the living documentation ties the features back to the original requirements, confirming that what was delivered corresponds to what the team originally discussed.

In this way, BDD reporting completes the circle that started with the initial conversations with business stakeholders. The stakeholders, business analysts, testers, and anyone else who participated in the conversations leading up to the scenarios and executable specifications see the conversations they had and the examples they discussed appear as part of the generated reports. This feedback loop is a great way to get buy-in from business stakeholders, who are often much more keen to contribute actively when they see the results of their contributions verbatim in the living documentation. In addition, because the reports are generated automatically from

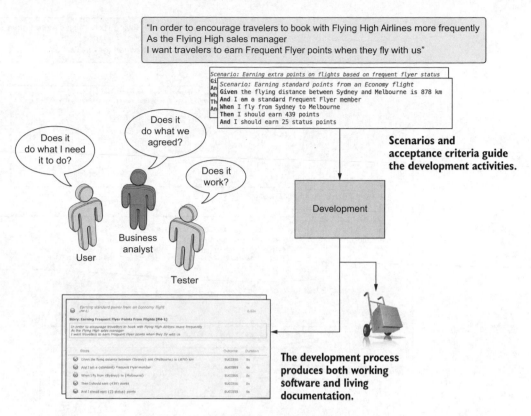

Figure 16.1 Living documentation provides feedback to the whole team, in particular to business analysts, testers, and business stakeholders. Living documentation can refer to feature files when they are executed and to the reports that are generated as a result of this execution.

the automated acceptance criteria, it's a fast and efficient way of providing feedback once it's set up (see figure 16.2).

Testers also use the living documentation to complement their own testing activities, to understand how features have been implemented, and to get a better idea of the areas in which they should focus their exploratory testing.

The benefits of living documentation shouldn't end when a project is delivered. When organized appropriately, living documentation is also a great way to bring new team members up to speed not only with what the application is supposed to do, but also how it does it. For organizations that hand over projects to a different team once they go into production, the benefits of this alone can be worth the time invested in setting up the living documentation.

But living documentation goes beyond describing and illustrating the features that have been built. Many teams also integrate their BDD reports with Agile project management or issue-tracking systems, making it possible to focus on the state of the fea-

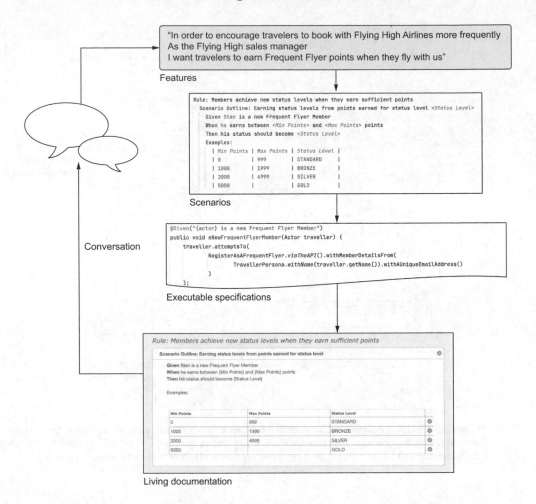

Figure 16.2   Living documentation is generated automatically from the executable specifications, which simplifies reporting and accelerates the feedback cycle.

tures planned for a particular release. Teams that do this typically rely on the living documentation to produce their release reports if they aren't generated automatically from the BDD reports.

   In the rest of this chapter, we'll look at some of these different aspects of living documentation in more detail. I'll illustrate many of the principles using Serenity reports and a few other similar tools, but the principles aren't specific to any particular tool set.

16.2   *Reporting on feature readiness and feature coverage*

One of the core concepts in BDD is something we call *feature readiness*. Features, in this sense, are just pieces of functionality that the stakeholders care about. Some teams use user stories in this role, and others prefer to distinguish user stories from higher-level features. The principle is the same in both cases: when the development team reports on progress, stakeholders are less interested in which individual tests pass or fail and are more interested in what functionality is ready to be deployed to production.

16.2.1 *Feature readiness: What features are ready to deliver*

In BDD terms, a feature can be considered ready (or done) when all of its acceptance criteria pass (see figure 16.3). If you can automate each of these acceptance criteria, then the automated test reports can give you a simple, concise view of the state of the features you're building. At this level, you're more interested in the overall result of all the scenarios associated with a feature than with whether individual scenarios pass or fail.

Most BDD tools provide at least some level of reporting on feature readiness, where scenario results are aggregated at the feature level. For example, Serenity provides feature-level reports directly from the underlying Cucumber feature files, as well as a concise, emailable version of this summary report that can be sent out to team members and key stakeholders (see figure 16.3).

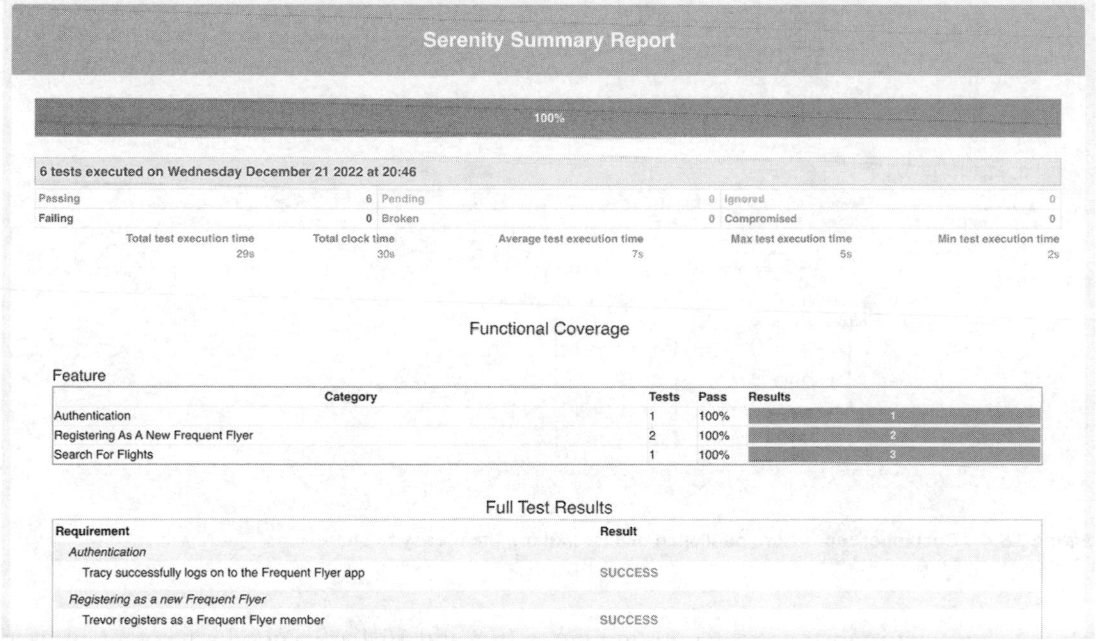

Figure 16.3   A Serenity BDD report providing a summary of the test results, organized by requirements

Standard Cucumber provides only basic feature reporting out of the box, but Smart-Bear, the company behind Cucumber, does propose a free online reporting service called Cucumber Reports (https://cucumber.io/blog/open-source/cucumber-reports/) that you can use to publish and share reports about any Cucumber tests online.

In figure 16.4, for example, you can see a feature report for a Cucumber project, generated using the `Cucumber Reports` library. In these reports the status of each feature is reported based on the overall result of the corresponding scenarios.

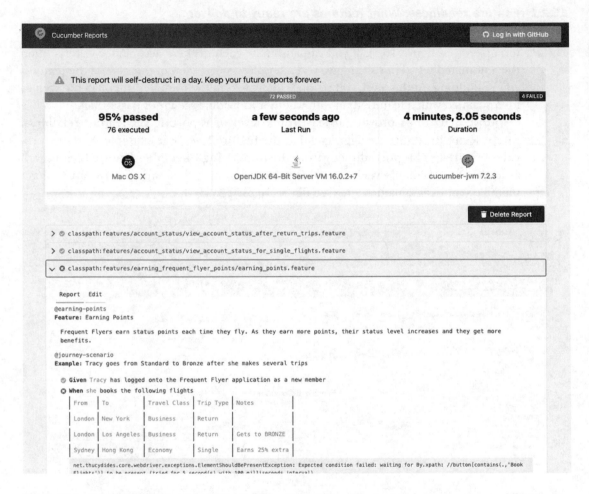

Figure 16.4 **Cucumber reports are published online, making them easy to share.**

Succinct reports like the ones in figures 16.3 and 16.4 are a good way to get an overview of the current state of the features under development, without drowning in the details of each scenario.

> **Generating Cucumber reports in your Cucumber project**
>
> You can activate this reporting in any Cucumber project (including one running with Serenity BDD) in several different ways:
>
> - By setting the `CUCUMBER_PUBLISH_ENABLED` environment variable to `true`
> - By creating a file called cucumber.properties in src/test/resources and setting the `cucumber.publish.enabled` property to `true`
> - By setting the publish property in the `@CucumberOptions` annotation to `true` in your test runner class
>
> Often it is useful to only generate and publish these reports as part of a continuous integration build job, so using the environment variable is generally the most common option.

16.2.2 *Feature coverage: What requirements have been built*

Feature-readiness reporting can go beyond simply aggregating conventional automated test results. Ideally, feature readiness should also take into account requirements that haven't been implemented and for which no automated tests exist. We'll call this more comprehensive form of feature readiness *feature coverage*.

Feature coverage tells you how many acceptance criteria have been defined and automated for each requirement. It also tells you what requirements have no automated acceptance criteria.

For example, suppose we want to allow confirmed users to log in to their Frequent Flyer accounts. Users can either register using a registration form or sign in via SSO using a third party such as Google or Facebook. However, for the current release, we only want to implement registration via the registration form. We could write a feature file to represent this requirement, along the following lines.

Listing 16.1   The Authentication feature file

```
Business Need: Authentication

    Registered Frequent Flyer members can access their account using their
➡ email and password

    Rule: 1) Frequent Flyers can authenticate by entering their credentials
➡ on the login page
```

This scenario is fully defined. ⊳
```
      Scenario: Trevor successfully logs on to the Frequent Flyer app
        Given Trevor has registered as a Frequent Flyer member
        And he has confirmed his email address
        Then he should be able to log on to the Frequent Flyer application

    Rule: 2) Frequent Flyers can sign in with SSO using their Google or
➡ Facebook account
      Example: Trevor logs in using his Google credentials
      Example: Trevor logs in using his Facebook credentials
```
These scenarios are listed as acceptance criteria but haven't been implemented.

Notice how the last two examples are empty? Cucumber allows us to define empty scenarios or examples like these ones to indicate that they have not been implemented.

In figure 16.5, you can see this in action. All of the implemented automated acceptance criteria in the Authentication feature pass. However, the feature coverage metric is only around 33% because two of the three scenarios remain to be implemented, so although all of the tests are green, this feature is only around one-third complete.

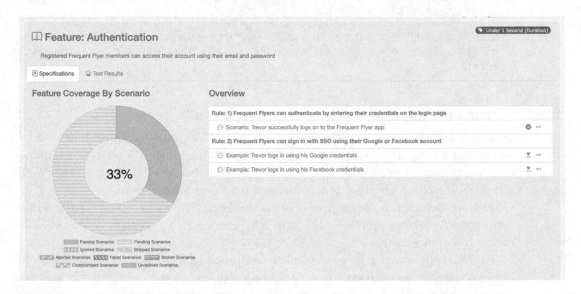

Figure 16.5   Incomplete scenarios are counted as "pending" in a feature coverage report.

Feature coverage isn't the same as code coverage. Traditional code coverage reports how many lines of code were exercised during the unit and integration tests. Code coverage can be a useful metric to tell developers what parts of the code base have not been well tested. However, code coverage can't tell you whether an application has been tested effectively or whether the application does what it is supposed to do, only how much code was executed during the automated tests.

The idea behind feature coverage is to give a fairer overall picture of project progress than you'd get by just reporting on test results. Feature coverage reports from the point of view of the requirements that have been defined rather than the tests that have been executed. Of course, there's a caveat: a feature coverage report will only be as thorough as the number of overall requirements it knows about. As you've seen, BDD practitioners, and Agile projects in general, avoid defining more detailed requirements up front than necessary. Stories and scenarios will typically be available for the current iteration, but not for much more; beyond that, the product backlog will typically contain higher-level features and Epics.

To produce this sort of high-level report, the BDD reporting tool needs knowledge about the application requirements beyond what can be obtained from the test reports. Test results can tell you what features were tested, but they can't tell you which features have no tests at all. One popular way to achieve this is to integrate the BDD reporting process with a digital product backlog.

16.3   *Integrating a digital product backlog*

In Agile projects, task boards are frequently used to keep track of project activity. A *task board* is a physical board or wall containing index cards that represent user stories, tasks, bug fixes, and other activities the team must undertake to complete the project. You can see a simple example in figure 16.6.

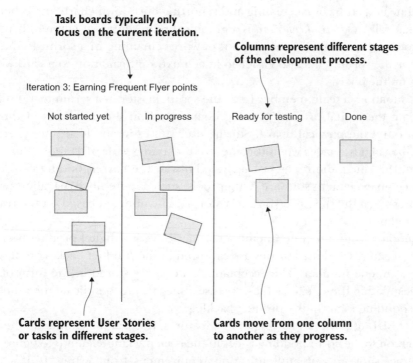

Task boards typically only focus on the current iteration.

Columns represent different stages of the development process.

Iteration 3: Earning Frequent Flyer points

| Not started yet | In progress | Ready for testing | Done |

Cards represent User Stories or tasks in different stages.

Cards move from one column to another as they progress.

Figure 16.6   A task board is a visual representation of the activities currently going on in a project.

The exact layout of a task board is very flexible and is generally different for each team and project, but the general principle is always the same. During an initial planning session, work is broken down into the user stories, tasks, and so on that need to be delivered during the current iteration. Each task or user story goes in a column on the board, based on its status (not started, in progress, done, etc.). Each day, team members get together in front of the task board to discuss the status of the task they're working on, possibly moving the cards from one column to another. The main advantage of this format is to let the whole team see at a glance what everyone is working on, making it easier to coordinate work and troubleshoot blockages.

Physical boards are excellent communication facilitators, and they provide great visibility for the current work in progress. But they do have their limitations. For example, they aren't optimal for teams that aren't co-located, they can be time-consuming to maintain, and there are many useful metrics that can be more easily tracked and visualized if the tasks are recorded electronically.

Because of these constraints, some teams prefer to keep track of work in some sort of issue-tracking or Agile project-management system, even if they still use a physical board for day-to-day organization and visibility. Some practitioners refer to this as a digital product backlog. This is the term we'll use going forward (because it's a lot easier to say than "Agile project-management software"). A digital product backlog can save you time and effort by calculating and reporting burndown charts and other metrics automatically. (A *burndown chart* is a graphical representation commonly used in Scrum projects that compares the amount of work remaining in a sprint to the work planned for the sprint.) It's also easier to attach extra information to a card without cluttering up the board.

In this situation, a team member (e.g., the scrum master in a scrum team) will typically update the digital product backlog items based on the outcomes of the daily meeting around the physical board. Storing user stories in an electronic system also has a number of advantages when it comes to integrating with BDD tools. In the simplest form, this integration may just include links to the corresponding card in the Agile project-management software. Other tools, such as Serenity BDD, allow two-way integration so that the state of a JIRA user story can be updated based on the result of the executed test.

One simple way to integrate Cucumber scenarios with a digital product backlog is to use tags. Features and user stories are captured in the product backlog tool, where they have a unique number. The acceptance criteria are stored in the form of BDD feature files. Within these feature files, you use a specific tag to indicate the number of the corresponding items in the product backlog.

Serenity BDD uses the `@Issue` tag to link features, rules, and examples in the living documentation to the corresponding issues in the issue tracking system (see figure 16.7). For example, suppose our authentication requirement from listing 16.1 is represented by a JIRA Epic FHFF-3, which contains two user stories (FHFF-1 and FHFF-4) that represent the two rules. We could add these annotations to the feature file from listing 16.1, to link the features, rules, and examples to the corresponding JIRA issues, as shown here:

```
@Issue:FHFF-3                    ◄───  Links the feature as
Business Need: Authentication          a whole to the JIRA
                                       Epic FHFF-3

Registered Frequent Flyer members can access their account using their
➥ email and password
```

```
@Issue:FHFF-1
Rule: 1) Frequent Flyers can authenticate by entering their credentials
  on the login page
    Example: Trevor successfully logs on to the Frequent Flyer app
      Given Trevor has registered as a Frequent Flyer member
      And he has confirmed his email address
      Then he should be able to log on to the Frequent Flyer application

@Issue:FHFF-4
Rule: 2) Frequent Flyers can sign in with SSO using their Google or
  Facebook account
    Example: Trevor logs in using his Google credentials
    Example: Trevor logs in using his Facebook credentials
```

Links the first rule to JIRA User Story FHFF-1

Links the second rule to JIRA User Story FHFF-4

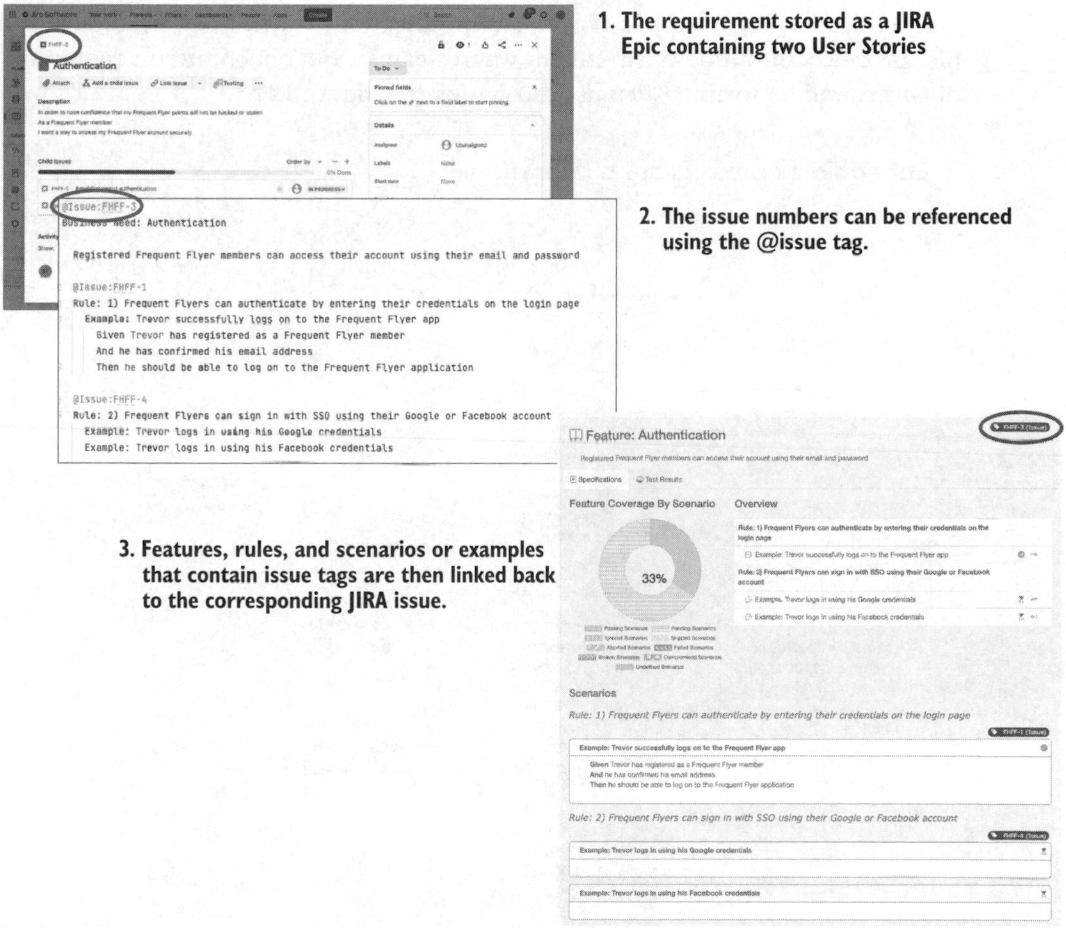

1. The requirement stored as a JIRA Epic containing two User Stories

2. The issue numbers can be referenced using the @issue tag.

3. Features, rules, and scenarios or examples that contain issue tags are then linked back to the corresponding JIRA issue.

Figure 16.7   Linking JIRA issues to feature files in a Serenity BDD report

NOTE You can configure Serenity BDD and Serenity JS to include links to JIRA issues by specifying the jira.url property in the serenity.conf file: jira.url =https://myorg.atlassian.net.

16.4 *Leveraging product backlog tools for better collaboration*

One of the disadvantages of the Gherkin format as a collaboration tool is that the feature files need to be stored in a version control system (such as Git). While it is relatively easy to publish living documentation using reporting tools such as Serenity BDD, writing and editing the feature files themselves is still more convenient to do in a development environment.

This can create a barrier for nondevelopers, who find it harder to collaborate on writing or updating the executable specifications. Some commercial tools, such as Cucumber Studio and Behave Pro, aim to make it easier for nondevelopers to collaborate on defining and writing executable specifications. Cucumber Studio, for example, provides an online environment where teams can collaborate on requirements discovery and on writing Cucumber scenarios (see figure 16.8).

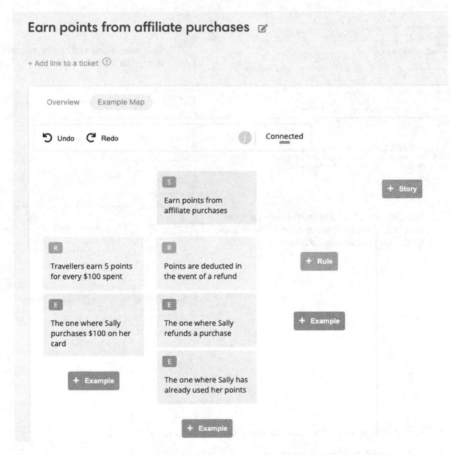

Figure 16.8   Cucumber Studio make it easy to run Example Mapping sessions online.

Behave Pro makes it possible to write acceptance criteria in Gherkin directly in JIRA (see figure 16.9) and have them synchronize automatically with your version control system. Both of these tools can also integrate with test execution so that test results can be fed back into the tool and be displayed alongside the executable specifications.

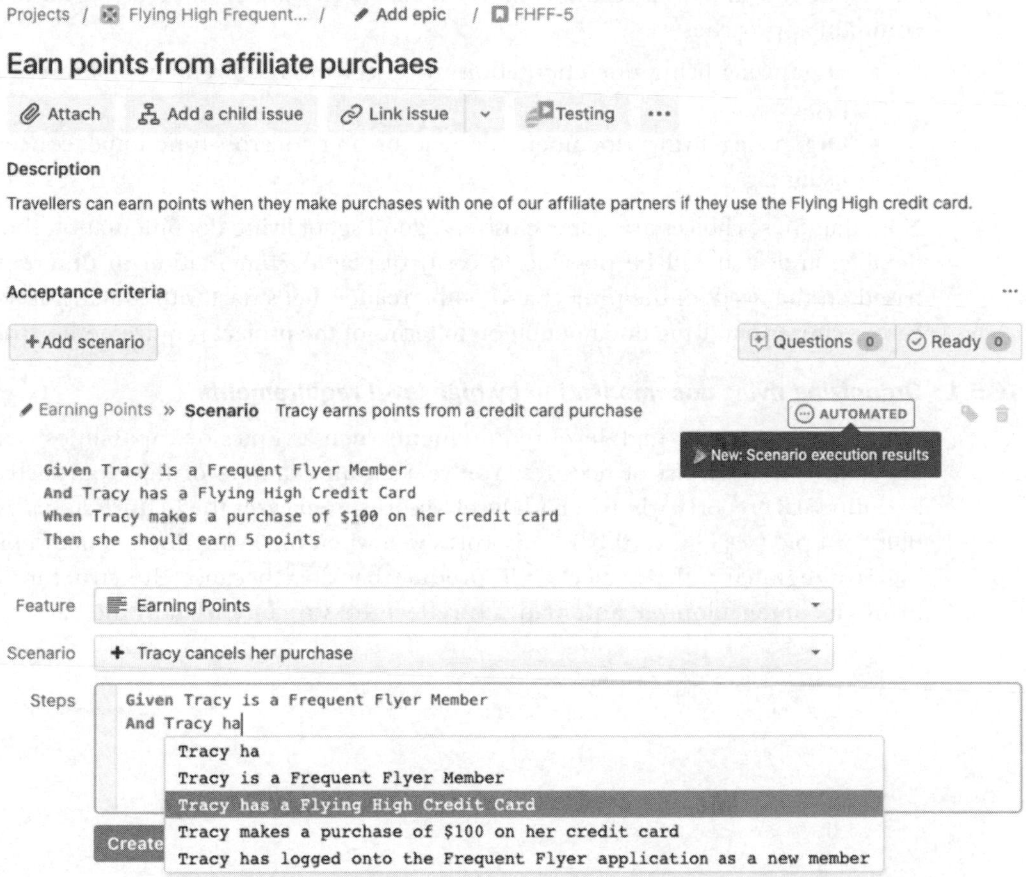

Projects / ⊠ Flying High Frequent... / ✏ Add epic / ▢ FHFF-5

Earn points from affiliate purchaes

⬤ Attach   ⛓ Add a child issue   🔗 Link issue   ⌄   🔲 Testing   •••

Description

Travellers can earn points when they make purchases with one of our affiliate partners if they use the Flying High credit card.

Acceptance criteria   •••

➕ Add scenario   ⊕ Questions 0   ⊘ Ready 0

✏ Earning Points » **Scenario** Tracy earns points from a credit card purchase   ⊙ AUTOMATED   🏷 🗑

▶ New: Scenario execution results

```
Given Tracy is a Frequent Flyer Member
And Tracy has a Flying High Credit Card
When Tracy makes a purchase of $100 on her credit card
Then she should earn 5 points
```

Feature   🟰 Earning Points   ▾

Scenario   ➕ Tracy cancels her purchase   ▾

Steps
```
Given Tracy is a Frequent Flyer Member
And Tracy ha|
```

```
Tracy ha
Tracy is a Frequent Flyer Member
Tracy has a Flying High Credit Card
Tracy makes a purchase of $100 on her credit card
Tracy has logged onto the Frequent Flyer application as a new member
```

Create

Figure 16.9 Some tools now allow you to work with feature files directly from issue tracking software such as JIRA.

These tools are still relatively new and immature and often lack support for the most recent Gherkin features. However, they are evolving fast, and it will certainly be worth evaluating them for your own projects when you need to determine the living documentation strategy.

16.5   Organizing the living documentation

If it's to be useful to the team as a whole, living documentation needs to be presented in a way that's easy to understand and navigate. For large projects, a flat list of features can quickly become unwieldy.

Fortunately, there are many ways to structure living documentation so that it's easier to navigate and, as a result, is more valuable. Here, we'll look at two of the most common approaches:

- Organizing living documentation to reflect the requirements hierarchy of the project
- Organizing living documentation according to cross-functional concerns by using tags

Note that these choices are not exclusive. A good set of living documentation should be flexible, and it should be possible to easily display documentation in different ways, based on the needs of the project and of the reader. Let's start with looking at how you can organize your living documentation in terms of the project requirements' structure.

16.5.1   Organizing living documentation by high-level requirements

Grouping features by high-level requirements such as Epics or capabilities is a good alternative to a flat list of features. You've seen an example of this approach in the Serenity BDD reports, where a high-level report summarizes the feature status by capability or Epic (see figure 16.10). This works well when the living documentation reporting is integrated with an electronic product backlog, because the structure of the living documentation will automatically reflect the structure used in the backlog tool.

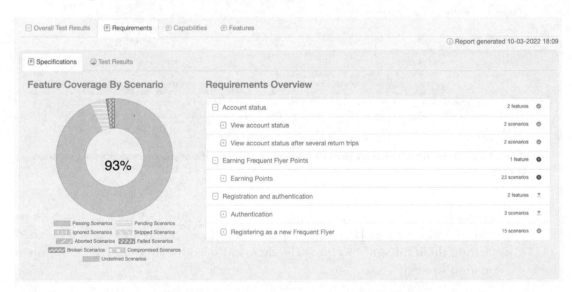

Figure 16.10   One useful way to organize living documentation is in terms of high-level requirements, such as Epics or capabilities.

Sometimes the structure that comes from this sort of hierarchical organization is a little too rigid. As you'll see in the next section, tags can offer a more flexible option.

16.5.2   *Organizing living documentation using tags*

There are times when it's useful to group features in a more free-form manner. For example, you might want to examine all the features related to particular nonfunctional requirements, such as security or performance, or all of the features that need to integrate with a particular external system.

Tags are an easy way to identify nonfunctional or cross-functional requirements like this. For example, the following scenario has been tagged as a security-related nonfunctional requirement:

> **Identifies this business rule, and the examples it contains, as relating to the Security/SSO nonfunctional requirement**

```
@Issue:FHFF-4
@security:sso          ◄────┘
Rule: 2) Frequent Flyers can sign in with SSO using their Google or Facebook
    account
  Example: Trevor logs in using his Google credentials
  Example: Trevor logs in using his Facebook credentials
```

16.5.3   *Living documentation for release reporting*

Living documentation is a great way to get a view of the overall project status from the point of view of the requirements. But for larger projects, the quantity of information can be a little overwhelming. It's useful to be able to focus on the work being done in the current iteration and mask out work that's already been completed or work that's scheduled for future releases.

There are many ways you can do this. One of the simplest is to use tags to associate features or individual scenarios with specific iterations. For example, you could assign a feature, rule, or scenario to iteration 1 in Cucumber by giving it an appropriate tag:

```
Feature: Earning Points

  Frequent Flyers earn status points each time they fly.
  As they earn more points, their status level increases and they get more
⇒ benefits.

  @release:iteration-1
  Rule: Members achieve new status levels when they earn sufficient points
    Scenario Outline: Earning status levels from points earned for status
⇒ level <Status Level>
      Given Stan is a new Frequent Flyer Member
      When he earns between <Min Points> and <Max Points> points
      Then his status should become <Status Level>
      Examples:
        | Min Points | Max Points | Status Level |
        | 0          | 999        | STANDARD     |
        | 1000       | 1999       | BRONZE       |
        | 2000       | 4999       | SILVER       |
        | 5000       |            | GOLD         |
```

You could then run a separate batch of acceptance tests for the features containing the `@release:iteration-1` tag, focusing only on the features scheduled for this iteration, or simply view the report page dedicated to this tag (see figure 16.11). This part of the report will contain only the scenarios and features that have been planned for this release, providing a clearer understanding of how ready the application is for release.

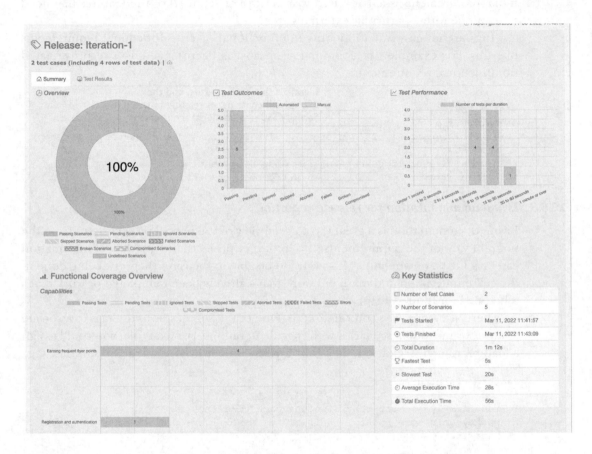

Figure 16.11   A release report focuses on requirements that have been scheduled for a particular release or iteration.

You don't have to stick with a single approach for your living documentation. In practice, teams often use a mix of several strategies for different purposes or different audiences. For example, a requirements-based organization is more effective for documenting what the application does as a whole and how it does it, whereas release-focused reporting is more relevant when reporting on progress and preparing release notes.

16.5.4 *Low-level living documentation*

Living documentation doesn't stop with the high-level requirements. Test-Driven Development (TDD) involves writing unit and integration tests in the form of low-level executable specifications, which form a major part of the technical documentation in a BDD/TDD project.

For technical living documentation, sophisticated reporting capabilities are less important than code readability and clarity. The primary audience of technical documentation is the developer who will need to maintain the code later on. Developers are used to reading code, so technical documentation in the form of well-organized, readable, annotated code samples is generally quite sufficient to help them understand the finer points of the code base. Many teams complement the low-level living documentation with light, higher-level architectural documentation, stored, for example, on a project wiki.

16.5.5 *Unit tests as living documentation*

Many modern unit testing tools make it easy express unit tests as living documentation. We saw in chapter 3 how we can use JUnit 5 in Java to write very readable unit and integration tests (see, for example, listing 3.3). There are also plenty of JavaScript testing tools that make writing clear, self-documenting unit tests very easy:

```
describe('FrequentFlyerController', () => {
    ...
    describe('When creating a new account', () => {

        it('should generate a new number for each account', async () => {
            const result = await controller.create(newFrequentFlyer);
            expect(result.frequentFlyerNumber).toBeDefined()
        })

        it('new Frequent Flyer accounts should be Pending', async () => {
            const result = await controller.create(newFrequentFlyer);
            const frequentFlyerNumber = result.frequentFlyerNumber;

            const frequentFlyerAccount =
        controller.findByFrequentFlyerNumber(frequentFlyerNumber)
            expect(frequentFlyerAccount.isActivated).toBeFalsy()
        });

        it('should return an error if the email is invalid ', async () => {
            const result =
        controller.create(frequentFlyerWithAnInvalidEmail);
            await expect(result).rejects.toThrow("Invalid email address");
        })
    });
    ...
});
```

But writing unit tests that make good technical documentation relies more on an attitude than on using a particular tool. The following NSpec specification, for example, also does a great job of explaining what feature it's describing and illustrating how an API should be used:

```
public class WhenUpdatingStatusPoints : nspec
{
    FrequentFlyer member;
    void before_each()
    {
        member = new FrequentFlyer();
    }
    void earning_status_points()
    {
        context["When cumulating Frequent Flyer points"] = () =>
        {
            it["should earn points for each flight"] = () =>
            {
                member.earnStatusPoints(100);
                member.earnStatusPoints(50);
              member.getStatusPoints().should_be(150);
            };
            it["should upgrade status when enough points are earned"] = () =>
            {
                member.earnStatusPoints(300);
                member.getStatus().should_be(Status.Silver);
            };
        };
    };
};
```

When a code base grows large, it can be hard to find the unit test that illustrates a particular feature. Many teams prefer to organize their unit tests in a package structure that mirrors the application structure. This approach has the advantage of making it easier to find the test class for a particular test, although this advantage is much less compelling with today's development environments, where it's very easy to find all the places in the code base where a particular class has been used.

This approach dates from the early days of unit testing. One of the original motivations was that Java classes in a given package could access protected fields of other classes in that package, so if the unit test class was in the same package as the class being tested, you could access protected fields as part of the unit tests.

From a BDD perspective, the argument for this approach is less compelling. A BDD-style unit test should provide a worked example of how to use a class and how the class is expected to behave. If you need to access protected variables, you may be binding your test code too tightly to the implementation, which runs the risk of making the unit tests more brittle.

This approach also assumes a very tight coupling between the classes under test and the features (or behavior) those classes are implementing. If you refactor a class, change its name, or break it into several smaller classes, for example, the requirement that these classes implement shouldn't change.

Having a test class for each production class can also hamper refactoring. A modern IDE will tell you at a glance if a method or a class isn't being used anywhere. Unless it's part of an API for an external client, a method that's never used anywhere can generally be deleted, which results in less code to maintain going forward.

For all these reasons, many organizations apply a looser association between test classes and production classes. For example, some teams find that test packages or directories organized in terms of functional slices are often easier to navigate, especially when you come back to a code base after a long period.

16.6 Living documentation for legacy applications

Many organizations have large legacy applications that are still very much in use and still need regular maintenance, updates, and releases. Many of these applications have few unit or integration tests and low test coverage, and they often lack technical or functional documentation.

The lack of automated tests for this sort of application makes it harder and riskier to deliver new features or bug fixes quickly. Releases are delayed by long testing cycles and regression issues. But for many organizations, rewriting the entire application isn't a viable proposition.

BDD offers some possible approaches that can relieve these symptoms and help teams to deliver changes to their legacy applications more safely and efficiently. One popular strategy that many teams adopt is to retrofit the legacy application with high-level acceptance tests, typically web tests for a web application. These acceptance tests both describe and document the existing system and help reduce the risk of regressions when new features are introduced. The tests are written in the same style as the automated acceptance criteria you've seen elsewhere in this book, and often with the same BDD-focused tools such as Cucumber and SpecFlow. The BDD reporting capabilities of these tools are a great way to document and communicate how people believe the application should behave.

Retrofitting unit testing is traditionally very difficult to do effectively because unit tests written too long after the code was written tend to be quite superficial. BDD unit tests specify the behavior of classes and components within these applications and are often the only place that this behavior is documented. When these specifications don't exist, it can be difficult to invent them after the fact, as it involves a deep understanding of how each class or component is expected to behave.

Despite these difficulties, BDD unit tests can provide excellent technical documentation, even for legacy applications. Some teams with mission-critical legacy applications that still require frequent and significant changes use BDD tests to document the most critical or high-risk parts of their application first, before expanding into less critical functionality. Unit tests are written in the spirit of documenting the current application behavior and giving code samples for how to use each class. This is a great way to provide technical documentation for the more critical parts of the application and to build up high-quality test coverage.

Summary

- Living documentation is a way of automatically reporting both what an application intends to do and how it does it.
- Living documentation provides information about features and requirements in addition to individual test results.
- If you store your requirements in a digital product backlog tool, it's useful to integrate BDD reporting from the automated acceptance criteria with the requirements from the product backlog tool.
- Living documentation can be organized in many ways, depending on what information needs to be retrieved.
- Living documentation can also be used to document the lower-level technical components of your system.
- Living documentation is also applicable for legacy systems, where it can be a very effective way of both documenting and testing an existing application.

index